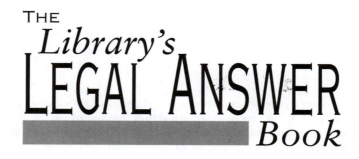

The *Library's* LEGAL ANSWER Book

MARY MINOW
TOMAS A. LIPINSKI

AMERICAN
LIBRARY
ASSOCIATION
CHICAGO   2003

While extensive effort has gone into ensuring the reliability of information appearing in this book, the publisher makes no warranty, express or implied, on the accuracy or reliability of the information, and does not assume and hereby disclaims any liability to any person for any loss or damage caused by errors or omissions in this publication.

This publication is designed to provide legal information for the library setting. This information is *not* provided as a substitute for legal advice. If legal advice or expert assistance is required, the services of a competent legal professional should be sought.

Design and composition by ALA Editions. Typeset in Sabon and Optima using QuarkXPress 5.0 on a PC platform

Printed on 50-pound white offset, a pH-neutral cover stock, and bound in 10-point cover stock by McNaughton & Gunn

The paper used in this publication meets the minimum requirements of American National Standard for Information Sciences—Permanence of Paper for Printed Library Materials, ANSI Z39.48-1992. ∞

Library of Congress Cataloging-in-Publication Data

Minow, Mary.
    The library's legal answer book / Mary Minow, Tomas A. Lipinski.
       p.   cm.
    Includes bibliographical references and index.
    ISBN 0-8389-0828-4 (alk. paper)
    1. Library legislation—United States. 2. Internet access for library users—Law and legislation—United States. I. Lipinski, Tomas A., 1958- II. Title.
    KF4315.M56 2003
    344.73'092—dc21   2002008095

Printed in the United States of America

07 06 05 04 03   5 4 3 2 1

To my parents and my husband, who believe nothing is impossible and whom I love more each day.

MARY MINOW

To my wife Eileen ("down a Boreen green came a sweet colleen"), whose support is ever-present and who lets me stay out late and play in the legal sandbox.

TOMAS A. LIPINSKI

Contents

∾ *Preface*

Every librarian encounters legal issues, sometimes every day of the week. This book is designed to alert librarians about potential legal trouble. It is a troubleshooter, not always a problem solver. Its purpose is to set off some alarm bells so you, the librarian, can stay away from trouble with the law.

You may be wondering who we are. Mary Minow is a librarian who went to law school, and Tom Lipinski is a lawyer who went to library school. Mary is a library law consultant. She has worked primarily in public libraries, but has experience with academic and special libraries, and with the information industry. Tom has worked as an attorney in private practice as well as in nonprofit legal sectors. His library experience is in academic law and urban public libraries. He is a tenure-track faculty member but continues to consult with libraries and schools on various legal and ethical issues.

This book is intended for librarians and their attorneys and will be particularly useful in addressing questions involving the public setting. It focuses on real questions and concerns that we have encountered over the years. Accordingly, we address many cyberlaw issues relevant to librarians, such as web page design and its accompanying linking, trademark, and defamation issues; patron privacy in Internet use; and the use of the Internet by Friends groups. We offer a grounding in federal copyright law and the tapestry of library privacy laws that are enacted at the state level. We look at issues of direct interest to librarians as professionals, such as liability for dispensing wrong information, writing inaccurate book reviews, and liability for latchkey children. We have included some general workplace issues involving employment law, and particularly the increasingly litigious areas of letters of reference, office romances, public employees' free speech rights, and harassment issues. We conclude with a key issue for library supporters—what are the legal limits on lobbying by Friends of the Library and others?

The information in this book does not constitute legal advice, but serves as a starting point that librarians and library lawyers may use in researching the law to apply to a particular situation. Different jurisdictions will have different laws, and may even apply the same laws differently. If legal advice or expert assistance is required, the services of a competent legal professional should be sought.

The law is becoming increasingly important to the library world. Rapid technological change has brought to the library new issues unheard of only a short time ago. The Internet, videorecorders, fax machines, and communications satellites have opened libraries to the world. Often the law lags behind, and we aim to help librarians as they race to keep up.

MARY MINOW

TOMAS A. LIPINSKI

⤳ *Acknowledgments*

An enormous debt of gratitude goes to my father, Newton Minow, and my friend, Cicely Wilson, who were there from the beginning and helped with every word. My father, a man of great vision and wisdom, advised me to write something each day, and to write plainly, removing or at least translating legalese whenever possible. Cicely, an indefatigable librarian who shares a real excitement for these issues, gave invaluable research assistance and always welcome advice. Thank you for the inspiration, editing, and constant reminders to write for readers.

Special thanks and appreciation go to Elaine Resnick, who told me the deadline to sign up for the LSATs was next Friday (and that registering for the LSATs didn't mean you had to take them, nor that you had to go to law school). When I somehow found myself in law school, I met Barbara Babcock, a professor who listens to students and has an uncanny ability to guide them to just where they should be. It was Professor Babcock who suggested I study library law, a specialty that I did not know existed.

This book would be much poorer without the time and specialized subject experience contributed by Henry Cohen, Gerald Gunther, and Kathleen Sullivan, mavens extraordinaire in First Amendment law. Peter Hirtle and Robert Kasunic generously shared some insights into the intricacies of copyright law. I appreciated the writings and review of the disability section by Barbara Mates and Cynthia Waddell. And thanks to Tom Barrington, we got some last-minute help on immunities.

Alfie Kohn and Joe Singer showed me how to organize my thoughts and research, and how to get started writing a book.

My appreciation for their encouragement and help with writing goes to Robert Bickal, Colleen Cayes, Karen Dyer, Andrea Gaines, Cheryl Gould, and Evy Posamentier.

Carol Johnson, LexisNexis, Paul Lomio, Erika V. Wayne, and the Robert Crown Law Library at Stanford Law School generously offered essential legal resource support.

The American Library Association fielded a strong team led by Patrick Hogan, who not only cajoled a book out of me, but gave me (and my library students at San Jose State University) an insightful view of copyright from the publisher's point of view. Many thanks to ALA managing editor Mary Huchting for carefully transforming a manuscript into a book, and to Judith Krug and the Office for Intellectual Freedom for their comments on the filters chapter.

My family is my touchstone and my pillar of support. My mother taught me never to take "no" for an answer, and the value of reaching out to others. My father taught me that a love of learning leads to a fulfilling life. My sister Nell has encouraged me to speak out and is helping me vanquish my apprehension. My sister Martha helped me get through law school and to ask the right questions. My sisters have brought David, Ben, Rachel, Joe, and Mira into my life and thus enriched it manyfold. My cousin David Feldman changed my life by healing my hands. My husband James has shown me the value of both candor and finding the time to enjoy life. Thank you all for coming into my life.

Finally, thanks to library folk and librarians everywhere for your questions, your answers, and your humor.

MARY MINOW

NOTES ON IMMUNITIES FOR PUBLIC ENTITIES AND PUBLIC EMPLOYEES

∽∽∽

General Framework on Library Liability and Immunity

Government-operated libraries, though subject to a wide range of lawsuits, have some weapons in their arsenal unavailable to privately funded
libraries. Governmental immunity doctrines are the first line of defense in
many lawsuits. This section provides a general overview of governmental
immunities. It also illustrates several library scenarios that test other statutory immunities.

Rationale for Governmental Immunity

It may surprise librarians to learn that there is a strong basis of sovereign
immunity, dating back to the common law, that still undergirds the tapestry of laws in place today. If there is not a law on the books that specifically
gives a party permission to sue the government for a particular claim, the
government enjoys immunity.

One commentator, Ann Judith Gellis, states that certain immunities
maximize a government's ability to allocate resources in furtherance of its

political agenda, thus preventing courts from second-guessing the costs and benefits of government decisions.[1] Put simply, when the government has to pay money damages, it is diverting funds from public services. Typically, the immunity only covers government when performing government functions, such as operating schools and libraries, and does not cover government when it performs proprietary functions, such as operating a municipal garage.

Why Libraries Get Sued, Despite Sovereign Immunity

First, anyone with the money for a filing fee can file suit in court. It takes a judge to dismiss a case, even one in which the library has immunity. Second, and more important, both the federal government and state governments have passed statutes that limit their common law immunity to allow the public to file suit.

"Tort Claims Acts" Limit Governmental Immunity

The Federal Tort Claims Act provides a significant waiver of the "sovereign immunity" of the government of the United States. It allows the United States to be sued and held liable for the negligent or wrongful acts and omissions of its employees while acting within the scope of their employment. Examples of allowable claims include property damage, personal injury, and death. The extent of government liability is about the same as that of a private person (subject to certain statutory exceptions) and is determined by the law of the place where the act or omission occurred.[2]

Similarly, state tort claims acts vary and may cover claims against "local public entities," the "state," and "public employees." Different states may include counties, cities, districts, public authorities, public agencies, and all political subdivisions in their acts. Public employees may be defined as any combination of officers, judicial officers, employees, and servants, whether or not compensated. Claims that are permitted may include premises liability, destruction of personal property, injuries, and the like. The laws often make a distinction between ministerial acts (those that obey instructions or laws) and discretionary acts (those that involve discretion, judgment, or skill), allowing liability only for the former.

Often there will be a limited time frame for parties to file suit, and a cap on money damages. To find out what a particular state's parameters for immunity (including immunity for employees) are, a good starting point is to look at the state's statutes or codes, and search for "tort claims act."

Immunity for Discretionary Functions

Both the Federal Tort Claims Act and the state tort claims acts allow for a great deal of governmental immunity, particularly under the "discretionary functions" exception. The federal act bars a claim "based upon the exercise or performance or the failure to exercise or perform a discretionary function or duty on the part of a federal agency or an employee of the Government, whether or not the discretion involved be abused."[3] States vary in the expansiveness of their immunity doctrines. Florida law, for example, has a narrow definition of the "discretionary functions" that bestow immunity. The Florida Supreme Court articulated a four-part test to identify discretionary functions of a local government:

> (1) Does the challenged act, omission, or decision necessarily involve a basic governmental policy, program, or objective? (2) Is the questioned act, omission, or decision essential to the realization or accomplishment of that policy, program, or objective as opposed to one which would not change the course or direction of the policy, program, or objective? (3) Does the act, omission, or decision require the exercise of basic policy evaluation, judgment, and expertise on the part of the governmental agency involved? (4) Does the governmental agency involved possess the requisite constitutional, statutory, or lawful authority and duty to do or make the challenged act, omission, or decision?[4]

In Florida, if all four of the above can be answered affirmatively, then the activity is deemed to be discretionary, and immunity applies. Note that exceptions may be written into a state statute, such as no waiver for public buildings.[5]

Examples of nondiscretionary duties in Florida, as determined by the courts, include a roadside stop and arrest of an individual driving with an expired inspection sticker, the negligent maintenance by city employees of a storm sewer system, the failure of a state caseworker to detect and prevent child abuse, the negligent maintenance of county swimming pools and failure to warn or correct known dangerous conditions, and the failure to protect a prison inmate from other inmates known to be dangerous.

In the *Mainstream Loudoun* case, citizens suing library trustees claimed that the trustees were exercising discretionary functions when they installed filters on library computers. The court, however, determined that the decision to adopt the filter policy was "legislative in nature," and thus the library board members were entitled to immunity.[6]

No Immunity for Civil Rights Violations

Although sovereign immunity is still wide-ranging, it does not apply to actions for federal civil rights violations.[7] For example, federal constitutional claims for free speech violations or racial discrimination are not given immunity under the Federal Tort Claims Act. The act also excludes workers' compensation and other claims. A party can recover under 42 U.S.C. §1983 if it can show that it was deprived of rights guaranteed by the Constitution or laws of the United States by a person acting under the color of state law.[8] Section 1983 authorizes liability to every person, who under color of any statute, ordinance, regulation, custom or usage, subjects or causes to be subjected, any person to be deprived of any rights, privileges, or immunities secured by the Constitution and laws. This would include suits for violation of First Amendment rights such as free speech and its corollary, the right to receive information.

No Immunity When Suit Seeks Injunction

Furthermore, there is generally no immunity when a party files suit for an injunction (e.g., requires a change in a policy), rather than monetary damages. This is significant in the library setting, when patrons are displeased with policies, such as Internet access; their lawsuits may not be barred by state immunity.

Employee Liability v. Governmental Liability

The immunity provisions for government and for government employees are not identical, and vary with the state statutes. There will be different provisions in the statutes that apply to employees, generally within the same tort claims acts, separate from those that apply to the government. Different types of employees may be treated differently, e.g., public officials (such as those elected or appointed to make laws) may be shielded to a greater extent than regular employees.

Absolute v. Qualified Immunity

Absolute immunity is a complete exemption from civil liability, usually afforded to public officials who perform legislative or judicial functions. Qualified immunity shields public officials and other public employees who are performing discretionary functions for acts that do not "violate clearly established statutory or constitutional principles of which a reasonable person would have known."[9] It can shield public employees from monetary suits, but not from requests for injunctive relief (court-ordered action, such as striking down part of a patron behavior policy).

A party going for the deep pocket will pursue the government itself, and try to establish "vicarious liability," that is, liability of the government due to the acts of its employees. In California, for example, the most common source of liability in its tort claims act is injuries caused by the acts or omissions of public employees. Under California law, to establish "vicarious liability" a plaintiff must demonstrate each of the following three conditions:

(1) the individual causing the injury is an employee;
(2) the employee's conduct is within the scope of his or her employment; and
(3) the employee's act or omission gives rise to a cause of action against that employee.[10]

In some cases, a party will be particularly interested in suing an employee because a library's immunities may be more expansive than the employees' immunity. For example, in California, the fraud immunity for public entities is broader than fraud immunity for public employees. There, the fraud immunity for employees excludes actual fraud, corruption, and actual malice, whereas the fraud immunity for public entities covers all injuries caused by both negligent and intentional misrepresentations of an employee.

If a party is successful in filing suit (i.e., it is not dismissed due to immunity), the library and the employees may still use any defense that would be available to a private person. For example, if a patron slips and falls, but is partly responsible for the accident—i.e., if the patron is partly at fault—some states will reduce the library's liability.

Other Statutory Immunity

Federal and state laws offer specific immunity to specified governmental parties under certain circumstances. Here are two examples especially relevant to libraries.

Volunteer Protection Act

Federal law offers volunteers some limited protection from liability. The Volunteer Protection Act applies to suits for damages in federal courts.[11] States often have similar statutes, such as the Texas Charitable Immunity and Liability Act: "a volunteer of a charitable organization is immune from civil liability for any act or omission resulting in death, damage, or injury if the volunteer was acting in good faith, and in the course and scope of his duties or functions within the organization." Under such acts, there are exceptions, such as the Texas act's exceptions for death, damage, or injuries arising from the operation or use of motor-driven equipment.[12]

Communications Decency Act:
Immunity for Providing Internet Access

The high-profile Communications Decency Act, 47 U.S.C. §230, was only *partly* struck down by the Supreme Court. Its remaining provisions have played a central role in recent library Internet cases. In a nutshell, a California appellate court found the law offered immunity to a library for offensive content distributed through its computers. A federal district court found the law *did not* offer immunity to a library that filtered its computers and was sued for violating the First Amendment.

Section 230 *does not* apply to violations of intellectual property rights such as trademark or copyright infringement.[13]

──────────────── CASE STUDY ────────────────

LOUDOUN COUNTY LIBRARY BOARD
HELD NOT IMMUNE

Absolute Immunity Argument Failed

Individual library board members were sued along with the library board as an entity in the landmark *Mainstream Loudoun v. Loudoun County Library* case. In that case, citizens sued the library for abridging the First Amendment when the library installed filters on every public computer terminal. The board members argued before the court that they enjoyed absolute immunity, a complete exemption from civil liability, generally given to government officials while performing legislative or judicial functions.[14]

The *Loudoun* court agreed that the board's role was legislative in nature, citing the Virginia state law that gives the board authority to govern the library.[15] However, the court found the board was also charged with "management and control of [the] free public library system."[16] In this capacity, the board members were not entitled to legislative immunity.

Qualified Immunity Argument Failed

Qualified immunity shields public officials from civil damages (money) liability, but it does not apply to injunctive relief (such as removing blocking software from library computers), nor does it prevent an award of attorneys' fees. In the *Loudoun* case, the library board was not given qualified immunity.[17]

Other Statutory Immunity Argument Failed: Library Not Immune

The Loudoun library board claimed immunity under the Communications Decency Act:

> (2) CIVIL LIABILITY—No provider or user of an interactive computer service shall be held liable on account of—
> (A) any action voluntarily taken in good faith to restrict access to or availability of material that the provider or user considers to be obscene, lewd, lascivious, filthy, excessively violent, harassing, or otherwise objectionable, whether or not such material is constitutionally protected; or
> (B) any action taken to enable or make available to information content providers or others the technical means to restrict access to material described in paragraph (1).
>
> 47 U.S.C. §230(c)(2)

The *Loudoun* court found that section 230 provided immunity from actions for monetary damages, but it did not immunize the library or the board from an action for injunctive relief (i.e., an order to remove blocking software from its computers). The court said that immunity did not extend to the First Amendment claim because "§230 was enacted to minimize state regulation of

Internet speech . . . §230 was not enacted to insulate government regulation of Internet speech from judicial review."[18]

Library Board Individual Members and Library Director Dismissed—Redundant Defendants

Finally, the library board argued that the suit against the individual board members was redundant because the library board *itself* was already a party. The Supreme Court has recognized that "official capacity suits generally represent only another way of pleading an action against an entity of which an officer is an agent."[19] The *Loudoun* court determined that a suit against the library board itself, if successful, would provide the plaintiffs with full relief against enforcement of the policy. The individual board members were dropped from the suit. Similarly, the suit against the director of the library was dropped, as the court determined he served solely as a "surrogate for the Board," and a judgment against him would not result in a change in library policy.[20]

--------- CASE STUDY ---------

LIVERMORE LIBRARY HELD IMMUNE

Library Immunity for Third-Party Content on the Internet

On the other hand, the law immunizes libraries from suits that would make them liable for information originating with a third-party user of the service.

> TREATMENT OF PUBLISHER OR SPEAKER—No provider or user of an interactive computer service shall be treated as the publisher or speaker of any information provided by another information content provider.
>
> 47 U.S.C. §230(c)(1)

In *Kathleen R. v. City of Livermore,* a mother filed several state claims against the library for the harm her son had undergone when he downloaded pornographic images from a library computer. The court granted immunity to the library, finding that section 230 prohibited "hold[ing] interactive computer services liable for their failure to edit, withhold or restrict access to offensive material disseminated through their medium."[21] The library was not "responsible, in whole or in part, for the creation or development" of any of the harmful matter accessible through its computers.[22] The federal statutory immunity precluded the state claims presented by the mother, of premises liability, waste of public funds, and public nuisance.

Emerging States' Rights Doctrine and Libraries

The U.S. Constitution, as originally written, described a federal government with limited powers. The rest were reserved to the states. Over time, the federal government increasingly passed legislation, including civil rights legislation, that applied to the states. Often it did this by using the Commerce Clause of the Constitution, i.e., the federal power to regulate commerce between the states. Recent Supreme Court decisions show a definite trend away from increasing federal power. The Court is giving new teeth to the Tenth and Eleventh Amendments, potentially affecting library liability regarding federal laws.

Tenth Amendment

The Tenth Amendment states that the powers not delegated to the federal government are reserved to the states or to the people.[23] Although it is too early to predict the ultimate effect of this emerging interpretation of the Tenth Amendment on libraries, it is possible that libraries in state government may have new defenses to some of the federal laws affecting them, such as the Americans with Disabilities Act and the Age Discrimination in Employment Act.

Eleventh Amendment

The Eleventh Amendment is difficult to interpret, as court decisions are inconsistent. It states that federal courts are not extended to lawsuits by citizens against the states.[24] Put simply, *state governments have immunity from some types of suits in federal courts.* In 1999, in separate cases, the

Supreme Court held that the Eleventh Amendment shielded states from some federal lawsuits concerning infringement of patent and trademark interests.[25] It is not yet known whether states will enjoy some immunity from copyright lawsuits, but it is an area to watch.[26]

Notes

1. Ann Judith Gellis, *Legislative Reforms of Governmental Tort Liability: Overreacting to Minimal Evidence,* 21 RUTGERS LAW JOURNAL 375 (1990).

2. 28 U.S.C. §1346(b), §1402(b), §2401(b), and §§2671–2680 (2000).

3. 28 U.S.C. §2680(a) (2000).

4. *Commercial Carrier Corp. v. Indian River County,* 371 So. 2d 1010, 1018 (1979).

5. *Howlett v. Rose,* 496 U.S. 356, 362–363 (1990), citing Florida cases that interpreted FLA. STAT. §768.28 (1989) that waives sovereign immunity for the state and its subdivisions, including municipalities.

6. *Mainstream Loudoun v. Loudoun County Library,* 2 F. Supp. 2d 783, 789 (E.D. Va. 1998).

7. 42 U.S.C. §1983 (2000).

8. *Parratt v. Taylor,* 451 U.S. 527, 535 (1981), overruled on other grounds, *Daniels v. Williams,* 474 U.S. 327 (1986).

9. *Harlow v. Fitzgerald,* 457 U.S. 800, 818 (1982), cited in *Mainstream Loudoun,* 2 F. Supp. 2d at 790.

10. CAL. GOV'T CODE §815.2 (2000).

11. 42 U.S.C. §14501 *et seq.* (1999).

12. TEX. CIV. PRAC. & REM. CODE ANN. §84.004(b) (2000).

13. *Gucci America v. Hall & Associates,* 2001 WL 253255 (S.D.N.Y. March 14, 2001).

14. See *Bogan v. Scott-Harris,* 523 U.S. 44 (1998) (local legislators enjoy absolute immunity even from civil liability under §1983f—or their legislative activities, as has long been the case with federal and state legislators), cited in *Mainstream Loudoun,* 2 F. Supp. 2d at 788.

15. VA. CODE ANN. §42.1-35, cited in *Mainstream Loudoun,* 2 F. Supp. 2d at 789.

16. *Mainstream Loudoun,* 2 F. Supp. 2d at 789.

17. *Mainstream Loudoun,* 2 F. Supp. 2d at 790.

18. *Mainstream Loudoun,* 2 F. Supp. 2d at 790.

19. *Monell v. Department of Soc. Servs.,* 436 U.S. 658, 690 n.55 (1978), cited in *Mainstream Loudoun,* 2 F. Supp. 2d at 790.

20. *Mainstream Loudoun,* 2 F. Supp. 2d at 791.

21. *Zeran v. America Online, Inc.,* 129 F.3d 327, 330 (4th Cir. 1997), cited in *Kathleen R. v. City of Livermore,* 87 Cal. App. 4th 684, 692 (2001).

22. 47 U.S.C. §230(f)(3), cited in *Kathleen R.,* 87 Cal. App. 4th at 692.

23. U.S. CONST. amend. X.

24. U.S. CONST. amend. XI.

25. *Florida Prepaid Postsecondary Education Expense Board v. College Savings Bank,* 527 U.S. 627 (1999) (dismissing patent claim); *College Savings Bank v. Florida Prepaid Postsecondary Education Expense Board,* 527 U.S. 666 (1999) (dismissing trademark and unfair trade practices claims).

26. Kenneth D. Crews, *Are State Universities* Immune *from Copyright Liability? The Constitution May Say* Yes!, *at* http://www.iupui.edu/~copyinfo/immunity.html (visited July 1, 2001).

1 LIBRARIES AND COPYRIGHT

Determining If a Work Is Copyrighted

Q1   As a general rule, are library-created newsletters, bibliographies, web pages, and the like protected by copyright?

Q2   When is a library publication not copyrighted because it is a "work of the United States Government"?

Q3   Does that mean that my library, which is not a federal library, can freely copy a bibliography published by a federal library?

Q4   If a federal librarian creates a work outside the scope of his or her employment, does the librarian hold a copyright to that work?

Q5   Are works published by state and local libraries copyrighted?

Q6   Would a state or local librarian's work be copyrightable?

Q7   Are all types of works created in a library copyrightable?

Copyright Holder Rights

Q8   What rights do copyright holders have?

Q9   When can libraries make copies of works?

Copyright Holder's Exclusive Rights

Reproduction

Derivative Works (Adaptations of Works)

Distribution
Performance and Display
  Location Clause
  Action (Transmission or Communication) Clause
Performance of Sound Recordings by Digital Transmission

Exceptions for Libraries and Users

Library "Fair Use" of Copyrighted Materials: Section 107

Q10   What does "fair use" mean?

Q11   What are the four "fair use" factors?

Q12   What exactly do the four factors really mean?

Purpose and Character of Use
  Commercial Use
  Transformative Use
Nature of the Work
Amount and Substantiality
  Amount
  Substantiality
Effect on the Market

Q13   Is it okay to use someone's copyrighted work for a library publication if it is comment or criticism?

Q14   Is it "fair use" for a library to make a copy for a patron if it is for research use only?

Q15   Does the opposite hold true? If a use falls outside "criticism, comment, news reporting, teaching (including multiple copies for classroom use), scholarship, or research," does it preclude a finding of fair use?

Q16   My supervisor gave me a sheet of Classroom Guidelines that tell me exactly how much I can copy, down to the number of words I can copy from a poem. Is this the legal limit?

Q17   If a work is unpublished, may the library assume it is "fair use" to use it?

Library Examples

Q18   Is it okay to copy pictures to make a thumbnail-image index to a collection?

Q19   Can a library show the chocolate factory assembly-line scene from *I Love Lucy* in a training workshop?

Q20   Can a library copy another library's bibliographies or pathfinders?

Q21   Can a library copy text, graphics, etc., from other web pages?

Q22   Is it fair use to copy an article for a library patron?

Q23   Is it fair use when a library copies an electronic article that it has leased from a vendor, even if the license restricts copying?

Library Interlibrary Loan, Preservation, and Replacements Exceptions: Section 108

Q24   What is the "library exception" known as section 108?

Q25   Does section 108 apply to my library?

Q26   What does section 108 mean when it says a notice of copyright or a legend must appear on the copy?

Q27   How does section 108 help libraries?

Q28   Does section 108 allow library staff to make personal copies?

Q29   Must library copying be done for nonprofit uses only?

Q30   Do the new copyright provisions passed in 1998 as part of the DMCA allow libraries to make digital copies?

Q31   When can a library make copies of unpublished works in its collection?

Q32   When can a library make copies to replace damaged copies of published works?

Q33   How does a library know when a format is "obsolete"?

Q34   If a used copy is available in the secondhand book market, or if the only available copy is priced at a premium, must the library purchase it rather than copy a work that is damaged?

Q35   May a library make a backup copy of a published work in anticipation of future damage?

Q36   Does this mean that if the titles in a library collection of videotapes are in the obsolete Beta format, a library could transfer them to VHS instead of buying new copies?

Q37   What if patrons demand a musical work on CD when the library only has an audiocassette tape version that is no longer available unused at a fair price, but an unused CD version is available at a fair price? Can the library copy the music onto a CD?

Q38   If an audiocassette tape is damaged, deteriorating, lost, or stolen, and a CD version of it is available, can the library make a copy with a CD burner?

Q39   When can a library make copies of an article or a small portion of a work for interlibrary loan?

Q40   When can a library make copies of an entire work or a substantial part of it for interlibrary loan?

Q41   Can the library make an extra copy for its files, in the expectation that there will be more interlibrary loan requests?

Q42   Can the library make copies of articles for reserves, e-reserves, or vertical files?

Q43   What does the law mean when it says "the library or archives has had no notice that the copy or phonorecord would be used for any purpose other than private study, scholarship, or research"?

Q44   What is the copyright warning notice that is required for display on order forms and at the place orders are taken?

Q45   I notice that the interlibrary loan provision of the copyright law does not seem to allow copies of entire works if a copy is available at a fair price. Does it allow a library to make a copy if the only "fair price" copy is a used copy?

Q46   What is the library's legal responsibility with respect to self-service photocopiers, scanners, computer printers, dual cassette players, or other reproducing equipment?

Q47   What is the difference between sections 108(d) and (e) and section 108(f)?

Q48   Are library patrons immune from copyright suits if they use a library photocopier?

Q49   A patron donated videotapes of news programs. May we add them to the collection?

Q50   Can I make a copy of a work, under section 108, even if I signed a licensing agreement that says I cannot make copies for any purpose?

Q51   When can my library make copies for interlibrary loan?

Q52   What are the CONTU Guidelines on Photocopying and Interlibrary Arrangements? Are these known as "the Rule of 5"?

Q53   Can my library make copies of articles for staff on a routing list?

Q54   I read that the term of copyright has been extended by twenty years. Is there an exception for libraries?

Q55   Can my library make a copy of a videotape or CD for interlibrary loan?

Library Lending Exceptions and the First Sale Doctrine: Section 109

Q56   May my library lend software as well as books?

Q57   If my library is part of a profit-making institution, may I still lend the software?

Q58   Can a nonprofit library, such as a public high school's media center, give used software to a grade school?

Q59   Can a nonprofit library, such as a public high school's media center, sell the software in a used book sale?

Q60   If my library legitimately purchases an electronic item, such as a journal article, may it lend or sell it under the first sale doctrine?

Performances and Displays: Section 110

Q61   Teachers show videos in their classrooms all the time, even videos that they check out from our library. Can we show the same videos as part of library programs?

Q62   We have educational programs in our meeting room. Is that "a similar place devoted to instruction"?

Q63   If two or three students are in the library and wish to view a video, is that permissible?

Q64   Can a library turn on the television or the radio for the public to enjoy?

Duration of Copyright: Sections 302–304

Patrons and Library Liability

Q65   If patrons are using my library's computers to copy material illegally, can my library be on the hook?

Q66   Our library does not get any financial benefit when patrons infringe. Can we still be "vicariously liable"?

Q67   Patrons have used our photocopiers for many, many years. We even get some direct financial revenue from this. Yet we've never been sued for "liability" or contributing to copyright infringement.

Q68   Can a library be liable when its patrons use its equipment to infringe copyright?

Q69   What if the library makes a copy at the request of a patron, as in interlibrary loan, or in response to a faxed or e-mailed request?

Q70   If we make the copies, it is usually because we got the request by fax or e-mail. Our patrons are not going to see this notice!

Q71   Should I put up the same notice next to my computers or computer printers where patrons make copies?

Liability and Remedies: Sections 501–504

Liability

Remedies

Appendix

When Works Pass into the Public Domain: Copyright Duration Rules

Notes

This chapter is an introduction to a variety of copyright issues, but presents them in the context of the library. Basic issues of ownership and liability are discussed. In addition, the concept of "fair use" (section 107) and the "library exception" in section 108 of the Copyright Revision Act of 1976 are discussed. Section 108 provides additional rights of reproduction and distribution to qualifying libraries. Every librarian should have a working understanding of these two important sections of the copyright law. In addition, section 109 (the "first sale doctrine") and section 110 (display and performance rights for specific user groups such as educators) are discussed. Understanding these provisions is important in applying the law to other areas such as the classroom, distance education, and the debate over license versus copyright. The questions posed and the answers provided will help the reader begin this process, though of course nothing can substitute for actually reading and understanding the provisions of each section. Finally, the new liability-limitation provisions for online service providers are discussed, provisions that the Digital Millennium Copyright Act of 1998 created. All of these topics need to be addressed before advanced topics such as website design issues can be understood. The law is under constant development, and most likely what is printed here will be somewhat out of date by the time it is published; however, the legal discussions in this chapter draw heavily upon the legislative history and the developing interpretations given by the courts. It is hoped that this approach will provide an overview of the various issues involved and will offer a sound footing upon which new developments in the law may be tracked, understood, and incorporated by readers into their daily practice.

DETERMINING IF A WORK IS COPYRIGHTED

Q1   As a general rule, are library-created newsletters, bibliographies, web pages, and the like protected by copyright?

It depends. The first issue to consider is who actually created the work. A library may copyright works that it creates, with some exceptions. If it is a federal government library, then the work is not protected. This is because section 105 of the copyright law states in simple terms that "Copyright protection under this title is not available for any work of the United States Government. . ."[1]

Q2   When is a library publication not copyrighted because it is a "work of the United States Government"?

A library publication is a "work of the United States Government" when it is prepared by an officer or employee of the United States government as part of that person's official duties.[2]

Q3   Does that mean that my library, which is not a federal library, can freely copy a bibliography published by a federal library?

In many cases this is true, but not always. First, you might think an agency is part of the federal government, when in fact it may be a quasi-federal government agency. For example, the United States Postal Service is *not* a United States government agency.[3]

Second, the United States government can actually *hold* copyright to works if it receives copyright ownership from third parties, transferred by assignment, bequest, or otherwise.[4]

Third, the U.S. government may publish a work that incorporates works produced by third parties. These works may be generated by grants, commissions, or other contracts; the copyright is still held by the third party unless transferred to the government.[5] Alternatively, a privately published work might be incorporated into a federal government publication, with permission granted to the government just for that one use. For example, a federal law library may publish a pathfinder that shows examples of how to use *Shepard's*, a citation index, *taken from a source that is copyrighted.* Although you could copy most of the pathfinder, you could not copy the portion that is copyrighted without permission. This is called a "reserved" portion. When a work or portion of a federal government publication is reserved (a third party claims copyright in some portion of the work), a reservation notice indicating which portion of the work is copyrighted should be included.[6] The unreserved portion of the work is in the public domain.

Q4   If a federal librarian creates a work outside the scope of his or her employment, does the librarian hold a copyright to that work?

It is possible for a federal government librarian to hold a copyright to a work created outside the scope of his or her employment. It may not be enough to show that the librarian created the work on his or her own time, however. The status of the work would turn on whether it is considered to be a "work made for hire," that is, a work prepared by the employee within the scope of his or her employment.[7] If the work was created outside of employment, it would generally not be considered a work of the U.S. government.[8]

Q5   Are works published by state and local libraries copyrighted?

They can be. Only works by the "United States Government" are "exempt" from copyright according to section 105. Thus, by definition, other governmental entities such as states and local municipalities may exert copyright in their publications.[9] There is a traditional exception to this for state statutes, judicial opinions, and regulations, but other works emanating from foreign, state, municipal, and local governments may be copyrighted.[10] If a local government adopts a privately written building code, it is even possible that the building code's copyright is still retained by its author or publisher.[11]

Some states have chosen to release their products into the public domain, although they are under no obligation to do so by the federal copyright law. Others opt to retain copyright. For example, the Oklahoma attorney general indicated that copyright might be claimed in works of the Oklahoma Historical Society.[12] Similarly, the Louisiana attorney general has stated that agencies of the state "may own the copyright in its capacity as a private person."[13]

Q6   Would a state or local librarian's work be copyrightable?

Like the federal employee example, a work created by a state employee "within the scope of his or her employment" would be subject to the "work made for hire" doctrine and thus the state could exert copyright ownership in the work. A work that is not related to librarianship, created outside the scope of employment, and fully created at home would belong to the librarian. It gets more complicated if the work does relate to librarianship, and a court would need to carefully determine the scope of the librarian's employment. In the much-cited *Marshall v. Miles Laboratories* case, a scientific researcher wrote an article at home during off-hours on technology and industrial chemicals. A federal court held that it was a "work made for hire," and belonged to his employer. The court relied heavily on the fact that Marshall's job description stated that he was responsible for researching and reporting information about advances in technologies.[14]

Q7   Are all types of works created in a library copyrightable?

No. The work must be original and fixed in a tangible medium of expression.[15] An oral workshop given by a librarian to a class is not copyrightable, unless it is fixed in a tangible medium, such as videotape. Handouts are copyrightable, if they are not the works of the federal government, or of a state government that has ceded its works into the public domain.

COPYRIGHT HOLDER RIGHTS

Q8   What rights do copyright holders have?

Copyright holders have a bundle of rights, known as "exclusive rights." This means that a library cannot intrude on those rights unless the library's use falls into one of the exceptions discussed below, or unless the library gets permission. The copyright holder's exclusive rights are: (1) the right to reproduce the copyrighted work in copies or phonorecords; (2) the right to prepare derivative works based upon the copyrighted work; (3) the right to distribute copies or phonorecords of the copyrighted work to the public by sale or other transfer of ownership, or by rental, lease, or lending; (4) the right, in the case of literary, musical, dramatic, and choreographic works, pantomimes, and motion pictures and other audiovisual works, to perform the copyrighted work publicly; and (5) the right, in the case of literary, musical, dramatic, and choreographic works, pantomimes, and pictorial, graphic, or sculptural works, including the individual images of a motion picture or other audiovisual work, to display the copyrighted work publicly, and in the case of sound recordings, to perform the copyrighted work publicly by means of a digital audio transmission.[16]

Copyright Holder's Exclusive Rights (Section 106)

- Reproduction
- Derivative works (adaptations of works)
- Distribution
- Performance
- Display
- Performance of sound recordings by digital transmission

Q9   When can libraries make copies of works?

Most of this chapter revolves around that question. The rights listed in section 106 of the copyright law are subject to numerous exceptions that help libraries and their users. The most important exceptions that help libraries are the section 107 "fair use," the section 108 "library exception," and the section 109 "first sale doctrine." In addition, a library can occasionally make use of other exceptions listed in the copyright law, such as the "backup of software" provision in section 117. All of the exceptions are found at 17 U.S.C. §§107–122.

The exceptions that help libraries are discussed in this chapter immediately after a detailed explanation of the copyright holder's rights.

Copyright Holder's Exclusive Rights

Reproduction

The right held by copyright owners to control reproduction (copies) of their works is the most important issue that libraries confront. Libraries are routinely requested to make copies for patrons through analog (photocopies) or digital means. Of course, if the work is in the public domain, there is no problem. Otherwise, the library must find the act of copying that fits into the specific categories listed in section 108, the "library exception," explained below. If the copying does not fit there, the library must evaluate whether or not it is a "fair use," which is a difficult balancing test. A final option is to see if another copyright exception applies. Unless the work is in the public domain, or the library can make a case for "fair use," the "library exception," or another specific exception, it must get permission from the copyright holder to make copies of the work in question.

Derivative Works (Adaptations of Works)

The right to prepare derivative works (adaptations of works) based upon the copyrighted work is one of the broadest rights that copyright owners possess. The copyright holder has the right to control (or deny) abridgements, annotations, art reproductions, condensations, dramatizations, editorial revisions, elaborations, fictionalizations, musical arrangements, and translations.[17] The key to understanding derivative works is that some portion of the original work is incorporated into the new work, the derivative work. If a school librarian adapts a book from her library shelf into a stage play for her students to perform, she first needs to get permission from the copyright holder, unless she can find an exception that covers her. Both the librarian and the original copyright holder have copyrightable interests in the new work, the stage play.

This should sound familiar to those who follow news stories about "film rights," such as the purchase of rights to John Grisham's novel *The Firm* by Paramount Pictures for $600,000, or the purchase of rights to Stephen Ambrose's book *Band of Brothers* by Tom Hanks and others for an HBO miniseries,[18] or the controversy surrounding books based on popular television shows such as *Twin Peaks, Seinfeld,* and *Star Trek.*[19]

Distribution

The copyright holder has the exclusive right to distribute copies of his or her work to the public by sale or other transfer of ownership, or by rental, lease, or lending. This is another important right that affects libraries. The term "public" is defined as beyond the "normal circle of a family and its social acquaintances,"[20] or at least "a substantial number of persons."[21]

Traditionally, courts have interpreted distribution to require some sort of "commercial" enterprise, one that is tied to the formal publication of the work. The description of distribution in section 106 of the copyright law is almost identical to the definition of "publication" in section 101: "distribution of copies or phonorecords of a work to the public by sale or other transfer of ownership, or by rental, lease, or *lending*"[22] (emphasis added). In addition, the legislative history refers to the section 106 "distribution" right as "publication."[23]

However, recent case law suggests an expanding view of distribution. This would mean that a library can not add illegally made copies to its collection, as the items' availability to patrons might be considered a distribution. In *Hotaling* v. *Church of Jesus Christ of Latter-day Saints,*[24] an unlawfully made microfiche copy of a text was made available and then distributed (lent) to members of the public through its availability in the library catalog. The court observed that "[w]hen a public library adds a work to its collection, lists the work in its index or catalog system, and makes the work available to the borrowing or browsing public, it has completed all the steps necessary for distribution to the public."[25] Because the library had an unlawfully made complete copy of one of the plaintiff's works on genealogy, the distribution of that material was unlawful.

Nonprofit, noncommercial status will not insulate a library from liability for an illegal "distribution" of a pirated work. This applies to "dubbed" videotapes and audiotapes that are "donated" by well-meaning users.

Performance and Display

Libraries can own films and videotapes yet not have the right to show them to the public. This is a "performance right," held by the copyright owner, who may fully license the rights to the library on a nonexclusive basis, or merely license the right to show (or "perform") such works on a one-time basis. Unlike the exclusive rights of reproduction, derivative, and distribution, the rights of public performance and display apply only to specified categories: literary, musical, dramatic, and choreographic works, pantomimes, and motion pictures and other audiovisual works. Performance rights do not apply to pictorial, graphic, or sculptural works, or to sound recordings transmitted nondigitally. (This is so because pictorial, graphic, and sculptural works are displayed rather than performed, whereas musical, dramatic, and choreographic works are performed rather than displayed.) Performance rights apply to motion pictures and other audiovisual works when the images are shown sequentially, while display rights apply when the images are shown nonsequentially.

The rights of performance and display apply only to those performances and displays that are "public." "To perform or display a work 'publicly' means to perform or display it at a place open to the public or at any place where a substantial number of persons outside of a normal circle of a family and its social acquaintances is gathered."[26]

LOCATION CLAUSE

The foregoing definition refers to "a place open to the public" and encompasses a wide range of library locations. It may not matter if a group of people know each other, if a student is working on an after-school project, or if members of the same household wish to see a library-owned video. The trigger is that the performance or display is made at a place open to the public or where people beyond the family or its social acquaintances might gather.

ACTION (TRANSMISSION OR COMMUNICATION) CLAUSE

The definition also has an "action (transmission or communication) clause." If the performance or display is transmitted or communicated to a place specified by the "location clause" or "to the public, by means of any device or process, whether the members of the public capable of receiving the performance or display receive it in the same place or in separate places and at the same time or at different times," the library may be infringing copyright.[27]

If a library allows patrons to view videos on its premises, it would trigger the location clause but not the action clause.[28] However, if the library placed an elevated monitor in each corner of the main reading room, and played videos related to various book-theme weeks, this would trigger the action (transmission or communication) clause as well.

Under certain conditions, such acts might still be allowable under other provisions of the copyright law (see the discussions of sections 107 and 110 in this chapter).

Performance of Sound Recordings by Digital Transmission

The last right covers only sound recordings and gives copyright holders the exclusive right to "perform the copyrighted work publicly by means of a digital audio transmission."[29] Sound recordings are works that result from the fixation of a series of musical, spoken, or other sounds. They do not include the sounds accompanying a motion picture or other audiovisual work. Sound recordings can be in any material objects, such as disks or tapes.[30] Because the recording is usually a record of someone singing or reading a preexisting copyrighted work, sound recordings are a form of derivative work. Before the passage of the Digital Performance Right in Sound Recordings Act of 1995,[31] sound recordings represented a significant category of copyrighted work denied the right of public performance. This act now gives copyright owners of sound recordings the rights to authorize certain digital transmissions of their works, including interactive digital audio transmissions. As amended by the Digital Millennium Copyright Act (DMCA) in 1998, the right now covers cable and satellite digital audio services, webcasters, and future forms of digital transmission. Most non-interactive transmissions are subject to statutory licensing at rates to be negotiated or, if necessary, arbitrated. Exempt from this bill are traditional radio and television broadcasts and transmissions to business establishments.

EXCEPTIONS FOR LIBRARIES AND USERS

As previously mentioned, the copyright holder's exclusive rights are subject to a series of exceptions; the most important exceptions for libraries are discussed here. As copyright law developed over the decades, courts recognized that some level of use by others should not impinge upon the rights of copyright owners. These rights are both general and specific.

Library "Fair Use" of Copyrighted Materials: Section 107

Q10   What does "fair use" mean?

Section 107 of the Copyright Revision Act contains the statutory expression of "fair use" rights. It explains when certain uses of copyrighted works are deemed fair and acceptable, e.g., for such purposes as criticism, comment, news reporting, teaching (including multiple copies for classroom use), scholarship, and research. The factors are somewhat nebulous by design, as Congress desired to provide a flexible interpretation. However, examining the language of section 107 in conjunction with several court cases provides guidance in applying the concept of "fair use" in library settings. There are four fair use factors that need to be considered in any fair use assessment. These will be discussed in detail below.

Q11   What are the four "fair use" factors?

By statute, the four factors are (1) the purpose and character of the use, including whether such use is of a commercial nature or is for nonprofit educational purposes; (2) the nature of the copyrighted work; (3) the amount and substantiality of the portion used in relation to the copyrighted work as a whole; and (4) the effect of the use upon the potential market for or value of the copyrighted work.[32]

Q12   What exactly do the four factors really mean?

Examining the four fair use factors in some detail is helpful in assessing whether a particular use would be considered fair use by a court. A court looks at a library's use of a copyrighted work based on each of the four factors, and then sums up the total. It then sometimes looks to other factors (the four factors are only illustrative) to see if the use, as a whole, is ultimately considered "fair" or not.

Fair Use Factors: "PNAM"—Purpose, Nature, Amount, Market

- The purpose and character of the use, including whether such use is of a commercial nature or is for nonprofit educational purposes

- The nature of the copyrighted work

- The amount and substantiality of the portion used in relation to the copyrighted work as a whole

- The effect of the use upon the potential market for or value of the copyrighted work[33]

Purpose and Character of Use

Most nonprofit, governmental, or academic library copying will fare well on the first factor when the copies are for nonprofit, educational use. If the library is in a corporate setting, or the library knows that the patron's use is for commercial advantage, the first-factor analysis can tip against the use.

The first factor, the purpose and character of the use, includes whether such use is of a commercial nature or is for nonprofit educational purposes. Is the use commercial or noncommercial? This is not a bright line or litmus test. However, if the use is commercial, the user must show that the commercial use does not adversely affect the market for the work. Conversely, if the use is noncommercial, the copyright owner must show harm that the use will have on the market for his or her work.

COMMERCIAL USE

The most important case on this subject for librarians is *American Geophysical Union* v. *Texaco, Inc.* In *Texaco,* company researchers (not librarians) made photocopies of a specialized journal for research and development. The *Texaco* court suggested that a "commercial use" has a more direct link to "commercial exploitation" than to the general for-profit nature of the entity using the work.[34]

There appear to be two separate lines of thought emerging among courts on this point: a "for-profit activity" versus a "commercial exploitation" criterion. Recent case law focuses on "exploitation" as opposed to the mere commercial nature of the use. This stands to reason, as most litigated uses are in conjunction with a commercial enterprise. For-profit is *not* necessarily an obstacle to "fair use." In the words of one commentator: "The fact that [the] defendant's book was sold for profit is not of itself determinative because if all uses for profit were to fail under this factor, practically no fair uses could be made at all."[35]

On the other hand, "commercial use" need not encompass profit seeking. Most recently, in *A&M Records, Inc.* v. *Napster, Inc.,* the Ninth Circuit concluded that the purpose of individuals who participated in the sharing of music through Napster technology was indeed commercial. The court explained that "[d]irect economic benefit is not required to demonstrate a commercial use. Rather, repeated and exploitative copying of copyrighted works even if the copies are not offered for sale, may constitute a commercial use. . . . In the record before us, commercial use is demonstrated by a showing that repeated and exploitative unauthorized copies of copyrighted works were made *to save the expense of purchasing authorized copies*" (emphasis added).[36] This is significant for any libraries that make an extra copy in order to save the purchase price of a second or backup copy. Courts have also looked to other considerations within the first factor: whether the use is private or personal or whether it is public, i.e., beyond the scope of normal family and friends.

TRANSFORMATIVE USE

Librarians sometimes want to know if they can make a copy of part of a video to create something new, like a multimedia presentation. Similarly, they may want to know if they can copy a book's cover art to create a flashier bibliography.

Copying part of a work (or even a whole work in some circumstances) in order to create a new work is often looked at more favorably by the courts than mere copying (to substitute for the original) without "transformation." Some courts have found that this transformation overrides the otherwise commercial nature of a use. "The more transformative the new work, the less will be the significance of other factors like commercialism, that may weigh against a finding of fair use."[37] The "transformation" must be more than a reproduction. For example, in creating a thumbnail index of pictures on a website, a court found the commercial nature of the site nonetheless transformative as it "was also of a somewhat more incidental and less exploitative nature than more traditional types of 'commercial use.'" Although the thumbnail images were complete copies, they had been transformed into a new product, an index to information on the Internet. In contrast to this, framing photographs of one website by another site was not transformative, was not fair use, and violated the copyright owner's exclusive right to display.[38]

However, merely copying articles to electronic bulletin boards, coursepacks, or library reference files is generally not a "transformative use." There is little that is transformative about copying the entirety or large portions of a work verbatim. In a recent case, the entire texts of articles on newspapers' websites were posted on another website so that registered site members could add commentary. The newspapers sued, alleging copyright infringement. The court found that the copying was verbatim, encompassed large numbers of articles, and occurred on an almost daily basis. The evidence supported a finding that the defendants engaged in extensive, systematic copying of the newspapers, and was not able to demonstrate that verbatim copying of the plaintiffs' articles was necessary to achieve the defendants' purpose of comment or criticism.[39] (See *Q13*.)

When courts look at the first factor, "the purpose and character of the use," they assess whether "the new work merely supersedes the objects of the original creation, or instead adds something new, with a further purpose or different character, altering the first with new expression, meaning, or message; it asks, in other words, whether and to what extent the new work is transformative."[40] The more transformative the new work, the less will be the significance of other factors, like commercialism, that may weigh against a finding of fair use."[41]

Creating a coursepack is not transformative, although it could be argued that in creating a new edited course reader a new work, a "derivative," is made. This argument presents another issue that courts are still exploring: make too transformative a use, and a derivative work is created, thus triggering another of the copyright owner's exclusive rights.[42] Likewise, making a copy for archival purposes (in a research file or a library vertical file) is also unlikely to be deemed transformative.[43]

Nature of the Work

The second factor in the fair use analysis focuses upon the nature of the copyrighted work that has been copied. An unpublished work will receive greater copyright protection than a published work. The rationale is that the creator has not had the chance to profit from an unpublished work.

A more important feature is whether the work is highly creative or is merely factual. There is a continuum of works from those that are most protected to those that are least protected (sometimes referred to as "thin copyrights").[44] The more creative the work, the stronger the copyright protection. The more factual the work (facts cannot be copyrighted), the weaker or "thinner" the copyright.

In the *Texaco* case, the scientific journal articles photocopied were "essentially factual in nature,"[45] but the content of excerpts (chapters from various books on political science and history) used to compile coursepacks in the *Michigan Document* case was "creative material."[46] Scientific articles enjoy less protection than creative excerpts. The newspaper articles pasted onto the electronic bulletin board in the *Free Republic* case were "predominantly factual. Consequently, defendants' fair use claim is stronger than it would be had the works been purely fictional."[47]

In *Kelly v. Arriba Soft Corp.*, Arriba operated a visual search engine on the Internet. It used a "crawler" to gather approximately two million images by the time of trial. The engine created thumbnail images, including ones of photographs taken by Leslie Kelly, a photographer specializing in California Gold Rush country. Although Arriba ultimately won the case, the second "fair use" factor, i.e., the nature of the work, weighed against the indexer because the photographs were creative, "artistic" work.[48] In another case, the modeling photographs published by a newspaper were viewed by the First Circuit as mostly factual.[49]

Amount and Substantiality

AMOUNT

Can a library copy an entire book, drawing, or journal article under the "fair use" exception? When the entire item is copied, it weighs against a fair use finding. The third factor is the amount and substantiality of the portion used in relation to the copyrighted work as a whole. While "amount" indicates how much has been taken, the courts have not established any bright line regarding how much is too much. The more of the work that is taken, the worse it is for the user. Libraries often make copies of an entire article. Based upon the copy-shop case law,[50] it might be suggested that once more than 5 to 10 percent of a work is taken there is a danger that this factor could weigh in against a finding of fair use. In many of the cases mentioned in this chapter, courts found the third factor weighed against a finding of fair use: copying a story from a newspaper onto an electronic bulletin board, photocopying an entire article from a journal (articles generally have their own copyright, apart from a copyright in the journal as a whole), and scanning a photograph are complete, 100-percent taking of works.

However, just because an entire work is copied, it does not mean that the full fair use analysis is over. As the Ninth Circuit summarized it, "[w]hile 'wholesale copying does not preclude fair use per se,' copying an entire work 'militates against a finding of fair use.'"[51]

At least one case has found that despite the copying of 100 percent of a series of pictures, the third factor, amount, came out neutral as to fair use. In *Nunez* v. *Caribbean International News Corp.,* a Puerto Rican newspaper published photographs of a nude Miss Universe contestant. The photographs had been taken by Sixto Nunez, who had distributed them to the modeling community. The newspaper won on a "fair use" defense; the pictures were newsworthy, and according to the court, "El Vocero admittedly copied the entire picture; however, to copy any less than that would have made the picture useless to the story. As a result, like the district court, we count this factor as of little consequence to our analysis."[52]

The third factor also looks at the substantiality of the portion used in relation to the copyrighted work as a whole. In other words, if the taking is of a small proportion of the work (measured quantitatively) but is nonetheless "substantial" to the work, this will weigh against a fair use. The seminal case in the area is the Supreme Court case *Harper & Row Publishers, Inc.* v. *Nation Enterprises*,[53] in which an excerpt from President Gerald Ford's memoirs was published in *The Nation* magazine. The excerpt was only a small proportion of the book. However, it was "the heart" of the book: the discussion of President Ford's pardon of President Nixon. This, in addition to other factors in the case, led the Court to find that using the excerpt was not fair use.

In another Supreme Court case, Acuff-Rose Music, the holder of the copyright to Roy Orbison's song "Oh Pretty Woman," sued the musical group 2 Live Crew. 2 Live Crew had copied the original's first line of lyrics and signature opening bass riff, the original's "heart." 2 Live Crew's lyrics quickly degenerate into lines such as "big hairy woman. . . ." The Court in this case found for fair use because the group's version was a parody, and in order to have a successful parody, taking the heart of the work was needed to conjure up the original song.[54]

Effect on the Market

When a library makes a copy, is it in place of making a purchase? Is the copy harming the potential for the work's sale in any way? This issue is the final fair use factor, and the effect on the potential market for the copyrighted work is generally considered the most important element of fair use, despite a Supreme Court decision to the contrary.[55]

The courts look not only at the impact on the market for the original work, but also on any secondary or residual market that has developed. An example of a "secondary market" is that which exists for coursepacks where several chapters or a number of pages of a book might be reproduced as part of a reader for students. The value of those chapters or pages is something less than the value (cost) of the entire book, and schools pay for the right to reproduce and include that "value." Thus, a secondary market has developed in addition to the primary market for sales of the entire book.

In *Texaco,* the market harm was the key to a decision against the user. The researchers copied journal articles, not entire journal issues. The court looked not only at the potential "sales of additional journal subscriptions, back issues and back volumes," but also the potential "licensing revenues and fees."[56] In *Texaco,* the secondary market was already established through clearinghouses such as the Copyright Clearance Center. However, it is unclear whether the secondary market must be well established or at least developing or have only the potential to develop before it will be considered. The Supreme Court has stated: "A challenge to a noncommercial use of a copyrighted work requires proof either that the particular use is harmful, or that if it should become widespread, it would adversely affect the potential market for the copyrighted work. . . . If the intended use is for commercial gain, that likelihood [of market harm] may be presumed. But if it is for a noncommercial purpose, the likelihood must be demonstrated."[57] However, the recent Ninth Circuit *Napster* decision considers the future or potential secondary market and a copyright owner's plan to "monetize" a resource in the future.[58] The court recognized harm "related to Napster's deleterious effect on the present and future digital download market."[59]

"To negate fair use," the Supreme Court has said that one need only show that if the challenged use "should become widespread, it would adversely affect the potential market for the copyrighted work."[60] In addition, *Napster* suggests that a copying or "reproduction" to forgo the purchase of a bona fide copy does in fact impact the economic rights of the copyright owner.[61]

As commercial vendors either express an interest or move into a market that makes smaller and smaller pieces of information available for purchase or license, there will be ample evidence for copyright owners to demonstrate secondary market harm.

Q13   Is it okay to use someone's copyrighted work for a library publication if it is comment or criticism?

Generally, yes. The four factors are preceded by a general comment:

> Notwithstanding the provisions of sections 106 and 106A, the fair use of a copyrighted work, including such use by reproduction in copies or phonorecords or by any other means specified by that section, for purposes such as criticism, comment, news reporting, teaching (including multiple copies for classroom use), scholarship, or research, is not an

infringement of copyright. In determining whether the use made of a work in any particular case is a fair use the factors to be considered shall include . . .[62]

However, just because a use falls within the listed categories of "criticism, comment, news reporting, teaching (including multiple copies for classroom use), scholarship, or research," it is not automatically a fair use. Rather, once it falls into one of these categories, it is then considered fair depending upon the four factors. Moreover, the list is not intended to be "exhaustive but illustrative."[63]

Q14   Is it "fair use" for a library to make a copy for a patron if it is for research use only?

Not necessarily. Research helps in finding fair use, but in itself, it is not enough. The confusion may arise from an informal understanding known as the "Gentlemen's Agreement" between librarians and publishers which predates the Copyright Act of 1976.[64] The Gentlemen's Agreement allowed a library to make a single copy of any printed material, even a complete copy of a book, if the purpose was for research and the copy was delivered to the scholar without any profit to the library. This may have given researchers the false impression that if a library could do this, an individual could too. Furthermore, researchers may erroneously believe that when Congress articulated the types of use for which a work might be considered fair, by a library or by an individual, it was expanding the list of acceptable uses beyond the mere "research" of the Gentlemen's Agreement, i.e., that complete copying for another listed purpose such as "teaching" is also acceptable per se. This is contrary to a plain reading of the statute and the legislative history. In fact, the House Judiciary Committee considered and rejected a blanket exemption for "educational and scholarly" purposes.[65] However, sometimes library copying will fall into fair use, after a careful analysis of all the factors. Furthermore, even if the copying does not appear to meet the fair use criteria, it may still be permissible under the "library exception," section 108.

Q15   Does the opposite hold true? If a use falls outside "criticism, comment, news reporting, teaching (including multiple copies for classroom use), scholarship, or research," does it preclude a finding of fair use?

No. The statute uses this phrase as an example. It says "*including* such use . . . for purposes such as criticism, comment," etc. Similarly, the four factors are not exhaustive, but illustrative: "the factors to be considered shall *include*. . ." Thus, fair use is not confined to these factors or purposes but must at a minimum consider the four factors.

Q16   *My supervisor gave me a sheet of Classroom Guidelines that tell me exactly how much I can copy, down to the number of words I can copy from a poem. Is this the legal limit?*

No. The Classroom Guidelines are the culmination of negotiations between private groups representing publishers and educators.[66] The guidelines are *not* the full extent of the library's rights under "fair use." Together, the groups set a "safe harbor," a set of guidelines that educators can use and know for certain that they are on safe legal ground. The guidelines represent a *floor*, not a *ceiling*, when it comes to fair use.

The preamble to the agreement states:

> The purpose of the following guidelines is to state the minimum standards of educational fair use under Section 107 [of the Copyright Act]. The parties agree that the conditions determining the extent of permissible copying for educational purposes may change in the future; that certain types of copying permitted under these guidelines may not be permissible in the future; and conversely that in the future other types of copying not permitted under these guidelines may be permissible under revised guidelines. Moreover, the . . . statement of the guidelines is not intended to limit the types of copying permitted under the standards of fair use under judicial decision and which are stated in Section 107. . . . *There may be instances in which copying which does not fall within the guidelines . . . may nonetheless be permitted under the criteria of fair use* (emphasis added).

These guidelines are *not* given the force of law in and of themselves. In some jurisdictions, however, courts have referred to the guidelines in their decisions.[67]

Librarians and library users may copy *more* than the rock-bottom amounts prescribed in the guidelines, provided they apply the four-factor fair use test. But by the same token, there may be some risk associated with reliance on these or any other of the so-called fair use guidelines that exist.[68] Moreover, recent precedent from the Second Circuit, while not referring to specifics, clearly contradicts the language of another fair use guideline, the Fair Use Guidelines for Educational Multimedia and Use of Digital Media in Student Assignments.[69]

Q17   If a work is unpublished, may the library assume it is "fair use" to use it?

No. Traditionally, unpublished works have received greater protection than published works. In 1992, Congress added a proviso to section 107 explicitly stating that "fair use" can apply to unpublished works: "The fact that a work is unpublished shall not itself bar a finding of fair use if such finding is made upon consideration of all the above factors."[70] This has been the only change to section 107 since its enactment in 1976. In the words of the House Judiciary Committee, the purpose of the amendment was "to clarify the intent of Congress that there be no per se rule barring claims of fair use of unpublished works."[71] Rather, "courts are to examine all four statutory factors set forth in Section 107, as well as any other factors deemed relevant in the court's discretion."[72]

Library Examples

In the following examples, the fair use factors are applied to various library situations. Note that no conclusions are drawn, in the absence of authoritative case law. Legal reasoning is offered, but the reader, like a judge, must draw her own conclusions. Several examples are provided to give the reader a sense of the fair-use factor analysis. The repetition in the reasoning should help you apply the reasoning to your own situation. Unfortunately, because fair use is a "flexible" concept, one never knows for certain whether a use would be considered fair use until a court decides the case. Libraries often make use of section 108, the "library exception," which is far more concrete, and is discussed immediately following these fair use examples.

Q18   Is it okay to copy pictures to make a thumbnail-image index to a collection?

Apply the four factors to this situation:

> *Purpose:* If nonprofit, educational, this will aid the library. The "transformative" use, i.e., using the images to create a new tool, will help a finding of fair use.

> *Nature of work:* As in *Kelly* v. *Arriba Soft*, a library's thumbnail index to pictures is likely to copy highly creative work, such as photographs or artwork, weighing against the user according to the second fair use factor.

Amount: Furthermore, the images are likely to be copied in their entirety, weighing against the user according to the third fair use factor. However, the quality of the images becomes important. In *Kelly,* the "reduction in size and resolution mitigates damage that might otherwise result from copying."[73] Therefore, the court concluded that the third factor only "weighs slightly against the fair use."

Market: If the thumbnail images can help a patron (or the library itself) substitute for the actual product, this will weigh against fair use. If, however, the images are of poor quality, the market harm may be minimized.

Q19   Can a library show the chocolate factory assembly-line scene from I Love Lucy in a training workshop?

Suppose a library wanted to give a program, for staff or for the public, about stress. It has a videotape of the episode of *I Love Lucy* that shows Lucy and Ethel working on a chocolate factory assembly line. The chocolates start speeding up at a rapid clip, and Lucy and Ethel resort to creative methods to keep up.

Purpose: An educational purpose will help; a commercial seminar will tilt away from fair use.

Nature of work: The television show is highly creative, not factual; this factor is likely to tilt away from fair use.

Amount: If the library used even just a few minutes of the episode, the *substantiality* of the portion would still weigh against fair use. This is also known as "the heart of the work."

Market: The scene is probably available to be licensed; not paying for a license could hurt the market for the work.

Q20   Can a library copy another library's bibliographies or pathfinders?

Recall that if the source is the federal government, or another level of government that has relinquished ownership to copyrights in its work, it is in the public domain. Recall also that there may be "reserved" portions within the pathfinder, such as an excerpt from a copyrighted work that will still need permission.

If the source is not in the public domain, either get permission or try to determine if the copying is fair use. Again, there is no case law, but a court might analyze this situation as follows:

Purpose: An educational purpose will help; a commercial purpose will tilt away from fair use.

Nature of work: The bibliography and pathfinder are mostly factual. In fact, citations cannot be copyrighted. However, the *compilation* of citations is copyrightable. This is a *thin copyright;* that is, the copyright owner has an ownership interest in the selection, arrangement, and presentation of the citations only. If there are original annotations, the copyright owner has ownership of these too, which are more creative than a mere recitation of facts.

Amount: The less proportion of the work used, the more likely it will be fair use. If there is a "heart of the work" that is used, that will weigh against fair use (unless the library copied the "heart" in order to make a parody of the original).

Market: If the original bibliography or pathfinder was available free of charge, the market harm is diminished. It is unlikely, however, that these items would be "draws" to bring in paying customers for other services.

Q21   Can a library copy text, graphics, etc., from other web pages?
A full discussion of this is in chapter 2, "Designing the Library Web Page."

Q22   Is it fair use to copy an article for a library patron?
Note: The next section of this chapter discusses section 108, the "library exception" to copyright law. This exception sometimes allows libraries to copy articles for patrons, even if fair use analysis fails.

Purpose: If the reason for the copy is personal or educational, this will help fair use. If it is commercial, this will hurt fair use.

Nature of work: If the work copied is from a factual reference book, such as a directory, this will help fair use. If it is highly creative, such as a novel or poetry, this will hurt fair use.

Amount: The less proportion copied, the more likely it will be fair use. If "the heart" of the work is copied, this will hurt fair use, unless essential for a parody.

Market: While it might be tempting to argue that a reproduction of a book for a public library patron or the copying of a video for use in a school media center is for a personal, educational, or otherwise nonprofit purpose, and one copy will not influence the market, this may not be true. Many products exist solely if not at least primarily in the nonprofit or educational or other limited market, like a textbook or workbook, auto-manual, multipart documentary video, etc. Justifying the reproduction, distribution, or display simply because it is for a good cause or purpose—the education of children—is not logical, as other users cannot simply make up the loss of sales if every library or school made the same rationalization, since the primary market for such sales is the library or school.

Q23   Is it fair use when a library copies an electronic article that it has leased from a vendor, even if the license restricts copying?

Today, libraries have shifted from owning copies of journal articles to licensing access to the articles in electronic form. When this is done, the license agreement, signed by the library (or a larger entity, such as the library's parent body or a library cooperative), dictates the terms of downloading, printing, interlibrary loans, etc.

Many resources are available today to help a librarian negotiate license terms that help preserve traditional uses, and it is critical that librarians ensure that these concerns are relayed to the persons who negotiate the library's licenses. The Association of Research Libraries, Yale University's Liblicense website, Arlene Bielefield and Lawrence Cheeseman's book *Interpreting and Negotiating Licensing Agreements,* and Lesley Ellen Harris's book *Licensing Digital Content* are particularly useful sources for libraries.[74]

The issue of whether a licensing agreement can override copyright law provisions is a complicated one. Although most copyright law provisions are essentially a "default" system of arranging rights and can be easily rearranged by contract (witness all publishing agreements), it is unclear whether or not someone can lose "fair use" rights by virtue of signing a contract.

In a related case, *ProCD* v. *Zeidenberg,* a controversial Seventh Circuit decision held that the license terms of a telephone directory database, SelectPhone, were enforceable, even though the license kept a user from copying a database that was not protected by copyright. The *ProCD* case had a complicating issue in that the license was not negotiated, but was rather a "shrinkwrap license," which was not reviewable at the time of purchase. This may suggest that other courts might view the signing away of fair use rights in a negotiated license agreement scenario as more palpable, in terms of the license's legal enforceability. In *ProCD,* a lower court had held that even if a shrinkwrap license was an enforceable contract under state law, federal law preempted it. Section 301(a) of the Copyright Act preempts "legal or equitable rights [under state law] that are equivalent to any of the exclusive rights within the general scope of copyright as specified by section 106 in works of authorship that are fixed in a tangible medium of expression and come within the subject matter of copyright as specified by sections 102 and 103."[75] But in a stunning turn of events for libraries, the appellate court questioned whether the state contract rights were equivalent to the exclusive rights within the general scope of copyright. It wrote: "A copyright is a right against the world. Contracts, by contrast, generally affect only their parties; strangers may do as they please, so contracts do not create "exclusive rights."[76] The appellate court upheld the contract.[77]

It is unclear whether the result might be different if a court were considering a nonprofit library's rights instead of commercial exploitation. Nonetheless, the lesson of *ProCD* for libraries is this: carefully scrutinize license agreements and negotiate terms that meet your library's needs, ideally retaining the section 108 and other rights that libraries have had in the analog world.

Library Interlibrary Loan, Preservation, and Replacements Exceptions: Section 108

Q24   What is the "library exception" known as section 108?

Section 108 permits libraries and archives to make copies for interlibrary loan, preservation, and replacements. Not every library qualifies for section 108 protection, and those that do must follow certain conditions, as discussed below. Unlike the painstakingly and uncertain case-by-case evaluation that libraries must make using a fair use analysis under section 107, the "library exceptions" presented in section 108 are detailed in the statute yet offer their own challenges, since each substantive section contains numerous conditions. Understanding the complexity and nuances of each subsection is the challenge here.

That said, it is important to remember that if a library does not qualify for section 108, or if the particular situation does not qualify, the copying might still be an acceptable "fair use." Furthermore, the copyright law lists a number of other exceptions that the library copying might qualify for.[78]

Q25   Does section 108 apply to my library?

It applies to most libraries. Section 108 requires that the library or archive be either open to the public or available to researchers in the field beyond its affiliated users. In other words, a school library that allows parents to access the collection would be "open to the public." A corporate library that allows outside researchers some access may also qualify.

Specifically, the law states that a library may enjoy section 108 protections if:

(1) the reproduction or distribution is made without any purpose of direct or indirect commercial advantage;

(2) the collections of the library or archives are
   (i) open to the public, or
   (ii) available not only to researchers affiliated with the library or archives or with the institution of which it is a part, but also to other persons doing research in a specialized field; and

(3) the reproduction or distribution of the work includes a notice of copyright that appears on the copy or phonorecord that is reproduced under the provisions of this section, or includes a legend stating that the work may be protected by copyright if no such notice can be found on the copy or phonorecord that is reproduced under the provisions of this section.[79]

Q26   What does section 108 mean when it says a notice of copyright or a legend must appear on the copy?

If the library finds a copyright notice on the work that it is copying from, it is typically in the front pages of a book, or at the beginning or end of an article.[80] This notice, e.g., "Copyright © 2001 Jane Author," must be added to the copy that the library makes. If a copyright notice does not appear, a "legend" can be stamped on the copy, saying that the work may be protected under copyright. For example: "Notice: This material may be protected by Copyright Law (Title 17 U.S.C.)."

Q27   How does section 108 help libraries?

Section 108 gives four circumstances in which libraries may make copies:

- Reproduction of unpublished works for "preservation and security" *for the library*
- Replacement of published works (that are damaged, deteriorating, lost, stolen, or in an obsolete format) *for the library*
- Reproduction *for a patron* of a serial or less than whole part of a work

- Reproduction *for a patron* of an entire or substantial portion of a work

Q28   Does section 108 allow library staff to make personal copies?

No. Section 108 liability limitation is for libraries and their employees only when performing actions within the scope of their employment. Personal copying is not covered by section 108, but would be subject to the fair use provisions of section 107.

Q29   Must library copying be done for nonprofit uses only?

Section 108 clearly states that reproduction or distribution must be made without any purpose of direct or indirect commercial advantage.[81] Unlike the evolving standard of "commercial" versus noncommercial in fair use, the section 108 standard appears to be more rigid. The district court in *Texaco* concluded that because the defendant used the copies as part of its overall commercial enterprise, it could not qualify for section 108(1) status:

> Section 108 authorizes library photocopying under narrowly specified circumstances. The circumstances do not apply. Section 108 is made applicable only 'if the reproduction . . . is made without any purpose of direct or indirect commercial advantage.' [Citation omitted] As noted above, Texaco makes the photocopies solely for commercial advantage. Texaco's $80 million dollar annual budget for scientific research, of which its photocopying represents a microscopic part, is not expended as an exercise in philanthropy. It is done for profit. Articles are photocopied to help Texaco's scientists in their profit-motivated research.[82]

Section 108, however, has a mixed legislative history. The House Report from the original enactment of section 108 in 1976 focused on the "immediate commercial motivation behind the reproduction or distribution itself, rather than to the ultimate profit-making motivation behind the enterprise in which the library is located."[83] The Senate Report suggests that Congress saw section 108 as limited to libraries or archives in nonprofit organizations. According to the Senate Report, it is "intended to preclude a library in a profit-making organization from providing photocopies of copyrighted materials to employees engaged in furtherance of the organization's commercial enterprise, unless such copying qualifies as a fair use, or the organization has obtained the necessary copyright licenses."[84] The Conference Report appears to strike a balance in stating that "isolated, spontaneous" copying or "participation by such a library or archive [in a for-profit organization without any commercial motivation] in interlibrary arrangements, would come within the scope of section 108."[85]

Q30   Do the new copyright provisions passed in 1998 as part of the DMCA allow libraries to make digital copies?

Only in the most limited of ways. Digital copies may *not* be distributed outside the library, except in the limited circumstances described below.[86] Congressional legislative history is very clear in its intent to limit digital copies:

> Although online interactive digital networks have since given birth to online digital "libraries" and "archives" that exist only in the virtual (rather than physical) sense on websites, bulletin boards and homepages across the Internet, it is not the Committee's intent that section 108 as revised apply to such collections of information. . . . The extension of the application of section 108 to all such sites would be tantamount to creating an exception to the exclusive rights of copyright holders that would permit any person who has an online website, bulletin board or a homepage to freely reproduce and distribute copyrighted works. Such an exemption would swallow the general rule and severely impair the copyright owner's right and ability to commercially exploit their copyrighted works.[87]

Q31   When can a library make copies of unpublished works in its collection?

Under section 108(b), a library may make up to three copies of an unpublished work for preservation or security, or up to three copies for deposit for research purposes in another library or archives (but that library must also qualify for section 108), if the copy is currently in the original library's collection, and any digital copies are not made available to the public outside the premises of the library.[88] This covers situations in which the library wants a backup copy (reproduction) or is willing to share a part of its collection (that is unpublished) with another library or archive (reproduction and distribution). Note that there is nothing in section 108 that requires a library or archive to share its collection.

The digital copy must not be "otherwise distributed" to the public outside the premises of the library or archives. Loading the digital collection on an in-house Intranet is permissible, but loading copies onto the library's website with access available to remote users is not. Furthermore, the receiving library or archive may not distribute the digital copy to another library or archive, i.e., the distribution is limited to the initial transfer ("is not otherwise distributed in that format"); that library would need to print out the digital copy that it received.[89] A library can mix and match, with one hard copy for circulation, one digital copy on its Intranet, and the third (digital) copy for transfer (under the conditions set forth above) to another library.

The Senate Report explained the committee's concern with making digitized library collections widely accessible: "This proviso is necessary to ensure that the amendment strikes the appropriate balance, permitting the use of digital technology by libraries and archives while guarding against the potential harm to the copyright owners' market from patrons obtaining unlimited access to digital copies from any location."[90]

Q32   When can a library make copies to replace damaged copies of published works?

Under section 108(c), a library may make up to three copies of a published work that is damaged, deteriorating, lost, or stolen, or if the existing format in which the work is stored has become obsolete. The library must, after a reasonable effort, determine that an unused replacement cannot be obtained at a fair price; and not make any digital copies available to the public outside the premises of the library or archives.[91]

If the library owns a book that is lost, stolen, or damaged, but the book is still available for purchase from the library's normal vendors, i.e., it is an "unused replacement" at a "fair price," the library must purchase a new copy. According to the legislative history, a "reasonable effort" will "always require recourse to commonly known trade sources in the United States, and in the normal situation also to the publisher or other copyright owners (if such owner can be located at the address listed in the copyright registration), or an authorized reproduction service."[92]

Q33   How does a library know when a format is "obsolete"?

A format is considered obsolete if the machine or device necessary to render perceptible a work stored in that format is no longer manufactured or is no longer reasonably available in the commercial marketplace.[92] Before 1998, the item itself had to be in jeopardy. The DMCA amendments added "or if the existing format in which the work is stored has become obsolete," which speaks to the status of the viewing or rendering technology, rather than the work itself.

Q34   If a used copy is available in the secondhand book market, or if the only available copy is priced at a premium, must the library purchase it rather than copy a work that is damaged?

No. The fact that a used "copy" is available in the secondhand book market, or the only unused copy is available but at a premium, does not prevent a library or archive from availing itself of section 108(c). The concept of a secondhand market applies to obsolete formats too, since a technology available only in secondhand stores "should not be considered reasonably available."[94]

Q35   May a library make a backup copy of a published work in anticipation of future damage?

No. A library may not make a backup copy of a published work in anticipation of its needing replacement at some future date or of its viewing or rendering technology becoming obsolete.

Q36   Does this mean that if some titles in a library collection of videotapes are in the obsolete Beta format, a library could transfer them to VHS instead of buying new copies?

In other words, does the "unused replacement" and "fair price" language refer only to the original Beta format or to the work in general? What if the tapes are available in VHS or on DVD? If the tapes are not replaceable as Beta, and no VHS or DVD is available, it is reasonable to transfer them to a newer format. The Senate Report, referring to section 108(c), states: "This provision is intended to permit libraries and archives to ensure that copies of works in their collections continue to be accessible and useful to their patrons."[95] The wording of the statute states that an "unused replacement cannot be obtained at fair price." However, if new VHS or DVD versions are now available at a fair price, the library would have to buy them. Otherwise, interpreting the subsection, for example, to allow the copying of obsolete formats onto VHS when new VHS versions are still available would amount to a right of perpetual reproduction in libraries. This right is triggered only when a replacement copy of the work can not be obtained in the normal marketplace.

*Q37   What if patrons demand a musical work on CD when the
library only has an audiocassette tape version that is no
longer available unused at a fair price, but an unused CD
version is available at a fair price? Can the library copy the
music onto a CD?*

The technology is not obsolete yet, as cassette players are still available for
sale in the primary market. Moreover, an unused replacement is still available at a fair price on CD. Thus, it is logical to conclude that the library
cannot copy the music onto a CD.

*Q38   If an audiocassette tape is damaged, deteriorating, lost, or
stolen, and a CD version of it is available, can the library
make a copy with a CD burner?*

No. Here, an unused replacement is available. Suppose that a CD version is
not available, then what? The library could burn the analog cassette tape on
to a CD, but it could not circulate it, since this would be making the 108(c)
copy available to patrons outside the physical premises of the library.

*Q39   When can a library make copies of an article or a small
portion of a work for interlibrary loan?*

Under section 108(d), a library may copy and send a copy of a periodical
article, a contribution to a copyrighted collection, or a small part of a
copyrighted work for interlibrary loan if:

- the copy becomes the property of the user;
- the library has no notice that the copy is for any purpose other than
  private study, scholarship, or research; and
- the library prominently displays a warning of copyright on its order
  forms, and posts the warning at the place where orders are
  accepted.

These provisions are clearly spelled out in section 108(d):

> The rights of reproduction and distribution under this section apply to a
> copy, made from the collection of a library or archives where the user
> makes his or her request or from that of another library or archives, of
> no more than one article or other contribution to a copyrighted collec-
> tion or periodical issue, or to a copy or phonorecord of a small part of
> any other copyrighted work, if—

(1) the copy or phonorecord becomes the property of the user, and the library or archives has had no notice that the copy or phonorecord would be used for any purpose other than private study, scholarship, or research; and

(2) the library or archives displays prominently, at the place where orders are accepted, and includes on its order form, a warning of copyright in accordance with requirements that the Register of Copyrights shall prescribe by regulation.[96]

Q40   When can a library make copies of an entire work or a substantial part of it for interlibrary loan?

Under section 108(e), a library can copy and deliver an entire work (or substantial part of it) when:

- the library undertakes a reasonable investigation and finds the work is not available at a fair price;
- the copy becomes the property of the user;
- the library had no notice that the copy is for any purpose other than private study, scholarship, or research; and
- the library prominently displays a warning of copyright on its order forms, and posts the warning at the place where orders are accepted.

Again, the copyright code clearly spells out these requirements, in section 108(e):

> The rights of reproduction and distribution under this section apply to the entire work, or to a substantial part of it, made from the collection of a library or archives where the user makes his or her request or from that of another library or archives, if the library or archives has first determined, on the basis of a reasonable investigation, that a copy or phonorecord of the copyrighted work cannot be obtained at a fair price, if—
>
> (1) the copy or phonorecord becomes the property of the user, and the library or archives has had no notice that the copy or phonorecord would be used for any purpose other than private study, scholarship, or research; and
>
> (2) the library or archives displays prominently, at the place where orders are accepted, and includes on its order form, a warning of copyright in accordance with requirements that the Register of Copyrights shall prescribe by regulation.[97]

Q41   Can the library make an extra copy for its files, in the expectation that there will be more interlibrary loan requests?

No. In both situations above, whether the copy is of an entire work or merely a portion of it, the law says that the copy must become the property of the user.[98] This clause, in fact, requires distribution of the reproduction. This prevents the library from using either section to build up its own collection.

Q42   Can the library make copies of articles for reserves, e-reserves, or vertical files?

Not under section 108. As in the example in question 41, the copy placed on reserve does not become the "property of the user." However, there may be fair use justifications for reserve copies. Each item should be evaluated on a case-by-case basis, using the fair use factors described in question 11.

Q43   What does the law mean when it says "the library or archives has had no notice that the copy or phonorecord would be used for any purpose other than private study, scholarship, or research"?

The statute uses the term "notice," but does nothing to provide the form or content of the notice, unlike the rather formal notice provisions of other sections of the copyright law, e.g., section 512, which pertains to the liability of online service providers. What if the librarian sees that the patron is wearing a T-shirt or security identification badge that says "ACME Document Reproduction Services" on it and the patron says "I need this for work" or "Charge the ILL fee to our account"? Does the library have "notice" according to law?[99] Turning a blind eye would seem to be stretching the law, looking to its spirit rather than to its letter. It would also raise ethical questions that are beyond the scope of this book, but are nonetheless of concern in the professional atmosphere of a library.

Q44   What is the copyright warning notice that is required for display on order forms and at the place orders are taken?

The second proviso, sections 108(d)(2) and 108(e)(2), requires that the "library or archives displays prominently, at the place where orders are accepted, and includes on its order form, a warning of copyright in accordance with requirements that the Register of Copyrights shall prescribe by regulation." These regulations have been promulgated and are now a familiar copyright warning notice. According to the regulation, the notice shall consist of a verbatim reproduction of the following:

> The copyright law of the United States (Title 17, United States Code) governs the making of photocopies or other reproductions of copyrighted material. Under certain conditions specified in the law, libraries and archives are authorized to furnish a photocopy or other reproduction. One of these specific conditions is that the photocopy or reproduction is not to be "used for any purpose other than private study, scholarship, or research." If a user makes a request for, or later uses, a photocopy or reproduction for purposes in excess of "fair use," that user may be liable for copyright infringement. This institution reserves the right to refuse to accept a copying order if, in its judgment, fulfillment of the order would involve violation of copyright law.[100]

Q45   I notice that the interlibrary loan provision of the copyright law does not seem to allow copies of entire works if a copy is available at a fair price. Does it allow a library to make a copy if the only "fair price" copy is a used copy?

Yes. This differs from the replacement criteria, section 108(c), which allows a library to copy an entire work to replace damaged, stolen, or lost copies even if a used copy is available. Section 108(e) does not contain the word "unused."[101] Thus if the copy is used, but otherwise available at a fair price, then the library or archive cannot use section 108(e) to justify copying the entire work or a substantial portion of it, but must instead consider purchasing the used copy.

Q46   What is the library's legal responsibility with respect to self-service photocopiers, scanners, computer printers, dual cassette players, or other reproducing equipment?

This is spelled out in section 108(f), which says:

> Nothing in this section— (1) shall be construed to impose liability for copyright infringement upon a library or archives or its employees for the unsupervised use of reproducing equipment located on its premises: *Provided,* That such equipment displays a notice that the making of a copy may be subject to the copyright law.

This provision limits the liability of the library or archive as a contributory infringer. "Two types of activities that lead to contributory liability are: (i) personal conduct that encourages or assists the infringement; and (ii) provision of machinery or goods that facilitate the infringement."[102] In commenting on the exemption for libraries that provide reproducing equipment, the authors of the White Paper on Intellectual Property noted that except for libraries, "no other provider of equipment enjoys any statutory immunity."[103] In return, libraries and archives must post a copyright warning on all equipment, photocopiers, computers, scanners, samplers, fiche readers/printers, or any sort of equipment that allows a patron to copy a copyrighted work.

Q47   What is the difference between sections 108(d) and (e) and section 108(f)(1)?

Section 108(f)(1) immunizes the library from secondary copyright liability for infringement by patrons on its premises. However, it does not provide any immunity, for example, when the library or its employees acting within the scope of their employment make infringing copies under 108(d) or (e).

Q48   Are library patrons immune from copyright suits if they use a library photocopier?

No. While the library may be immune from claims of contributory infringement, the patron is not: nothing "excuses a person who uses such reproducing equipment or who requests a copy under subsection (d) from liability for copyright infringement for any such act, or for any later use of such copy or phonorecord, if it exceeds fair use as provided by section 107."[104]

Q49   A patron donated videotapes of news programs. May we add them to the collection?

As long as the library meets the requirements of section 108, it can copy and lend a limited number of copies and excerpts of an audiovisual news program.[105] The House Report says that this exemption is intended to apply to the daily newscasts of the national television networks, which report the major events of the day. It does not apply to a documentary (except documentary programs involving news reporting as that term is used in section 107), or to magazine-format or other public affairs broadcasts dealing with subjects of general interest to the viewing public.[106]

Programs such as *60 Minutes* or *20/20* would not qualify; the purpose is rather to "make off-the-air videotape recordings of daily network newscasts for limited distribution to scholars and researchers for use in research."[107] The Conference Report echoes this intent to allow a library to reproduce (by videotape, audiotape, etc.) newscasts, interviews, etc., and "to distribute a limited number of reproductions of such a program on a loan basis."[108] However, both the House and Conference reports use language suggesting that the qualifying library or archive make the copy of the news program, rather than use a copy made by a patron.

Q50 *Can I make a copy of a work, under section 108, even if I signed a licensing agreement that says I cannot make copies for any purpose?*

No. A library cannot use section 108 to override any contractual obligations assumed at any time by the library when it obtained a copy of a work in its collections.[109] Be careful when signing licensing agreements. If your parent organization or a cooperative signed the licensing agreement, get a copy and read it. A library's ability to participate in interlibrary loan might be limited by the license agreement the library signed when it acquired the item for its collection.

Q51 *When can my library make copies for interlibrary loan?*

According to section 108, the copies must be made without any purpose of direct or indirect commercial advantage.[110] There have been no court cases interpreting this language, but the legislative history suggests that "[p]articipation by such library or archives in interlibrary arrangements would come within the scope of the section 108."[111]

The library is prohibited from making systematic multiple copies.[112] A library may make a single copy of an item for a patron. Additional copies may be made of the same material on separate occasions.[113] Specific quantitative limits are suggested in the CONTU Guidelines on Photocopying and Interlibrary Arrangements.

Q52 *What are the CONTU Guidelines on Photocopying and Interlibrary Arrangements? Are these known as "the Rule of 5"?*

The CONTU Guidelines on Photocopying and Interlibrary Loan Arrangements were written by the National Commission on New Technological Uses of Copyright Works (CONTU) in a report for Congress.[114] They have since become part of the de facto rules on quantitative limits on interlibrary lending.

The guidelines are also known as "the Rule of 5," although this is not a legal limit, and is better characterized as "the Suggestion of 5."[115] Stated simply, the rule says that within any calendar year, a borrowing library should not borrow more than five articles from the same periodical title published within five years of the date of the request. If a library received a request on January 1, 2003, for two articles from the same journal, one from fall 1999 and the other from spring 1997, the library would count the former but not the latter. Borrowing libraries are to keep three years of records of all requests made and filled.

Q53 Can my library make copies of articles for staff on a routing list?

If a library distributes a list of new journal articles to people on a routing list, the library should be careful not to make systematic copies of the articles for staff. If the copying is part of a library's routine table of contents distribution and periodical reproduction service, then it is most likely systematic. The Senate Report had some harsh words for libraries and archives involved in various common practices, suggesting that these are in fact "systematic" and prohibited by section 108(g), such as a lending/collection development consortium, a routing/photocopying service, and a collection development plan among branches of the same library to avoid multiple subscriptions.[116] It can be argued, however, that the Conference Report, and its adoption of the Rule of 5, supersede the Senate Report.

Q54 I read that the term of copyright has been extended by twenty years. Is there an exception for libraries?

There is a very weak exception for libraries. Section 108(h) was added by recent copyright term-extension legislation.[117] The term-extension legislation extended the duration of current copyrighted protection for works protected as of December 31, 1998, by an additional twenty years. However, the library and archive community was given a special exemption. These institutions do not need to recognize the additional twenty-year extension if the purpose of the reproduction, distribution, display, or performance of a published work is for preservation, scholarship, or research, and the work is not subject to normal commercial exploitation.

Section 108(h) states:

> For purposes of this section, during the last 20 years of any term of copyright of a published work, a library or archives, including a nonprofit educational institution that functions as such, may reproduce, distribute, display, or perform in facsimile or digital form a copy or phonorecord of

such work, or portions thereof, for purposes of preservation, scholarship, or research,

if the library or archive after a "reasonable investigation" determines that none of the following conditions apply:

> the work is subject to normal commercial exploitation; . . . a copy or phonorecord of the work can be obtained at a reasonable price; or . . . the copyright owner or its agent provides notice pursuant to regulations promulgated by the Register of Copyrights that either of the conditions set forth above apply, i.e., the work is still subject to normal commercially exploitation or is available at a reasonable price.[118]

This exception is somewhat hollow, since the most desirable works for which the library would like to ignore the additional twenty-year copyright term extension are those that a copyright owner would still attempt to exploit commercially. Furthermore, there is no simple test to determine if a work is subject to a normal commercial exploitation.

Q55 Can my library make a copy of a videotape or CD for interlibrary loan?

Not under section 108. While a library may make a copy of a journal article (a literary work) for interlibrary loan, it may not make a copy of a videotape cassette (an audiovisual work), musical work, pictorial, graphic, or sculptural work, or a motion picture.[119] This prohibition does not apply to 108(b) or (c) rights, however; that is why the discussion earlier posed the question of the replacement of damaged video or cassette tapes under 108(c). It is acceptable, however, if a pictorial or graphic work, published as an illustration, diagram, or similar adjunct to a work, is copied.

However, do not forget "fair use." Depending on the circumstances, it is possible that a copy could be made, after evaluating the four factors. In fact, the House Report says:

> In the case of music, for example, it would be fair use for a scholar doing musicological research to have a library supply a copy of a portion of a score or to reproduce portions of a phonorecord of a work. Nothing in section 108 impairs the applicability of the fair use doctrine to a wide variety of situations involving photocopying or other reproduction by a library of copyrighted material in its collections, where the user requests the reproduction for legitimate scholarly or research purposes.[120]

Library Lending Exceptions and
the First Sale Doctrine: Section 109

The "first sale doctrine" is at the foundation of public libraries in the United States. Although the right to distribute a work is an "exclusive right" maintained by the copyright holder, the Supreme Court has said that it only applies to the "first sale" of the item.[121] Once a library buys an item, it may lend, resell, or do whatever it chooses with it.

In contrast to the American first sale doctrine, other nations such as Canada, the United Kingdom, and Australia operate under a "public lending right" system. Such systems pay royalties to authors *after* the book has been sold, based on the number of times it gets checked out of the library. In enacting the Public Lending Right Bill in 1985, the Australian minister at that time said: "Public Lending Right (PLR) is an internationally recognised concept of compensation paid to authors to recompense them for income lost by the free multiple use of their books in public lending libraries."[122]

In the United States, on the other hand, the first sale doctrine "assures the copyright owner that, until she parts with ownership, she has the right to prohibit all others from distributing the work. On the other hand, once a sale has occurred, the first sale doctrine allows the new owner to treat the object as his own."[123] In other words, the right of control created by the copyright law ends after the first sale of the work, whether a book, video, CD, etc.

This concept is embodied in section 109:

> Notwithstanding the provisions of section 106(3), the owner of a particular copy or phonorecord lawfully made under this title, or any person authorized by such owner, is entitled, without the authority of the copyright owner, to sell or otherwise dispose of the possession of that copy or phonorecord.[124]

The term "object" here refers to the physical embodiment of the copyrighted work, as opposed to the copyright itself. The first sale doctrine applies to this physical embodiment of the work. This is one reason the U.S. Copyright Office rejected the extension of section 109 into cyberspace and the creation of a digital first sale doctrine:

> Digital transmission of a work does not implicate the alienability of a physical artifact. When a work is transmitted, the sender is not exercising common-law dominion over an item of personal property; he is exer-

cising the central copyright of reproduction with respect to the intangible work. . . . The underlying purpose of the first sale doctrine is to ensure the free circulation of tangible copies.[125]

Q56   May my library lend software as well as books?

Yes, if a nonprofit library lends the program for nonprofit purposes. Also, the library must affix the following notice to the packaging that contains the computer program, verbatim:

Computer Programs Notice:
Warning of Copyright Restrictions

The copyright law of the United States (Title 17, United States Code) governs the reproduction, distribution, adaptation, public performance, and public display of copyrighted material. Under certain conditions specified in law, nonprofit libraries are authorized to lend, lease, or rent copies of computer programs to patrons on a nonprofit basis and for nonprofit purposes. Any person who makes an unauthorized copy or adaptation of the computer program, or redistributes the loan copy, or publicly performs or displays the computer program, except as permitted by title 17 of the United States Code, may be liable for copyright infringement. This institution reserves the right to refuse to fulfill a loan request if, in its judgement, fulfillment of the request would lead to violation of the copyright law.[126]

The notice must be affixed by means of a label cemented, gummed, or otherwise durably attached to the copies or to a box, reel, cartridge, cassette, or other container used as a permanent receptacle for the copy of the computer program. The notice must be printed in such manner as to be clearly legible, comprehensible, and readily apparent to a casual user of the computer program.[127]

Q57   If my library is part of a profit-making institution, may I still lend the software?

No. The software and music industry, concerned that software and CD resale shops would undermine the market for their products, lobbied Congress for an exception to the first sale doctrine, one that would give a carve-out or return to the copyright owner of some level of control over subsequent transfers, including resales of these two types of works.

The Computer Software Rental Amendments Act of 1990[128] addressed these concerns by amending section 109 to provide for an exception to the first sale doctrine with respect to two categories of works.

> [N]either the owner of a particular phonorecord nor any person in possession of a particular copy of a computer program (including any tape, disk, or other medium embodying such program), may, for the purposes of direct or indirect commercial advantage, dispose of, or authorize the disposal of, the possession of that phonorecord or computer program (including any tape, disk, or other medium embodying such program) by rental, lease, or lending, or by any other act or practice in the nature of rental, lease, or lending.[129]

Thus the right to dispose of a computer program or phonorecord by "rental, lease, or lending" requires the permission of the copyright owner.

However, section 109(b) provides that this exception to the first sale doctrine "shall [not] apply to the rental, lease, or lending of a phonorecord for nonprofit purposes by a nonprofit library or nonprofit educational institution."[130] In other words, there is an exception to the exception for "nonprofit library and nonprofit educational institutions" for the rental, lease, or lending of phonorecords, such as a music CD.

In an attempt to balance the rights of owners and users, Congress recognized the potential for abuse and so required that libraries remind patrons of their obligations to honor the copyright of others.

> The Committee does not wish, however, to prohibit nonprofit lending by nonprofit libraries and nonprofit educational institutions. Such institutions serve a valuable public purpose by making computer software available to students who would not otherwise have access to it. At the same time, the Committee is aware that the same economic factors that lead to unauthorized copying in a commercial context may lead library patrons also to engage in such conduct.[131]

Q58   Can a nonprofit library, such as a public high school's media center, give used software to a grade school?

A nonprofit educational institution can transfer (give or "donate") a copy of a software program to another school. The transfer of possession of a lawfully made copy of a computer program by one nonprofit educational institution to another or to faculty, staff, and students does not constitute rental, lease, or lending for direct or indirect commercial purposes and is permitted.[132]

Q59   Can a nonprofit library, such as a public high school's media
       center, sell the software in a used book sale?

No, the exemption is only for transfer to another nonprofit educational
institution.[133]

Q60   If my library legitimately purchases an electronic item, such
       as a journal article, may it lend or sell it under the first sale
       doctrine?

The chances are good that the library signed a licensing agreement that
dictates specific terms as to the use of the electronic articles. If the licensing agreement is silent, it is a difficult question as to what constitutes a
legitimately purchased copy in the digital world. The U.S. Copyright
Office believes that the first sale doctrine does not cover electronic articles
such as an e-book, even if acquired by sale.[134]

Performances and Displays: Section 110

Section 110 helps libraries and others use copyrighted materials with
respect to performances and displays.

Q61   Teachers show videos in their classrooms all the time, even
       videos that they check out from our library. Can we show the
       same videos as part of library programs?

Generally not. Teachers have a special exception for

> performance or display of a work by instructors or pupils in the course
> of face-to-face teaching activities of a nonprofit educational institution,
> in a classroom or similar place devoted to instruction, unless, in the case
> of a motion picture or other audiovisual work, the performance, or the
> display of individual images, is given by means of a copy that was not
> lawfully made under this title, and that the person responsible for the
> performance knew or had reason to believe was not lawfully made.[135]

Several points should be made regarding the provisions of this section.
First, the performance or display in subsection (1) must be made "by in-
structors or pupils"; it cannot be done by other students not in the class.
Second, the exemption applies to any type of work. In other words, there
is no limitation on the type of work that may be performed or displayed
in a classroom. Possible categories of works include motion picture or

audiovisual works (a videocassette, for example), nondramatic literary works (a novel, for example), musical works (a song), dramatic works (a stage play), or dramatico-musical works (a Broadway musical). "To 'perform' a work means to recite, render, play, dance, or act it, either directly or by means of any device or process or, in the case of a motion picture or other audiovisual work, to show its images in any sequence or to make the sounds accompanying it audible."[136]

The major limitation on this very broad section 110(1) exemption is that it must occur within the context "of face-to-face teaching activities of a nonprofit educational institution, in a classroom or similar place devoted to instruction." This means that while the students and teacher need not see each other, "it does require their simultaneous presence in the same general area."[137] Remote broadcasts (i.e., distance education) are not allowed (but are covered by subsection (2) of section 110), but as long as the instructor and pupils are in the same building or general area the exemption would apply. This would allow for a transmission from one room to another because all the students could not physically fit into the same lecture hall.

The "teaching activity" language requires that the content of the material be related to the curriculum. While showing a Hollywood film adaptation of *Romeo and Juliet* would qualify in a literature class, a showing of the horror film *Scream* as an end-of-the-semester reward would not. The "teaching activities" do not include performances or displays, "whatever their cultural or recreational value or intellectual appeal, that are given for the recreation or entertainment of any part of their audience."[138]

Q62   *We have educational programs in our meeting room.*
        Is that "a similar place devoted to instruction"?

The section 110(1) exemptions must be in a bona fide educational environment to students enrolled in the class.[139] For example, showing a video to the school's Spanish Club members that meet in the library would not qualify. Showing a videocassette at a public library meeting room as part of a travel program would also not qualify. If a library rents out its meeting room, it would be wise to require groups to secure all necessary performance licenses and exempt the library from any penalties for any failure on their part to do so.

Q63   *If two or three students are in the library and wish to view*
        a video, is that permissible?

There is some debate over whether the ad hoc gathering of two or three patrons—for example, students in the library working on a school project—would also infringe copyright. The question is whether the viewing is a public performance (calling one of the exclusive rights of a copyright owner into play) for which a performance right is needed. The law states that a public display or performance is one that is made in a public place "where a substantial number of persons outside of a normal circle of a family and its social acquaintances is gathered."[140] Students from a classroom would meet the public performance criteria.

If the video viewing takes place in an academic or school library, the section 110 exemption may apply if in fact the library space also serves as a "classroom or similar place devoted to instruction."[141] An affirmative answer to this question in a public library is far less certain, since it would seem that the viewing of the video by two or three patrons there, even if each of them knew each other, might be a public performance because the library in general is "a place open to the public . . . where a substantial number of persons outside of a normal circle of a family and its social acquaintances" may gather.

There have not been any court cases clarifying public library video viewing. However, one could argue that even the small grouping constitutes a "public performance," needing a license. In cases involving video viewing in video stores, courts held that although the viewings were in booths, they were public performances, because the stores where the booths were located were "public."[142] This contrasted with private viewing in a hotel room, which a court found was *not* a public performance because hotel rooms, once rented for occupancy, were deemed "private."[143] A videotape system installed in a hotel for remote operation by hotel guests, who used it for transmitting selected videotapes for viewing on television sets in their hotel rooms, was a public performance requiring copyright license, because of the transmission.[144]

On the other hand, arguments have been made that video viewing in small groups in a public library may sometimes be "fair use," depending on the purpose, nature, amount viewed, and effect on the market.[145] (See question 11 for more on "fair use.") But again, this result uses section 107, not section 110.

Q64   Can a library turn on the television or the radio for the public to enjoy?

Generally, a library may allow patrons to view CNN broadcasts through a television console or play the local classical music station on a normal radio for the enjoyment of patrons. The "purpose is to exempt from copyright liability anyone who merely turns on, in a public place, an ordinary radio or television receiving apparatus of a kind commonly sold to members of the public for private use."[146] However, a concert-sized jumbo-tron or speaker system would not be the sort of apparatus contemplated in the law.[147]

If the transmission received is of a nondramatic musical work (a song, for example) intended to be received by the general public, originated by a radio or television broadcast station licensed as such by the Federal Communications Commission, or, if an audiovisual transmission, by a cable system or satellite carrier,"[148] then limitations on the number of receiving units used exist. The size of the library matters. If the library has "less than 2,000 gross square feet of space (excluding space used for customer parking and for no other purpose),"[149] multiple devices such as monitors are acceptable. But if the library has more than 2,000 gross square feet of space (excluding space used for customer parking), then there may be up to six loudspeakers in the library (and up to four in one room),[150] and up to four audiovisual devices (and no more than one in any one room). A screen for the audiovisual device may not be larger than fifty-five inches (measured on the diagonal).[151]

While a library in the latter category (more than 2,000 gross square feet) could have a standard television monitor (less than fifty-five inches) that receives broadcasts for patron viewing, it could not place a monitor in each corner of the library stack area. It could, however, place one monitor in the main reading room, one in the children's area, and another in the checkout alcove or entrance hall, making sure not to exceed the limit on total receiving devices ("not more than 4 audiovisual devices").[152]

DURATION OF COPYRIGHT: SECTIONS 302–304

Determining whether an older work is still protected by copyright law is complicated for several reasons. First, Congress has altered the term of copyright on numerous occasions. Second, Congress also conceptually changed the triggering act, moving from formalistic registration and notice provisions to a current system of having the work in theory protected from its creation. These are two quite different events. Finally, restoration pro-visions may actually restore the copyright of certain works of foreign origin whose copyright was lost due to factors other than expiration, e.g., renewal requirements. The restoration rules are complex and beyond the scope of this introduction.[153]

In general, a work is not eligible for copyright restoration under U.S. law if it is no longer protected in its country of origin. The current term of duration for published works created after March 1, 1989, is the life of the author plus 70 years. If the work is an anonymous, pseudonymous, or a work for hire the duration is the shorter of 95 years from publication or 120 from creation.

Before the 1989 date, but after January 1, 1978, if a work was pub-lished without notice of copyright but later registered, the same duration rules apply. If the same work was published during this period without copyright notice but not subsequently registered, it is in theory in the public domain. The complexity of even these introductory duration guide-lines underscores the confusion that resulted when the United States moved away from formal registration and notice requirements.

For a work published before the 1978 date, the operative trigger was the publication of the work. If the work was published with notice and the work's copyright was renewed, the duration is 95 years (28-year period, plus a renewal of 47, and a recent extension of 20 years for a total of 95 years). The final 20-year extension was added in 1998.[154] Before that recent extension, the term was 75 years (1998 − 75 = 1923). In other words, works published with proper notice before 1923 are no longer protected by copyright and are in the public domain. Works published after 1922 are potentially still protected. However, if the work was published with notice between 1923 and 1963 (before the term renewal was made automatic) but the copyright was not renewed, the work is in the public domain.

If the work was published with notice between 1923 and 1963 and the copyright was in fact renewed, or the work was published with notice between 1964 and 1978 (when renewal was automatic, but notice was still required), then in either case the duration of copyright is 95 years from publication (and the earliest a work would fall under the public domain would be 2018). This demonstrates the impact of the new term extension legislation: a work published in 1928, and still protected in 1998, had its term of copyright extended by 20 years.

The duration rules are slightly different for unpublished works but are simpler due to the absence of "publication" dates. For works created on or after January 1, 1978, the same life plus 70 (known author) or 95/120 (anonymous, pseudonymous, or a work for hire) rules apply. For works created before 1978 but unpublished at the time the new law took effect in 1978 (the 1976 Copyright Revision Act had a delayed "effective" date), there are two alternatives. If the work is somehow published before January 1, 2003, then the duration of copyright is for the life of the author plus 70 years or December 31, 2047, whichever is greater. If the work is created before 1978 but not published until after December 31, 2002, then the duration is the life of the author plus 70 years. For unpublished works when the death date of the author is not known, the duration is 120 years from creation. (For a table of the copyright duration rules, see the appendix to this chapter.)[155]

PATRONS AND LIBRARY LIABILITY

Q65   If patrons are using my library's computers to copy material illegally, can my library be on the hook?

It is possible. If the library facilitates the copying, has the right and ability to control the copying, and gets a financial benefit such as charging for use of the equipment, it can be sued under the legal doctrine of "vicarious infringement." The library need not have known about the infringement. Another legal claim, though less likely in the library environment, is "contributory infringement."[156] To be contributorily liable, the library must have known (or had reason to know) of the infringing act, and induced, caused, or contributed to the act of infringement.

Q66   Our library does not get any financial benefit when patrons infringe. Can we still be "vicariously liable"?

The argument that you get no financial benefit will help if you go to court. On the other hand, the copyright owner will try to argue that the library is getting some financial benefit—perhaps a need to buy fewer copies of a CD-ROM, or a less extensive performance license. Even if the library argues that it would not buy more copies, or that the source is a free Internet resource, a financial benefit can result when material "acts as a draw" for customers, as demonstrated in the recent *Napster* decision.[157] If the infringing activity brings in more patrons and the library's increased user base helps it get increased funding, a copyright owner could argue that the library is getting a financial benefit. A more direct link could be shown if the library charges beyond cost recovery for access to equipment such as Internet workstations or CD burners, or for use of performance or display space.

Q67   *Patrons have used our photocopiers for many, many years.*
       We even get some direct financial revenue from this. Yet
       we've never been sued for "liability" or contributing to
       copyright infringement.

You are right to notice that the underlying issue (library liability for patron copying) is exactly the same as when patrons use library photocopiers. However, the American Library Association lobbied successfully for a specific copyright provision that protects libraries when patrons use photocopiers or any other reproducing equipment. Section 108(f)(1) exempts a library from liability for the unsupervised use of "reproducing equipment located on its premises" provided that the equipment displays a notice that the making of a copy may be subject to the copyright law.[158] You may notice that the law does not specifically say "photocopiers only." This provision logically protects libraries for other types of equipment, but it has not been tested for equipment such as computers or scanners. Moreover, there are other activities that a patron might engage in and that the library might illegally assist in beyond the use of reproducing equipment via 108(f)(1), such as unlawful displays or performances of copyrighted materials.

Q68   *Can a library be liable when its patrons use its equipment*
       to infringe copyright?

Chapter 2, "Designing the Library Web Page," discusses the relevant concepts of vicarious and contributory liability. Most libraries have had photocopy machines and are familiar with the recommended notice to be posted by those machines:

NOTICE: THE COPYRIGHT LAW OF THE UNITED STATES (TITLE 17 U.S. CODE) GOVERNS THE MAKING OF PHOTOCOPIES OR OTHER REPRODUCTIONS OF COPYRIGHTED MATERIAL. THE PERSON USING THIS EQUIPMENT IS LIABLE FOR ANY INFRINGEMENT.

The law does not specify the exact wording. Many libraries use the notice depicted here.

Q69   *What if the library makes the copy at the request of a patron, as in interlibrary loan, or in response to a faxed or e-mailed request?*

The law requires that a specific notice be posted at the place the orders are accepted. It must say:[159]

**NOTICE: WARNING CONCERNING
COPYRIGHT RESTRICTIONS**

The copyright law of the United States (Title 17, United States Code) governs the making of photocopies or other reproductions of copyrighted material.

Under certain conditions specified in the law, libraries and archives are authorized to furnish a photocopy or other reproduction. One of these specific conditions is that the photocopy or reproduction is not to be "used for any purpose other than private study, scholarship, or research." If a user makes a request for, or later uses, a photocopy or reproduction for purposes in excess of "fair use," that user may be liable for copyright infringement.

This institution reserves the right to refuse to accept a copying order if, in its judgment, fulfillment of the order would involve violation of copyright law.

The displayed warning must be printed on heavy paper or other durable material. It must have at least an 18-point typeface. The sign must be displayed prominently, in such a manner and location as to be clearly visible, legible, and comprehensible to a casual observer within the immediate vicinity of the place where orders are accepted.[160]

Q70   *If we make the copies, it is usually because we got the request by fax or e-mail. Our patrons are not going to see this notice!*

Technically, if you display the notice where the orders are *received,* you are in compliance with the law. To comply with the spirit of the law, it is recommended that you routinely send the notice as a part of your e-mail or fax reply. The law also requires that the library put the work's own copyright statement (e.g., "Copyright © 2003 Mary Minow") on the copy. This statement is typically found at the beginning or end of a work. If and only if no copyright statement for the actual work can be found, the library may substitute a statement that the work may be protected by copyright.[161] Libraries often use a rubber stamp, "Warning! This work may be protected by copyright," for this purpose.

Q71 Should I put up the same notice next to my computers or computer printers where patrons make copies?

Yes. Post the notice not only by your photocopiers, but also next to any "reproducing equipment" that can print or make copies of digital material. You should also put the notice on the website or other portal screens that patrons use to access copyrighted material.

Q72 Will the notice protect me if patrons make copies of digital material that the library leases from a vendor?

No. Bear in mind any contractual obligations that your library (or its parent institution, or consortium) signed in order to get the digital information. The relationship between contract law and copyright law is complicated and not completely settled.[162] It is best to ensure that your licensing agreements are written with the library patrons' needs in mind, including provisions for fair use. For an excellent source on negotiating license agreements that are geared for library patrons, see Yale University's Liblicense website. It gives sample contract clauses beneficial to libraries, an excellent glossary of contract terms, and other useful tips.[163]

Q73 I don't need to worry about library patrons making illegal copies off our Internet-access computers, when everything on the Internet is free anyway, right?

The bad news is that the Internet is not always as free as it seems. For example, if pirated content (music or movies, for example) is posted on the Internet, patrons who copy that material can be infringing copyright. The good news is that you may be protected by a new provision in the copyright law, known as the "online service provider" provisions of the Digital Millennium Copyright Act.[164]

Q74 Is my library covered under the "online service provider" (OSP) provisions?

If your library offers Internet access to the public, it is considered an "online service provider" with regard to copyright law. This is because it provides connections for digital online communications for users, to material of the users' choosing, without modifying the content sent or received. The term "online service provider" thus refers to a provider of online services or network access or an operator of facilities for the provision of these services.[165] For further treatment of these issues, see Jay Dratler Jr.,

Cyberlaw: Intellectual Property in the Digital Millennium; and Tomas Lipinski, "Legal Issues in Web-Based Distance Education," in *Handbook of American Distance Education,* edited by Michael G. Moore.[166]

Q75 What protection does my library get under the OSP provisions?

It depends on what copying activities your library computers are involved with. Note that the OSP provisions will protect the library from liability for acts of its patrons, but *not* acts by library employees. Once the library qualifies for protection under section 512, any liability it has is limited to injunctive relief, with no monetary damages of any kind. The law distinguishes between four different functions that library computers are involved with when electronic copies are made:

(1) Transitory copies
(2) Cached copies
(3) Information residing on library computers at the direction of users
(4) Information location tools such as links or online directories

The law automatically protects your library for the "transitory" and "cached" copies it makes, under the conditions set forth below. The law *can* protect your library for "information residing on systems" (posted by others) and "information location tools" (i.e., linking) if the library designates an agent and then follows the procedures specified in section 512(g).[167]

The first two categories refer to transmissions that occur automatically.

1. *Transitory copies.* Transitory copies are made automatically in the operation of a network, where the library computers act merely as a conduit. The library is not liable for copies made in transient transmissions as long as the library does not (1) initiate the transmission, (2) facilitate the transmission by any other than automatic means, (3) select the recipients of the materials by any other than automatic means, (4) make copies of the materials for any longer than ordinarily necessary to transmit the materials to the user, or (5) modify the materials transmitted.[168]

2. *Cached copies.* Computers can be set to cache copies of materials in order to save bandwidth and reduce waiting time on subsequent requests for the same material. The library is not liable for cached copies if (1) the library doesn't itself make the material available, (2) the patron transmits the copy to a third party, and (3) the materials are stored only by automatic means. The following conditions must be met: the library (*a*)

must not modify the materials, (*b*) must comply with general industry standards with regards to refreshing, reloading, or updating material, (*c*) must not interfere with technology associated with the material that returns "hit" information to the party that posted the material, (*d*) must not interfere with passwords or fee requirements, and (*e*) must expeditiously remove or disable access upon notification of claimed infringement.[169]

The third and fourth categories do not involve "automatic" copying by computers, and libraries have an increased chance of being liable. However, if the library designates an agent (required for posting situations, recommended for others) and follows procedures outlined in section 512 of the Copyright Act (see below), it can greatly limit its liability to at most injunctive relief alone.

3. *Information residing on library computers at the direction of users.* The library is not liable if storage of information on library computers is done at the direction of patrons if the library (1) does not have knowledge that the material is infringing, (2) does not receive a financial benefit from the infringing activity, if the library has the right and ability to control the activity, and (3) upon notification of claimed infringement responds expeditiously to remove or disable access to the material.

The library must designate an agent to receive notifications of claimed infringements.

4. *Information location tools such as links or online directories.* What if the library puts a link on its home page to a site filled with pirated music or videos? The library is not liable if it (1) does not have knowledge that the material is infringing, (2) does not receive a financial benefit directly from the infringing activity, if the library has the right and ability to control the activity, and (3) upon notification of claimed infringement, responds expeditiously to remove or disable access to the material.[170]

The library need not designate an agent to receive notifications of claimed infringements, but it is recommended to do so.

Q76   *How does a library "designate an agent" to receive notifications of claimed infringements, as required for the last two categories, "information residing on library computers" and "information location tools"?*

The Copyright Office website explains how to designate an agent.[171] There is a $20 fee. Although you are not required to use a specific form, the site gives a suggested format for providing the required information: name, address, telephone number, and e-mail of agent, as well as name and address of the library.[172] To check to see if your library (or its parent institution) has designated an agent, you can check the Copyright Office's website, which lists all agents.[173] You must also post the agent's information on your own website. An example of this can be seen at the Contra Costa County Library website.[174]

Q77   If I designate an agent, am I "inviting" copyright owners to go after my library?

Probably not. The person who signs the notification of claimed infringement is subject to the penalty of perjury. The law states that the copyright owner's notice to the library must be in writing, directed to the designated agent, and include the following:

(1) A physical or electronic signature of a person authorized to act on behalf of the copyright owner
(2) Identification of the work that is allegedly infringed
(3) Identification of the material that is to be removed (or access disabled)
(4) Contact information of the complaining party
(5) A statement that the above information is accurate, under penalty of perjury[175]

Failure to comply substantially with these requirements means the notification will not be valid.

Q78   If I get a legal claim that meets these requirements, what must I do?

To gain protection under this provision of the Copyright Act, you must promptly remove or block access to the item(s) in the notice. In addition, one court has ruled that the notice a copyright owner sends need not be "perfect" before your responsibility to act on it is triggered.[176]

Q79   I see that the Copyright Act has procedures for counter-notification by a party who thinks that the "take down" was wrongly done. How does this apply to my library?

This provision applies mainly to mainstream Internet service providers, who may be taking down documents posted by subscribers.[177] The subscribers then have an opportunity to respond. It is not as likely to apply to libraries, especially outside of a school or university setting. Libraries could possibly take down material that a patron stored on a library computer (an act that was probably not consistent with library policy, whether or not the document was infringing). Alternatively, a library could take down a link or directory that the library itself posted, again not a likely source for an outside complaint. Nevertheless, if there is a "counter-notice" to the library to "put back" the material because the patron says that it is not infringing copyright, the library must "put back" the material within ten business days, unless the matter is referred to court.

For further information, see section 512(g)[178] of the Copyright Act, or read a helpful legal memo by Arnold Lutzker, written for the Association of Research Libraries.[179]

*Q80   Doesn't it invade the privacy of our patrons if the library
        is checking to see what copies they are making?*

The Copyright Act explicitly states that the library is not required to monitor its service or access material in violation of law (such as the Electronic Communications Privacy Act) in order to be eligible for liability limitations.[180]

*Q81   What happens if my library designates an agent and then
        decides not to take down a link or follow through on the rest
        of the procedures?*

That is your library's choice. You may prefer to handle the claim in another way. The OSP provision merely provides you certain protections if you wish to seek them. As always, seek legal counsel in handling any legal claim.

LIABILITY AND REMEDIES: SECTIONS 501–504

Liability

If a library violates one of the exclusive rights of the copyright, it can be sued for copyright infringement. According to the copyright law, this is true even if the library is part of state or local government.[181] However, the courts are currently taking an unusual approach to state liability in the area of many federal laws. The Eleventh Amendment of the United States Constitution states:

> The judicial power of the United States shall not be construed to extend to any suit in law or equity, commenced or prosecuted against one of the United States by citizens of another state, or by citizens or subjects of any foreign state.[182]

Recent U.S. Supreme Court decisions have interpreted the Eleventh Amendment to immunize states from certain federal laws. In *Florida Prepaid Postsecondary Education Expense Board* v. *College Savings Bank*[183] and *College Savings Bank* v. *Florida Prepaid Postsecondary Education Expense Board,*[184] the Supreme Court ruled that states cannot be sued in federal court for patent or trademark infringement, since Congress overstepped its bounds when passing legislation making states subject to suit. The immunity would only apply to a state law library, state university library, etc., since municipalities, counties, and other political subdivisions, such as a public school district, do not partake in a state's Eleventh Amendment immunity,[185] and thus remain liable for copyright infringement.

The Fifth Circuit expanded the concept to include claims of copyright infringement.[186] A district court has also held that the Eleventh Amendment immunity applies to misappropriation claims.[187] This does not mean that states' libraries and archives should infringe copyright with reckless abandon, since Senator Patrick Leahy and others in Congress have vowed to close this gap.[188] Several bills have since been introduced to restore the liability of states.[189] These did not pass, but it is expected that similar versions will be reintroduced in the 107th Congress. Even without this legislation, states may still find themselves liable, since immunity can always be waived by agreements such as a license agreement.

Remedies

Q82   If my library loses a copyright lawsuit, what are the legal consequences?

Assuming a library is successfully sued, several remedies are available to the copyright owner. First, the copyright owner may seek an injunction.[190] The injunction can be temporary or permanent and, if granted, could order the library to remove infringing material from its website or to cease the further display or distribution of off-air tapes or the circulation of infringing copies of material. The copyright owner may also seek to have the infringing copies impounded pending the outcome of the litigation and destroyed as a final remedy.[191] These remedies are considered "equitable."

Another set of remedies involves money or "damages." There are two types of damages that the copyright owner can recover: statutory or actual. The copyright owner may receive one but not both sorts.

Actual Damages

The copyright owner is entitled to recover the actual damages suffered by him or her as a result of the infringement, and any profits of the library that are attributable to the infringement and are not taken into account in computing the actual damages.[192] If a library has loaded a software program onto eleven computers when it only purchased a single copy for a single installation and the program cost $99.99, damages would be $999.90 (ten programs loaded without permission at $99.99 each). If a library made five copies of a book in excess of fair use, the loss (damage) to the copyright owner would represent the price of five copies, i.e., the lost sales from the five copies photocopied.

Statutory Damages

Statutory damages are the bane of copyright defendants. The copyright owner may elect an award of damages set by the copyright statute. The statute requires that each infringement be calculated at no less than $750 and up to $30,000, as the court considers just.[193] Statutory damages can add up rapidly, since the dollar amount, determined by the court, applies to each work infringed. Statutory damages in the *UMG Recordings, Inc. v. MP3.com, Inc.* case approached $118 million:

> Weighing not only the foregoing factors but all the other relevant factors put before the Court, the Court concludes, and hereby determines, that the appropriate measure of damages is $25,000 per CD. If defendant is right that there are no more than 4,700 CDs for which plaintiffs qualify for statutory damages, the total award will be approximately $118,000,000; but, of course, it could be considerably more or less depending on the number of qualifying CDs determined at the final phase of the trial scheduled for November of this year.[194]

Statutory damages may reach $150,000 per work where there is evidence of "willfulness"[195] or be reduced to $200 if the court finds that "such infringer was not aware and had no reason to believe that his or her acts constituted an infringement of copyright."[196]

Libraries and Actual Damages

Most important to libraries is a provision in section 504 that eliminates statutory damages if:

(1) the infringer believed and had reasonable grounds for believing that his or her use of the copyrighted work was a fair use; and

(2) the infringer was an employee or agent of a nonprofit educational institution, library, or archives acting within the scope of his or her employment; or

(3) [was] such institution, library, or archives itself which infringed by reproducing the work in copies or phonorecords.[197]

However, for a library to avail itself of the provision, there must a reasonable belief that the act that triggered the claim of infringement was a fair use. If so, then the costly statutory damages are waived and the library would be liable only for the actual damages, which may be far less. For example, actual damages could be the value of a second or third copy of a reproduced book or the royalty due the "performance" of a video loaded on the library website and made available for patron viewing. Given the increased awareness of copyright violations in all library settings, coupled with the availability of cases providing judicial insight into the application of copyright law in new environments, like the *Napster* case, the standard for arguing what is a reasonable belief of fair use is getting higher.

Attorney's Fees

The prevailing party (this may be the plaintiff or the defendant) may also be awarded attorney's fees and cost at the court's discretion.[198]

Criminal Penalties

There are also provisions for criminal penalties. Generally, a criminal copyright infringement requires that the infringement be executed with intent ("willfully") and for "commercial advantage" or "financial gain." A defendant could face up to 5 years in prison if the offense consists of the copying or distribution, including by electronic means, during any 180-day period, of 10 or more copies of one or more copyrighted works, which have a total retail value of more than $2,500. The defendant could face up to 10 years if the offense is a second or subsequent offense. In any other case, the defendant may be imprisoned up to one year.

Criminal infringement need not include the selling of the illegal copy, but exchanging or trading it for another copyrighted work, such as by uploading or downloading software on an electronic bulletin board or website.[199]

If the copying was not done for commercial advantage or financial gain, criminal penalties may still be imposed at a lesser degree. A defendant can face up to one year in prison if the total retail value of the copies is up to $1,000. If the defendant made at least 10 copies and the retail value is more than $1,000, he can face up to 3 years in prison. If it is a second or subsequent offense, he could face up to 6 years.[200]

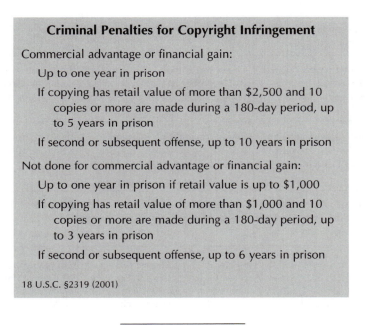

Criminal Penalties for Copyright Infringement

Commercial advantage or financial gain:

    Up to one year in prison

    If copying has retail value of more than $2,500 and 10 copies or more are made during a 180-day period, up to 5 years in prison

    If second or subsequent offense, up to 10 years in prison

Not done for commercial advantage or financial gain:

    Up to one year in prison if retail value is up to $1,000

    If copying has retail value of more than $1,000 and 10 copies or more are made during a 180-day period, up to 3 years in prison

    If second or subsequent offense, up to 6 years in prison

18 U.S.C. §2319 (2001)

APPENDIX

*When Works Pass into the Public Domain: Copyright Terms for the Archivist**

UNPUBLISHED WORKS		
Type of Work	Copyright Term	What Will Become Public Domain on January 1, 2003
Unpublished works	Life of the author + 70 years	Works from authors who died before 1933
Unpublished anonymous and pseudonymous works, and works made for hire (corporate authorship)	120 years from date of creation	Works created before 1883
Unpublished works created before 1978 that are published before January 1, 2003	Life of the author + 70 years or December 31, 2047, whichever is greater	Nothing. The soonest the publications can enter the public domain is January 1, 2048
Unpublished works created before 1978 that are published after December 31, 2002	Life of the author + 70 years	Works of authors who died before 1933
Unpublished works when the death date of the author is not known**	120 years from date of creation†	Works created before 1883†

* These charts were published in Peter B. Hirtle, *Recent Changes to the Copyright Law: Copyright Term Extension,* ARCHIVAL OUTLOOK, January–February 1999. They are based in part on Laura N. Gasaway's chart, *When Works Pass into the Public Domain,* at http://www.unc.edu/~unclng/public-d.htm, and similar charts found in Marie C. Malaro, A LEGAL PRIMER ON MANAGING MUSEUM COLLECTIONS 155–156 (Washington, D.C.: Smithsonian Institution Press, 1998). Gasaway's chart is also available at http://cidc.library.cornell.edu/copyright/.

** These works may still be copyrighted, but certification from the Copyright Office is a complete defense to any action for infringement.

† Presumption as to the author's death requires a certified report from the Copyright Office that its records disclose nothing to indicate that the author of the work is living or died less than 70 years before.

PUBLISHED WORKS		
Time of Publication	**Conditions**	**Public Domain Status**
Before 1923	None	In public domain
Between 1923 and 1978	Published without a copyright notice	In public domain
Between 1978 and March 1, 1989	Published without notice and without subsequent registration	In public domain
Between 1978 and March 1, 1989	Published without notice and with subsequent registration	70 years after death of author, or if work of corporate authorship, the shorter of 95 years from publication, or 120 years from creation
Between 1923 and 1963	Published with notice but copyright was not renewed[††]	In public domain
Between 1923 and 1963	Published with notice and the copyright was renewed[‡]	95 years after publication date
Between 1964 and 1978	Published with notice	95 years after publication date
After March 1, 1989	None	70 years after death of author, or if work of corporate authorship, the shorter of 95 years from publication, or 120 years from creation

†† A 1961 Copyright Office study found that fewer than 15 percent of all registered copyrights were renewed. For textual material (including books), the figure was even lower: 7 percent.

‡ A good guide to investigating the copyright and renewal status of published work is Samuel Demas and Jennie L. Brogdon, *Determining Copyright Status for Preservation and Access: Defining Reasonable Effort,* LIBRARY RESOURCES AND TECHNICAL SERVICES 41, no. 4 (October 1997), at 323–334.

Notes

1. 17 U.S.C. §105 (2000).

2. 17 U.S.C. §101 (2000).

3. H.R. REP. NO. 94-1476, at 60 (1976).

4. 17 U.S.C. §105.

5. H.R. REP. NO. 94-1476, at 56–57 (1976); *Schnapper v. Foley,* 667 F.2d 102 (D.C. Cir. 1981), *cert. denied* 455 U.S. 948 (1982).

6. *See* U.S. Copyright Office, Circular 1: *Copyright Basics* 5 (1993) (discussing the use of reserved portions in United States government works).

7. 17 U.S.C. §101.

8. *Schnapper,* 667 F.2d 102, *cert. denied* 455 U.S. 948.

9. *National Conference of Bar Examiners v. Multistate Legal Studies, Inc.,* 495 F. Supp. 34 (N.D. Ill. 1980), *aff'd* 692 F.2d 478 (7th Cir. 1982), *cert. denied* 464 U.S. 814 (1983).

10. *Building Officials & Code Administration and Code Technology,* 628 F.2d 730, 735 (1st Cir. 1980).

11. *Veeck v. Southern Building Code Congress International,* No. 99-40632 (E.D. Tex. Feb. 2, 2001).

12. 14 Op. Att'y Gen. Okla. 317 (1982) (No. 82-167).

13. 1983 La. AG LEXIS 387, at 2 (July 27, 1983).

14. *Marshall v. Miles Laboratories, Inc.,* 647 F. Supp. 1326, 1330 (N.D. Ind. 1986).

15. 17 U.S.C. §102 (2000).

16. 17 U.S.C. §106 (2000).

17. H.R. REP. NO. 94-1476, at 62 (1976), reprinted in 1976 U.S. CODE CONGRESSIONAL AND ADMINISTRATIVE NEWS 5659, 5675.

18. Mississippi Writers Page, *John Grisham, at* http://www.olemiss.edu/depts/english/ms-writers/dir/grisham_john (visited April 20, 2001); *Book Buzz, from Book to Screen, at* http://suspense.net/buzz/book-to-screen.htm (visited April 20, 2001).

19. *Twin Peaks Productions, Inc. v. Publications International, Ltd.,* 996 F.2d 1366 (2d Cir. 1993) (TWIN PEAKS: A COMPLETE GUIDE TO WHO'S WHO AND WHAT'S WHAT); *Castle Rock Entertainment, Inc. v. Carol Publishing Group, Inc.,* 150 F.3d 132 (2d Cir. 1995) (THE SEINFELD APTITUDE TEST); *Paramount Pictures Corp. v. Carol Publishing Group, Inc.,* 11 F. Supp. 2d 329 (S.D.N.Y. 1998), preliminary injunction *aff'd* 1999 U.S. App. LEXIS 9218 (2d Cir. 1999) (unpublished opinion) (JOY OF TREK).

20. 17 U.S.C. §101 (2000).

21. Jay Dratler Jr., 1 INTELLECTUAL PROPERTY LAW: COMMERCIAL, CREATIVE, AND INDUSTRIAL PROPERTY §6.01[3], at 6-14 (2000).

22. 17 U.S.C. §101.

23. H.R. REP. NO. 94-1476, at 61–62 (1976), reprinted in 1976 U.S. CODE CONGRESSIONAL AND ADMINISTRATIVE NEWS 5659, 5674–5675.

24. *Hotaling v. Church of Jesus Christ of Latter-day Saints,* 118 F.3d 199 (4th Cir. 1999).

25. *Hotaling,* 118 F.3d at 203.

26. 17 U.S.C. §101.

27. 17 U.S.C. §101.

28. See *Columbia Pictures Industries, Inc. v. Professional Real Estate Investors, Inc.,* 866 F.2d 278, 282 (9th Cir. 1989).

29. 17 U.S.C. §106(6) (2000).

30. 17 U.S.C. §101.

31. Pub. L. No. 104-39, 109 Stat. 336-344 (codified at 17 U.S.C. §§101, 111, 196, 114, 119, 801–803. See also S. REP. No. 104-128, at 10 (1995), reprinted in 1994 U.S. CODE CONGRESSIONAL AND ADMINISTRATIVE NEWS 356, 357.

32. 17 U.S.C. §107 (2000).

33. 17 U.S.C. §107.

34. *American Geophysical Union v. Texaco, Inc.,* 60 F.3d 913, 922 (2d Cir. 1993).

35. Stephen Fraser, *The Conflict between the First Amendment and Copyright Law and Its Impact on the Internet,* 16 CARDOZO ARTS AND ENTERTAINMENT LAW JOURNAL 1, 25 (1998).

36. *A&M Records, Inc. v. Napster, Inc.,* 239 F.3d. 1004, 1015 (9th Cir. 2001).

37. *Campbell v. Acuff-Rose Music,* 510 U.S. 569, 579 (1994) (citation omitted).

38. *Kelly v. Arriba Soft Corp.,* 77 F. Supp. 2d 1116, 1119 (C.D. Cal. 1999), *aff'd* 280 F.3d 934 (9th Cir. 2002).

39. *Los Angeles Times v. Free Republic,* 2000 U.S. Dist. LEXIS, at *24 (C.D. Cal. 2000).

40. *Campbell,* 510 U.S. at 579 (quotation and citation omitted).

41. *Campbell,* 510 U.S. at 579.

42. *Princeton University Press v. Michigan Document Services,* 99 F.3d 1381, 1388–1389 (6th Cir. 1996).

43. *American Geophysical Union v. Texaco, Inc.,* 60 F.3d 913, 922–924 (2d Cir. 1993).

44. David G. Luettgen, *Functional Usefulness vs. Communicative Usefulness: Thin Copyright Protection for the Nonliteral Elements of Computer Programs,* 4 TEXAS INTELLECTUAL PROPERTY LAW REVIEW 233 (1996).

45. *American Geophysical Union,* 60 F.3d at 925.

46. *Princeton University Press,* 99 F.3d at 1389.

47. *Los Angeles Times v. Free Republic,* 2000 U.S. Dist. LEXIS, at *55 (C.D. Cal. 2000).

48. *Kelly v. Arriba Soft Corp.,* 77 F. Supp. 2d 1116, 1120 (C.D. Cal. 1999), *aff'd* 280 F.3d 934, 943 (9th Cir. 2002) ("photographs used for illustrative purposes are generally creative in nature").

49. *Nunez v. Caribbean International News Corp.,* 235 F.3d 18, 23 (1st Cir. 2000) ("the photographs were not artistic representations . . . we find that the impact of their creativity on the fair use finding is neutral").

50. *Basic Books, Inc. v. Kinko's Graphics Corp.,* 758 F. Supp. 1522 (S.D.N.Y. 1991); *Princeton University Press,* 99 F.3d at 1389.

51. *Worldwide Church of God v. Philadelphia Church of God,* 227 F.3d 1110, 1118 (9th Cir. 2000), quoting *Hustler Magazine, Inc. v. Moral Majority, Inc.,* 796 F.2d 1148, 1155 (9th Cir. 1986).

52. *Nunez v. Caribbean International News Corp.,* 235 F.3d 18, 24 (1st Cir. 2000).

53. *Harper & Row Publishers, Inc. v. Nation Enterprises,* 471 U.S. 539 (1985).

54. See *Campbell v. Acuff-Rose Music,* 510 U.S. 569, 588 (1994).

55. *Campbell,* 510 U.S. 569, 591 ("market harm is a matter of degree, and the importance of this factor will vary, not only with the amount of harm, but also with the relative strength of the showing of the other factors").

56. *American Geophysical Union v. Texaco, Inc.,* 60 F.3d 913, 927–931 (2d Cir. 1993).

57. *Sony Corporation of America v. Universal City Studios, Inc.,* 464 U.S. 417, 451 (1984).

58. *A&M Records, Inc. v. Napster, Inc.,* 114 F. Supp. 2d 895, 902 (N.D. Cal. 2000), *aff'd* 239 F.3d 1004 (9th Cir. 2001).

59. *A&M Records, Inc.,* 239 F.3d 1004, 1017.

60. *Harper & Row Publishers, Inc. v. Nation Enterprises,* 471 U.S. 539, 568 (1985), quoting *Sony Corporation of America v. Universal City Studios, Inc.,* 464 U.S. 417, 451 (1984).

61. *A&M Records, Inc.,* 239 F.3d 1004, 1017.

62. 17 U.S.C. §107 (2000).

63. See H.R. REP. NO. 94-1476 (1976), reprinted in U.S. Copyright Office, Circular 21: REPRODUCTION OF COPYRIGHTED WORKS BY EDUCATORS AND LIBRARIANS 8 (1993).

64. *See* Randall Coyne, *Rights of Reproduction and the Provision of Library Services,* 13 LAW LIBRARY JOURNAL 485, 488–489 (1991).

65. H.R. REP. NO. 94-1476, reprinted in U.S. Copyright Office, REPRODUCTION OF COPYRIGHTED WORKS, at 9.

66. The agreement that was reached became part of the legislative history of the Copyright Revision Act of 1976. H.R. REP. NO. 94-1476, at 68 (1976).

67. See, e.g., *Marcus v. Rowley,* 695 F.2d 1171, 1178 (9th Cir. 1983); and *Basic Books, Inc. v. Kinko's Graphics Corp,* 758 F. Supp. 1522, 1550 (S.D.N.Y. 1991).

68. Kenneth D. Crews, *The Law of Fair Use and the Illusion of Fair-Use Guidelines,* 62 OHIO STATE LAW JOURNAL 599 (2001).

69. *Universal City Studios, Inc. v. Corley,* 273 F.3d 429, 459 (7th Cir. 2001).

70. Pub. L. No. 12-492, 106 Stat. 3145 (1992); 17 U.S.C. §107 (2000).

71. H.R. REP. NO. 102-836, at 1 (1992), reprinted in 1992 U.S. CODE CONGRESSIONAL AND ADMINISTRATIVE NEWS 2553, 2553.

72. H.R. REP. NO. 102-836, at 9 (1992), reprinted in 1992 U.S. CODE CONGRESSIONAL AND ADMINISTRATIVE NEWS 2553, 2561.

73. *Kelly v. Arriba Soft Corp.,* 77 F. Supp. 2d 1116, 1120 (C.D. Cal. 1999).
74. Association of Research Libraries, *at* http://www.arl.org (visited May 17, 2001); Yale University Liblicense, *at* http://www.library.yale.edu/~llicense/index.shtml (visited May 17, 2001); Arlene Bielefield and Lawrence Cheeseman, INTERPRETING AND NEGOTIATING LICENSING AGREEMENTS: A GUIDEBOOK FOR THE LIBRARY, RESEARCH, AND TEACHING PROFESSIONS (1999); Lesley Ellen Harris, LICENSING DIGITAL CONTENT: A PRACTICAL GUIDE FOR LIBRARIANS (2002).
75. 17 U.S.C. §301(a) (2000).
76. *ProCD v. Zeidenberg,* 86 F.3d 1447, 1454 (7th Cir. 1996).
77. *ProCD,* 86 F.3d at 1447.
78. See 17 U.S.C. §§109–121 (2000).
79. 17 U.S.C. §108(a) (2000).
80. For detailed information on the regulations concerning placement of the copyright notice, see 37 C.F.R. §201.20.
81. 17 U.S.C. §108(a).
82. *American Geophysical Union v. Texaco, Inc.,* 802 F. Supp. 1, 27 (S.D.N.Y. 1992), *aff'd,* 60 F.3d 913, 917, 921 (2d Cir. 1993).
83. H.R. REP. NO. 94-1476 (1976), reprinted in U.S. Copyright Office, Circular 21: REPRODUCTION OF COPYRIGHTED WORKS BY EDUCATORS AND LIBRARIANS 18 (1993).
84. S. REP. NO. 94-473 (1976), reprinted in U.S. Copyright Office, Circular 21: REPRODUCTION OF COPYRIGHTED WORKS BY EDUCATORS AND LIBRARIANS 23 (1993).
85. H.R. CONF. REP. NO. 94-1733 (1976), reprinted in U.S. Copyright Office, Circular 21: REPRODUCTION OF COPYRIGHTED WORKS BY EDUCATORS AND LIBRARIANS 8 (1993).
86. Pub. L. No. 105-304, 112 Stat. 2889, Title IV (1998); Pub. L. No. 105-298, 112 Stat. 2827, Title I (1998).
87. S. REP. NO. 105-190, at 62 (1998).
88. 17 U.S.C. §108(b) (2000).
89. *See* Dwayne K. Butler and Kenneth D. Crews, *Copyright Protection and Technological Reform of Library Services: Digital Change, Practical Application, and Congressional Action,* in LIBRARIES, MUSEUMS, AND ARCHIVES: LEGAL ISSUES AND ETHICAL CHALLENGES IN THE NEW INFORMATION ERA 257, 268–69 (Tomas A. Lipinski ed., 2001).
90. S. REP. NO. 105-190, at 61–62.
91. 17 U.S.C. §108(c) (2000).
92. H.R. REP. NO. 94-1476 (1976), reprinted in U.S. Copyright Office, Circular 21: REPRODUCTION OF COPYRIGHTED WORKS BY EDUCATORS AND LIBRARIANS 19 (1993).
93. 17 U.S.C. §108(c)(2).
94. S. REP. NO. 105-190, at 62.
95. S. REP. NO. 105-190, at 62.
96. 17 U.S.C. §108(d).
97. 17 U.S.C. §108(e).

98. 17 U.S.C. §108(d)(1) and (e)(1) (2000).

99. Specifically, 17 U.S.C. §108(d)(1) or §108(e)(1).

100. 37 C.F.R. §201.14 (2000).

101. But see H.R. REP. NO. 94-1476, at 60 (1976), reprinted in U.S. Copyright Office, Circular 21: REPRODUCTION OF COPYRIGHTED WORKS BY EDUCATORS AND LIBRARIANS 19 (1993), indicating that the "scope and nature of a reasonable investigation to determine that an unused copy cannot be obtained will vary according to the circumstances of a particular situation."

102. *ITSI T.V. Prods., Inc. v. California Authority of Racing Fairs,* 785 F. Supp. 854, 861 n.13 (E.D. Cal. 1992).

103. Information Infrastructure Task Force, INTELLECTUAL PROPERTY AND THE NATIONAL INFORMATION INFRASTRUCTURE: THE REPORT OF THE WORKING GROUP ON INTELLECTUAL PROPERTY RIGHTS 111, n.357 (1995), *available at* http://www.uspto.gov/web/offices/com/doc/ipnii/ipnii.doc (visited May 17, 2001).

104. 17 U.S.C. §108(f)(2) (2000), read in tandem with 17 U.S.C. §108(f)(1).

105. 17 U.S.C. §108(f)(3).

106. H.R. REP. NO. 94-1476, at 60, reprinted in U.S. Copyright Office, REPRODUCTION OF COPYRIGHTED WORKS, at 19–20.

107. H.R. REP. NO. 94-1476, at 60, reprinted in U.S. Copyright Office, REPRODUCTION OF COPYRIGHTED WORKS, at 20.

108. H.R. CONF. REP. NO. 94-1733 (1976), reprinted in U.S. Copyright Office, Circular 21: REPRODUCTION OF COPYRIGHTED WORKS BY EDUCATORS AND LIBRARIANS 23 (1993).

109. 17 U.S.C. §108(f)(4).

110. 17 U.S.C. §108(a)(1) (2000).

111. H.R. CONF. REP. NO. 94-1733, reprinted in U.S. Copyright Office, REPRODUCTION OF COPYRIGHTED WORKS, at 23.

112. 17 U.S.C. §108(g)(2) (2000).

113. 17 U.S.C. §108(g)(1).

114. See H.R. CONF. REP. NO. 94-1733, reprinted in U.S. Copyright Office, REPRODUCTION OF COPYRIGHTED WORKS, at 22–23.

115. Robert Wedgeworth, The Fall 1993 Horace S. Manges Lecture: *Copyright and Libraries: Act II,* 17 COLUMBIA-VLA JOURNAL OF LAW & THE ARTS 418, 420 (Summer 1993).

116. S. REP. NO. 94-473 (1976), reprinted in U.S. Copyright Office, Circular 21: REPRODUCTION OF COPYRIGHTED WORKS BY EDUCATORS AND LIBRARIANS 17 (1993) (examples (1), (2), and (3)).

117. Pub. L. No. 105-298, 112 Stat. 2827, Title I (1998).

118. 17 U.S.C. §108(h)(2)(A)–(B) (2000).

119. 17 U.S.C. §108(i) (2000).

120. H.R. REP. NO. 94-1476, at 60 (1976), reprinted in U.S. Copyright Office, Circular 21: REPRODUCTION OF COPYRIGHTED WORKS BY EDUCATORS AND LIBRARIANS 21 (1993).

121. *Bobbs-Merrill Co. v. Straus,* 210 U.S. 339 (1908).

122. Public Lending Right Scheme, *Outline of Public Lending Rights, at* http://www. dca.gov.au/plr.html (visited April 21, 2001).

123. Arthur R. Miller and Michael H. Davis, INTELLECTUAL PROPERTY, PATENTS, TRADEMARK, AND COPYRIGHT IN A NUTSHELL 328 (3d ed. 2000).

124. 17 U.S.C. §109(a) (2000).

125. U.S. Copyright Office, *DMCA: Section 104 Report (A Report of the Register of Copyrights Pursuant to Section 104 of the Digital Millennium Copyright Act) (2001)* 87, *at* http://www.copyright.gov/reports/studies/dmca/dmca_study.html.

126. 37 C.F.R. §201.24 (1999).

127. 37 C.F.R. §201.24.

128. Pub. L. No. 101-650 (Title VIII), 104 Stat. 5134 (1990).

129. 17 U.S.C. §109(b)(1) (2000).

130. 17 U.S.C. §109(b).

131. H.R. Rep. No. 101-735, at 8 (1990).

132. 17 U.S.C. §109(b)(1)(A).

133. 17 U.S.C. §109(b)(1)(A).

134. On Oct. 28, 1998, H.R. 2281, the Digital Millennium Copyright Act (DMCA), was enacted into law. Section 104 of the DMCA directed the Register of Copyrights and the Assistant Secretary of Commerce for Communications and Information to prepare a report for Congress examining the effects of the amendments made by title 1 of the DMCA, and the development of electronic commerce on the operation of sections 109 and 117 of title 17, United States Code, and the relationship between existing and emerging technology and the operation of such sections. The report was released in the fall of 2001: U.S. Copyright Office, *DMCA: Section 104 Report (A Report of the Register of Copyrights Pursuant to §104 of the Digital Millennium Copyright Act) (2001), at* http://www. copyright.gov/reports/studies/dmca/dmca_ study.html.

135. 17 U.S.C. §110(1) (2000).

136. 17 U.S.C. §101 (2000).

137. H.R. REP. NO. 94-1476, at 56–57 (1976), reprinted in 17 U.S.C.A. §110 (Historical and Statutory Notes).

138. H.R. REP. NO. 94-1476, at 56–57 (1976), reprinted in 17 U.S.C.A. §110 (Historical and Statutory Notes).

139. 17 U.S.C. §110(1).

140. 17 U.S.C. §101.

141. 17 U.S.C. §110(1).

142. *Columbia Pictures Industries, Inc. v. Aveco, Inc.,* 800 F.2d 29 (3d Cir. 1986); *Columbia Pictures Industries, Inc. v. Redd Horne, Inc.,* 749 F.2d 154 (3d Cir. 1984).

143. *Columbia Pictures Industries, Inc. v. Professional Real Estate Investors, Inc.,* 866 F.2d 278 (9th Cir. 1989).

144. *On Command Video Corp. v. Columbia Pictures Industries, Inc.,* 777 F. Supp. 787 (N.D. Cal. 1991).

145. *See* James S. Heller, *Copyright: The Public Performance Right in Libraries: Is There Anything Fair About It?* 84 LAW LIBRARY JOURNAL 315 (1992); J. Wesley Cochran, *Why Can't I Watch This Video Here? Copyright Confusion and Performance of Videocassettes and Videodiscs in Libraries,* 15 HASTINGS COMMUNICATIONS AND ENTERTAINMENT LAW JOURNAL 837 (1993).

146. H.R. REP. NO. 94-1476, at 56–57 (1976), reprinted in 17 U.S.C.A. §110 (Historical and Statutory Notes).

147. 17 U.S.C. §110(5)(A) (2000).

148. 17 U.S.C. §110(5)(B).

149. 17 U.S.C. §110(5)(B)(i).

150. 17 U.S.C. §110(5)(B)(i)(I).

151. 17 U.S.C. §110(5)(B)(i)(II).

152. 17 U.S.C. §110(5)(B)(i)(I).

153. A brief overview is found in Michael S. Shapiro and Brett I. Miller, A MUSEUM GUIDE TO COPYRIGHT AND TRADEMARK 37–41 (1999). A thorough review is found in Jay Dratler Jr., 1 INTELLECTUAL PROPERTY LAW: COMMERCIAL, CREATIVE, AND INDUSTRIAL PROPERTY §6.04[3], at 6-96.12 to 6-154 (2000).

154. Sonny Bono Term Extension Act, Pub. L. No. 105-298, 112 Stat. 2827 (1998).

155. These duration guidelines were published in chart form by Peter B. Hirtle, adapted from Laura N. Gasaway's chart *at* http://cidc.library.cornell.edu/copyright (visited May 17, 2001).

156. *Intellectual Reserve, Inc. v. Utah Lighthouse Ministry, Inc.,* 75 F. Supp. 2d 1290 (D. Utah 1999).

157. *A&M Records, Inc. v. Napster, Inc.,* 239 F.3d 1004, 1023 (9th Cir. 2001), citing *Fonovisa v. Cherry Auction, Inc.,* 76 F.3d 259, 263–264 (9th Cir. 1996) (stating that financial benefit may be shown "where infringing performances enhance the attractiveness of a venue").

158. "Nothing in this section—(1) shall be construed to impose liability for copyright infringement upon a library or archives or its employees for the unsupervised use of reproducing equipment located on its premises: *Provided,* That such equipment displays a notice that the making of a copy may be subject to the copyright law . . ." 17 U.S.C §108(f)(1) (2000).

159. "A Display Warning of Copyright and an Order Warning of Copyright shall consist of a verbatim reproduction of the following notice, printed in such size and form and displayed in such manner as to comply with paragraph (c) of this section." 37 C.F.R. §201.14(b).

160. "Form and manner of use. (1) A Display Warning of Copyright shall be printed on heavy paper or other durable material in type at least 18 points in size, and shall be displayed prominently, in such manner and location as to be clearly visible, legible, and comprehensible to a casual observer within the immediate vicinity of the place where orders are accepted." 37 C.F.R. §201.14(c).

161. 17 U.S.C. §108(a)(3) (2000).

162. See *ProCD v. Zeidenberg*, 86 F.3d 1447 (7th Cir. 1996) (contract law preempts copyright law). This case is widely discussed and criticized in law reviews. See, e.g., Kell Corrigan Mercer, Casenote, *Consumer Shrink-Wrap Licenses and Public Domain Materials: Copyright Preemption and Uniform Commercial Code Validity in* ProCD v. Zeidenberg, 30 CREIGHTON LAW REVIEW 1287 (1997); Jennett M. Hill, Note, *The State of Copyright Protection for Electronic Databases Beyond* ProCD v. Zeidenberg: *Are Shrinkwrap Licenses a Viable Alternative for Database Protection?* 31 INDIANA LAW REVIEW 143 (1998).

163. Yale University Library, *Liblicense: Licensing Digital Information, A Resource for Librarians, at* http://www.library.yale.edu/~llicense/index.shtml (visited April 4, 2001). *See also* Arlene Bielefield and Lawrence Cheeseman, INTERPRETING AND NEGOTIATING LICENSING AGREEMENTS: A GUIDEBOOK FOR THE LIBRARY, RESEARCH AND TEACHING PROFESSIONS (1999); and Lesley Ellen Harris, LICENSING DIGITAL CONTENT: A PRACTICAL GUIDE FOR LIBRARIANS (2002).

164. 17 U.S.C. §512 (2000).

165. 17 U.S.C. §512 (k)(1).

166. Jay Dratler Jr., CYBERLAW: INTELLECTUAL PROPERTY IN THE DIGITAL MILLENNIUM (2000); and Tomas Lipinski, *Legal Issues in Web-Based Distance Education*, in HANDBOOK OF AMERICAN DISTANCE EDUCATION (Michael G. Moore ed., 2002).

167. 17 U.S.C. §512(g) (2000).

168. 17 U.S.C. §512(a) (2000).

169. 17 U.S.C. §512(b) (2000).

170. 17 U.S.C. §512(d) (2000).

171. U.S. Copyright Office, *Designation by Service Provider of Agent for Notification of Claims of Infringement, at* http://www.loc.gov/copyright/onlinesp/index.html#agent (visited April 4, 2001).

172. 17 U.S.C. §512(c) (2000).

173. U.S. Copyright Office, *Directory of Service Provider Agents for Notification of Claims of Infringement, at* http://www.loc.gov/copyright/onlinesp/list/index.html (visited April 4, 2001).

174. Contra Costa County Library, *at* http://www.contra-costa.lib.ca.us/policies/policies.html (visited July 3, 2001).

175. 17 U.S.C. §512(c)(3).

176. *ALS Scans, Inc. v. Remorq Communications*, 239 F.3d 619 (4th Cir. 2001) (notice adequate if copyright owner "substantially complied" with statutory requirements, specificity is not required for collections of multiple infringing works).

177. 17 U.S.C. §512(g) (2000).

178. 17 U.S.C. §512(g).

179. Arnold P. Lutzker, Susan J. Lutzker, and Carl H. Settlemyer III, *The Digital Millennium Copyright Act: Highlights of New Copyright Provision Establishing*

Limitation of Liability for Online Service Providers, at http://www.arl.org/info/frn/copy/osp.html (visited April 4, 2001).

180. 17 U.S.C. §512(m) (2000).

181. "As used in this subsection, the term 'anyone' includes any State, any instrumentality of a State, and any officer or employee of a State or instrumentality of a State acting in his or her official capacity. Any State, and any such instrumentality, officer, or employee, shall be subject to the provisions of this title in the same manner and to the same extent as any nongovernmental entity." 17 U.S.C. §501 (2000).

182. U.S. CONST. amend. XI.

183. *Florida Prepaid Postsecondary Education Expense Board v. College Savings Bank,* 527 U.S. 627 (1999).

184. *College Savings Bank v. Florida Prepaid Postsecondary Education Expense Board,* 527 U.S. 666 (1999).

185. *Mt. Healthy School District Board of Education v. Doyle,* 429 U.S. 274, 280 (1977).

186. *Rodriguez v. Texas Commission on the Arts,* 871 F.3d 552 (5th Cir. 2000).

187. *Boyd v. University of Illinois,* 1999 U.S. Dist. LEXIS 15348 (S.D.N.Y. 1999).

188. Brenda Sandburg, *Universities May Lose IP Immunity,* LEGAL INTELLIGENCER, Sept. 13, 2000, at 4.

189. S. 1259, 106th Cong. (1999) (Trademark Amendments Act of 1999, restoring liability for trademark dilution); S. 1835, 106th Cong. (1999) (Intellectual Property Protection Restoration Act of 1999, restoring the remedies for violations of intellectual property rights by states, and for other purposes).

190. 17 U.S.C. §502 (2000).

191. 17 U.S.C. §503(a) and (b) (2000).

192. 17 U.S.C. §504(b) (2000).

193. 17 U.S.C. §504(c) (2000).

194. *UMG Recordings, Inc. v. MP3.com, Inc.,* 2000 U.S. Dist. LEXIS 13293, at *18 (S.D.N.Y. 2000).

195. 17 U.S.C. §504(c)(2).

196. 17 U.S.C. §504(c)(2).

197. 17 U.S.C. §504(c)(2).

198. 17 U.S.C. §505 (2000); *Fogerty v. Fantasy, Inc.,* 127 L. Ed. 2d 455, 114 S. Ct. 1023 (1994).

199. See *United States v. LaMacchia,* 871 F. Supp. 535 (D. Mass. 1994). The No Electronic Theft (NET) Act amended to section 506 in 1997 (Pub. L. No. 105-147, 111 Stat. 2678) closed the so-called *LaMacchia* loophole; prior to amendment, the infringement had to involve a more traditional financial transaction such as a sale of pirated works.

200. 17 U.S.C. §506 (2000) and 18 U.S.C. §2319 (2000).

2 DESIGNING THE LIBRARY WEB PAGE

Linking on the World Wide Web

Q1 May my library's web page freely link to others?

Q2 What is deep-linking?

Q3 May my library's web page include "deep links"?

Q4 How do I know if I need permission to deep-link?

Q5 Our library does not use robots, but rather people to find the deep links. Is that legal?

Q6 How will my nonprofit library be treated if it engages in the practice of deep-linking?

Q7 What are the consequences of deep-linking without permission?

Q8 What legal concerns should I consider if my library's web page uses frames?

Q9 Are there other legal concerns about linking?

Q10 Does my library's nonprofit status shield it from liability?

Trademarks

Q11 When does a library need to be concerned with trademark law in designing the library's web page?

Q12   Briefly, what are some of the underlying principles of trademark law?

Q13   What is trademark infringement?

Q14   What is trademark dilution?

Hypothetical Library Cases

> "James Dean" and "Barney" Cases
>
> "McRead" Promotion

Q15   If my library uses someone's trademark, either inadvertently or deliberately, is it on better footing in a dilution lawsuit if its use is noncommercial?

Q16   Does a library have a First Amendment right to comment or criticism using someone else's trademark?

Q17   When is a library's use of a trademark considered "fair use"?

Hypothetical Case: Library Puts PBS Logo on Its Website as a Link

> Fair Use Defense

Trademarks in Metatags

Q18   Will a library ever want to use trademarked phrases in its metatags?

Q19   What would be an acceptable use of a trademark metatag by a library?

Trademarks in Library Domain Names

Q20   A Public Library has a registered domain name with the acronym "APL" in it. What happens if "APL" is a trademark belonging to someone else?

Rights of Privacy and Publicity

Q21   May the library put pictures of patrons on its web page?

Copyright and the Library Website: Liability for Direct, Contributory, and Vicarious Infringement

Q22   How might a library be liable for copyright infringement on the Web?

Direct Infringement on the Web

Q23   Our library put up a web page some time ago. Do we need to worry that someone is going to come after us for copyright infringement?

Q24   What if my library created its own web page, but borrowed ideas and facts from other web pages?

Q25   What if my library copied some of another website's content?

Q26   Can my library's web page always link to other websites?

Q27   Can I use graphics from another site if I don't copy them, but merely link to them?

Q28   What about regular links, that is, hyperlinks (HREFs)? My page has a long list of links.

Q29   Can my library provide its own indexes to materials on the Web, such as a thumbnail-image index to pictures that are on the Web?

Q30   Have libraries ever been held accountable for direct copyright infringement?

Contributory and Vicarious Infringement

Q31   Can a library be liable if its web page links to infringing material?

   Innocent Linking

   Contributory Infringement: Linking to Sources Known to Contain Infringing Material

Q32   How does a library or educational institution know if the other site is infringing someone's copyright?

Q33   Would a library that encouraged patrons to download music or video with Napster or similar technology be liable as a contributory infringer?

Q34   What would be the result if a library site contained links to a site that shows patrons how to decode encrypted copyrighted material?

Q35   What should libraries know about copyright infringement when linking to sites in other countries?

Vicarious Infringement

Q36   Is the library itself legally responsible if the library's webmaster or other technical employee is actually the person writing the web page, posting, or framing copyrighted materials without permission?

Q37   What if the library doesn't know that its webmaster is infringing copyright—can it still be held vicariously liable?

Q38   If the webmaster is an independent contractor, can the library still be held liable for copyright infringement?

Q39   If the library patrons are using library equipment to create websites that infringe copyright, can the library be liable?

Liability for Republication of Defamatory Material on the Library Website

Q40   What does a library need to know about defamation?

Q41   But libraries are not responsible for removing all defamatory materials in their collections, are they?

Q42   What about defamatory information located on a library's website? Is a library protected the same as it is in the print environment?

Q43   What if a library web page simply links to another site that contains defamatory material? Can the library be held liable for defamation?

Q44   Could a library or educational institution linking to a site of defamatory material be cast in the role of a republisher and thus be liable?

General Rules for Linking on the World Wide Web

Notes

∽∽∽

This chapter discusses the use of websites in various library settings, with a special emphasis on the noncommercial or nonprofit library, such as a local public library, school, college, or university library, or those of other philanthropic organizations. While the legal problems involving library web spaces are many, the purpose here is to introduce the issues of linking, posting, or framing in a web space that in turn can raise issues of trespass, trademark, copyright, and defamation. Each area is dealt with in turn, stressing how the application of recent case law may impact the practices of organizations such as libraries in their use of information available on the World Wide Web.

LINKING ON THE WORLD WIDE WEB

Q1   *May my library's web page freely link to others?*

If the link is nothing more than a simple cross-reference, copyright permission is not usually required. There is no copyright violation, because by placing a link on your page, you are not actually copying another website's copyrighted expression, but merely its address.[1] Further, one court has found a First Amendment right of third parties to link to another's website without permission.[2] The court found the right to link superseded any commercial or proprietary right of website owners to control access to their site. However, if the link implies an endorsement or affiliation,[3] other legal claims such as trademark and unfair competition may arise. Some litigation trends suggest there may be a limited right to control linking to commercial and to a lesser extent noncommercial sites, particularly when links create a commercial advantage for one site at the expense of another. An especially hot area for litigation involves the practice of "deep-linking." In essence, there is no absolute right to link, and much depends on the circumstances. Some web publishers will send a cease and desist letter or commence litigation in order to curtail or modify the linking practices of others to their site. A brief examination of a site's posted notices or licenses will help avoid these letters.

Q2   What is deep-linking?

Deep-linking is the practice of bypassing introductory home pages and thereby bypassing a site's own content and advertising. The practice of deep-linking is commonly done to get right to the item of interest—a service that libraries may be particularly adept at offering in the pursuit of expedience and convenience for their patrons.

Q3   May my library's web page include "deep links"?

Many commercial site owners believe it is within their prerogative to restrict deep-linking.[4] The legal basis for an unauthorized deep link is typically not rooted in copyright theory.[5] Rather, it is usually based on some other property right such as trespass[6] or misappropriation.[7] In fact, the first significant case to deal with deep-linking focused on unfair competition laws. Ticketmaster sued Microsoft when Microsoft deep-linked to "Seattle Sidewalks," bypassing Ticketmaster's top-level page and advertising.[8] Microsoft settled the case by agreeing to link to Ticketmaster's top-level page. No legal precedent was set, but the cautious approach for libraries is to be aware of bypassing top-level pages with advertising.

The legal claim of "trespass" has become increasingly important as web robots, crawlers, and spiders are used to access the content of other owners' websites. In an important legal case, "virtual trespass" was claimed when Bidder's Edge, Inc., used a software robot to gather information from the eBay site in contravention of eBay's policy (stated on its website) of not allowing such information collection.[9] The court accepted eBay's characterization of the unauthorized access to its site as a trespass and granted a preliminary injunction, stopping Bidder's Edge's practice.[10] In an extended discussion, the court negotiated the often difficult task of applying real (physical) world legal concepts to virtual space:

> [I]t is black letter law in California that an injunction is an appropriate remedy for a continuing trespass to real property. [citation omitted] If eBay were a brick and mortar auction house with limited seating capacity, eBay would appear to be entitled to reserve those seats for potential bidders, to refuse entrance to individuals (or robots) with no intention of bidding on any of the items, and to seek preliminary injunctive relief against non-customer trespassers eBay was physically unable to exclude. The analytic difficulty is that a wrongdoer can commit an ongoing trespass of a computer system that is more akin to the traditional notion of a trespass to real property, than the traditional notion of a trespass to chattels, because even though it is ongoing, it will probably never amount to a conversion.[11]

The court concluded that under the circumstances, Bidder's Edge's ongoing violation of eBay's fundamental property right to exclude others from its computer system potentially caused sufficient irreparable harm (the legal standard used when issuing a preliminary injunction) from reduced system performance, system unavailability, or data losses.[12]

The case was settled in March 2001. As part of the settlement, Bidder's Edge paid eBay an undisclosed amount of money and dropped its appeal.[13]

Q4   How do I know if I need permission to deep-link?

In many instances, you can determine whether or not you have permission to deep-link by reading the legal pages of the sites you are linking to. The legal page may contain the terms and conditions of use the site owner may require of its visitor, such as a "no deep link rule" without permission. For example, the Ticketmaster site only forbade linking for commercial purposes. On the other hand, the enforceability of the provisions on sites that merely post terms and conditions of use, without any positive assent by the site visitor or linking site such as a web-click mechanism, is yet to be tested squarely in court. Two commentators go so far as to suggest that linking of any kind is of concern only when it occurs for commercial purposes.[14] However, it should be observed that in the brick and mortar world, the argument that one's use is noncommercial or nonprofit is a weak defense to a charge of trespass on someone's property; adapting the rationale to cyberspace would likewise offer little help to the library. However, the sort of harm identified by the eBay court would typically not result from the mere linking or deep-linking to a website by a library or a number of libraries.

Q5   Our library does not use robots, but rather people to find the deep links. Is that legal?

While it is not clear-cut, there is legal support for the argument that any harm from deep-linking may be offset by a benefit to the linked-to site. In a later case, Tickets.com deep-linked into Ticketmaster.[15] This time, referencing the *eBay* decision, the court squarely faced the trespass issue, in addition to copyright. The difference between the trespass issue in the *eBay* litigation and the later *Tickets.com* case is that the *Tickets.com* court found the elements of a physical harm and obstruction of basic function lacking (known as "trespass to chattels"). Deep-linking into the Ticketmaster site was, in comparison to the number of hits to the Ticketmaster site, "very small and there is no showing that the use interferes with the regular business of TM [Ticketmaster]. If it did, an injunction might well issue."[16]

The court looked at the loss of advertising revenue as a harm but saw as much potential benefit from the deep link as potential harm:

> While TM sees some detriment in T.Com's operation (possibly in the loss of advertising revenue), there is also a beneficial effect in the referral of customers looking for tickets to TM events directly to TM. (In fact, other companies, who presumably pay a fee, are allowed to refer customers directly to the internal Web pages of TM, presumably leading to sale of TM tickets despite hypothetical loss of advertising revenue by not going through the TM home Web page.) Accordingly, while the trespass theory has some merit, there is insufficient proof of its elements in this case to justify a preliminary injunction. Further, there appears to be a lack of irreparable injury (required for this theory).[17]

In a copyright case, discussed in a following section of this chapter, a court in the Central District of California also ruled against a claim regarding the loss of advertising space as a recoverable harm. There a search engine enabled users to deep-link directly to the pages containing retrieved images, and thereby bypass the "front page" of the originating website. As a result, these users would be less likely to view all of the advertisements on the website or view the site's entire promotional message. Yet the court found "no evidence of any harm or adverse impact."[18] If these cases are any indication, most courts, given the proper evidence, would conclude that a trespass has occurred if there is a finding of either monetary harm (loss of advertising revenue resulting from the bypassed pages) or a functional harm (systems usability) at least greater than the benefit from increased site visits. In other words, the question for the deep-linking site is whether the intended deep link would cause some economic or functional harm to the site owner's operation, since the site owner must be able to demonstrate such harm to succeed at trial.

Q6   *How will my nonprofit library be treated if it engages in the practice of deep-linking?*

It is difficult to predict how a commercial website owner might react to a nonprofit library that bypasses several pages of advertising to its site, advertising that arguably might attract (from the commercial site owner's perspective) the patron of the library. This is regardless of whether the linking site—the library, museum, archive, or educational institution—is a nonprofit organization itself. While one link from a library website would not seem to rise to the level of the repeated deep-linking performed by the Bidder's Edge robots in the *eBay* case, either in terms of monetary harm or functional harm, librarians need to be aware of the potential downside to deep-linking practices.

The fact that the library that uses or "trespasses" the site is noncommercial or nonprofit may also influence a court faced with a legal challenge from a website owner against a deep-linking library. But be wary of using the nonprofit rationale as a pattern of practice. Many commercial sites to which a library might deep-link may rely on the nonprofit market of schools and libraries for the majority of their customers, such as a textbook vendor's website. Bypassing the advertising on these sites could hurt the ability of these website owners to generate revenue from their client base (the nonprofit school and library community) in the same way a commercial site might rely on other commercial visitors or the consuming public to visit and read the advertising on its site. Netiquette might also suggest that if the site linked to by the library is a commercial site that the linking party, the library patron, might legitimately patronize as a paying customer, then permission to deep-link could be sought.

Q7   What are the consequences of deep-linking without permission?

Most likely the offended site would contact the library and request the library refrain from deep-linking. At this point the library could evaluate whether it desired to continue the link and face a possible court challenge, which might resolve in its favor or withdraw the deep link at that time. Alternatively, it could negotiate a compromise such as adding or substituting a link to the site's home page.

Q8   What legal concerns should I consider if my library's web page uses frames?

Unlike the links discussed earlier, which allow the patron to reach out to another site, framing allows the use of "inline" links that pull in materials from other sites. The patron need never leave the original site. The first case to challenge the legality of framing reached a settlement agreement in which the framer was permitted to retain conventional links subject to revocation of fifteen days' notice.[19] The best practice is to get permission when using inline links with frames.

As indicated in the preceding chapter, the court in *Kelly* v. *Arriba Soft Corp.* concluded that the framing of photographs on another website was not fair use and violated the copyright owner's exclusive right of display. So if a frame is a display, then the library should make sure that its use of the framed contents is a fair use.[20] What was different between the two scenarios in *Arriba*—a thumbnail index of photographs (right of reproduction) is a fair use versus the framing of photographs (right of display), which is not a fair use—was that the framing of copyrighted material was not transformative, but a substitute for the original; furthermore, the framing was likely to harm the market for the photographs; thus two additional fair use factors favored the plaintiff copyright owner.

Q9   Are there other legal concerns about linking?

Yes. Patrons that use adaptive technology such as screen readers need separations between links such as text or punctuation. New legal guidelines have been developed, and extensive discussion as to whom the guidelines apply is provided in chapter 4, "Digital Library Resources and Patrons with Disabilities."

Q10   Does my library's nonprofit status shield it from liability?

No. Regardless of which direction the law ultimately takes, the fact remains that an institution that is deemed not-for-profit or has an "educational" purpose when it does in fact in-link does not mean that the institution may ignore the developing precedent. Just as the nonprofit institution—be it a library, museum, archive, school, college, or university—cannot freely copy or display without limit from copyrighted materials simply because it is nonprofit, that same institution cannot ignore the property rights, real or virtual, of others. This position is underscored in situations where the primary market for the protected work is a nonprofit one, educational, for example.

The final lesson of *Ticketmaster, eBay,* and their progeny is that proprietors of commercial sites often believe that it is within their prerogative to control linking to their sites. The law is still developing, and libraries should continue to monitor these developments. If noncommercial libraries link to commercial sites or even to other noncommercial sites (i.e., sites that are not-for-profit but still potentially partisan or in competition with other nonprofit organizations), the most conservative course of action would be to check the site's legal page, link only to the site's home page, or seek permission for the deep link.[21] Entering into a web link agreement is another possibility.[22] However, other concerns may arise; for example, the appearance of a commercial product or service endorsement by the nonprofit entity may be prohibited by the entity's own bylaws. This type of tacit or implied endorsement may run afoul of nonprofit institutional restrictions as contained in the entity's governing articles or bylaws. Furthermore, a web link agreement raises its own complicating issues, e.g., review of contract or approval by institutional legal authority (general counsel). In the alternative, in commercial settings, when an actual association does in fact exist and it is not disclosed or the link is made in such a way as to disguise the association, it may give rise to a claim of unfair competition.[23] It may be easier to just obtain a simple (written) permission to deep-link to a commercial website, similar to the copyright permissions routinely obtained for the use of copyrighted materials. A record of this permission to link could be kept on file with the appropriate staff member.

TRADEMARKS

Q11   When does a library need to be concerned with trademark law in designing the library's web page?

Trademark issues can arise if the library uses a logo, design, or other trademarked symbol or mark as a "hot" button to activate a link, to insert as a metatag, or as part of a library's domain name.

*Q12   Briefly, what are some of the underlying principles
of trademark law?*

Trademark law is governed by both a federal and a state scheme of pro-tection. A trademark owner's value in a mark is tied to the relative dis-tinctiveness of the mark; for example, the mark "Amazon.com" distin-guishes that company's services from competitors' similar services. "Brand-ing" has become increasingly important, and if a library's web page uses someone else's trademark, even inadvertently, it could face some legal challenges of infringement.

Q13   What is trademark infringement?

Trademark infringement would occur if a library's conduct is "likely to cause confusion, or cause mistake, or to deceive" as to the "origin, spon-sorship, or approval" of the defendant's (the library or educational insti-tution's) goods or services.[24] In other words, the library could be accused of interfering with the distinctiveness of the plaintiff-trademark owner's use of a particular mark in relation to that owner's goods or services. Trademark owners strive to maintain that distinctiveness when tying spe-cific marks, words, sounds, colors, and logos to the provision of their spe-cific products and services.

Q14   What is trademark dilution?

The use of a mark by someone other than the trademark owner may tend to confuse consumers or, in a special form of trademark infringement, it may "dilute" the strength of the mark by harming the good name of the mark (tarnishment) or by decreasing the value of the mark (blurring) by its use on dissimilar products and services. Special protection against dilu-tion is awarded to famous marks under federal law.[25] Many states also have anti-dilution statutes. While tarnishment is arguably something libraries might not engage in by design, it is not unfathomable.

Hypothetical Library Cases

"James Dean" and "Barney" Cases

Suppose a library compiled a website display or exhibit related to popular cultural icons protected by trademark, such as the late actor James Dean[26] or the children's dinosaur character Barney.[27] Let's suppose the library creates promotional material suggesting that no matter how "cool" one tries to appear, unless one visits the library instead of running wild, an early grave awaits (just as it awaited the glamorous young actor of the 1950s). Or that if the dinosaurs had visited their libraries a bit more often they would not be extinct (or at least would not now be represented by an oversized and overstuffed bumbling purple character). Both are negative reflections on the original trademark characters. Let's also say that no actual image of James Dean or Barney is used, but the characterization is similar enough to suggest to viewers a recollection of the original marks— yet no one would confuse the designs of the library with the originals, and without confusion there can be no trademark infringement. Since dilution does not require that the use of the other mark cause confusion among consumers,[28] a library might accidentally harm the dilution rights of a famous mark owner.[29] The library display benefits, it rides the coattails, so to speak, of the original marks of James Dean and Barney. Both are arguably famous marks under the federal statute, and in fact, both the James Dean[30] and Barney[31] marks have been the subject of tarnishment or tarnishment-like litigation. Dilution in this sense protects against "tarnishment of the reputation of the plaintiff's mark by association with something unsavory, unwholesome, or of poor quality."[32] Alternatively, the library might use the appeal of James Dean or Barney in its own promotional literature—in a manner similar to the "Read" promotional posters of the American Library Association—to sell some of its own publications such as greeting cards, T-shirts, or other library memorabilia.

"McRead" Promotion

Suppose a library designs and sells a series of "McRead" posters that say "over one billion read," referring to the books available in the library. This could dilute the mark of McDonald's. Others have tried to benefit from the name recognition of the famous fast-food chain's mark to no avail in cases involving a hotel chain (McSleep)[33] and a bakery product (McBagel).[34] Dilution by blurring is a "whittling away of an established mark's selling power through its use on dissimilar products or services."[35]

Q15   *If my library uses someone's trademark, either inadvertently or deliberately, is it on better footing in a dilution lawsuit if its use is noncommercial?*

Yes. Assessing the federal Trademark Dilution Act of 1995,[36] one commentator suggests that application of the act "will turn on whether the challenged trademark use was for commercial or noncommercial purposes."[37] The federal dilution statute is triggered only when the library engages in a commercial act in conjunction with the use of the mark. This suggests a safe harbor: a noncommercial use of a mark (in criticism, comment, or parody, and in educational or personal uses in general) can never be the subject of a dilution claim.[38] The plain language of the statute also supports this interpretation,[39] although one commentator[40] suggests this interpretation may raise constitutional commercial free speech issues, i.e., impermissible disadvantage imposed upon a category (commercial) of protected speech. Regardless of the noncommercial dilution safe harbor, unauthorized use of the mark may still subject the user to a claim of general trademark infringement.

*Q16   Does a library have a First Amendment right to comment
        or criticism using someone else's trademark?*

The greater the extent of actual comment, criticism, or even parody in the library's use of a trademark, the greater is the likelihood of a successful First Amendment defense. Presumably, a library or archive could seek First Amendment refuge for the use of a trademark in an exhibit or display when its use is part of a broader protected educational criticism or social commentary.[41] Parody is a way of claiming that no likelihood of confusion exists "because consumers will get the joke."[42] If, through the use of a mark in parody, it is clear the user is in no way implying or suggesting sponsorship, endorsement, etc., then the rights of the trademark owner have not been infringed. While parody may in effect be a "defense" to a claim of trademark infringement,[43] not every display that confuses or reduces distinctiveness (infringes trademark) or tarnishes or blurs (dilutes) is intended to be parody.[44] It is also difficult to claim that a "bright line" exists between commercial and noncommercial uses of a trademark in parody.[45] However, the parody is clearly less protected if it involves a commercial use of the mark in parody than if it involves a noncommercial use of the mark in parody. It is less protected if placed on a library T-shirt for sale and distribution than if it is part of a library web page or an in-house display.

Q17   When is a library's use of a trademark considered "fair use"?

"Fair use" in trademark law is based on the similar concept in copyright law, i.e., that an intellectual property owner's right to control the uses of his or her work is limited by certain rights of public access to the work. Those rights are embodied in the concept of fair use. However, in trademark law the fair-use rights of persons other than the trademark owner are far more limited and far less developed by the courts than they are in copyright law.

There are two types of trademark fair use, descriptive and nominative, and the library might engage in practices that might invoke either or both types as a defense. *Descriptive fair use* of a trademark can occur when the

> use of the name, term, or device charged to be an infringement is a use, otherwise than as a mark, of the party's individual name in his own business, or of the individual name of anyone in privity with such party, or of a term or device which is descriptive of and used fairly and in good faith only to describe the goods or services of such party, or their geographic origin.[46]

For example, if a library were to use the words "Hot Picks" to describe the library's products or services—in a reading corner, exhibit, display, or special collection featuring recent best-sellers or seasonal favorites—it might not realize it is using a defendant's trademark belonging to someone else.[47] If a library's catalog record contains a self-made subject heading for "world beat music," the label "world beat music" is too generic to impinge upon someone else's trademark when merely used as a descriptive term.[48] In both the "Hot Picks" and "world beat music" examples, the library does not use either as a trademark; rather, its use of another's trademark is merely descriptive of something else.

Nominative trademark fair use is a concept created by the courts to determine when the use of another's mark to reference the trademark owner's product or service is a fair use. The fair use is of the name of the trademark owner's product or service; the fair use "names" (nominative), represents, or identifies the trademark owner's mark. Under this doctrine, a library is allowed to use the plaintiff's trademark to identify the plaintiff's products and services and the relationship of those products or services to the defendant's products or services.

The test for nominative fair use, as articulated by a recent court case, is in three parts: (1) the product must not be readily identifiable without the use of the trademark, (2) no more of the trademark is used by the library than is reasonably necessary to identify the product, and (3) the user must not act in such a way as to suggest sponsorship or endorsement by the plaintiff.[49] In the *New Kids on the Block* case, a court allowed a

900-phone number vote for your favorite New Kid on the Block, since there was no way to identify what the contest or poll was about without using the actual trademarked name of the teen idol singing group. Only as much of the trademark that was necessary was used, and the poll service disclaimed any association with the New Kids on the Block band itself.

Hypothetical Case: Library Puts PBS Logo on Its Website as a Link

Let's suppose a library places the "faces" logo of the Public Broadcasting Service (PBS) on its website (or in its online catalog) and uses it as a prompt or logo-link (clicking on the logo activates the link). Activating the logo-link takes patrons or students to the PBS site where they can locate additional information regarding the documentaries that PBS airs. The PBS mark is in fact protected by federal trademark.[50] The library may intend no harm; it uses the logo-link as a convenient and visually appealing way to allow patrons to seek out additional information, such as other related video titles. Although the purpose behind this use might be reasonable—education or personal use—this use nonetheless may disturb or interfere with the distinctiveness or strength of the mark.

Placing the PBS "faces" logo on the library website could also be analyzed under a "dilution by blurring" framework. Blurring might occur if the library designed its own PLS (Public Library Services) faces logo. If this logo began popping up on library websites across the country, it could be viewed as diluting the strength of the PBS mark. The use of the PLS faces logo by all of these other "public" institutions blurs the distinctiveness of the original PBS faces mark. PBS might be concerned that such use of the logo confuses viewers of the library website as to the connection between the public library that circulates in its collection tapes of various PBS programs and the franchised public television stations on which those programs are shown. It might be logical to believe that this "harmless" non-commercial use by a library or even a multitude of uses by a multitude of libraries would not interfere with the PBS trademark. However, the problem for PBS will come when a competitor uses the PBS logo as a trademark and PBS then desires to halt that use. If the competitor can show that PBS does nothing to police the use of its mark or that consumers are generally confused about the origin of the PBS mark (public libraries versus public broadcasting), PBS will lose its case. The competitor would try to demonstrate that web users have come to view the PBS mark as an indicator of documentary or reference-type resources in general, whether available from the local library or from the PBS video store or its 800 toll-free service, for example. Survey and marketing studies would be performed to substantiate these claims. As part of its litigation strategy against the library, PBS would need to demonstrate an association in the public mind between the PBS mark and the library's goods or services.[51]

Fair Use Defense

An analysis of the library's situation under the nominative fair-use defense might look like this: (1) Is there some other way to identify PBS videos in the library collections without use of the PBS faces logo? Certainly there is. (2) Must the library use the faces logo, or could it get the message across by using only the abbreviation "PBS" or the name "Public Broadcasting Service"? It could use the latter. (3) Did the library act in such a way as to suggest sponsorship or endorsement by PBS? If this were the only concern, a disclaimer on the library website disavowing any connection or formal relationship between the two is advisable.

Although the library might want to use the PBS trademark to indicate that its collection contains educational videos from PBS, "where a defendant uses a plaintiff's distinctive lettering style, color scheme, or logo, the nominative fair-use defense likely will fail."[52] Use of the PBS logo in the virtual catalog or exhibit to indicate PBS holdings by the library or as a hot-link to take users to the PBS.org site would be unlikely to survive the fair use test.[53] The use of a trademarked domain name such as "PBS.org" on the library website or online catalog would not meet the same fate, since there would be no other way of effectively identifying the Public Broadcasting Service; one couldn't very well refer to the latter as "that entity where the Ken Burns *Civil War* and *Baseball* documentaries first aired."

Trademarks in Metatags

Q18   *Will a library ever want to use trademarked phrases in its metatags?*

Metatags are tags that summarize the content of web pages.[54] If contacting the library's website counts as a circulation or visit, then indeed the library may be interested in doing all it can to promote access to and contact with its website, as opposed to another site of similar information. Likewise, an educational institution that launches a copycat degree or certificate program may want to deflect prospective students to its mirror program instead of the more established program. This may be especially true if budget allocations are based upon output measures such as visits per year per capita or enrollments. The library might use a trademarked word or phrase as a metatag cue to attract a "hit." If so, the library is likely to run afoul of the trademark law. In a recent case, an appellate court upheld a preliminary injunction barring one company from using the similarly worded trademark of a competitor in its domain name and metatags.[55] While misled customers would eventually realize the guise, the "initial interest confusion" was sufficient to raise valid trademark concerns.

Q19 *What would be an acceptable use of a trademark metatag by a library?*

When metatags contain another party's trademark merely to indicate a fair use of the trademark in the website's visible contents, use of the trademark in the metatags will likely be protected.[56] Under these restrictions, merely using the name "Public Broadcasting Service" as a metatag in an attempt to promote institutional holdings containing the complete PBS video library might qualify as an acceptable nominative use of a metatag mark.

Trademarks in Library Domain Names

Trademark law allows the use of the same name by different entities, so long as there is no likelihood of confusion by consumers as to the source, sponsorship, or affiliation of the goods or services involved. Parties in the physical world have geographical and product-specific ranges; in the online world, however, those territories can merge.

Q20 *A Public Library has a registered domain name with the acronym "APL" in it. What happens if "APL" is a trademark belonging to someone else?*

It depends. Under the old Domain Name Dispute Policy administered by Network Solutions, Inc. (NSI; the company that at one time had exclusive administration over several top-level domains), the APL trademark owner needed merely to give NSI a trademark registration certificate to initiate a challenge. The library would need to reply by submitting its own trademark registration to NSI, with a registration date prior to the dispute. If unable to do so, the domain would be taken away from the library, and a lot of time and money was needed to fight this. Under the new Internet Corporation for Assigned Names and Numbers (ICAAN) policy, the trademark owner has to show the library acted in bad faith. That is, did the library grab a trademarked domain name in the hopes of selling it for a million dollars later? It's a complicated issue that is still evolving.[57] Unfortunately, old domain names are still treated under the old policy. New domains registered after November 4, 1999, by an authorized register, such as Network Solutions, Inc., use the new policy. For further information, see the Internet Corporation for Assigned Names and Numbers Uniform Domain Name Dispute Resolution Policy.[58]

Bad-faith domain names are now illegal in the United States under the 1999 Anti-Cybersquatting Consumer Protection Act.[59] To prevail under the act, the owner of a trademark or service mark must meet two requirements. First, the owner must prove that the domain name holder has a "bad faith intent to profit" from that mark.[60] Second, the owner must demonstrate that the holder "registers, traffics in, or uses a domain name" in a way that harms the owner's commercial interests.[61] The law was passed to combat the practice of unscrupulous domain registrants who routinely register the domain names of famous companies and then offer to sell the registered domain name to the company—for a sizable fee, of course.[62]

RIGHTS OF PRIVACY AND PUBLICITY

The rights of privacy and publicity recognize that an individual has certain interests in his or her name, voice, picture, likeness, and other identifying characteristics. These rights exist separately from trademark and copyright. The rights of privacy and publicity vary significantly from state to state, and state statutes and case law should be consulted.

The right of privacy protects persons from unwanted public exposure and resulting emotional harm. It encompasses four types of harm: (1) intrusion upon seclusion, (2) public disclosure of private facts, (3) publicly placing another in a false light, and (4) appropriation of a name or likeness.[63] These rights usually terminate at death.

The right of publicity is the right of a person, especially a public figure or celebrity, to control the commercial value of his or her name, likeness, or other identifying characteristic and to prevent others from unfairly appropriating the name or likeness for commercial gain.[64] These rights sometimes survive death as descendible property rights. California, for example, protects both privacy and publicity rights for seventy years after death.[65]

Q21   May the library put pictures of patrons on its web page?

The context of the images is significant. If an embarrassing picture is taken at a library event (which is arguably a public event), the patron's right to challenge the publication of the picture is limited. If the picture was taken in a private setting (such as a home), the patron's privacy rights are strong, and the picture should only be posted with permission given by the patron. The next important question is the purpose of using the pictures. If the pictures are part of a news or opinion story, the library's use is more likely to be shielded under the First Amendment. If the use is primarily for commercial or advertising purposes, permission should be acquired. The use of a candid picture of librarians helping children in order to promote the library's reading program may be considered advertising, *even for non-commercial purposes*. Great care should be taken when using images of children, as courts are highly protective of children's privacy rights. Moreover, the library should take into account ethical as well as legal considerations. Pedophiles may be able to quickly locate or be attracted to a child, even with no further identification, when a picture of the child is posted on the website of the local library.

COPYRIGHT AND THE LIBRARY WEBSITE: LIABILITY FOR DIRECT, CONTRIBUTORY, AND VICARIOUS INFRINGEMENT

Copyright infringement occurs when the work at issue is protected by copyright and those in question violated one of the exclusive rights of the copyright owner. It would be folly to assume that simply because a library may exist in a nonprofit or educational setting it is immune from liability for copyright infringement. Not only is this a dangerous and incorrect legal assumption, but recent case law also demonstrates that nonprofit organizations such as libraries are increasingly the targets of infringement litigation. The expansion of library services into web pages only serves to underscore this reality, as the stakes appear to be higher on both sides: infringement is easier to accomplish and traces of the infringement are easier to discover.

Q22   How might a library be liable for copyright infringement on the Web?

There are several possibilities. Either the library is liable because of its own actions or the actions of its employees (known as direct copyright infringement), or it is liable because of its patrons' actions (contributory or vicarious infringement). Thus there are actually three ways to infringe on copyright. The first type falls under a primary theory of liability and is called direct copyright infringement. This is the actual infringement, i.e., an exercise of the owner's exclusive rights in excess of fair use. An example would be a library employee or patron who loads a digitized version of a VHS movie on to the library website without permission from the copyright owner. There are also two types of secondary liability whereby an intermediary or "secondary" party may be liable for the acts of a direct infringer. This secondary liability comes in two forms: contributory and vicarious liability. The former relates to conduct, the latter to relationship.

To be a contributory infringer, one must have knowledge of a direct infringing activity and must induce, cause, or materially contribute to the infringing conduct.[66] If a library creates a digital video exchange page on its website where patrons can upload and download pirated movies, it would be found to have materially contributed to the infringement of the patrons who actually post the digitized VHS recordings.

In vicarious liability, two elements are required: (1) the vicarious infringer must have the right and ability to supervise or control the infringing activity, and (2) it must have a direct material interest in the infringing activity.[67] Suppose the library video exchange page is a members-only page: patrons have to pay an extra $25 per year to access that area of the site. The more movies that are loaded on to the page by patrons (i.e., the more infringement that occurs), the more popular the page becomes, the more special memberships are sold, and the more money is raked in by the library. The library is a vicarious infringer since it could control the activity, i.e., it could shut down the page, and it has a direct financial interest in that the greater the amount of infringement, the more money the library makes from it. Employers are also thought to be vicariously liable for copyright infringement by their employees.

Direct Infringement on the Web

Reproducing protected material without permission is the most common violation by direct infringement of the copyright owner's rights, as when one posts the copyrighted material of another without permission onto a website. (Arguably this is also a "display," another right of the copyright owner.) In *Marobie-F* v. *National Association of Firefighter Equipment Distributors*,[68] a tax-exempt organization that loaded several volumes of the plaintiff's clip art onto its website without permission violated not only the right of reproduction but also the right of display.

Q23 *Our library put up a web page sometime ago. Do we need to worry that someone is going to come after us for copyright infringement?*

If you created your own content and expression in the web page, there should be no cause for concern. A plaintiff needs to show that actual copying has taken place (a rarity in most copyright infringement), or that there is an unexplainable likeness (the legal standard of "substantial similarity") and the defendant had access to the original. Even in the event that your page happens to look like another's, if both parties independently create similar web pages, without ever even seeing each other's, there's no copyright infringement, since copyright law supports the concept of independent parallel creation.

Q24 *What if my library created its own web page, but borrowed ideas and facts from other web pages?*

Ideas and facts are not protected by copyright. Many people misunderstand this. Copyright protects the expression of ideas and facts, but not the ideas or facts themselves. For example, if another website has a colorful, animated page that promotes its library's reading program, this may have given you the idea to create a colorful, animated page that promotes your reading program. But if your page has a different design and different words, it is highly unlikely that a court would find that you copied the other website's expression. In fact, one court stated in passing that copying both protected and unprotected expression from a website in order to extract the unprotected content was acceptable.[69]

However, other legal concepts such as misappropriation must be considered. Several cases have arisen in Internet settings where one website operator extracted factual data from competing sites.[70] If the information

to the whole, and (4) the effect of the use upon the potential market for the copyrighted work. Regarding the first factor, the purpose of use was deemed fair, even though the Arriba Soft site was commercial. The court noted that "it was also of a somewhat more incidental and less exploitative nature than more traditional types of 'commercial sites.'"[73] The index also was transformative because the thumbnail index was "designed to catalog and improve access to images on the Internet,"[74] favoring fair use. ("Transformative uses" that create new works tip in favor of fair use.) Regarding the second factor, i.e., the nature of the copyrighted work, the photographs were highly creative, weighing against fair use. Most significant in this case is the court's discussion of the third factor, the amount or substantiality of the portion of the work used. The photographs were presented by Arriba Soft in their entirety, but the "reduction in [their] size and resolution mitigates damage that might otherwise result from copying."[75] This is a somewhat unique distinction to draw, as if to say the format or functionality of the reproduction affects the amount or substantiality of it. In spite of this 100-percent taking, the court mildly stated that the "third factor weighs slightly against fair use."[76] The fourth factor weighed in favor of fair use, since the court found no evidence of market harm; this is not the same as saying that none could be conceived of with similar facts, only that the plaintiff merely failed to demonstrate this.

What is significant is the court's refuting the "lost advertising revenue" argument that so many website proprietors have tried to use in asserting harm to their economic interests. The plaintiff argued that the link from the thumbnail to the full-size image was made possible through a deep link into the site where the original image resides; this deep link bypassed the potential advertising or promotional pages of the original site. The court concluded that the overall use was fair because of the transformative and functional nature of the use in the first factor and the lack of market harm.

Factually, this case may parallel many library activities involving the use of metadata and the creation of indexes to materials on the Web. While libraries may gain some solace from this decision, they should be careful not to interfere with the market for the original work. It will help if the library adds to the original site's market potential through the "functional" presentation (as part of an index, for example) of the work, making it easier for web users to find and patronize the original site from which material is copied or framed or to which material is linked.[77] It is possible that the indexes will create more benefit to the target site in terms of publicity and traffic than harm to the site through lost advertising.

Q30   Have libraries ever been held accountable for direct copyright infringement?

Yes. A case involving direct infringement of a copyright holder's right to distribute involved the library of the Church of Jesus Christ of Latter-day Saints. An unlawfully made copy of a fiche item was in the collection and listed in its catalog for use in one of its genealogical libraries. The statute of limitations (three years) for infringement based upon unauthorized reproduction had passed. However, the court found that the library had continually directly infringed by "distributing" the fiche when it made the work available to the public through its collection.[78] The court observed that "[w]hen a public library adds a work to its collection, lists the work in its index or catalog system, and makes the work available to the borrowing or browsing public, it has completed all the steps necessary for distribution to the public."[79] Because the library had unlawfully made a complete cover-to-cover copy of one of the plaintiff's works on genealogy, the distribution of that material was also unlawful.[80]

In the web environment, a library that improperly loads copied material onto its website is also distributing the work, and is directly engaging in an unlawful distribution of copyrighted material as long as the material is available to the public. As long as the material remains posted on the library website, infringement is considered to be continually occurring daily and the statute of limitations would be three years from each daily unauthorized posting (distribution).[81]

Contributory and Vicarious Infringement

Q31   Can a library be liable if its web page links to infringing material?

This question brings up a discussion of contributory infringement. Contributory copyright infringement can occur when "one who, with knowledge of the infringing activity, induces or causes, or materially contributes to the infringement of another."[82] It is conceivable that a link to a site that is known to contain infringing material or is otherwise highly suspect, along with encouragement to patrons to download content from that site, would meet the standards of contributory infringement.

Innocent Linking

If the library unintentionally links to infringing material, it is not knowingly contributing to infringement. Based on the interconnectedness of the Web and the theory that no more than "six degrees of separation" stand between any two websites on the planet, it would not take too much to bring the Web to its knees if this theory was used. In a recent California case, a photographer sued a website owner whose site linked to unauthorized copies of the photographer's work. The court dismissed the complaint, finding no significant participation in the infringement on the defendant's part.[83] The law of third-party liability in copyright law is very well developed, however, and libraries should proceed with caution when linking to suspect sites.

Contributory Infringement: Linking to Sources Known to Contain Infringing Material

On the other hand, the library should beware if it does knowingly link to infringing material. In the *Utah Lighthouse Ministry* case, the Church of Jesus Christ of Latter-day Saints won a lawsuit against a website operator who posted copyrighted material from a Mormon Church instructional handbook without permission on a personal website.[84] A court ordered the defendants to cease display of the church's material. The defendants removed the infringing pages, but placed a note on their web page that the handbook was online elsewhere. The note included a description (but not an active link) of how visitors to their site could locate three other sites where the full text of the handbook could be obtained. The defendants also included the texts of several e-mails that encouraged subsequent browsing of the handbook by site visitors and encouraged them to get one of three full-text versions of the handbook to copy and send to others.[85] The court concluded that the defendants actively encouraged the infringement of the plaintiff's copyright.

Q32   How does a library or educational institution know if the other site is infringing someone's copyright?

In the *Utah Lighthouse Ministry* case, the defendants knew that any source of the handbook would be an infringing source of material, as the Mormon Church never publicly released the handbook. In other less obvious instances, some commentators[86] suggest that in today's litigious Internet environment, becoming familiar with the nature and content of the site to which one links is prudent, if not a necessity. (This is called a "should have known" standard.) The deciding factor may be one of plain reasonableness. While actual knowledge is not always needed, there must be at least some reason to know of the site's infringing nature. This does not require the library to check every site to which it links or to which it refers patrons. Use a "mirror" test. Look at yourself in the mirror and ask, "Why am I linking or referring to this site, and is there any reason to suspect it is not legitimate?" Does the site have 2,000 theatrical movies downloadable for free? In light of the attention that *Napster* and other cases have received, heading that same way is unwise, since all users of copyrighted material (including libraries) now have a better idea of what is acceptable and what is unacceptable.

The issue here is the potential to commit a contributory infringement through a referral; through a verbal or written communication, as in the *Utah Lighthouse Ministry* case; or through a bookmark or other link referral, accompanied by encouragement to copy, repost, etc. In the *Utah Lighthouse Ministry* case, the court ordered the defendants to "remove from and not post on [their] Web site addresses to Web sites that defendants know or have reason to know, contain material alleged to infringe plaintiff's copyright."[87] This case has serious implications for library web pages and for the library reference or referral process. If library patrons are directed to known sources of digital formats posted on infringing sites, and encouraged to engage in infringing conduct by viewing, downloading, and forwarding that infringing material, there may be liability for contributory infringement.

Q33   Would a library that encouraged patrons to download music or video with Napster or similar technology be liable as a contributory infringer?

It may be. Consider the following example. Is it reasonable to suspect that a contemplated link from a library or other educational or nonprofit referral to a site containing more than 5,000 digital music or video files downloadable to visitors without charge would be a link to an infringing site? Unless the URL is that of Columbia.com, Capitol.com, or some other known record company or distributor, it is entirely reasonable and prudent to assume that the site contains infringing material. (This is the "reason to know" concept.) To conclude that the digital music library site is less than legitimate, especially considering the publicity that illegal music and video downloading from the Web have received, is consistent with developing precedent, and providing the link or referral without further investigation would seem unwise. Unless there is some other clear guarantee from the site of its compliance with the copyright law, it would be unwise to alert patrons or students to its existence or otherwise induce, cause, or materially contribute to patrons' use of the site. This example would also appear to have implications for curtailing the conduct of overeager reference staff who direct patrons to known or likely sources of infringing material.

Q34   What would be the result if a library site contained links to a site that shows patrons how to decode encrypted copyrighted material?

Using a different provision of the copyright law, 17 U.S.C. §1201, a court recently prohibited the posting of links to decoding software.[88] The court applied the anti-trafficking provisions of the copyright law, observing that "the anti-trafficking provision of the DMCA [Digital Millennium Copyright Act] is implicated where one presents, holds out or makes a circumvention technology or device available, knowing its nature, for the purpose of allowing others to acquire it."[89]

The defendants linked to sites that contained de-encryption software (DeCSS) and "urged others to post DeCSS in an effort to disseminate DeCSS and to inform defendants that they were doing so."[90] The court concluded that either having a link to a site consisting solely of the infringing software or linking to a site containing the software (or containing a link to another site with the software) along with additional information, in light of the active encouragement of infringement, satisfied the "offered, provided or otherwise trafficked in" requirement of the DMCA. The decision was affirmed on appeal.[91] The appellate court was not sympathetic to the rights of users when it analogized the use of decryption codes to that of "a skeleton key that can open a locked door, a combination that can open a safe, or a device that can neutralize the security device attached to a store's products. DeCSS enables anyone to gain access to a DVD without using a DVD player."[92] However, unlike a skeleton key, the DeCSS computer code also contains speech. Even so, the court concluded that section 1201 did not violate the free speech rights of the defendants who posted and linked to DeCSS.

The court's most disturbing language, dicta that cast doubt on the common practice of many users, concerns the digital copying of material in exercise of fair use rights:

Third, the Appellants have provided no support for their premise that fair use of DVD movies is constitutionally required to be made by copying the original work in its original format. . . . One example is that of a school child who wishes to copy images from a DVD movie to insert into the student's documentary film. We know of no authority for the proposition that fair use, as protected by the Copyright Act, much less the constitution, guarantees copying by the optimum method or in the identical format of the original . . . the DMCA does not impose even an arguable limitation on the opportunity to make a variety of traditional fair uses of DVD movies, such a commenting on their content, quoting excerpts from their screenplays, and even recording portions of the video image and sounds on film or tape by pointing a camera, a camcorder, or a microphone at a monitor as it displays the DVD movie.[93]

In other words, the common practice of students digitally clipping or cutting and then pasting a piece of a digital work (the dicta spoke to DVDs but arguably could be applied to other digital works) for use in educationally related products is not necessarily a fair use. The appellate court seems to suggest that the legally preferred way to copy a DVD video clip for various fair uses would be to videotape the screen on which the DVD is shown and record the sound as the DVD is playing—sort of like Ebert and Roper using a camcorder to videotape a movie they're reviewing and showing that clip later in their television show. If this is a correct assessment of fair use of material in digital environments, then the common practices of many users—including many schools and libraries—would have to be significantly modified.

Q35   What should libraries know about copyright infringement when linking to sites in other countries?

Relevant cases that have arisen in other countries include a Dutch court which ruled that Internet service providers (ISPs) that provide access or a link to a site that displays copyrighted work without consent are infringing the copyright of the owner of the posted work.[94] *Religious Technology Center* v. *DataWeb B.V.* involved writings by L. Ron Hubbard, the founder of the Church of Scientology, which were posted without permission. The Dutch court explained that although the ISP was not a publisher of the infringing works, infringement resulted when an ISP had a link that led to the reproduction of the material *and* the ISP was aware of the infringing material. Foreign courts may impose liability more readily than U.S. courts.

Vicarious Infringement

Q36   Is the library itself legally responsible if the library's webmaster or other technical employee is actually the person writing the web page, posting, or framing copyrighted materials without permission?

Yes, the library is vicariously responsible for the infringement of its employees. Vicarious infringement is found when one has the "right and ability to supervise the infringing activity and also has a direct financial interest in such activities."[95] The employer is responsible for the acts of its employee, but not vice versa. Vicarious liability is grounded in the tort concept of respondent superior, which means literally "let the superior answer," thus the employer answers for the acts of its employees.

Q37   What if the library doesn't know that its webmaster is infringing copyright—can it still be held vicariously liable?

Yes. Vicarious liability in employment settings does not require knowledge of the infringement by the vicarious defendant.[96] Only contributory infringement requires knowledge. That is why it is often said that standards of liability for both direct and vicarious infringement are "strict" liability standards. However, like contributory infringement, a direct infringement—a result of the action of the librarian-employee—must underlie the vicarious liability.

Q38   If the webmaster is an independent contractor, can the library still be held liable for copyright infringement?

Yes. The doctrine of vicarious liability is also applicable in independent contractor settings, i.e., the acts of the independent contractor are imputed to the contracting institution.[97]

Q39   If the library patrons are using library equipment to create websites that infringe copyright, can the library be liable?

Yes. More discussion on the relationship between librarians, patrons, and copyright is available in chapter 1, "Libraries and Copyright." But note here that an employment setting is not even always required to impute liability. In a famous case, a swap-meet purveyor was found liable for the bootleg tapes sold by vendors who rented space at the swap meet.[98]

LIABILITY FOR REPUBLICATION OF DEFAMATORY MATERIAL ON THE LIBRARY WEBSITE

Q40   What does a library need to know about defamation?

In order to successfully sue a library because of defamation on its website, a plaintiff must show that he or she has been exposed to contempt or public ridicule, injuring his or her professional standing in the community.[99] The four elements of a claim for defamation are (1) a false and defamatory statement, (2) that is published to one or more third parties without privilege, (3) by a publisher who is at least negligent in communicating the information, and (4) that results in presumed or actual damage.[100]

Q41   But libraries are not responsible for removing all defamatory materials in their collections, are they?

That's correct. Libraries are not responsible for the defamatory statements contained within material residing in their collections, catalogs, or exhibits. This is because the law draws a distinction between a true publisher of a defamatory statement and a mere distributor of a defamatory statement. "Examples of such distributors include libraries, bookstores, and news vendors."[101]

Q42   What about defamatory information located on a library's website? Is a library protected the same as it is in the print environment?

In cyberspace, libraries that may have been safe in the past from defamation actions may now be exposed to liability. Technological advances can blur the legal distinction between conduit (distributor) and information creator (author, publisher, or republisher).[102] As libraries move from their traditional role as "information distributors" to "information publishers," it is essential that they have a fundamental grasp of the parameters of a defamation action.[103]

Q43   What if a library web page simply links to another site that contains defamatory material? Can the library be held liable for defamation?

A library that cuts, pastes, grafts, or otherwise edits content onto its website has arguably moved beyond the function of a mere conduit, distributor, or secondary publisher and is now acting more like a primary publisher or the editor of a newspaper. As yet it is unclear whether a link to another site that contains defamatory material makes the linking site also liable to the defamed party.

Q44   *Could a library or educational institution linking to a site of defamatory material be cast in the role of a republisher and thus be liable?*

A mere link would appear unlikely to be a republication,[104] but a link provided in the context of a website containing other recommended links for patrons or students to consult places the library into the editing function that may serve as a trigger for publisher/republisher liability. In traditional media such as print, radio, etc., there is a conflict of opinion on this question. One case held that a radio broadcast that calls attention to a defamatory magazine is not liable for "republication or publication,"[105] yet the *Restatement of Torts*[106] suggests that a person who gives a copy of his or her newspaper to another, calling attention to the defamatory article, is liable. It may depend on whether the library merely acts as an intermediary, providing a functional service such as the thumbnail index in the Kelly copyright case, or whether the library edits and presents the material to such an extent as to make it its own. A recent statute[107] has been interpreted to protect service providers for defamation and other tort harms in online settings as long as the content originated with a third party.[108] Moreover, the developing case law suggests that an intermediary is never responsible for the content of third parties, even if it reposts or resends the content.[109]

GENERAL RULES FOR LINKING ON THE WORLD WIDE WEB

The following is a simple list of rules to follow when linking to other sites from the library's website. Understand that the law is in a state of constant flux, and so these recommendations present the most conservative position. Taking a more aggressive position is, of course, a determination each library needs to make on its own. It is a given that by the time this book is published the law will have developed further. However, the following rules would appear to be representative of a safe harbor.

1. Check to see whether the website you are linking to has a statement regarding linking or framing. Some sites post a position on linking and framing, i.e., whether it is allowed and under what circumstances (noncommercial, to home page only, notice requirement, etc.). If you frame a portion of the site, a fair use analysis should be made consistent with the cases in this chapter, chapter 1, and other precedent.
2. When linking, it is safer to use the name of the linked site than a logo or design to activate the link, since they may be protected by trademark. A logo may look attractive, but it raises issues of trademark and dilution.
3. Do not deep-link to commercial sites unless you have permission to do so. If the site is one which the library or its patrons might normally patronize, deep-linking to it might harm the economic interests of that site. However, there is some trend in the courts to disavow the merits of these claims. It may also depend on the number of deep-link hits your link generates; again this would affect the amount of economic harm the deep link causes. When framing, the point is to never portray or present the linked site in a fashion that distorts the original site in any way, as could be done, for example, by obscuring advertising on a commercial site, framing only portions of a site, or deep-linking past membership information on an organizational site. Even so, some site owners believe that entry to their web space must always be via the home page. Likewise, make sure to identify the use of any framing technology that copies or distorts the original source of the material.
4. It might be prudent to make clear to your site's viewers that links are for informational purposes only, and that a provided link is not to be taken by patrons as an endorsement or approval of the linked site or of material on that site, and does not grant the right to do anything other than view material at the linked site. A disclaimer on the library website can serve this function.

Notes

1. *Ticketmaster Corp. v. Tickets.com, Inc.,* 2000 U.S. Dist. LEXIS 4553 (C.D. Cal. 2000) (in-link not a copyright infringement).
2. *American Civil Liberties Union of Georgia v. Miller,* 977 F. Supp. (N.D. Ga. 1998) (state statute regulating linking to commercial sites unconstitutional).

3. David Ensign, Legal Liability for Linking, COPYRIGHT AND NEW MEDIA LAW NEWSLETTER, vol. 5, no. 4 (2001), at 3; Michael Rustad and Cyrus Daftary, E-BUSINESS LEGAL HANDBOOK §4.02[F][1] at 253 (2002) ("Linking, however, may infringe trademarks by implying association between the initial site and the linked site").

4. Jeffrey R. Kuester and Peter A. Nieves, *Hyperlinks: A Form of Protected Expression?* NATIONAL LAW JOURNAL, Jan. 26, 1998, at C10.

5. Matt Jackson, *Linking Copyright to Homepages,* 49 FEDERAL COMMUNICATIONS LAW JOURNAL, 731, 749 (1997) ("Since A merely provides a link to the server where B is located, the author of A should not be liable for direct infringement. A useful analogy is a telephone answering system. One can program a number into speed dial and then call the number to reach a business's answering machine and listen to their outgoing message. B's server is like an answering machine. When B's author places B on the server, it is akin to placing an outgoing message on the answering machine. The URL that designates B's location is the "phone number" used to reach the answering machine. When the author of A creates a link to B, she has essentially put B's phone number (the URL) into a speed dial memory. When the user selects the link, the user's Web browser "calls" B's server. B's answering machine (the server) then transmits the outgoing message (B) to the user's Web browser for the user to view. The crucial point is that A does not control the *distribution* of B. If B's author no longer wants to *distribute* B, she can take the document off the server or restrict access with encryption or passwords. So even if a copy of B has been distributed, the *distribution* is being made by the author of B, not A.") (emphases added). But see *Kelly v. Arriba Soft Corp.,* 280 F.3d 934 (9th Cir. 2002), where the court concluded that a frame link of a copyright owner's photographs posted on a website by another website violated the owner's exclusive right of display.

6. I. Trotter Hardy, *The Ancient Doctrine of Trespass to Web Sites,* JOURNAL OF ONLINE LAW, October 1996, article 7 (available in the LEXIS-NEXIS Legnew Library); Mark D. Robbins, *Electronic Trespass: An Old Theory in a New Context,* COMPUTER LAWYER, July 1998, at 1.

7. Bruce P. Keller, *Condemned to Repeat the Past: The Reemergence of Misappropriation and Other Common Law Theories of Protection for Intellectual Property, in* LEGAL AND BUSINESS ASPECTS OF THE INTERNET 1997 at 339 (PLI Course Handbook Series no. 217, 1997); Richard Raysman and Peter Brown, *Dangerous Liaisons: The Legal Risks of Linking Web Sites,* NEW YORK LAW JOURNAL, April 8, 1997, at 3.

8. *Ticketmaster Corp. v. Microsoft Corp.,* 97 Civ. 3055 (C.D. Cal., filed April 28, 1997).

9. *eBay, Inc. v. Bidder's Edge, Inc.,* 100 F. Supp. 2d 1058 (N.D. Cal. 2000).

10. *eBay, Inc. v. Bidder's Edge, Inc.,* 100 F. Supp. 2d 1058, 1067 (N.D. Cal. 2000). *See also* Jeffrey D. Neuburger and Stefania R. Geraci, *Web Site Metabrowsers,* NATIONAL LAW JOURNAL, July 24, 2000, at B9.

11. *eBay, Inc.,* 100 F. Supp. 2d at 1067 (footnote omitted).

12. *eBay, Inc.,* 100 F. Supp. 2d at 1067.

13. Troy Wolverton, *EBay, Bidder's Edge End Legal Dispute,* CNET News.com, March 1, 2001, *available at* http://news.cnet.com (visited July 8, 2001).

14. Barry J. Brett and Gilbert C. Hoover IV, *Exploring the Brave New World of Internet Litigation,* NEW YORK LAW JOURNAL, Aug. 29, 2000, at 1.

15. *Ticketmaster Corp. v. Tickets.com, Inc.,* 2000 U.S. Dist. LEXIS 12987 (C.D. Cal. 2000).

16. *Ticketmaster Corp.,* 2000 U.S. Dist. LEXIS 12987 at *17.

17. *Ticketmaster Corp.,* 2000 U.S. Dist. LEXIS 12987 at *17–18.

18. *Kelly v. Arriba Soft Corp.,* 77 F. Supp. 2d 1116, 1120–1121 (C.D. Cal. 1999).

19. *Washington Post v. TotalNews,* 97-1190 (PLK), Order of Dismissal, *at* http://legal.web.aol.com/decisions/dlip/washorde.html (visited July 8, 2001).

20. *Kelly v. Arriba Soft Corp.,* 280 F.3d 934 (9th Cir. 2002).

21. Richard Raysman and Peter Brown, *Recent Linking Issues,* NEW YORK LAW JOURNAL, Feb. 8, 2000, at 3.

22. See, e.g., AMERICAN BAR ASSOCIATION, *Section of Business Law: Committee of the Law of Commerce in Cyberspace: Subcommittee on Interactive Services,* in WEB-LINKING AGREEMENTS: CONTRACTING STRATEGIES AND MODEL PROVISIONS (1997) for sample language to use in link agreements.

23. *National Association of Recording Merchandisers, Inc. v. Sony Corp. of America,* No. 0CV-164 (EGS) (D.D.C., Jan. 31, 2000) (complaint alleges that Sony's practice of linking from its site to a Sony-controlled website that sells Sony music, without revealing to website visitors that both sites are controlled by Sony, constitutes unfair competition).

24. 15 U.S.C. §§1114(1) and 1125(a)(1)(A) (2000).

25. 15 U.S.C. §1125(c) (2000).

26. Federal trademark registration 73-668814.

27. Federal trademark registration 26-900103.

28. F. Lawrence Street, LAW OF THE INTERNET §4-2(d), at 380 (2000); Dratler, 2 INTELLECTUAL PROPERTY LAW §10.03, at 10-42.

29. *Original Appalachian Art Works, Inc. v. Topps Chewing Gum, Inc.,* 642 F. Supp. 1031 (N.D. Ga. 1986).

30. *CMG World Wide, Inc. v. American Legends,* 49 D 109607 (D. Ind., filed July 22, 1996).

31. *Lyons Partnership v. Giannoulas,* 179 F.3d 384 (5th Cir. 1999).

32. Jay Dratler Jr., 2 INTELLECTUAL PROPERTY LAW: COMMERCIAL, CREATIVE AND INDUSTRIAL PROPERTY §10.03[2], at 10-56 (2000).

33. *Quality Inns Int'l, Inc. v. McDonald's Corp.,* 695 F. Supp. 198 (D. Md. 1988).

34. *McDonald's Corp. v. McBagel's Inc.,* 649 F. Supp. 1268 (S.D.N.Y. 1986).

35. Kent D. Stuckey, INTERNET AND ONLINE LAW §7.03[1], at 7-49 (2000).

36. Pub. L. No. 104-98, 109 Stat. 985.

37. Theodore C. Max, *Dilution Act May Limit Commercial Parodies,* NATIONAL LAW JOURNAL, May 20, 1996, at C13.

38. Stuart I. Graff, *Could Mark Owners Sue Media for Generic Use?* NATIONAL LAW JOURNAL, Oct. 19, 1998, at C6.

39. 15 U.S.C. §1125(c)(4)(B) (2000).

40. Max, *Dilution Act,* C13.

41. *L.L. Bean, Inc. v. Drake Publishers, Inc.,* 811 F.2d 26, 31 (1st Cir. 1987) (parody of a well-known merchandiser's trademark in an adult magazine was permissible because it was artistic in nature and therefore did not constitute commercial speech); *Jordache Enterprises, Inc. v. Hogg Wyld, Ltd.,* 828 F.2d 1482 (10th Cir. 1987) (no likelihood of dilution for the use of "Lardasche" in a competing manufacturer's sale of large-size women's jeans; parody tends to increase public identification of a plaintiff's mark with the plaintiff, not weaken it); *Bally Total Fitness Holding Corp. v. Farber,* 29 F. Supp. 2d 1161 (C.D. Cal. 1998) (no trademark infringement when a website called "Bally's Sucks" used a trademark name in criticizing the health club chain, nor was there tarnishment (dilution) because of this name "link" between the sites).

42. David Bernstein and Thomas H. Prochnow, *Defense to Infringement: When the First Amendment Protects Trademark Parodies,* NATIONAL LAW JOURNAL, August 1998, at 1.

43. 15 U.S.C. §1125(c)(4) (2000).

44. *Lyons Partnership v. Giannoulas,* 179 F.3d 384 (5th Cir. 1999) (baseball mascot "The Chicken's" assault of the Barney character in his act was a parody).

45. Robert W. Erb and Harold Traub, *To Some Big Names, Commercial Parody Is No Laughing Matter,* NATIONAL LAW JOURNAL, Jan. 24, 1993, at S5.

46. 15 U.S.C. §1115(b)(4) (2000).

47. A travel agency, federal trademark registration 74-651170; a monthly book catalog, federal trademark registration 73-751642.

48. *Richards v. Cable News Network, Inc.,* 15 F. Supp. 2d 683 (D. Or. 1998) (although the plaintiff continued to hold the trademark rights in the phrase "world beat" for prerecorded reggae music, the plaintiff could not preclude CNN's use of the term in its generic sense in connection with CNN's television show or website).

49. See *New Kids on the Block v. News America Publishing,* 971 F.2d 302, 308 (9th Cir. 1991).

50. Federal trademark registration 73-034891.

51. Jay Dratler Jr., 2 INTELLECTUAL PROPERTY LAW: COMMERCIAL, CREATIVE AND INDUSTRIAL PROPERTY §10.03[2], at 10-56 (2000).

52. David M. Kelly and Jonathan M. Gelchinsky, *"No Fair! Stop Using My Marks":* *A Look at Trademarks and the Fair-Use Defense on the Internet,* INTELLECTUAL PROPERTY TODAY, July 1999, at 16.

53. Fair use test as articulated in *New Kids on the Block,* 971 F.2d at 308.

54. Michael Rustad and Cyrus Daftary, E-BUSINESS LEGAL HANDBOOK 1174 (2002) ("Metatags are HTML tags which provide information that describes the content of the web pages a user will be viewing . . . Many search engines have now incorporated reading metatags as part of the indexing results").

55. *Brookfield Communications, Inc. v. West Coast Entertainment Corp.,* 174 F.3d 1036 (9th Cir. 1999).

56. Mark D. Robbins, *The Emerging Law of Web Sites: Trademarks in Metatags,* INTELLECTUAL PROPERTY STRATEGIST, July 1999, at 1.

57. For a detailed discussion of the ICAAN and the Uniform Dispute Resolution Policy, *see* Michael Rustad and Cyrus Daftary, E-BUSINESS LEGAL HANDBOOK §4.03[K] at 317–351 (2002).

58. Internet Corporation for Assigned Names and Numbers, *Uniform Domain Name Dispute Resolution Policy, at* http://www.icann.org/dndr/udrp/policy.htm (visited July 7, 2001).

59. The Anti-Cybersquatting Consumer Protection Act amends section 43 of the Lanham Act, 15 U.S.C. §1125, by adding a subsection (d).

60. 15 U.S.C. §43(d)(1)(A)(i).

61. 15 U.S.C. §43(d)(1)(A)(ii).

62. The most famous dealer in domain name futures is Dennis Toeppen; see *Panavision International, L.P. v. Toeppen,* 141 F.3d 1316 (9th Cir. 1998).

63. RESTATEMENT (SECOND) OF TORTS §652A (1976).

64. For a more detailed discussion of privacy and publicity rights in a library setting, *see* Tomas Lipinski, *Tort Theory in Library, Museum, and Archive Collections, Materials, Exhibits, and Displays: Rights of Privacy and Publicity in Personal Information and Persona,* in LIBRARIES, MUSEUMS, AND ARCHIVES: LEGAL ISSUES AND ETHICAL CHALLENGES IN THE NEW INFORMATION ERA 47 (Tomas A. Lipinski ed., 2002); and *Legal Issues Involved in the Privacy Rights of Patrons,* in LIBRARIES, MUSEUMS, AND ARCHIVES 95.

65. CAL. CIV. CODE §3344.1 (2001).

66. *A&M Records, Inc. v. Napster, Inc.,* 239 F.3d 1004, 1019 (9th Cir. 2001), citing *Gershwin Publishing Corp. v. Columbia Artists Mgmt, Inc.,* 443 F.2d 1159, 1162 (2d Cir. 1971).

67. *A&M Records, Inc.,* 239 F.3d at 1022, quoting *Gershwin* at 1162.

68. *Marobie-F v. National Association of Firefighter Equipment Distributors,* 983 F. Supp. 1167 (N.D. Ill. 1997); 2000 U.S. Dist. LEXIS 1022 (N.D. Ill. July 28, 2000). See also *Kelly v. Arriba Soft. Corp.,* 280 F.3d 934 (9th Cir. 2002).

69. *Ticketmaster Corp. v. Tickets.com, Inc.,* 2000 U.S. Dist. LEXIS 12987 (C.D. Cal. 2000).

70. *Fred Wehrenberg Circuit of Theatres, Inc. v. Moviefone, Inc.,* 73 F. Supp. 2d 1044 (E.D. Mo. 1999), movie listings not "hot news" under *Motorola* standard (high cost, time-sensitive, commercial free-riding, parties in direct competition, reduce

incentive to collect, i.e., missing the incentive element), see *NBA v. Motorola,* 105 F.3d 841 (2d Cir. 1997); *Pollstar v. Gigmania, Ltd.,* 2000 U.S. Dist. LEXIS 21035 (E.D. Cal. 2000) (court "declines to decide this issue at the present time" but observes that the "claim was pled with sufficiency as a 'hot news' claim").

71. For a comprehensive global perspective, see *The Link Controversy Page* by Stefan Bechtold *at* http://www.jura.uni-tuebingen.de/~bes1/lcp.html (visited July 3, 2001).

72. *See* Dan Wallach, *Dilbert Page Hack Archives, at* http://www.cs.rice.edu/~dwallach/ dilbert (visited July 3, 2001). For United Media's current policy concerning reprints of Dilbert comics, *see* http://www.unitedmedia.com/uminfo/um_faq.html (visited June 24, 2001).

73. *Kelly v. Arriba Soft Corp.,* 77 F. Supp. 2d 1116, 1119 (C.D. Cal. 1999).

74. *Kelly,* 77 F. Supp. 2d at 1119.

75. *Kelly,* 77 F. Supp. 2d at 1120.

76. *Kelly,* 77 F. Supp. 2d at 1120.

77. *Ticketmaster Corp. v. Tickets.com, Inc.,* 2000 U.S. Dist. LEXIS 12987 at 17 (C.D. Cal. 2000) ("While TM sees some detriment in T.Com's operation (possibly in the loss of advertising revenue), there is also a beneficial effect in the referral of customers looking for tickets to TM events directly to TM").

78. *Hotaling v. Church of Jesus Christ of Latter-day Saints,* 118 F.3d 199 (4th Cir. 1999).

79. *Hotaling,* 118 F.3d at 203.

80. *Hotaling,* 118 F.3d at 203.

81. 17 U.S.C. §507(b) (2000).

82. *Gershwin Publishing Corp. v. Columbia Artists Management, Inc.,* 443 F.2d 1159, 1162 (2d Cir. 1971).

83. See *Bernstein v. JC Penney, Inc.,* 1998 U.S. Dist. LEXIS 19048. The suit was based on a photographer's claim (Bernstein) that a cosmetic company and retailer (JC Penney) promoted its perfume on the JC Penney site, endorsed by a celebrity. The company site linked to a site operated by an Internet company which in turn linked to other websites which contained the infringing photographs. The case never reached final resolution, suggesting that the "contributory infringement" theory may be a tough one for plaintiffs to win in this situation.

84. *Intellectual Reserve, Inc. v. Utah Lighthouse Ministry, Inc.,* 75 F. Supp. 2d 1290 (Dist. Utah 1999).

85. *Intellectual Reserve, Inc.,* 75 F. Supp. 2d at 1294 (citing *Marobie-F v. National Association of Firefighter Equipment Distributors,* among others).

86. Richard Raysman and Peter Brown, *Recent Linking Issues,* NEW YORK LAW JOURNAL, Feb. 8, 2000, at 3.

87. *Intellectual Reserve, Inc.,* 75 F. Supp. 2d at 1295.

88. *Universal City Studios v. Reimerdes,* 82 F. Supp. 2d 211 (S.D.N.Y. 2000); 111 F. Supp. 2d 294, 325 (S.D.N.Y. 2000) (permanent injunction), *aff'd sub. nom. Universal Studios, Inc. v. Corley,* 273 F.3d 429 (2d Cir. 2001).

89. *Universal City Studios v. Reimerdes,* 111 F. Supp. 2d at 325 (permanent injunction), *aff'd sub. nom. Universal Studios, Inc. v. Corley,* 273 F.3d 429 (2d Cir. 2001).

90. *Universal City Studios v. Reimerdes,* 111 F. Supp. 2d at 325 (permanent injunction), *aff'd sub. nom. Universal Studios, Inc. v. Corley,* 273 F.3d 429 (2d Cir. 2001).

91. *Universal Studios, Inc. v. Corley,* 273 F.3d 429, 453 (2d Cir. 2001).

92. *Universal Studios, Inc. v. Corley,* 273 F.3d at 453.

93. *Universal Studios, Inc. v. Corley,* 273 F.3d at 459.

94. *Religious Technology Center v. DataWeb B.V.,* No. 96/1048 (Dist. Ct. of The Hague, Civil Law Sector, June 9, 1999).

95. *Fonovisa, Inc. v. Cherry Auction, Inc.,* 76 F.3d 259, 262 (9th Cir. 1996).

96. John W. Hazard Jr., COPYRIGHT LAW IN BUSINESS AND PRACTICE ¶7.08, at 7-72–75 (2000).

97. *Southern Bell Telephone and Telegraph v. Associated Telephone Directory,* 756 F.2d 801 (1985).

98. *Columbia Pictures Industries v. Redd Horne, Inc.,* 749 F.2d 154 (3d Cir. 1984).

99. W. Page Keeton et al., PROSSER AND KEETON ON THE LAW OF TORTS 117 (5th ed. 1984).

100. F. Lawrence Street, LAW OF THE INTERNET §6-2(b), at 625 (2000).

101. James M. Talbott, NEW MEDIA: INTELLECTUAL PROPERTY, ENTERTAINMENT AND TECHNOLOGY LAW §10.4, at 10-4 (1999); Kent D. Stuckey, INTERNET AND ONLINE LAW, §2.03[3], at 2-33 (2000).

102. Cynthia L. Counts and C. Amanda Martin, *Libel in Cyberspace: A Framework for Addressing Liability and Jurisdictional Issues in This New Frontier,* 59 ALBANY LAW REVIEW 1083 (1996); Talbott, NEW MEDIA §10.15.

103. A more thorough discussion of these concepts is found in Tomas A. Lipinski, Elizabeth Buchanan, and Johannes J. Britz, *Sticks and Stones and Words That Harm—Liability vs. Responsibility: Section 230 and Defamatory Speech in Cyberspace,* ETHICS AND INFORMATION TECHNOLOGY, Fall 2002 (forthcoming).

104. Brenda Sandburg, *Hyperlink Blast Sparks a Libel Suit,* NATIONAL LAW JOURNAL, Feb. 21, 2000, at A4.

105. *MacFadden v. Anthony,* 117 N.Y.S.2d 520 (Sup. 1952).

106. RESTATEMENT (SECOND) OF TORTS §581, comment c, illustration 3 (1977).

107. 47 U.S.C. §230.

108. *Zeran v. America Online, Inc.,* 129 F.3d 327 (4th Cir. 1997); *Blumenthal v. Drudge,* 992 F. Supp. 44 (D.C. 1998); *Ben Ezra, Weinstein & Co. v. America Online, Inc.,* 206 F.3d 980 (10th Cir. 2000), *cert denied* 531 U.S. 824 (2000); *Does v. Franco Productions,* 2000 U.S. Dist. LEXIS 8645 (N.D. Ill. 2000); *Stoner v. eBay, Inc.,* 56 U.S.P.Q.2d (BNA) 1852 (2000); *Doe v. America Online, Inc.,* 783 So. 2d 1010 (2001).

109. See *Barrett v. Clark,* 2001 WL 881259 (Cal. Super. Ct. 2001) (unpublished).

3

FILTERS AND OTHER RESTRICTIONS ON INTERNET ACCESS

Internet Access Restrictions and the Law

Q1   What guidance does my library have to ensure patrons' rights to information on the Internet?

Q2   Can libraries or librarians be criminally liable for having obscene, indecent, or controversial materials in their collections?

Q3   Do patrons have a right to legal materials that are inappropriate?

Q4   Do children have the same rights as adults to materials?

Q5   Who determines whether materials on the Internet are legal or illegal?

Q6   Can you give examples of materials that have been judged obscene?

Q7   Do patrons have a right to unfiltered Internet access in private school libraries or other private libraries?

Q8   Does the ALA's *Library Bill of Rights* guarantee access for library patrons in any type of library?

Q9   May parents put restrictions on their children's access to the Internet at a public library?

Types of Internet Access Restrictions

Q10   Is it legal to have the librarian determine appropriate sites, e.g., use a "tap on the shoulder" policy?

124

Q11   Do public school libraries have a different responsibility than public
libraries?

Appendix A

Appendix B

*Definitions of Child Pornography, Obscenity, and
Material "Harmful to Minors"*

>   Child Pornography
>   Obscenity
>   Materials "Harmful to Minors"

Notes

෨෨෨

This chapter will discuss the legal concepts underlying the issue of
filters on library Internet terminals. The relevant First Amendment
principles, particularly with regard to public forum access, can be found
in chapter 6, "Meeting Rooms and Displays."

On May 31, 2002, a federal district court struck down the provision
of the Children's Internet Protection Act (CIPA) that required public
libraries that receive certain federal funds to use technology that blocks or
filters Internet sites containing "child pornography," "obscenity," or
material that is "harmful to minors."[1] At the time this book went to press,
the case was slated to be heard by the U.S. Supreme Court. To stay abreast
of the current status of the case, see the ALA Office for Intellectual
Freedom's CIPA website at http://www.ala.org/cipa.

A companion law, the Neighborhood Children's Internet Protection
Act (NCIPA), was not challenged. It requires libraries that receive certain
funds to institute Internet safety policies.

INTERNET ACCESS RESTRICTIONS
AND THE LAW

*Q1   What guidance does my library have to ensure patrons' rights
to information on the Internet?*

The American Library Association has extensive resources on its website.
Pay particular attention to *Libraries & the Internet Toolkit* and the CIPA
site at http://www.ala.org/cipa for updated information.[2]

*Q2   Can libraries or librarians be criminally liable for having obscene,
indecent, or controversial materials in their collections?*

No. Obscenity law imposes liability on those who create and post illegal
materials on the Internet, not on those who merely provide access to such
content. Federal obscenity law prohibits obscenity on federal property, in
the mail, on radio and television, in interstate commerce and on interstate
highways and railroads, even when the obscene material is transported
intrastate.[3] State laws vary in specifying exactly what is defined as
obscene, but it may not, in any case, be more restrictive than the limits set
by the *Miller* case.

In *Miller* v. *California* in 1973, the U.S. Supreme Court formulated the
constitutional standard for obscenity that is still in use today:

> (a) whether "the average person, applying contemporary community
> standards" would find that the work, taken as a whole, appeals to the
> prurient interest, . . . (b) whether the work depicts or describes, in a
> patently offensive way, sexual conduct specifically defined by the appli-
> cable state law, and (c) whether the work, taken as a whole, lacks serious
> literary, artistic, political, or scientific value.[4]

Furthermore, a provision of the federal Telecommunications Act of 1996
states that "No provider or user of an interactive computer service shall
be treated as the publisher or speaker of any information provided by
another information content provider." This provision prohibits holding
interactive computer services liable for their failure to edit, withhold, or
restrict access to offensive material.[5]

In 2001, a California appellate court explicitly found that this immunity applied to library Internet access.[6] Even school libraries, which are
subject to CIPA, are not criminally or civilly liable. The penalty for noncompliance is a cut in the applicable federal funds to the library.

Q3 Do patrons have a right to legal materials that are inappropriate?

Yes, both adults and children have First Amendment rights to materials that do not fall within the ambit of "illegal material." Inappropriate, indecent, or sexually explicit materials that do not fit under federal or state statutes' definitions of child pornography, obscenity, or "harmful to minors" materials may not be restricted by a public library. Public libraries are government entities, and the First Amendment restrains the government from making content-based speech restrictions, unless to do so would further a "compelling need" and the method chosen was the least restrictive alternative.

Q4 Do children have the same rights as adults to materials?

Not exactly. In a school library setting, the Supreme Court has limited minors' right to receive information if the information is "educationally unsuitable"—but not based on a school's disapproval of the content of the information.[7]

More broadly (inside and outside school settings), the Court has allowed restrictions on material that is "harmful to minors,"[8] though this material may not be restricted as to adults. Essentially, this is material that is considered "obscene" for minors even if the materials are protected for adults. Most states have enacted so-called "harmful to minors" obscenity statutes. The CIPA legislation and the Child Online Protection Act legislation (also struck down by the courts, but final status as yet unknown) unsuccessfully attempted to set a national standard for material "harmful to minors." (See the appendix for definitions.)

A helpful legal analysis of minors' rights to receive information under the First Amendment can be found at the ALA website.[9]

Q5 Who determines whether materials on the Internet are legal or illegal?

Only a court of law—not citizens' groups, clergy, or librarians—can determine the legal status of materials. The types of speech that courts have determined to fall outside the broad umbrella of the First Amendment are very narrowly defined. These categories are child pornography, obscenity, and material that is "harmful to minors." Determinations as to whether a particular Internet site falls within these categories is determined by the legal definition and by an actual court decision examining the material.

It should be noted that in some states, *even materials that may be judged by a court to be obscene or "harmful to minors"* may be permissible in a library collection, or when used for bona fide research purposes per state law.[10]

Q6   *Can you give examples of materials that have been judged obscene?*

In practice, prosecuting obscenity cases is very difficult. Jeffrey Douglas, a Santa Monica lawyer, has tracked nationwide obscenity prosecutions since 1987. He found that of the materials that have been judged obscene—by a judge or a jury—there are several common elements: explicit showing of excretion, bestiality, necrophilia, incest, or any type of non-consensual sex. He notes that taken as a whole, language is important, and this is one of the reasons that all—or most—adult magazines have literary content.[11] The adult industry has a growing number of web pages that offer legal information regarding the Internet distribution of adult materials. According to one of them, "If you can prove that the content on your adult website has some literary, artistic, political, or scientific value, the criminal charges against you might be dismissed . . . In light of this, you might want to consider displaying or linking to content that has something other than masturbatory value such as information about health care issues in the adult entertainment industry, safe sex information, a discussion of fetishes, or political links to other websites."[12]

Legal definitions of child pornography, obscenity, and "harmful to minors" material are found in the appendix at the end of this chapter.

Q7   *Do patrons have a right to unfiltered Internet access in private school libraries or other private libraries?*

Usually not. Generally, private institutions may make restrictions with regard to information access. The First Amendment is a restraint on *governmental* actions, not on private actions. There are exceptions, however. In California, for example, the state constitution's First Amendment is stronger than the corresponding amendment in the U.S. Constitution[13] and its laws extend free speech guarantees to students in private schools.[14]

Q8   *Does the ALA's* Library Bill of Rights *guarantee access for library patrons in any type of library?*

The ALA's *Library Bill of Rights* is a professional code of ethics that bolsters access to all kinds of library materials for patrons, regardless of age.

It has no force of law in and of itself. However, it is often adopted by libraries' governing authorities, giving children's access rights the force of law in public entities, and can serve as a governing directive for private entities that adopt it. See the ALA's *Libraries & the Internet Toolkit* site for further information.[15]

*Q9   May parents put restrictions on their children's access to the
        Internet at a public library?*

The First Amendment does not hinder parents in any way from restricting their children's access to information. The First Amendment restricts *government,* e.g., a public library, from imposing restrictions. The CIPA district court has suggested (without evaluating their constitutionality) that policies that require parental approval are less restrictive than the CIPA law that required blocking software.[16]

If the constitutionality of such policies were to be evaluated, one question would likely concern how involved the government is in creating those restrictions. The difference between "opt-in" and "opt-out" alternatives could be significant. If a library's policy allows open access, but allows parents to "opt-in" a restriction for their child, that shows the parents are making the decision to restrict. If, on the other hand, a library's policy defaults to restrictions on children, but allows parents to "opt-out" of the restrictions by signing a permission slip, that evinces a far greater degree of government restriction. If parents are required to sign in person at the library, the burden becomes even greater, since many parents work full time or are otherwise not available, even if their intent is to secure open access for their children.

Types of Internet Access Restrictions

1. *Restrictions on content.* Public libraries and public academic libraries may not deny access to "inappropriate" or "offensive" sites, since those terms have no legal meaning under state, federal, or constitutional law as described above. Contrast this with most school libraries, in which materials may be restricted to those that are deemed by the school board to be "educationally suitable."

2. *Restrictions on games and chat.* These are *protocol* restrictions, not content restrictions per se. As such, they would likely be judged at a lower standard than content restrictions. Courts would likely use either an inter-

mediate scrutiny standard or a "rational review" standard—in either case, a court is likely to uphold such restrictions if uniformly and fairly applied.

3. *Restrictions on conduct.* These restrictions do not invoke the First Amendment. Rules of patron conduct while using the Internet are not free speech issues, and librarians should not hesitate to use rules of conduct similar to other conduct rules in place in the library. Note that only the conduct may be restricted. The mere tendency of certain Internet sites to encourage unlawful acts is insufficient reason for banning it. The proper method to deter harassment, masturbation, etc., is to remove the patron from the library, revoke library privileges, or call the police.[17]

Q10   Is it legal to have the librarian determine appropriate sites, e.g., use a "tap on the shoulder" policy?

It's not clear. The library would need to come up with objective standards to define what is "inappropriate," "sexually explicit," or whatever term it chose. In addition to failing to match the legal categories of materials that may be prohibited ("child pornography," "obscenity," and "harmful to minors" material), this could raise the serious legal issue of "unbridled discretion in a government official."

In the *Mainstream Loudoun* case, the federal district court looked at a library that had placed filters on all library computers. Its policy allowed patrons to request the library to unblock sites. Patrons had to submit written requests that included their names, telephone numbers, and detailed explanations of why they desired access to the blocked site. The library staff then would decide whether the request should be granted.[18]

The court noted that the unblocking policy amounted to a "standardless discretion" by library staff. This imposed an unconstitutional chilling of the patrons' rights to free speech. It cited the Supreme Court case *Lamont* v. *Postmaster General,* in which a federal statute directed the postmaster general not to deliver "communist propaganda" without a written request from the customer.[19] The requirement that citizens publicly petition the government for access to disfavored speech was found to have a "severe chilling effect."[20] In *Loudoun,* library patrons needed not only to petition, but to seek discretionary approval, unlike the automatic approval in *Lamont.* The court saw this as more chilling of the public's right to free speech than the *Lamont* Supreme Court case.

In 1992, the Supreme Court examined a case in which a county administrator was empowered to determine how much to charge for parade permits, based on his own judgment of what would be reasonable to pay for police protection and administrative costs. The Court determined that in the absence of objective factors, the First Amendment prohibited the "vesting of such unbridled discretion in a government official."[21]

The CIPA district court acknowledged that a "tap on the shoulder" delegates to librarians substantial discretion to determine which websites a patron may view. It noted that this discretion was no less problematic when a library delegates the decisions to a filtering company. The court mentioned that one alternative for libraries that are experiencing problems would be to review Internet history log files, and then track down abuses to a particular patron. Taps on children's shoulders when children are observed viewing material that is likely to be "harmful to minors" would be a less restrictive alternative to the use of filters. The constitutionality of such "taps" was not at issue in the case, however.

Q11 *Do public school libraries have a different responsibility than public libraries?*

Yes. Teachers have a different legal relationship with their students than public librarians have with their patrons. In the landmark Supreme Court case *Board of Education* v. *Pico,* students brought suit when the school board removed books that it characterized as "anti-American, anti-Christian, anti-[Semitic], and just plain filthy."[22] Schools serve in loco parentis, unlike public libraries, and courts allow greater latitude in school-issued restrictions on student speech than in other public institutions that do not serve "in place of the parent." A plurality of the justices found that a school board must be permitted "to establish and apply their curriculum in such a way as to transmit community values," but that it may not remove school library books in order to deny access to ideas with which it disagrees for political reasons. Instructively, a *Pico* dictum notes that the challenged books in the school library were not entirely banned to the children, inasmuch as they were available at the local public library, which had in fact put the books on display.[23]

APPENDIX A

Librarians can find an excellent analysis of constitutional and federal child pornography and obscenity law through the Congressional Research Service. See especially Henry Cohen, *Child Pornography: Constitutional*

Principles and Federal Statutes, CRS Report for Congress, Congressional Research Service (updated June 26, 2002); and Henry Cohen, *Obscenity and Indecency: Constitutional Principles and Federal Statutes,* CRS Report for Congress, Congressional Research Service (updated June 5, 2002).

APPENDIX B

Definitions of Child Pornography, Obscenity, and Material "Harmful to Minors"

Child Pornography

CONSTITUTION

According to the Supreme Court, child pornography is a category of speech that is not protected by the First Amendment.[24] It is not legal to have child pornography in the home.[25] It is not legal to look at child pornography for research or journalistic purposes.[26]

CHILD PORNOGRAPHY LAW

The federal child pornography statute defines "child pornography" as "any visual depiction" of a minor under eighteen years old engaging in "sexually explicit conduct." "Sexually explicit conduct" is defined in child pornography as actual or simulated "(A) sexual intercourse, including genital-genital, oral-genital, anal-genital, or oral-anal, whether between persons of the same or opposite sex; (B) bestiality; (C) masturbation; (D) sadistic or masochistic abuse; or (E) lascivious exhibition of the genitals or pubic area of any person.[27]

In 1996 Congress passed the Child Pornography Prevention Act, which added a definition of "child pornography" that includes depictions of images that "appear to be" of minors engaging in sexually explicit conduct. On April 16, 2002, the Supreme Court held this provision unconstitutional to the extent that it prohibited pictures that were not produced with actual minors.[28]

Additionally, each state has child pornography laws.[29]

Obscenity

The legal definition of "obscenity" is far narrower than the common usage of the term.

The constitutional definition of "obscenity," according to the Supreme Court, applies to "material whose predominant appeal is to a shameful or morbid interest in nudity, sex, or excretion" and not to "materials that provoked only normal sexual reactions."[30] This is a refinement of the *Miller* decision, which is discussed below.

CONSTITUTION

The U.S. Supreme Court, in the famous *Miller* v. *California* decision, established a three-pronged test to determine whether a work is obscene:

(a) whether the "average person, applying contemporary community standards" would find that the work, taken as a whole, appeals to the prurient interest,

(b) whether the work depicts or describes, in a patently offensive way, sexual conduct specifically defined by the applicable state law, and

(c) whether the work, taken as a whole, lacks serious literary, artistic, political, or scientific value.[31]

The first two prongs of the Miller test—the prurient interest and patent offensiveness—are issues of fact for a jury to determine, applying contemporary community standards and federal or state law. The third prong does not rely on a particular community's sensibilities. Courts instruct juries to use a "reasonableness standard"; the inquiry is "not whether an ordinary member of any given community would find serious literary, artistic, political, or scientific value in allegedly obscene material, but whether a reasonable person would find such value in the material, taken as a whole."[32]

The legal definition of "obscenity" is extraordinarily narrow. As Kathleen Sullivan, now dean of Stanford Law School, wrote in 1992, "The first two parts of this test are incoherent: to put it crudely, they require the audience to be turned on and grossed out at the same time."[33]

Note: In some situations, courts have upheld zoning regulations of sexually explicit material that is not obscene. The restrictions are not an outright ban, and must be narrowly tailored to combat secondary effects such as crime.[34] In the only case on point to date, a federal district court judge did not find the "secondary effects" argument viable when a library claimed that Internet filters were needed to prevent a hostile working environment and to prevent the viewing of illegal materials. The court found that neither of those claims were secondary effects.[35]

FEDERAL OBSCENITY LAWS

Congress passed the Communications Decency Act (47 U.S.C. §223) as part of its Telecommunications Act of 1996.[36] The "indecent transmission" provision and the "patently offensive display" provision were struck down by the Supreme Court in *Reno* v. *ACLU*.[37] The act also prohibited the knowing transmission of obscene messages to any recipient under eighteen years of age. This provision was not challenged and remains part of the law today.[38] Therefore, a website that may be legally permissible in California may be illegal in another state such as Tennessee. The liability for obscene material falls on producers and distributors, not "mere conduits," such as libraries (see question 2).

STATE OBSCENITY LAWS

States generally pattern their laws on the *Miller* decision.[39] What is not commonly understood is that the *Miller* decision sets a ceiling on permissible statutes regarding obscenity. States may define "obscenity" more liberally than the *Miller* decision. For example, the California Penal Code's section 311 states:

> As used in this chapter, the following definitions apply:
>
> (a) "Obscene matter" means matter, taken as a whole, that to the average person, applying contemporary statewide standards, appeals to the prurient interest, that, taken as a whole, depicts or describes sexual conduct in a patently offensive way, and that, taken as a whole, lacks serious literary, artistic, political, or scientific value.
>
> (1) If it appears from the nature of the matter or the circumstances of its dissemination, distribution, or exhibition that it is designed for clearly defined deviant sexual groups, the appeal of the matter shall be judged with reference to its intended recipient group.
>
> (2) In prosecutions under this chapter, if circumstances of production, presentation, sale, dissemination, distribution, or publicity indicate that matter is being commercially exploited by the

defendant for the sake of its prurient appeal, this evidence is probative with respect to the nature of the matter and may justify the conclusion that the matter lacks serious literary, artistic, political, or scientific value.

(3) In determining whether the matter taken as a whole lacks serious literary, artistic, political, or scientific value in description or representation of those matters, the fact that the defendant knew that the matter depicts persons under the age of 16 years engaged in sexual conduct, as defined in subdivision (c) of Section 311.4, is a factor that may be considered in making that determination.

Materials "Harmful to Minors"

The Supreme Court has ruled that states may prohibit access by minors to material deemed "harmful to minors."[40] Until the Child Online Protection Act (COPA) and the Children's Internet Protection Act (CIPA) were passed, there was no federal "harmful to minors" law. As this book went to press, COPA had been enjoined by the Third Circuit. On May 13, 2002, the Supreme Court vacated the Third Circuit's opinion and sent the case back down for further proceedings. The Supreme Court kept the preliminary injunction, however, and the statute, at present, is still not in effect. On May 31, 2002, the U.S. District Court for Eastern Pennsylvania struck down CIPA as unconstitutional so far as public libraries were concerned. Since the final court decisions have yet to be made, the two statutes' definitions of material that is "harmful to minors" are given below.

The Children's Internet Protection Act (CIPA) as written applied only to schools and libraries that use these federal funding programs: Library Services and Technology Act, Title III of the Elementary and Secondary Education Act, and the Universal Service discount program known as the E-rate (Public Law No. 106-554). A federal district court struck down its application to public libraries, but the application to schools was not challenged and is still in effect.[41]

CIPA defines "material that is harmful to minors" as:

any picture, image, graphic image file, or other visual depiction that—

(i) taken as a whole and with respect to minors, appeals to a prurient interest in nudity, sex, or excretion;

(ii) depicts, describes, or represents in a patently offensive way with respect to what is suitable for minors, an actual or simulated sexual act or sexual contact, actual or simulated normal or perverted sexual acts, or a lewd exhibition of the genitals; and

(iii) taken as a whole, lacks serious literary, artistic, political, or scientific value as to minors.[42]

Note: This statute refers to minors as persons under seventeen years of age. It differs from the COPA definition (below) in three respects. CIPA applies only to images, whereas COPA applies to images and words. CIPA does not apply community standards, and CIPA does not include an image of the "post-pubescent female breast" as "harmful to minors."

Current Status: Although a federal district court has struck down the application of CIPA to public libraries, the final word will come from the Supreme Court. To get updates on the case, see http://www.ala.org/cipa.

The Child Online Protection Act (COPA) would define materials harmful to minors differently, but this law has never gone into effect. The day after COPA was signed into law, it was challenged in federal court and an injunction was soon granted. COPA defines "material that is harmful to minors" as pictures or words that:

(i) the average person, applying contemporary community standards, would find, taking the material as a whole and with respect to minors, is designed to appeal to, or is designed to pander to, the prurient interest;

(ii) depicts, describes, or represents in a manner patently offensive with respect to minors, an actual or simulated sexual act or sexual contact, an actual or simulated normal or perverted sexual act, or a lewd exhibition of the genitals or a post-pubescent female breast; and

(iii) taken as a whole, lacks serious literary, artistic, political, or scientific value as to minors.[43]

Current Status: The Supreme Court sent the COPA case back to the lower court for further proceedings. It kept the preliminary injunction, which stops enforcement of the law.[44]

Unless COPA or CIPA is upheld by the Supreme Court, the "harmful to minors" laws will remain at the state level, outside the context of school libraries.

Notes

1. *American Library Association v. United States,* 201 F. Supp. 2d. 401 (E.D. Pa. 2002). *See also* Mary Minow, *The Children's Internet Protection Act: The Recent District Court Decision, in Context, for Librarians and Library Patrons,* LLRX.com (June 17, 2002), *at* http://www.llrx.com/features/cipa.htm (visited July 13, 2002).

2. American Library Association, *Libraries & the Internet Toolkit: Tips and Guidance for Managing and Communicating about the Internet, at* http://www.ala.org/alaorg/oif/internettoolkit.html (visited Feb. 25, 2002); and the ALA's CIPA website, *at* http://www.ala.org/cipa (visited Feb. 25, 2002).

3. 18 U.S.C. §1460-1470 (2001). *See* Henry Cohen, *Obscenity and Indecency: Constitutional Principles and Federal Statutes,* CRS Report for Congress, Congressional Research Service (updated May 17, 2002), for an excellent summary of obscenity law.

4. *Miller v. California,* 413 U.S. 15, 24 (1973).

5. 47 U.S.C. §230(c)(1) (2000).

6. *Kathleen R. v. City of Livermore,* 87 Cal. App. 4th 684, 697 (Cal. App. 1st Dist. 2001), citing *Blumenthal v. Drudge* 992, F. Supp. 44, 49 (D.D.C. 1998). These cases refer to 47 U.S.C. §230(c)(1).

7. *Board of Education, Island Trees Union Free School District No. 26 v. Pico,* 457 U.S. 853, 871 (1982).

8. *Ginsberg v. New York,* 390 U.S. 629 (1968).

9. Jenner & Block, Memorandum, *Minors' Rights to Receive Information under the First Amendment* (August 1998), *at* http://www.ala.org/alaorg/oif/minor_jb.html (visited Feb. 26, 2002).

10. For a thorough analysis of statutory exemptions, *see* Ian L. Saffer, Note, *Obscenity Law and the Equal Protection Clause: May States Exempt Schools, Libraries, and Museums from Obscenity Statutes?* 70 NEW YORK UNIVERSITY LAW REVIEW 397 (May 1995). Saffer examines statutory exemptions and distinguishes different characteristics: display of materials v. distribution of materials, and obscenity v. harmful matters.

11. Kristen Delguzzi, *Flynt Uncovering All the Bases: Hustler Publisher Unable to Bait Local Authorities,* CINCINNATI INQUIRER, May 19, 1997.

12. Adultweblaw, *at* http://www.adultweblaw.com/laws/obscene.htm (visited June 2, 2001).

13. See *Pruneyard Shopping Center v. Robins,* 447 U.S. 74 (1980).

14. "School districts operating one or more high schools and private secondary schools shall not make or enforce any rule subjecting any high school pupil to disciplinary sanctions solely on the basis of conduct that is speech or other communication that, when engaged in outside of the campus, is protected from governmental restriction by the First Amendment to the United States Constitution or Section 2 of Article 1 of the California Constitution." CAL. EDUC. CODE §48950(a) (2001).

   "No private postsecondary educational institution shall make or enforce any rule subjecting any student to disciplinary sanctions solely on the basis of conduct that is speech or other communication that, when engaged in outside the campus or facility of a private postsecondary institution, is protected from governmental restriction by the First Amendment to the United States Constitution or Section 2 of Article 1 of the California Constitution." CAL. EDUC. CODE §94367(a) (2001).

15. American Library Association, *Libraries & the Internet Toolkit: Tips and Guidance for Managing and Communicating about the Internet,* at http://www.ala.org/alaorg/oif/internettoolkit.html (visited Feb. 25, 2002).

16. *American Library Association v. United States,* 201 F. Supp. 2d 401 (E.D. Pa. 2002).

17. *American Library Association,* No. 01-1303.

18. *Mainstream Loudoun v. Loudoun County Library,* 2 F. Supp. 2d 783, 797 (E.D. Va. 1998).

19. *Mainstream Loudoun,* 2 F. Supp. 2d at 791, citing *Lamont v. Postmaster General,* 381 U.S. 301 (1943).

20. *Mainstream Loudoun,* 2 F. Supp. 2d at 797.

21. "There are no articulated standards either in the ordinance or in the county's established practice. The administrator is not required to rely on any objective factors. He need not provide any explanation for his decision, and that decision is unreviewable. Nothing in the law or its application prevents the official from encouraging some views and discouraging others through the arbitrary application of fees. The First Amendment prohibits the vesting of such unbridled discretion in a government official." *Forsyth County, Ga. v. Nationalist Movement,* 505 U.S. 123, 133 (1992).

22. *Board of Education, Island Trees Union Free School District No. 26 v. Pico,* 457 U.S. 853, 857 (1982).

23. *Board of Education, Island Trees Union Free School District No. 26,* 457 U.S. at 915.

24. *New York v. Ferber,* 458 U.S. 747 (1982).

25. *Osborne v. Ohio,* 495 U.S. 103 (1990).

26. See, e.g., *United States v. Matthews,* 209 F.3d 338 (4th Cir. 2000).

27. 18 U.S.C. §2256 (2000).

28. *Ashcroft v. Free Speech Coalition,* 122 S. Ct. 1389 (2002).

29. See U.S. Dept. of Health and Human Services, *Child Abuse and Neglect State Statutes Elements: Crimes No. 30, Child Pornography* (current through Dec. 31, 1999), for the text of each state statute, *at* http://www.calib.com/nccanch/pubs/stats00/pornog.pdf (visited Feb. 26, 2002).

30. *Brockett v. Spokane Arcades,* 472 U.S. 491, 498 (1985).

31. *Miller v. California,* 413 U.S. 15 (1973).

32. *Pope v. Illinois,* 481 U.S. 497, 500–501 (1987). The difficulty inherent in these criteria is summed up in Justice Antonin Scalia's concurrence: "I must note, however, that in my view it is quite impossible to come to an objective assessment of (at least) literary or artistic value, there being many accomplished people who have found literature in Dada, and art in the replication of a soup can. Since ratiocina-

tion has little to do with esthetics, the fabled "reasonable man" is of little help in the inquiry, and would have to be replaced with, perhaps, the "man of tolerably good taste"—a description that betrays the lack of an ascertainable standard. If even handed and accurate decision making is not always impossible under such a regime, it is at least impossible in the cases that matter. I think we would be better advised to adopt as a legal maxim what has long been the wisdom of mankind: Degustibus non est disputandum. Just as there is no use arguing about taste, there is no use litigating about it. For the law courts to decide 'What is Beauty' is a novelty even by today's standards." *Pope,* 481 U.S. at 504–505.

33. Kathleen M. Sullivan, *Girls Lean Back Everywhere: The Law of Obscenity and the Assault on Genius,* NEW REPUBLIC, Sept. 28, 1992, at 35 (book review).

34. *Young v. American Mini Theaters, Inc.,* 427 U.S. 50 (1976); and *Renton v. Playtime Theaters, Inc.* 475 U.S. 41 (1986).

35. *Mainstream Loudoun v. Loudoun County Library,* 24 F. Supp. 2d 552 (E.D. Va. 1998).

36. Telecommunications Act of 1996, Pub. L. No. 104-104, 110 Stat. 56.

37. *Reno v. ACLU,* 521 U.S. 844 (1997).

38. See 47 U.S.C. §223(a)(1)(B) (2000).

39. The Morality in Media website has links to current state and federal obscenity statutes. *See* http://www.moralityinmedia.org/nolc/statutesIndex.htm (visited Feb. 26, 2002).

40. *Ginsberg v. New York,* 390 U.S. 629 (1968).

41. *American Library Association v. United States,* No. 01-1303 (E.D. Pa. 2002).

42. Children's Internet Protection Act, section 1703(b), H.R. 4577, 107th Cong.; final version passed into law as Pub. L. No. 106-554 (Dec. 21, 2000), codified at 20 U.S.C. §9134 and 47 U.S.C. §254(h).

43. 47 U.S.C. §231(e)(6) (2000).

44. 122 S. Ct. 1700, 2002 U.S. Dist. LEXIS 3421 (2002) ("The scope of our decision today is quite limited. We hold only that COPA's reliance on community standards to identify 'material that is harmful to minors' does not by itself render the statute substantially overbroad for purposes of the First Amendment. We do not express any view as to whether COPA suffers from substantial overbreadth for other reasons, whether the statute is unconstitutionally vague, or whether the District Court correctly concluded that the statute likely will not survive strict scrutiny analysis once adjudication of the case is completed below. While respondents urge us to resolve these questions at this time, prudence dictates allowing the Court of Appeals to first examine these difficult issues").

4 DIGITAL LIBRARY RESOURCES AND PATRONS WITH DISABILITIES

Q1 Does the Americans with Disabilities Act (ADA) apply to digital resources in libraries, such as library and online databases and websites?

Q2 How does the ADA treat private libraries differently from public libraries?

Q3 How do I know if my library is providing "effective communication"?

Q4 What are "auxiliary aids and services"?

Q5 What is an "undue burden"?

Q6 What is a "fundamental alteration"?

Q7 What are Title II (public) and Title III (private) libraries and organizations?

Q8 Are all private libraries considered "Title III" libraries?

Q9 Are any libraries not subject to the ADA at all?

Q10 How does a library make its web pages accessible to people with disabilities?

Q11 What does it mean to be "accessible" in the electronic environment?

Q12 Is electronic text considered accessible?

Q13 What are the accessibility standards for electronic information?

Q14 Do these electronic accessibility standards have the force of law?

Q15 What are the Section 508 Standards?

Q16 Do the Section 508 Standards allow libraries a phase-in period?

Q17 Is there a phase-in period for state and local libraries?

Q18   What is required of a Title II library that must provide "program access"?

Q19   What does it mean to say that a Title III library must make accommodations if "readily achievable"?

Q20   What are the Web Content Accessibility Guidelines (WCAG)?

Q21   What are the WCAG Priorities?

Q22   Does my public library need to provide access to older materials such as microfilmed newspapers?

Q23   Is a public university library held to the same standards as a public library when providing access to materials?

Q24   Can the library wait until a specific request is made before providing access?

Q25   How do I know if my library has a "comprehensive policy"?

Q26   How does my library determine which adaptive equipment will satisfy our legal obligation?

Q27   If my library already has a speech synthesizer, must it get a different one to meet a specific patron request?

Q28   What if a public library leases space from a private business? How does this affect liability under the ADA?

Q29   Do library support groups such as Friends of the Library, my library foundation organization, and my library association have to make sure their websites are accessible to users with disabilities?

Q30   Does my library trustee board have to make sure its website is accessible to patrons with disabilities?

Q31   If an association or group has no meetings and only publishes a web page, would a court consider it a "public accommodation"?

Q32   How are disability laws enforced?

Q33   What are the penalties a library faces if it is judged to be noncompliant with the ADA?

Appendix

Additional Online Resources

Federal Law

Federal Standards

State Laws

Cases

Notes

This chapter discusses the legal requirements to make electronic information in libraries accessible to patrons with disabilities. In the early years of the digital world, information was primarily text. Digital text, such as computerized card catalogs, opened up access to many library patrons with disabilities. Visually impaired readers can manipulate electronic text by enlarging it, turning it into braille, and even turning it into synthesized speech.

Today, libraries are increasingly purchasing, leasing, and creating electronic content. Some disabled patrons cannot readily come to a library at all. Remote access can bring the library to them, but only if the websites are accessible.

Ironically, as technology has grown more sophisticated with graphics and streaming video and audio, digital information has actually become less accessible to people with disabilities. "Screen readers" can no longer "read" these features unless the features are accompanied by text explanations.

Although not many cases have been reported that deal with the Americans with Disabilities Act (ADA) and access to information, many complaints have been filed and settled at the administrative level. Early indications show a legal responsibility for both public and private libraries to make accessible to patrons with disabilities all the electronic information that is available to nondisabled patrons. The following are key standards and guidelines regarding electronic access that apply to public and private libraries.

> The federal guidelines known as the Electronic and Information Technology Accessibility Standards (or Section 508 Standards), that are issued by the Architectural and Transportation Compliance Board (known as the Access Board), require all electronic information and information technology used by the federal government to be accessible to individuals with disabilities. Although the standards are specific to the federal government, they impact state and local libraries and the private sector if they wish to do business with the federal government.

> The World Wide Web Consortium sets forth voluntary guidelines specific to web pages. These are known as the Web Accessibility Initiative's Web Content Accessibility Guidelines (WCAG). These form the basis of the Section 508 Standards with regard to web pages. These guidelines are helpful for libraries that create their

own web pages. One free tool to help libraries start evaluating whether their web pages comply with these guidelines is the Center for Applied Special Technology's diagnostic website, Bobby, at http://www.cast.org/bobby.

Both private and public libraries must make all electronic information equally accessible to disabled and nondisabled patrons. While libraries generally have no obligation to make material available at all, once they do so, they may not discriminate on the basis of disability.

Making materials "accessible" encompasses a range of options, from librarian readers to adaptive information technology.

Information technology is generally considered "accessible" if it can be used in a variety of ways that do not depend on a single sense or ability. For example, information in audio formats can become visual through captioning. Information in visual formats, such as electronic text, can be translated into audio or tactile formats with the use of screen readers, speech synthesizers, and braille equipment. Digital images can be captioned with text and then similarly turned into audio or tactile formats.

Electronic text is raw material that allows "accessibility" to people who may have a wide range of disabilities. With readily available adaptive technology, it can easily be turned into large type, synthesized speech, and refreshable braille—a technology that turns text into braille output using one row of pins that are reused again and again.

The greater the library's resources, as measured by its purchases of technology for nondisabled patrons, the greater the expectation that the library will provide adaptive technology for disabled patrons.

The greater the library's control over the electronic information, the greater the expectation is that it will be accessible. For example, a higher level of accessibility is expected of library-created web pages and digitized collections than of purchased or leased materials. However, as commercial materials increasingly adhere to federal guidelines, the expectation increases that libraries will purchase accessible materials.

Q1   *Does the Americans with Disabilities Act (ADA) apply to digital resources in publicly funded libraries, such as library and online databases and websites?*

Yes. The ADA applies to the information and services in libraries, just as it applies to the physical buildings. State and local disability laws may also apply. Federal libraries must also comply with Section 508 Standards, both in creating and purchasing electronic information.

Q2   How does the ADA treat private libraries differently from public libraries?

State and local public libraries are covered under Title II of the Americans with Disabilities Act and are subject to stricter levels of compliance than private libraries, which are covered under Title III. In general, private libraries are treated separately and not equally with public ones. Several excellent books and articles discuss the specific legal requirements for both types of libraries.[1]

Both public and private libraries, however, must ensure that they provide *effective communication* to their patrons, providing *auxiliary aids and services*. Although case law is still newly emerging, early decisions and government communications indicate that for the most part, public and private libraries have the same legal burden: both must provide *reasonable accommodations* for patrons unless to do so would create an *undue burden* or a *fundamental alteration*. The questions and answers that follow will apply to both public and private libraries unless specifically indicated otherwise. In areas where the law treats private and public libraries differently, or where cases refer specifically to public or private institutions, the discussion will identify the libraries as "Title II" (public) or "Title III" (private) libraries.

Q3   How do I know if my library is providing "effective communication"?

The ADA requires that communication for persons with disabilities must be "as effective as" that provided to nondisabled persons. It defines "effective communication" as encompassing three components: timeliness of delivery, accuracy of translation, and provision in a manner and medium appropriate to the significance of the message and the abilities of the individual with the disability.[2] Both Title II and Title III libraries must provide "effective communication."[3]

To illustrate the interpretation of this in a library, one ruling stated:

> When looking at exactly which of its resources a library is obligated to provide in an accessible medium, the short answer is any resources the library makes available to nondisabled patrons must be made accessible

to blind patrons. This includes the library catalogue, the archived microfiche, daily newspapers, and the Internet (if that is a service provided to sighted patrons).

A categorical decision by a public library not to even consider a request by a patron for a particular alternative format is in most instances a violation of Title II. However, when determining what alternative format is most appropriate, a library may take into account how frequently the material is used by patrons and the longevity of the material's usefulness. For instance, more serious consideration should be given to translating into Braille frequently used reference materials which have a long "shelf-life" than would be true for daily newspapers. Moreover, the basic purpose of the library may be taken into account in shaping the library's obligations to make its resources available to its patrons, including its patrons with disabilities.

The ruling continued:

When making purchases and when designing its resources, a public entity is expected to take into account its legal obligation to provide communication to persons with disabilities that is "as effective as" communication provided to nondisabled persons. At a minimum, a public entity has a duty to solve barriers to information access that the public entity's purchasing choices create, particularly with regard to materials that with minimal thought and cost may be acquired in a manner facilitating provision in alternative formats. When a public institution selects software programs and/or hardware equipment that are not adaptable for access by persons with disabilities, the subsequent substantial expense of providing access is not generally regarded as an undue burden when such cost could have been significantly reduced by considering the issue of accessibility at the time of the initial selection.[4]

Q4   What are "auxiliary aids and services"?

Auxiliary aids and services include a wide range of services and devices that promote effective communication. Examples of auxiliary aids and services for individuals who are deaf or hard of hearing include qualified interpreters, note-takers, computer-aided transcription services, written materials, telephone handset amplifiers, assistive listening systems, telephones compatible with hearing aids, closed-caption decoders, open and closed captioning, telecommunications devices for deaf persons (TDDs), videotext displays, and exchange of written notes.

Examples for individuals with vision impairments include qualified readers, taped texts, audio recordings, brailled materials, large-print materials, and assistance in locating items. Examples for individuals with speech impairments include TDDs, computer terminals, speech synthesizers, and communication boards.[5]

Q5   What is an "undue burden"?

An "undue burden" means significant difficulty or expense incurred in complying with standards. In determining whether an action would result in an undue burden, the factors to be considered include the following:

The nature and cost of the action

The overall financial resources of the site or sites involved in the action; the number of persons employed at the site; the effect on expenses and resources; legitimate safety requirements that are necessary for safe operation, including crime prevention measures; or the impact otherwise of the action upon the operation of the site

The geographic separateness, and the administrative or fiscal relationship of the site or sites in question to any parent corporation or entity

The overall financial resources of any parent corporation or entity; the overall size of the parent corporation or entity with respect to the number of its employees; and the number, type, and location of its facilities

The type of operation or operations of any parent corporation or entity, including the composition, structure, and functions of the workforce of the parent corporation or entity[6]

In determining whether acquiring electronic information technology that meets all or part of the applicable technical provisions of the Access Board's standards would impose an undue burden, a library must consider and document all resources available to its program.[7]

Note that showing an undue burden may not be enough to allow a library off the hook. Under the federal guidelines concerning electronic information, even if a federal agency can show an "undue burden," it must still provide information and data to individuals with disabilities by an alternative means of access. For example, if an agency wishes to purchase a computer program that generates maps denoting regional demographics, but determines that it would constitute an undue burden to purchase an accessible version of such a program, the agency would be required to make the information provided by the program available by alternative means to users with disabilities. Alternative means of access focus on the provision of the information and data in an accessible manner—as opposed to the accessibility of the product itself. Alternative means of access for an individual who is blind might mean providing a hard-copy description of the information in braille or providing an assistant to help guide the user through the information. Alternative means may include, but are not limited to, voice, fax, relay service, text telephone (TTY), qualified sign language interpreters, Internet posting, captioning, text-to-speech synthesis, readers, personal assistants, and audio descriptions.[8]

Q6   What is a "fundamental alteration"?

A library is not required to alter its acquisition requirements if the alteration would be so fundamental that the library would no longer be procuring electronic information technology that met its needs.

An FAQ (frequently asked question) on the federal guidelines for electronic information technology gives the following example. If an agency needs to meet certain security needs by acquiring secure telephone units that are all analog, the agency would not be required to buy digital phones if such phones failed to meet the agency's security needs even if the digital phones fully meet the applicable technical provisions of the Access Board's standards and the analog phones meet only some of the applicable technical provisions.[9]

*Q7   What are Title II (public) and Title III (private)
       libraries and organizations?*

Title II libraries are those *operated by* state and local government, not merely institutions that receive some measure of government funding. Title III libraries are operated by private organizations. School and academic libraries are classified by the type of parent organization they are in. Refer to figure 1 to determine if your library is considered public or private under the ADA.

Although this distinction is generally quite clear, the question may be difficult when a library has both public and private features. For example, a municipal library, as a department of the township, would be a public entity covered by Title II. The factors to be considered include whether the library is operated with public funds, whether the library employees

Title II: State and Local Government	Title III: Public Accommodations
(Private Ownership)	(Public Ownership)
Public libraries, museums, and archives (city, county, special district)	Private school libraries, museums, and archives
Public school libraries	Private academic libraries, museums, and archives
Public academic libraries, museums, and archives	Most private corporate libraries, museums, and archives

FIGURE 1
Americans with Disabilities Act: Public and Private Libraries

are considered government employees, whether the library receives significant assistance from the government by provision of property or equipment, and whether the library is governed by an independent board that is selected by the members of a private organization or is elected by the voters or appointed by elected officials.

Q8   Are all private libraries considered "Title III" libraries?

Yes, with very few exceptions. Virtually all private libraries are considered Title III libraries under the ADA. Legally, Title III covers organizations and businesses that are "public accommodations." Title III specifically mentions private libraries in its definition of public accommodations: "Place of public accommodation means a facility, operated by a private entity, whose operations affect commerce and fall within at least one of the following categories . . . [a] museum, library, gallery, or other place of public display or collection. . . ."[11] Under the ADA, a public accommodation is any private entity, regardless of size, that offers goods and

Factors Used in Distinguishing Public from Private Libraries

- whether the library is operated with public funds

- whether the library employees are considered government employees

- whether the library receives significant assistance from the government by provision of property or equipment

- whether the library is governed by an independent board selected by the members of a private organization, or is elected by the voters or appointed by elected officials[10]

services to the public. Only religious entities and certain private clubs are exempt.[12] The definition of "public accommodations" may be quite broad, as evidenced by the recent Supreme Court case concerning the golfer Casey Martin. The Court found that the PGA Tour was a "public accommodation" even though only qualified golfers could participate.[13]

As this book went to press, however, one federal district court narrowly defined "public accommodations" as physical spaces. It dismissed a lawsuit filed by a disability advocacy group claiming that a website owned by Southwest Airlines was not accessible. In the case of *Access Now* v. *Southwest Airlines* (S.D. Fla. Oct. 18, 2002), the court said that Title III governed only physical places of accommodation. Despite the dismissal of the case, it's clear that more such lawsuits are coming. Access Now has already filed suit against American Airlines claiming that its site violates the ADA, and many other websites are making changes to avoid such suits.

Q9   Are any libraries not subject to the ADA at all?

Yes. A few exceptions exist. Religious entities are exempt, including their libraries. Private clubs and their libraries that are not open to the public are also exempt.[14]

Q10   How does a library make its web pages accessible to people with disabilities?

Information technology is generally considered "accessible" if it can be used in a variety of ways that do not depend on a single sense or ability. For example, a system that provides output only in audio format would not be accessible to people with hearing impairments, and a system that requires mouse actions to navigate would not be accessible to people who cannot use a mouse because of dexterity or visual impairments.[15]

Q11   What does it mean to be "accessible" in the electronic environment?

The Department of Justice says that "accessibility" means that the user need not rely on a sole sense to receive information. The prime directive of accessibility is to *separate content from form*. That is, if the information is presented visually, make sure it can also be presented in audible or tactile formats. If the information is presented in audible format, make sure it can also be presented in a visual or tactile format.

Q12   Is electronic text considered accessible?

Yes, coupled with adaptive equipment, electronic text is an ideal format for accessibility. Through the use of adaptive equipment such as screen readers, electronic text can be enlarged, read by speech synthesizers, or turned into braille. In early DOS days, electronic text opened up a world of information to people with visual and learning disabilities. Today, however, increasingly sophisticated multimedia programs are not always readable. Electronic information standards have developed over recent years to address this critical issue.

Q13   What are the accessibility standards for electronic information?

Accessibility standards are based on the principle of "universal design." In the physical world, we see universal design features in ramps and in the placement of light switches at heights that patrons in wheelchairs can reach, etc. Many of these features are helpful to a wide variety of users, such as parents with baby strollers and library shelvers with book trucks. Many libraries make an effort to purchase equipment such as microfilm readers that have the operating controls at the bottom of the machine rather than the top so that patrons in wheelchairs can use the equipment without assistance and so the controls are more convenient for other seated patrons.

The two major sets of standards are the Electronic and Information Technology Accessibility (or Section 508) Standards issued by the Architectural and Transportation Barriers Compliance Board (the Access Board) and the Web Content Accessibility Guidelines (WCAG) issued by the World Wide Web Consortium Web Accessibility Initiative.

Q14   Do these electronic accessibility standards have the force of law?

Section 508 Standards have the force of law, with regard to federal agencies. The Web Content Accessibility Guidelines are voluntary in nature. In addition, access to services is required by law under existing federal and state laws. The National Federation of the Blind recently filed a lawsuit against America Online under the Americans with Disabilities Act. The two parties reached a settlement agreement that required the company to make its online service accessible to people with disabilities.[16]

Q15   What are the Section 508 Standards?

The Electronic and Information Technology Accessibility Standards are required by section 508 of the Rehabilitation Act. The Access Board, the same federal agency that issues the ADA Accessibility Guidelines for Buildings and Facilities (ADAAG), issues Section 508 Standards. Libraries and their architects are already familiar with ADAAG, the guidelines that specify acceptable ramp slopes, height of grab bars, width of aisles and doorways, etc.[17]

These standards apply directly to federal libraries, with a narrow exemption for national security. Section 508 does not apply to general recipients of federal funds, and does not directly regulate the private sector.[18] Section 508 Electronic Information and Technology Standards concern all aspects of electronic and information technology, from web pages to electronic databases, keyboards, and telecommunications. Section 508 Standards concerning web page design are largely based on the Priority One Guidelines of the Web Content Accessibility Guidelines.[19]

Q16   Do the Section 508 Standards allow libraries a phase-in period?

Yes. This is analogous to the physical world, in which older buildings need not conform to ADAAG. The Section 508 Standards apply to all federal contracts awarded on or after June 25, 2001. Persons with disabilities may file administrative complaints or bring civil actions in federal court against agencies that fail to comply with the requirements of section 508 as of June 21, 2001.

Q17   Is there a phase-in period for state and local libraries?

Section 508 does not directly apply to state and local libraries. However, electronic accessibility has been addressed by the Department of Justice's Office for Civil Rights (OCR-DOJ), which has compared phasing in electronic accessibility standards with phasing in building standards in Title II libraries. When Title II libraries make purchases or design their own resources, they are expected to provide effective communication to patrons with disabilities. Specifically, public libraries have a duty to solve barriers to information access that their purchasing choices create, particularly with regard to materials that with minimal thought and cost may be acquired in alternative formats. When a public library selects software or hardware that is not adaptable for access by persons with disabilities, a subsequent substantial expense of providing access is not generally regarded as an undue burden when such cost could have been significantly reduced by considering the issue of accessibility at the time of the initial selection.[20]

Note, however, that in the physical world, Title II libraries *must nevertheless provide program access* unless to do so would create an undue burden or a fundamental alteration. That is, the programs and services of the library must be made available to people with disabilities in some manner. For example, books on the second floor of a building without an elevator must be retrieved for a patron who makes a request. Title III libraries, by contrast, are required to make accommodations only if it is *readily achievable* to do so.

Q18   What is required of a Title II library that must provide "program access"?

A public library must operate each service, program, or activity so that the service, program, or activity, when viewed in its entirety, is readily accessible to and usable by individuals with disabilities.[21] For example, in a case in Oregon, a university student requested independent access to the library's CD-ROM system that provided periodical articles. The Office for Civil Rights determined that the library was required to provide access to "library programs." In this case, reference librarians serving as readers were determined to be a sufficient auxiliary aid.[22]

Q19   What does it mean to say that a Title III library must make accommodations if "readily achievable"?

"Readily achievable" means easily accomplishable and able to be carried out without much difficulty or expense. In determining whether an action is readily achievable, the factors to be considered include the following:

The nature and cost of the action needed

The overall financial resources of the site or sites involved in the action; the number of persons employed at the site; the effect on expenses and resources; legitimate safety requirements that are necessary for safe operation, including crime prevention measures; or the impact otherwise of the action upon the operation of the site

The geographic separateness, and the administrative or fiscal relationship of the site or sites in question to any parent corporation or entity

The overall financial resources of any parent corporation or entity; the overall size of the parent corporation or entity with respect to the number of its employees; the number, type, and location of its facilities

The type of operation or operations of any parent corporation or entity, including the composition, structure, and functions of the workforce of the parent corporation or entity[23]

Examples of typical accommodations include staff retrieving books for a patron, adding a simple ramp, and the like.

Q20   What are the Web Content Accessibility Guidelines (WCAG)?

The Web Content Accessibility Guidelines, issued by a nonprofit international organization, the World Wide Web Consortium, promote the interoperability of the Web. The standards cover web pages and no other electronic information. Although the standards do not have the force of law, it is conceivable that a legislative body could pass a law or ordinance incorporating these standards by reference. Fourteen guidelines serve as general principles of accessible design. Each guideline is associated with one or more checkpoints describing how to apply that guideline to particular features of web pages. An appendix to the guidelines, "List of Checkpoints for the Web Content Accessibility Guidelines 1.0," presents the checkpoints sorted by priority. A summary chart is included in this appendix.[24]

Q21   What are the WCAG Priorities?

The WCAG Priorities, as of July 2001, are:

> *Priority One.* A web content developer *must* satisfy this checkpoint. Otherwise, one or more disabled groups will find it impossible to access information in the document. Satisfying this checkpoint is a basic requirement for some groups to be able to use web documents.

> *Priority Two.* A web content developer *should* satisfy this checkpoint. Otherwise, one or more disabled groups will find it difficult to access information in the document. Satisfying this checkpoint will remove significant barriers to accessing web documents.

> *Priority Three.* A web content developer *may* address this checkpoint. Otherwise, one or more disabled groups will find it somewhat difficult to access information in the document. Satisfying this checkpoint will improve access to web documents.[25]

Q22   Does my public library need to provide access to older materials such as microfilmed newspapers?

Yes. The library must provide the means to make its materials accessible to patrons with disabilities. It has many choices as to how it can accomplish this. Many libraries use staff or volunteers to help patrons access library catalogs and materials. Others provide adaptive equipment that translates printed text into audible speech or refreshable braille.

Libraries must make sure that the resources that are available to the general public are accessible to patrons with disabilities as well. This includes, for example, the library catalog, archived microfiche, and daily newspapers. A categorical decision by a public library not to even consider a request by a patron for a particular alternative format is, in most instances, a violation of Title II. However, when determining what alternative format is most appropriate, a library may take into account how frequently the material is used and the longevity of the material's usefulness. For instance, more serious consideration should be given to translating into braille frequently used reference materials, which have a longer "shelf-life" than would be true for daily newspapers.[26]

Federal regulations make a distinction between public and private libraries' obligations regarding library materials. A private library is not required "to alter its inventory to include accessible or special goods that are designed for . . . individuals with disabilities," but must provide those materials through interlibrary loan "at the request of an individual with disabilities, if, in the normal course of operations, it makes special orders on unstocked goods, and if the accessible or special goods can be obtained from a supplier with whom the public accommodation customarily does business."[27]

Q23   *Is a public university library held to the same standards as a public library when providing access to materials?*

The basic purpose of the library may be taken into account in terms of making library resources generally available. A recent OCR decision says that the primary mission of the university library is to support and enhance the curricula of the university. A university may, in appropriate circumstances, allocate or set priorities in use of resources consistent with the fundamental purpose of the university library, "but may not condition access to services, such as the microfiche collection, upon a showing of academic or course related relevance if those services are available to nondisabled students without such a showing."[28]

Q24   *Can the library wait until a specific request is made before providing access?*

No. The library's obligation is to provide immediate access. Title II libraries may not simply respond to individual requests for accommodation on an ad hoc basis. Public entities have an affirmative duty to establish a comprehensive policy in advance of requests for auxiliary aids or services.[29] Again, if the library has a comprehensive policy that includes an effective means to provide access, for example, by using staff to read material aloud, it may wait for specific requests to do so.

Q25   How do I know if my library has a "comprehensive policy"?

The Department of Education's Office for Civil Rights has noted that a recognized good practice in establishing a comprehensive policy is to consult with the disability community, especially those members most likely to request accommodations.[30]

Q26   How does my library determine which adaptive equipment will satisfy our legal obligation?

For both Title II and Title III libraries that are not subject to Section 508 Standards, the test is whether the library is offering auxiliary aids and services that provide *effective communication* with the library patron. Title II libraries must also give *primary consideration* to the specific request by the patron with the disability.

If the library is subject to Section 508 Standards, it should look at those standards as controlling. Otherwise, these standards may be considered a good source of specific standards in demonstrating that the library has effective communication.

Q27   If my library already has a speech synthesizer, must it get a different one to meet a specific patron request?

The Department of Education's Office for Civil Rights has said that when a user requests adaptive technology software that is different from software already in use at the library, it is reasonable to consider expert opinion. That is, if the library is using a

> widely used program that is generally regarded by knowledgeable experts as reliable for access by persons with that type of disability (e.g., blindness), the person with the disability may well be required to learn the program selected by the institution. On the other hand, if the public institution has installed a program that is generally regarded by knowledgeable experts as providing cumbersome inferior access to persons with visual impairments, the person with the disability may rely upon the Title II provision requiring that "primary consideration" be given to his/her

request for the institution to purchase the software with which s/he is proficient.[31]

Specific equipment advice is readily available in print and online.[32]

Q28   What if a public library leases space from a private business? How does this affect its liability under the ADA?

In cases of joint ventures, leases, or other relationships between government entities and public accommodations, the practical result of the relationship will usually be that the facility has to comply with the highest standard represented by both Titles. Each entity is generally liable only for its failure to ensure compliance with the portion of the law that applies to it. If a state or local government contracts with a private entity, it must ensure that it operates in a manner that satisfies the government's Title II obligations.[33]

Q29   Do library support groups such as Friends of the Library, my library foundation organization, and my library association have to make sure their websites are accessible to users with disabilities?

Friends of the Library, library foundations, and library associations are clearly *not* Title II organizations. That is, they are *not* part of state or local government. However, they are almost certain to be "public accommodations," and subject to Title III.

Q30   Does my library trustee board have to make sure its website is accessible to patrons with disabilities?

Yes. If the trustee board is part of state or local government, i.e., elected or appointed by elected officials, then it is a Title II entity. Therefore, Title II accessibility guidelines would be applied to web access. This is true even if it is a volunteer board that meets infrequently.

Q31   If an association or group has no meetings and only publishes a web page, would a court consider it a "public accommodation"?

This was a central issue in two recent lawsuits. In *National Federation of the Blind* v. *America Online*, an online service was sued because its web pages were not accessible to persons with visual impairment. The case was settled, without offering a legal precedent. The settlement agreement ensured that the next version of America Online's software (AOL 6.0) would be compatible with screen reader-assistive technology. The agreement also specified that AOL would undertake steps to assure that the existing and future content of AOL-developed areas of the AOL service would be largely accessible to the blind.[34] In *Hooks* v. *OKBridge,* the Department of Justice filed an amicus brief supporting the position that an Internet bridge tournament is a "public accommodation," and hence subject to Title III. The appellate court's decision is unpublished.[35]

Also of interest is a landmark Australian case, in which a blind sports enthusiast filed a legal complaint against the Sydney Organising Committee for the Olympic Games, claiming that significant portions of the Olympic website were inaccessible to someone with a refreshable braille reader. He won his case, and the Olympic Committee was ordered to make its website accessible by "(i) including ALT text on all images and image map links on its web site; (ii) providing access to the Index of Sports from the Schedule page; and (iii) providing access to the Results Tables to be used on the web site during the Sydney Olympic Games."[36]

Although this case has no official bearing on U.S. law, the issues are relevant, and the Australian Disability Discrimination Act has many similarities to the Americans with Disabilities Act. A prudent position for an American organization that exists or communicates only on the Internet is to assume that it is a "public accommodation" subject to the ADA, especially if the website is open to the public.

Q32   How are disability laws enforced?

The Americans with Disabilities Act is not enforced by an agency that comes to your library to make inspections. Disability laws are primarily triggered when individuals and groups file complaints. Under Titles II and III, an individual may file an administrative complaint or file suit in court without exhausting administrative remedies.[37] Complaints are filed with the Department of Justice, Civil Rights Division. The Department of Justice refers your complaints to the appropriate agency, including the Department of Education, Office for Civil Rights (OCR), which is responsible for ensuring that all educational institutions and public libraries comply with the requirements of all federal civil rights laws, including section 504 (the Rehabilitation Act of 1973) and Title II of the ADA. The OCR opinions are generally accorded considerable weight by the courts in interpreting the requirements of these laws.

*Q33   What are the penalties a library faces if it is judged
to be noncompliant with the ADA?*

Monetary damages are not recoverable in the private suits. Only injunctive relief is available, i.e., an order that facilities be made accessible, auxiliary aids or services be provided, or alternative methods be provided. Monetary damages *are* recoverable in suits filed by the U.S. attorney general. The attorney general is authorized to bring a lawsuit where there is a pattern or practice of discrimination or where an act of discrimination raises an issue of general public importance. Courts may order compensatory damages of up to $50,000 for the first violation and $100,000 for any subsequent violation to remedy discrimination if the Department of Justice prevails in such suits.[38]

APPENDIX

Additional Online Resources

Bobby: An Accessibility Tool to Check Accessibility of Library Web Pages

"Bobby" is a free online utility that lets you type in your library's URL and check its accessibility to disabled patrons per the World Wide Web Consortium's guidelines. See http://www.cast.org/bobby.

International Center for Disability Resources on the Internet

This is a nonprofit corporation that focuses on the field of accessible electronic and information technology. See http://www.icdri.org, and see in particular the writings and presentations of Cynthia Waddell, at http://www.icdri.org/cynthia_waddell.htm.

World Wide Web Consortium: Web Content Accessibility Guidelines

These voluntary guidelines promote the interoperability of the Web and cover web pages in depth. See http://www.w3.org/TR/WAI-WEB CONTENT.

Federal Law

29 U.S.C. §794(d) (2001). The Rehabilitation Act Amendments strengthen section 508 of the Rehabilitation Act and require access to electronic and information technology provided by the federal government. The amend-

ments apply to all federal agencies when they develop, procure, maintain, or use electronic and information technology.

See also U.S. Department of Justice, *A Guide to Disability Rights Laws* (August 2001). This excellent guide to federal disability laws, including the Americans with Disabilities Act, the Telecommunications Act, and the Rehabilitation Act, is at http://www.usdoj.gov/crt/ada/cguide.htm.

Federal Standards

36 C.F.R. pt. 1194 (2001). Electronic and Information Technology Accessibility Standards, or Section 508 Standards. These are issued by the Architectural and Transportation Barriers Compliance Board, were published in the *Federal Register* on December 21, 2000, and became effective in 2001. The standards cover web pages, (based in part on the World Wide Web Consortium's guidelines), communications equipment, and other information technology. See http://www.access-board.gov/sec508/508standards. htm. See also Web-Based Intranet and Internet Information and Applications, at http://www.access-board.gov/sec508/guide/1194.22.htm.

State Laws

State laws may require libraries to conform to higher standards of accessibility. To check a state's disability laws, see Cornell Law School, Legal Information Institute, *Disability Law: An Overview,* at http://www.law. cornell.edu/topics/disability.html.

Cases

National Federation of the Blind v. *America Online* (settled July 26, 2000).[39] In its settlement agreement, AOL agreed to ensure that its next version of software (AOL 6.0) would be compatible with screen reader-assistive technology. See http://www.nfb.org/Tech/accessibility.htm. The National Federation of the Blind also filed a lawsuit against the Connecticut attorney general's office in April 2000, claiming it provided links to four inaccessible online tax-filing services. The sites have since been made accessible.[40]

California State University–Los Angeles, Region IX, O.C.R. Complaint No. 09-97-2002, 1997 NDLR (LRP) LEXIS 525; 11 NDLR (LRP) 71 (April 7, 1997). Complaint said the university's library failed to provide access to blind and low-vision students. This strongly worded opinion required a university library to select accessible software programs and/or hardware equipment for students with disabilities.

Notes

1. See, e.g., Library Buildings, Equipment and the ADA: Compliance Issues and Solutions: Proceedings of the LAMA Buildings and Equipment Section Preconference (Susan E. Cirillo and Robert E. Danford eds., 1996); How Libraries Must Comply with the Americans with Disabilities Act (ADA) (Nancy C. Pack and Donald D. Foos eds., 1992).

2. O.C.R. Region IX, Complaint No. 09-97-2002, *California State University–L.A.,* 1997 NDLR (LRP) LEXIS 525; 11 NDLR (LRP) 71 (April 7, 1997).

3. 42 U.S.C. tit. 3, §§12181–89 (2000); Americans with Disabilities Act Accessibility Guidelines (ADAAG), 28 C.F.R. pt. 36 (2000), section 504 of the Rehabilitation Act of 1973, as amended; 29 U.S.C. §794, section 504 regulations; 45 C.F.R. 84.

4. O.C.R. Region IX, Complaint No. 09-97-2002, *California State University–L.A.,* 1997 NDLR (LRP) LEXIS 525; 11 NDLR (LRP) 71 (April 7, 1997).

5. *Americans with Disabilities Act Technical Assistance Manual III-4.3300, available at* http://www.usdoj.gov/crt/ada/taman3.html (visited June 25, 2001).

6. 28 C.F.R. §36.104 (2000).

7. 36 C.F.R. §1194.4 (2000).

8. *Acquisition of Electronic and Information Technology under Section 508 of the Rehabilitation Act, Frequently Asked Questions, at* http://www.section508.gov.

9. *Acquisition of Electronic and Information Technology, Frequently Asked Questions, at* http://www.section 508.gov.

10. U.S. Department of Justice, Letter DJ No. 182-06-00019 to Suffolk Cooperative Library System, New York (May 3, 1992), *available at* http://www.usdoj.gov/crt/foia/cltr011.txt (visited June 25, 2001).

11. 42 U.S.C. §12181 (2000); 28 C.F.R. §36.104 and .104(8) (2000).

12. 28 C.F.R. §36.104.

13. *PGA Tour v. Casey Martin,* U.S. No. 00-24 (decided May 29, 2001).

14. 28 C.F.R. §36.104.

15. U.S. Department of Education, *Q & A, Title IV-Rehabilitation Act Amendments of 1998, Section 508: Electronic and Information Technology (n.d.) at* http://www.usdoj.gov/crt/508/archive/deptofed.pdf.

16. See *National Federation of the Blind v. America Online* Accessibility Agreement, *at* http://www.nfb.org/Tech/accessibility.htm (visited Feb. 28, 2002).

17. See Americans with Disabilities Act Accessibility Guidelines (ADAAG), 28 C.F.R. 36, app. A (1999), for the full specifications.

18. U.S. Department of Justice, *Section 508: Frequently Asked Questions (FAQ), at* http://www.usdoj.gov/crt/508/archive/old508faq.html (visited June 26, 2001).

19. For full listing, see 65 Fed. Reg. 63 (proposed March 31, 2000), *available at* http://frwebgate.access.gpo.gov/cgi-bin/getdoc.cgi?dbname=2000_register& docid=00-7719-filed.pdf. For a summary chart of the Section 508 Standards, *see* the appendix at this location.

20. O.C.R. Region IX, Complaint No. 09-97-2002, *California State University–L.A.,* 1997 NDLR (LRP) LEXIS 525; 11 NDLR (LRP) 71 (April 7, 1997).

21. 28 C.F.R. §35, subpart D (2000).

22. O.C.R. Region X, Complaint No. 10-91-2019, *University of Oregon,* 1992 NDLR (LRP) LEXIS 1129; 5 NDLR (LRP) 219 (June 30, 1992).

23. 28 C.F.R. §36.104 (2000).

24. *See* http://www.w3.org/TR/WAI-WEBCONTENT/full-checklist.html.

25. W3C Web Content Accessibility Guidelines are *available at* http://www.w3.org/TR/1999/WAI-WEBCONTENT-19990505.

26. O.C.R. Region IX, Complaint No. 09-97-2002, *California State University–L.A.,* 1997 NDLR (LRP) LEXIS 525; 11 NDLR (LRP) 71 (April 7, 1997).

27. 56 Fed. Reg. 35598 (1991), codified at 28 C.F.R. §36.

28. O.C.R. Region IX, Complaint No. 09-97-2002, *California State University–L.A.,* (citing O.C.R. Region IX, Complaint No. 09-96-2056, *San Jose State University* (Feb. 7, 1997)).

29. See *Tyler v. City of Manhattan,* 857 F. Supp. 800 (D. Kan. 1994), cited in O.C.R. Region IX, Complaint No. 09-97-2002, *California State University–L.A.*

30. O.C.R. Region IX, Complaint No. 09-97-2002, *California State University–L.A.*

31. O.C.R. Region IX, Complaint No. 09-97-2002, *California State University–L.A.*

32. An excellent print source is Barbara T. Mates, ADAPTIVE TECHNOLOGY FOR THE INTERNET: MAKING ELECTRONIC RESOURCES ACCESSIBLE TO ALL (2000). This book gives useful current information on available adaptive technologies for library patrons' use with electronic information resources, e.g., large-print keytops for persons who are visually impaired, high contrast and simple fonts for online public-access catalogs and web pages, the ability to change font size, contrast, and colors, the use of white space to reduce distraction, etc. Another useful print source is ACCESSIBLE LIBRARIES ON CAMPUS: A PRACTICAL GUIDE FOR THE CREATION OF DISABILITY-FRIENDLY LIBRARIES (Tom McNulty ed., 1999). For Internet accessibility, *see* the International Center for Disability Resources on the Net, *at* http://www.icdri.org (visited June 26, 2001).

33. Lisa Huggins, *You Can Get There from Here: Program Accessibility Requirements under the Americans with Disabilities Act,* 56 ALABAMA LAWYER 363 (November 1995).

34. National Federation of the Blind and AOL Press Release, *National Federation of the Blind and America Online Reach Agreement in Accessibility* (July 26, 2000).

35. Amicus Curiae Brief for Appellant, *Hooks v. OKBridge,* No. 99-50891 (W.D. Tex. Sept. 13, 2000), *at* http://www.usdoj.gov/crt/briefs/hooks.pdf (visited June 26, 2001). For an overview of the ADA and the Internet, *see* Paul Taylor, *The Americans with*

Disabilities Act and the Internet, 7 BOSTON UNIVERSITY JOURNAL OF SCIENCE & TECHNOLOGY LAW 26 (Winter 2001), *available at* http://www.bu.edu/law/scitech/OLJ7.htm (visited June 26, 2001).

36. *Bruce Lindsay Maguire v. Sydney Organising Committee for the Olympic Games,* Human Rights and Equal Opportunity Commission, No. H99/115 (Aug. 24, 2000), *at* http://scaleplus.law.gov.au/html/ddadec/0/2000/0/DD000120.htm (visited June 26, 2001).

37. U.S. Department of Justice, Civil Rights Division, Disability Rights Section, *A Guide to Disability Rights Laws* (Sept. 1, 1998), *at* http://www.usdoj.gov/crt/ada/cguide.htm (visited July 11, 2001).

38. The remedies are those set forth in section 505 of the Rehabilitation Act, 29 U.S.C. §794a, 42 U.S.C. §12188 (2000). *See also* U.S. Department of Justice, Civil Rights Division, Disability Rights Section, *Enforcement, at* http://www.usdoj.gov/crt/ ada/ enforce.htm (visited July 11, 2001).

39. Complaint *at* http://www.nfb.org (visited June 5, 2000).

40. Joel Schettler, *Equal Access to All: New Federal Accessibility Guidelines for Electronic Information Technology May Open New Roads to the Online Learning Superhighway,* TRAININGMAG.COM (January 2002), *at* http://www.trainingmag.com/training/search/search_display.jsp?vnu_content_id=1230447.

5 LIBRARY RECORDS AND PRIVACY

A New York Court

Reading the Wisconsin Statute

Interpreting the Oregon Statute

Understanding State Laws That Protect Patron Privacy in Libraries

Q10   What is the general nature of the state laws protecting patron privacy in libraries?

Understanding the Statutory Context

Defining the Four Elements

Institution

Q11   Is my library covered by my state's library privacy laws?

Q12   What if it's unclear which library institutions my state's statute covers?

Target Record or Information

Q13   What information about patrons, exactly, is protected by law?

Records

Information

Neither Records nor Information: The Power of Librarian Observation

Action

Q14   What acts are prohibited?

Q15   May a library routinely print circulation receipts that reveal a patron's name, library registration number, and the title of the circulated items to distribute to patrons as a record of the transaction upon check-out?

Q16   If a library releases a "record" containing private patron information in violation of the statute, what remedy does the patron have?

Exceptions: Consent, Parents, Administrative, Court Orders, etc.

Q17   What types of exceptions are typical in state confidentiality laws?

Consent

Parents and Guardians

The Michigan Experience

Q18   If the state law is silent on the issue of parental access to children's library records, what should the library do?

Q19   If my state law allows disclosure of patron information under certain conditions, do the patrons have any right to be notified and contest?

Applying Library Confidentiality Statutes in Practice

Q20   What if faculty members would like others to pick up materials for them?*:*

   Library Administration

   Criminal or Civil Legal Proceedings

Q21   What is a subpoena duces tecum?

Q22   My state requires a court order. Is that the same as a subpoena?

Q23   Must any court order be complied with immediately?

Q24   My state only requires "a lawfully issued subpoena." How do I know if it is "lawfully issued"?

Q25   Is a search warrant a court order?

Q26   What should the library do if law enforcement (or someone else) comes into the library with a subpoena?

Q27   How should the library challenge the subpoena in court?

Q28   What if the librarian *wants* to comply with the subpoena?

Q29   Can you give an example of a case where law enforcement successfully obtained library records?

Q30   Can you give an example of a case where law enforcement was unsuccessful in obtaining library records?

Q31   My library belongs to a consortium, and I'm concerned that my patrons' records are out of my control. How can I ensure that each library in the consortium adheres to the same privacy guarantees that my library does?

Q32   What does the American Library Association recommend when drafting a library confidentiality policy?

Conclusion

Appendix

State Library Confidentiality Statutes

Notes

W hat should a library do if the police come in and ask for Internet-use records or circulation records? The library profession traditionally has strongly protected patron privacy rights. Without a sense of privacy about reading habits, a "chilling effect" takes place. That is, some patrons will no longer feel free to surf the Internet or check out certain books, because they are fearful that others, from spouses to the police, will see their reading trail.[1]

Children pose special issues. Unlike schools or school libraries, public libraries are not legally positioned to act in loco parentis, that is, to act in the "place of the parent." Yet because parents and society care deeply about protecting children, even public libraries are pressured to act in loco parentis. Some patrons want libraries to honor parental wishes when it comes to Internet use, R-rated video check-outs, or the circulation of other library materials. Many librarians wonder where the rights of a child in his or her own privacy end and where the rights of parents begin.

The present state of privacy law is based mostly on state law, with many variations from state to state. This chapter will discuss patron privacy in general terms, drawing examples from the variety of state approaches to protecting patron privacy, and will prepare a librarian to read and understand his or her own state privacy statute. It cannot be overemphasized that a library must follow the laws in its own state when drafting policy, and not those of another state or of some general notion of privacy. In addition, it should be noted that the state statutes are the starting point in researching state library privacy laws. Attorney generals' opinions and court cases and other administrative rulings interpreting the laws should also be checked.

An important point for librarians to know is that library policies may often go further toward protecting patron privacy than state law as long as they are not in conflict with that state law.

Q1   What does federal law say about public library patron privacy?

Federal law does not explicitly protect public library patrons. In fact, the word "privacy" does not even appear in the United States Constitution, although the Supreme Court has determined that it is implied.[2]

The Fourth Amendment asserts that individuals have rights against unreasonable searches and seizures of their persons, houses, papers, and effects:

The right of the people to be secure in their persons, houses, papers, and effects, against unreasonable searches and seizures, shall not be violated, and no Warrants shall issue, but upon probable cause, supported by Oath or affirmation, and particularly describing the place to be searched, and the persons or things to be seized.[3]

The Ninth Amendment indirectly addresses privacy. Basically, it says that individual citizens retain any rights not specifically mentioned or written into the Constitution.[4] The Tenth Amendment leaves powers to the states that are not given to the federal government by the Constitution, and although this amendment had been widely ignored for years, the Supreme Court has been strengthening it steadily over the past few years.[5]

Perhaps due to the less than clear articulation of privacy in the federal Constitution, the United States' legislative approach to informational privacy is best described as piecemeal. There is no overarching federal privacy law that protects patrons' reading interests, with the exception of video check-outs.

Q2   How does the USA PATRIOT Act affect libraries?

The Uniting and Strengthening America by Providing Appropriate Tools Required to Intercept and Obstruct Terrorism Act of 2001,[6] or USA PATRIOT Act, is not a stand-alone law, but an act that amends over a dozen federal statutes.

Although it is too soon to know how these changes will affect libraries, library advocates have focused on the surveillance provisions and the impact such provisions could have on intellectual freedom.

The act amends the Foreign Intelligence Surveillance Act of 1978 (FISA)[7] to allow its lower thresholds for court orders to be used when "a significant purpose of the surveillance is to obtain foreign intelligence information." The pre-PATRIOT standard required that law enforcement demonstrate that the "sole or main purpose" of the surveillance was to gather foreign intelligence information.[8] This change is critical; it allows the lower FISA standards to be used outside of the foreign intelligence context.

Q3   Can the federal government obtain library records under the PATRIOT Act?

One of the most controversial sections of the PATRIOT Act for library advocates is section 215. This amends FISA to authorize the director of the

FBI or his or her designee to "make an application for an order requiring the production of any tangible thing (including books, records, papers, documents, and other items) for an investigation to protect against international terrorism or clandestine intelligence activities."[9] Once granted, this order entitles the FBI to procure any library records, including circulation and Internet use records. Moreover, the process is sealed, and librarians who are given a section 215 order may not discuss the order with anyone (except those that need to know, such as a lawyer). The provision states that "[a]n order under this subsection shall not disclose that it is issued for purposes of an investigation described in subsection (a)" and "[n]o person shall disclose to any other person (other than those persons necessary to produce the tangible things under this section) that the Federal Bureau of Investigation has sought or obtained tangible things under this section."[10]

In other words, the order cannot disclose its purpose, and a library receiving the order is prohibited from disclosing its occurrence. Because of this, reports of library incidents will be limited; do not expect to read about such investigations in the next issue of the ALA's *Newsletter on Intellectual Freedom.*

Q4   Is there a conflict between this provision of the PATRIOT Act and the First Amendment?

The act includes a proviso that any application issued under section 215 to a "United States person is not conducted solely upon the basis of activities protected by the first amendment to the Constitution." However, since the proceedings are sealed and the issuance of the order comes with a gag order, it is virtually impossible for librarians to monitor this. The U.S. attorney general is required to report twice a year to the respective House and Senate intelligence committees on the number of requests and orders issued.

Q5   Does the PATRIOT Act supersede state laws?

If there is a conflict, federal law will supersede state law. The PATRIOT Act lowers the threshold to issue court orders, but it does not appear to conflict with state laws that require court orders (or state laws that merely require subpoenas).

Q6   Does my state have a library confidentiality law?

Each state and the District of Columbia have some sort of protection for library records. Forty-eight states and the District of Columbia include protection within a statutory scheme.[11] The two remaining states, Kentucky and Texas, have issued attorney general opinions that suggest that library records are protected under state privacy laws in general.[12] (For a table of state library confidentiality statutes, see the appendix at the end of this chapter.)

Within the statutory framework, a number of states do not have stand-alone library confidentiality statutes, but instead add "public" library records as an exception to the states' general open records laws.[13] The legal significance of this placement is important. If the privacy statute exists as an exception to a state's open records laws, the other provisions of the state's open records law also apply. These provisions might define what a record is, indicate the conditions for consent for release to a third party, and the penalty for an improper release of the record by the record custodian.

The *Privacy Journal* has ranked the fifty states into tiers in terms of their overall privacy protection. Library record confidentiality is one factor in the ranking, which looks also at medical records, drivers licenses, etc. The library confidentiality issue is included with the simple question: "Does the state make the records of library patrons confidential by law?"[14]

*Q7   When, if ever, should I give out records of patron
        Internet use?*

This is a complicated question. Unlike automated circulation systems which generally delete circulation transactions that are no longer active, computers connected to the Internet may continue to store an "electronic trail" of where your patrons have been and what subjects they have been researching.

Electronic Tracks

Computers can track not only the sites visited, but also the queries entered, and the information a patron fills into an online form. Internet browsers can be asked by a website to store a "cookie" on the library's hard drive. This "cookie" file might hold a password, or a running compilation of web pages visited and articles downloaded. The computer thus tracks the subjects of the research. The library network administrator can see what websites a patron has visited, and even the next patron can check the cookie file to see the "history" of websites visited. Cookie files can be easily deleted, however, and browsers can be set to reject cookies. Computers can be set to automatically clear their cache, and electronic shredders can also be used.

Q8   *Are my library's automated Internet history logs considered a "public record" that must be made available to the public on request?*

"Public records" laws are determined state by state, and a definitive answer is not possible. If a state includes these electronic logs as "public records," then the issue becomes whether or not the identification of users is exempt from disclosure and what steps must be followed when and if records are destroyed.[15]

A recent lawsuit on this issue was filed in New Hampshire under Rev. Stat. Ann. 91-A, the state's open records or "Right-to-Know" law. A father asked to see a school's computer Internet logs, because he was concerned that the school's acceptable use policy was not an adequate safeguard to protect his children from pornographic images. The school did not turn over the records at the father's initial request, saying that the Internet searches included student IDs and passwords that make the students personally identifiable. In November 2000, the Superior Court in Rockingham County ordered the school to turn over the logs without personally identifying information of the student searches. In January 2001, the court found that the school had intentionally deleted the logs after the father filed suit and that the school misled the court into believing the logs still existed. The court found the school to be in contempt of court and ordered it to produce the remaining records and pay the father his costs and attorney's fees.[16]

Libraries may want to carefully consider the consequences of keeping Internet history log files, as well as other sources that create records of patrons' activity in the library such as bookmarks, caches, etc.

Internet Service Providers

Some libraries use outside Internet service providers (ISPs). All of a patron's Internet behavior and messages can easily be tracked by the ISP. At this point, protection is out of the control of the library (except for the internal sign-up identification). ISPs often have little incentive to fight subpoenas and may not even allow their subscribers sufficient time or notice to do so, either.[17] Libraries that use outside ISPs should choose carefully to find one that best matches the library's privacy policy.

Data Mining

A concern for libraries that use filtering products designed to screen out objectionable sites is "data mining." In January 2001, the story broke that the Pentagon had bought a database called "Class Clicks" from a popular Internet filter company, N2H2. Class Clicks reported on aggregate data of the websites that 14 million students visited on the Internet and how much time they spent at each one. N2H2 had also sold the data to Roper Starch Worldwide, a marketing research firm, as well as to the U.S. Department of Defense.[18] This effort was withdrawn as a result of the publicity.

Library Sign-Up Lists

Libraries use different methods to allow patrons to use Internet computers, ranging from no sign-ups to paper waiting lists to automated card systems. The practical choices that the library makes can have legal consequences. The libraries that keep no records, use anonymous sign-ups, or destroy sheets immediately have nothing to turn over to a requester. The libraries that do keep records, even for short durations such as a week, are subject to inquiries by law enforcement officers or others who wish to track down the identity of a library patron who was at a certain terminal at a certain time. One solution for libraries that need accountability and require patron identification is to use a "pass system." That is, the patron shows ID to library staff, but the ID is not recorded in any way. The patron receives an anonymous "pass" for the Internet terminal.

Q9   *How do the different states handle library patron information regarding Internet use?*

If the library does choose to keep records with patron identification, the disclosure of the records is subject to both state law and the library's own confidentiality policy. It will not be unusual to find that neither has been updated to directly answer the question, and that sign-up lists do not fit into the state law's categories, which may be limited to circulation or borrower registration records. It may be time to draft an updated confidentiality policy for the library. See question 32 below for help on starting that process. It may also be time to get involved in writing to legislators to update the state law. Not only can the language of the statute itself offer guidance, but court or administrative decisions can assist in interpreting a state library statute. Unfortunately, many libraries are left with only the state statute as a guide. Consider the following examples of how three similar state statutes might be interpreted and applied to some of the Internet settings discussed: by a court, by a plain reading of the statute, and by an administrative ruling or opinion.

A New York Court

The landmark court case on this issue was tried in New York state.[19] New York has a strong patron confidentiality provision that protects "personally identifying details" regarding the users of "computer database searches" in public, free association, school, college, and university libraries and library systems.[20] A printing company in Wisconsin, Quad Graphics, found that someone was using its computers to make long-distance telephone calls. This sort of information may in fact be the focus of inquiry, as in the *Quad/Graphics* case, in which a private company attempted to obtain access to library records that would identify the specific individuals associated with a list of nine passwords. The company tracked the passwords to a public library in York and tried to get the names of the patrons under the New York Freedom of Information Law. The library did not give the records, and prevailed in court. The court found that the information was protected, relying on the statute and its legislative history. The New York Assembly had issued a supporting memorandum to the law, calling the library a "unique sanctuary of the widest possible spectrum of ideas." The library must protect the confidentiality of its records in order to insure its readers' right to read anything they wish, "free from the fear that someone might see what they read and use."[21]

Although this is a significant decision for New York, because library confidentiality laws are unique to each state, each state court will still need to rely on its own state law. Although we do not yet have reported cases, an analysis of sample states is offered later in this chapter.

Reading the Wisconsin Statute

Consider the Wisconsin statute as another example. Section 43.30 indicates that "records of any library which is in whole or part supported by public funds, including the records of a public library system, indicating the identity of any individual who borrows or uses the library's documents or other materials, resources, or services may not be disclosed except . . ."[22] The focus is not upon the person and his or her confidentiality, nor upon the release of certain information, but upon the release of records that include certain information, i.e., those records that "indicat[e] the identity of" persons who use the library or borrow its materials. Many statutes contain similar language: protection is tied to a record that contains personally identifiable information.[23]

Would this approach protect a reference log sheet of library card numbers and resources used or a web transaction log of computer network passwords and sites visited? In other words, what is the status of records that do not identify a particular patron but relate to or reference a specific individual through indirect means such as a password or number? Could this information be disclosed? What about state statutes that protect any registration or circulation records?

It would appear that the information would not be protected if the statute protects only certain types of records such as circulation or registration, since neither the reference log sheet nor the web transaction log is a circulation or registration record.

The narrow phrasing of statutes that tie the definition of "record" to the borrowing of library materials would suffer the same infirmity, since one does not "borrow" computer access or some other service in the same way as a book, periodical, video, etc. It would depend on how the statute discusses what sort of identifying information is protected. While a library card number or password may be unique, it may not "identify" a patron. A statute drafted broadly enough to include all conceivable uses of library space, services, and resources would provide greater protection.

Interpreting the Oregon Statute

This would also be the result with the Oregon statute, which specifies the "records of a library, including circulation records, showing use of specific library material by a named person or consisting of the name of a library patron together with the address or telephone number or both of the patron."[24] A "record" like a reference log sheet or web transaction log, which consists of a list of patron numbers or passwords and the various uses of library, remote, or Internet resources, would not seem to qualify. However, an earlier state attorney general's opinion interpreting the Oregon public records law (section 192.501) indicated that any "personal information" contained in public library records without condition is exempt from the public records law,[25] and this might be interpreted to provide broader protection than name-associated information in section 192.502(22). While the logs might be considered records, there is no "named person" revealed by the release of a mere number or password. Again, can a registration number or password alone identify a patron? It might be able to distinguish the use of one library item or website by one patron from the use made of that resource by another patron, but in and of itself such a number or unique character string cannot identify a patron without additional information.

UNDERSTANDING STATE LAWS THAT PROTECT PATRON PRIVACY IN LIBRARIES

Assessing the status of the law in each state is beyond the scope of this chapter, but it might be helpful to organize any reading of a state's library privacy statute into several elements that may facilitate your understanding of that particular library privacy statute's strengths and weaknesses.

Take special notice of the following elements, all of which are discussed in greater depth throughout this chapter:

- Institution
- Target record or information
- Action
- Exceptions

Q10   *What is the general nature of the state laws protecting patron privacy in libraries?*

First, obtain and read a complete copy of your state's statute and review it carefully, since there is great variation from state to state. A library's policy should be drafted or revised in keeping with the state law, and when possible, should expand the privacy rights of patrons.

Understanding the Statutory Context

Most if not all privacy statutes prohibit the release of library patron information to third parties. A number of states prohibit the release of patron information outright, but there may be several exceptions. Understanding the nuances of coverage is critical, e.g., how the protected patron information is defined. A second approach is taken by states that present library confidentiality as an exception to a state's open records laws. These statutes more accurately operate to merely remove the public library patron record from the general definition of public records and thus limit the reach of the "public" or "open" records law. However, these records may still be subject to disclosure through a subpoena.

Defining the Four Elements

The "institution" indicates which libraries in the state the law covers. The "target record or information" is also an important element, since different states protect different aspects of patron privacy. Most of the discussion of coverage centers around what type of record is protected, i.e., what sort of information must be in a record before it will be considered a "record" for purposes of the statute and thus its contents protected. The state statutes generally define a "circulation or registration" record, with different states giving different definitions. Patron privacy is often limited to certain types of acts ("action"). In general, a "release" of patron information to a third party is prohibited, but sometimes a parent is not considered to be a third party, thus release of the patron record to a parent may not be an "action" proscribed by the statute. Most significant are the "exceptions," including the release of patron records subject to a valid search warrant, subpoena, or court order.

Institution

Q11   Is my library covered by my state's library privacy laws?

To analyze this, look at the "institution" clause in your state statute. Different states include different types of library institutions in their statutes. Most statutes contain language that protects patrons in all libraries in a given state that are "funded in whole or in part" by public funds. A number of states make an exception to general open or public records laws for library patron information, and this exception would also apply to all types of "public" libraries, those that generate public records. In addition, a few states offer expanded coverage by protecting patron privacy in all libraries that are "open to the public." And finally, several state statutes specifically apply to private libraries, often in certain restrictive categories such as schools and colleges.

Most states define "public" libraries as those funded with public resources[26] or operated by an arm of the state.[27]

A second approach is taken by several states that include a list of the specific types of "public" libraries covered by statute.[28] This may include, as in Arkansas, extending protection to "the patrons of public, school, academic, and special libraries and library systems supported in whole or in part by public funds."[29]

A third approach ties confidentiality to the public nature of library clientele, i.e., libraries open to or serving the public. For example, the Ohio law includes any library that "is open to the public," including a "library that is created and maintained by a public or private school, college, university or other educational institution."[30] Similarly, Michigan, Missouri, and Tennessee define "library" to potentially include those operated by private entities, as long as the library is "open to the public."[31] Incorporating the "open to the public" approach, North Carolina makes this clear by adding to the definition of covered libraries "or any private library open to the public."[32] The New Hampshire statute makes it clear that protection extends to users "of public or other than public libraries."[33] South Carolina includes "private" within its list of covered libraries (but the "private" library must still be "supported in whole or in part by public funds" in order to be covered by the statute).[34] Nevada uses the following language: "of a public library or other library which contain the identity of."[35] This also suggests application to libraries "other" than those merely funded in whole or in part with public monies. However, the Nevada law, section 239.013, is part of chapter 239, dealing with the public records portion of the Nevada statutes. This suggests that the record would initially be generated by a public entity and so by operation may apply only to libraries funded by public monies.

Under these or similar statutes, a library would still need to secure public funding or be open to the public, i.e., have some public nexus, in order to trigger application of the statute. Thus a parochial grade school library would not in all likelihood qualify, but a parochial school receiving state or local support through a voucher or textbook support, e-rate, or similar Internet assistance program might qualify.

New Jersey lists categories of libraries such as "a library maintained by a state or local governmental agency, school, college, or industrial, commercial or other special group, association or agency," and then adds "whether public or private,"[36] offering protection to patrons at libraries beyond the public setting. Similar to the "open to the public" language,

Illinois indicates that libraries which offer some public benefit should be covered: "any public library or library of an educational, historical, or eleemosynary institution."[37] South Carolina merely states,[38] as do a number of states,[39] that any library funded in whole or in part by public funds or one "receiving public funds"[40] is subject to the provisions of the statute.

Q12   What if it's unclear which library institutions my state's statute covers?

Either courts or administrators sometimes give further interpretations of which institutions are covered. For example, the Wisconsin statute[41] does not apply to school libraries per se, since the statute fails to list the "types" of public libraries covered by the statute. If there is no specific mention of the statute's application to public K–12 environments, either toward inclusion or exclusion, it is recommended that the state department of instruction or appropriate agency be contacted to determine if the agency has made an administrative interpretation of the statute. For example, there is an indication from the Wisconsin Department of Public Instruction that the state statute would in fact protect the privacy of K–12 students in public school settings against parental and administration inquiries.[42] Note: School library records may also be protected under the federal Family Educational Right to Privacy Act (FERPA).[43]

Another option is to seek a formal interpretation of the statute from the office of the state attorney general. This request for a formal opinion is generally made by the director of state education or instruction, the head of state library services, or by the appropriate agency head in other cases, such as the administrator of state courts for a court library.

Target Record or Information

Q13   What information about patrons, exactly, is protected by law?

A review of various states' privacy statutes reveals two approaches. The first focuses on patron *records*. The second focuses on protecting patron *information*.

Records

In the first approach, the statute indicates the *type of record* protected. "Registration and circulation" records are most common,[44] though some states limit protection to "circulation" records.[45] The heading of the

Maryland statute identifies the section as relating to "circulation records," then the text uses the language "circulation record or other item, collection, or grouping of information about an individual."[46] Both Georgia and West Virginia protect "circulation and similar records,"[47] without explicitly naming registration records. Statutes that use a particular term like "registration" or "circulation" or simply "record" but then define the contents of the record more specifically offer additional guidance, but generally result in a more limited coverage. The definition of the term "record" can be narrow, as in Pennsylvania: "[r]ecords related to the circulation of library materials which contain the names or other personally identifying details regarding the users."[48] It can be broad, as in South Dakota: "[a]ll public library records containing personally identifiable information are confidential . . . personally identifiable means any information a library maintains that would identify a patron."[49] A middle approach is taken by South Carolina: "[r]ecords related to registration and circulation of library materials which contain names or other personally identifying details regarding the users of."[50]

Some states make it clear that the term "record" is to be read broadly, protecting a wide variety of information that might be created regarding a patron. For example, both Arkansas and New York take this approach. The Arkansas statute states: "including, but not limited to, circulation of library books, materials, computer database searches, interlibrary loan transactions, reference queries, patent searches, requests for photocopies of library materials, title reserve requests, or the use of audiovisual materials, films, or records."[51] The New York statute states: "including but not limited to records related to the circulation of library materials, computer database searches, interlibrary loan transactions, reference queries, requests for photocopies of library materials, title reserve requests, or the use of audio-visual materials, films or records."[52]

A single word can make quite a difference. California takes the middle approach of protecting "registration and circulation" records. California defines "registration records" to include "any information which a library requires a patron to provide in order to become eligible to borrow books and other materials." California defines "circulation records" to include "any information which identifies the patrons borrowing particular books and other materials."[53] Some may see the term "borrowing" as more limited than the word "using." A patron's interaction with the Internet in a library is less like a "borrowing" of library material, and more of a "use" of library material. This "use" is akin to merely browsing a particular area of the library stacks, or flipping through a few magazines. The browsing or flipping is not "borrowing" in the common sense of the term; neither is it "borrowing" in librarians' view, nor in many statutes, yet browsing and flipping would surely be using a library's services or materials. Therefore, a record of patron names on sign-up lists would be neither a registration nor a circulation record in California, since a library user normally is not said to "borrow" Internet or network access. Similarly, Florida prohibits the release "in any manner [of] any information contained in such records ["registration and circulation records of every public library"]."[54] Yet the statute giveth and the statute taketh away, as the Florida statute proceeds to define registration and circulation records with the more narrow focus of "borrow" instead of "use." Furthermore, if "borrowing" can be said to be synonymous with "circulation," then it is even more limiting, since a record of a patron's request to use material from closed stacks would not be "borrowing" in a narrow sense.

Others will argue that the term "borrowing" has a broader reach, including "using." For example, if a patron takes a book off the shelf, reads it and leaves it behind, the patron has appropriated the material for his or her own use during that time.[55]

Information

The second approach focuses on protecting *information in records,* as opposed to the records themselves. This is a much broader approach, prohibiting the release of the underlying information contained in the records. Florida links the registration and circulation record to the patron "borrow[ing] books or other materials" but states that a "person may not make known in any manner any information contained in such records." Thus, if network password information is also contained in a patron's registration or circulation record or both, then the registration or circulation record as well as the password list would be protected, regardless of whether the password information itself can identify a particular individual. This might in fact occur, since a registration record might contain a patron's network password as well as his or her library card or registration number, etc. Under a reading of the Florida statute, the master password list would be protected because the passwords also appear in the registration records of patrons and the statute forbids release of "any information contained in such records."

The Maryland statute protects "any circulation record or other item, collection, or grouping of information about an individual that . . . identifies the *use* a patron makes of that library's materials, services, or facilities" (emphasis supplied).[56] It is likely that a master list of sign-ups qualifies for protection in Maryland at least as far as the "borrowing" versus "use" issue is concerned, as would other "documentation" that might indicate what stacks patrons visited or what magazines they browsed, for example, a security camera tape that records patrons' use of materials.

Confidentiality may be targeted at so-called identity information such as "name, addresses or other personal identifying information of people who have used material made available to the public by a library."[57] For example, the South Dakota statute ("All public library records containing personally identifiable information are confidential") defines "personally identifiable" as "any information a library maintains that would identify a patron."[58] Some states that use the "personally identifiable information" phrase condition protection upon the existence of the information in certain types of records such as "circulation or registration." The "record" is what is protected, but the record qualifies for protection only if it contains "any information that would identify a patron." Maryland protects a "record or other item, collection, or grouping of information about an individual that . . . contains an individual's name or identifying number, symbol, or other identifying particular assigned to the individual."[59] Thus a password, registration number, or symbol identifying that a particular patron is a senior citizen and subject to additional library services would all be protected information in Maryland.

Louisiana expands the concept of protection beyond a single person to include material "loaned to or used by an identifiable individual or group of individuals."[60] Oklahoma also provides for the protection of "records indicating which of its documents or other materials, regardless of format, have been loaned to or used by an identifiable individual or group."[61] Again, whether such an approach is broader may depend upon what triggers the underlying prohibition.

States like Florida,[62] Minnesota,[63] and Alaska[64] protect the underlying information regardless of its embodiment, as opposed to the majority of states that protect either a certain type of record or a certain type of record if it contains a certain type (personally identifying) of information. The latter statute is seemingly a compromise of the "underlying information" and "type of record" approaches, prohibiting disclosure of "*any record* or other information which identifies a person" (emphasis supplied).[65]

Neither Records nor Information:
The Power of Librarian Observation

What if a reference librarian or library page shelving books is asked what the person sitting at the table second from the window was reading during the afternoon? The librarian or page, while not compelled to do so, could reveal what he or she observed the individual reading without violating privacy statutes in many states. If the state statute uses the term "record," then the information revealed by the librarian's observation is not protected. If the statute protects "information," depending on how the statute is written, it may be protected. If in having a librarian or clerk notice that it was in fact Mr. Smith reading ABC book this afternoon, no record has been created. While library privacy statutes do not compel disclosure in such instances, the important fact is that a literal reading of such a statute that protects only "records" may not prohibit the disclosure. The result might be different if the third party asked whether the librarian or clerk could determine whom the person sitting at the second window is. It would depend on whether the prohibited disclosure focuses upon a type of record (arguably the observation of the person is not a record) or upon the release of information whether or not contained in a type of record (like a person's name). Some may argue, however, that even a librarian's memory of a record (she remembers what a patron read from a completed transaction) is protected.

The Colorado or a similar statute, for example, could be interpreted to prevent such disclosures: "shall not disclose any record or other information which identifies a person as having requested or obtained specific materials or service or as otherwise having used the library."[66] A similar result might derive from the Arizona statute, as it does "not allow disclosure of any record or other information which identifies a user of library services as requesting or obtaining specific materials or services or as otherwise using the library."[67] The recollection of the reading habit of Mr. Smith earlier in the day (ABC book) would be "other information" and it would "identif[y]" him as having "obtain[ed] specific materials or services or as otherwise [having] us[ed] the library."

Suppose a law enforcement officer came into the library, showed the librarian a picture of a man with a beard, and asked if the librarian noticed whether this patron had visited the library in the past few days. Further, the librarian is asked what the patron was observed reading. Most state privacy statutes would not prohibit such information from disclosure; the information is not contained in a record, nor could it in any sense be considered "personally identifiable." Obviously this may or may not be the level (or lack thereof) of confidentiality that most libraries would like to offer to their patrons. These problems underscore the value of having an approved (by the appropriate governing authority) confidentiality policy that protects the privacy of library and archive patrons to the extent desired (an extent often beyond the coverage provided by statute) and having staff knowledgeable as to its contents, application, and enforcement. Patrons should also be made aware of this policy as well.

Action

Q14   What acts are prohibited?

The third factor, action, considers what the library may not do. In general, this involves the actual disclosure to third parties of the protected "record" or "information."

Q15   May a library routinely print circulation receipts that reveal a
patron's name, library registration number, and the title of
the circulated items to distribute to patrons as a record of the
transaction upon check-out?

To answer this question, look first at the state statute and then at the library's own policy. Virtually all states and libraries that protect library patron confidentiality are concerned with disclosure to a third party, not the patron. What if the patron leaves the receipt in one of the items he or she returns? When the item is next checked out to another patron, the subsequent borrower of the item comes into possession of the previous patron's receipt with name, registration number, and a list of the items the patron recently borrowed. Has the library violated the statute? The answer is no, because it was the patron who left the receipt in the item upon return. This action by the patron, even if by mistake, could be construed as a consensual release of information. (Most state statutes allow for the release of information subject to patron consent; see the discussion in the following section, "Exceptions: Consent, Parents, Administrative, Court Orders, etc.") While the library arguably did not violate the privacy of the patron, sensitive information may nonetheless have been revealed. One state legislature had the foresight to anticipate the problem this might cause and requires libraries in its state to "use an automated or Gaylord-type circulation system that does not identify a patron with circulated materials after materials are returned."[68] Arguably this statute may still not prohibit the printing of circulation receipts; it just requires the use of a system that does not maintain historical circulation information.

Q16   *If a library releases a "record" containing private patron information in violation of the statute, what remedy does the patron have?*

Several states provide for specific remedies if the privacy statute is violated; the unauthorized release is a misdemeanor or petty offense.[69] Other states, which structure library patron privacy as an exception to their open records law, may subject the library to the same sort of penalty that any custodian of public records would face for the improper release of confidential information. This would depend upon the particulars of a state's open records law. For example, the *Los Angeles Times* requested a list of patron names with the largest overdue fines at the Los Angeles Public Library. When the library refused the request, the *Times* filed a public records lawsuit, and five months later the library agreed to produce a list of patrons with outstanding fines of more than $1,000.[70]

Most states, however, offer no actual remedy or punishment for a violation of a state library confidentiality statute. Regardless of this odd fact, under traditional common tort law (the law dealing with injury or harm to a person or thing), a patron would have an action for invasion of privacy against the library and record custodian. This lack of statutory punch means that the best offense a library can have in protecting patron privacy is a well-developed and implemented policy, since the after-the-fact remedy is little deterrence against unintended disclosure by inattentive or unconcerned staff.

Exceptions: Consent, Parents, Administrative, Court Orders, etc.

Q17   *What types of exceptions are typical in state confidentiality laws?*

Exceptions fall typically into three categories: consent, library administration, and criminal or civil legal proceedings. Some library confidentiality statutes contain no exceptions. However, most states do list one or more exceptions. The consent of the patron or data subject is a common exception; most states require that it be in writing. Not all states allow for a consensual release, however. A narrow though illogical reading of these statutes would lead to a conclusion that a release could not be made even with the permission of the person to whom the record or information relates. Other common exceptions are administrative: to assist the library in collecting fines or overdue materials, facilitate interlibrary loan, or maintain the normal operation of the library. Another significant type of exception relates to law enforcement matters or other legal proceedings. Typical here are exceptions for a court order or subpoena, with exceptions for a search warrant far less common. Finally, as mentioned in a preceding question, some privacy provisions are created as an exception to a state's open records law. Consequently, the exceptions for disclosure in the open records law under which private or privileged material in an open record may nonetheless be disclosed, may also apply to library records.

Consent

Consent is a problem area. Many state privacy statutes allow the release of patron records with the consent of the record subject. Many statutes require that the consent must be in writing.[71] In addition, Maine requires that the "records may only be released with the express written permission of the patron involved."[72] Mississippi also requires that the written consent be "express."[73] Montana requires the consent to be on approved library forms.[74] Michigan leaves the particulars of written consent to the library ("procedure and form of giving written consent . . . may be determined by the library").[75] New Hampshire, New Jersey, and Wisconsin allow for consent to be provided by the data subject but none requires that it be in writing.[76]

Other state statutes are silent on the issue of consent. Does this mean that information released to a third party in those states is prohibited, even when made with the consent of the record subject? Although it may seem obvious that a patron can knowingly consent to see his or her own records, it may depend on the way the statute is written.

The Circulation Standing Committee of the Library Information Network for Community Colleges in Florida researched Florida law in 1993, and found a substantial difference between the use of the terms "confidential" and "private" in that state. "Confidential" meant that the contents of the record were not available to anyone, *including the person the record represents,* unless express permission is stated within the statute. "Private" meant the individual retained inherent "rights of privacy" which prohibited others from learning about the contents of the record.[77]

If consent is not one of a statute's explicit exceptions, then the library should not allow the release of information even to a family member who wishes to pick up items placed on reserve, *even with the consent of the patron.* Another interpretation, however, would find that consent by the patron is an implied exception. Again, the efficacy of comparing one state library privacy statute to one or more dissimilar statutes is tenuous at best. The most that can be concluded is that in those states silent on the issue of consent and with no mention of any exceptions whatsoever, it is logical to imply an exception by consent of the patron. In those states with particular consent provisions, the requirements for consent must be followed.[78] Thus a state requiring consent to be in writing could not honor a phone request from spouse A to allow the library to release reserve or hold items to spouse B, even if spouse B is waiting at the check-out desk for the material.

In states that tie library privacy to open records laws,[79] it is advisable to check the conditions, if any, under which a library patron may waive protection and allow release of the record. Some states allow for a consent exception either in writing (Arizona, Arkansas, California, Colorado, Georgia, Maine, Michigan, Mississippi, Missouri, Montana, New Mexico, North Carolina, Oklahoma, Tennessee, and West Virginia) or by any means (New Hampshire, New Jersey, and Wisconsin). Other states, however, list at least one exception,[80] but fail to also indicate patron consent as one of those listed exceptions. A strict reading of such a statute may thus exclude consent as an exception, although other exceptions are included. Yet common sense allows consent, and it may be argued that it is implied as a delegation of information by the patron.

Parents and Guardians

The topic of implied consent becomes an issue when discussing the rights of parents to access the library records of their minor children. Again, some state open records laws may indicate in specific terms that parents have legal "consent" (perhaps "automatic" consent is a more descriptive but less legal phrase to use) to access any public record regarding their minor child.[81] A reading of various state statutes reveals one of three trends. First, a state may specifically grant a right of parental access.[82] Second, a statute may suggest that parents do not have an access right to the library records of minor children by specifically including "school"—and thus presumably K–12 environments where minor children abound—in the inclusion of the types of "public" libraries protected by the statute. Third, the statute may be silent on the matter, but a court or administrative agency may interpret the statute to protect the privacy rights of minors. But in addition to the parental access that may be allowed as a result of "automatic" consent language, this may still leave a category of statutes open to interpretation. Many statutes are simply silent on the matter of child versus parental rights but a court or administrative agency may interpret the statute to protect the privacy rights of minors. Courts can expand a state law by interpreting it broadly. For example, a recent New York court indicated in dicta (a dictum is an observation that a court makes that is not central to its holding or decision) that the state's privacy law would protect a child's circulation record in a public library against parental curiosity (as well as protect one spouse's record against the other).[83]

Some states limit the access right to parents alone, though most include legal guardians as well. No state makes any distinction between a custodial and a non-custodial parent. It is logical to conclude that when a library privacy statute is silent, the statute in fact protects minor children in the same way as adult patrons and the library may not release the protected information to the parent. As a practical matter, parents may be able to access this information by nature of and in the course of the daily supervisory activities of parenting, but at least the public library may not facilitate this access by releasing the information directly to the parent. Again, these statutory gaps or oversights belie the value of having a precise, articulated confidentiality policy.

Many parents assume that they can ask a public library for a listing of what items their children have currently checked out. In some states they are entitled to this information; in others they are not. The issue becomes especially thorny in libraries where the parents are deemed responsible for paying fines.

THE MICHIGAN EXPERIENCE

Michigan offers a good illustration of this dilemma. Michigan amended its law in 1996 to prohibit releases of patron information unless ordered to do so by a court (giving the library notice and the opportunity to be heard) *or* unless it has the "written consent of the person liable for payment for or return of materials identified in that library record."[84] In other words, the person who pays the bill (most likely the parent) must consent to the release of the record.

The amended law *does not require* a library to adopt a policy of disclosing the library record of a young patron even if a parent or guardian consents to such disclosure. The choice is with the library. The statute requires that the consent of the person financially responsible is needed, but this is not the same as saying that the person financially responsible has a right to see the record, although it is a logical conclusion or result, i.e., parents financially responsible may view the records of their children, since the only persons who need to consent under the statute *are* the parents. Some libraries may continue to uphold the confidentiality of the record, even when the materials involved are overdue. Other libraries may take advantage of the amendment and seek the assistance of persons who may be ultimately responsible for the return of the materials or the payment of fines or replacement costs.[85]

> Unless ordered by a court after giving the affected library notice of the request and an opportunity to be heard on the request, a library or an employee or agent of a library shall not release or disclose a library record or portion of a library record to a person without the written consent of the person liable for payment for or return of the materials identified in that library record.
>
> Library Privacy Act[86]

One strategy when registering children for library cards is to distinguish between financial responsibility (by the parent) and access to the contents of the child's records. In practice, especially with circulation systems that allow a patron to look up his or her own record, a parent may have no difficulty finding the information. Here, the library is not actively giving out the records. Another strategy is to not hold parents financially responsible. Many libraries have no fines on children's materials, and at least one holds only the child responsible, offering volunteer work if a book is lost or damaged.[87]

Q18   If the state law is silent on the issue of parental access to children's library records, what should the library do?

While a library cannot take away a parental right of access if granted by state law, a library may interpret a silent statute to include children under the umbrella of its protection. In these optional cases, how does a library balance the privacy rights of children with the family responsibilities of parents? In many libraries, parents are required to authorize (declare parental assumption of financial responsibility for damages, fines, loss, etc.) before the library issues a card to a minor patron. Parents should be informed when making such an authorization that the signature represents a promise of financial responsibility or commitment, not a right to access the record of the child. The Michigan statute allows parental access precisely because of the financial responsibility of the parent. It states that release of information may not be made "without the written consent of the person liable for payment for or return of the materials identified in that library record."[88] If a parent is identified as the individual responsible "for [the] payment . . . or return of the materials identified in that library record," then the parent would have consent by virtue of being named as the responsible party in the record. Michigan also holds parents liable for the acts of "an unemancipated minor, living with his or her parents or parent, who has maliciously or wilfully destroyed real, personal, or mixed property which belongs to the municipal corporation, county, township, village, school district, department of the state, person, partnership, corporation, association, or religious organization incorporated or unincorporated";[89] this might include damage or loss to library property. A number of states have similar statutes,[90] but Michigan is the only state with a library confidentiality statute that even suggests a parental (financial) responsibility statute might somehow trigger parents' access to the library records of their minor child. As a practical matter, since most parents control the use of their children's library card, this should not be an issue. What is important is the sense of propriety that is maintained by the library when the library is not directly involved in the release of information to parents. Parents may be able to access this information on their own through maintenance of their child's library borrowing and use activities.

Even when a state law allows parental access in its library confidentiality law, it is not always clear what is meant. Alabama and South Dakota both use the term "parent" alone,[91] while other states include "custodian" or "guardian."[92] Does that mean that in these two states a non-custodial parent would have the right to access the library records of a minor child while a custodial grandparent would not? A plain reading of the statute suggests so. This issue might also arise in the majority of states where there is no parental access provision whatsoever, but the library concludes that parents nonetheless have access, either by operation of other laws (consent vis-à-vis the open records law, for example), or by an articulated library policy. Consider the situation where a non-custodial parent wants to see a child's record, perhaps to obtain the recently changed home phone number of the ex-spouse or to stop a child from using the Internet at the library. In Wyoming, a state with a "custodial parent or guardian" clause, the non-custodial parent would not have access to the record and the library would have to honor the protection provided by the statute—no release, except to custodial parent—and this would entail the possibility of sensitive questions by the library staff in order to obtain the information necessary to enforce the statute. Having a policy that resolves these questions, whether in favor of child confidentiality or parental access, and that is consistent and not in contradiction to the statute, is encouraged.

Q19   *If my state law allows disclosure of patron information under certain conditions, do the patrons have any right to be notified and contest?*

Some statutes specifically provide for the legal right of library representation before the records are released. For example, the New Mexico statute provides that "the library shall have the right to be represented by counsel at any hearing on disclosure or release of its patron records."[93] The Michigan statute requires that before any court order may issue, a library must first be given "notice of the request [for release] and an opportunity to be heard on the request" and further that the "library may appear and be represented by counsel at a hearing" in order to determine whether the order should in fact issue.[94] In the District of Columbia, after the library receives a subpoena, the library is required to send a copy of the subpoena along with a statutorily prescribed notice to the patron to whom the subpoena relates.[95] The notice indicates that the patron has the right to challenge the subpoena. There is a delay purposely built in to allow for a patron challenge to the subpoena: "The public library shall not make available any subpoenaed materials until 10 days after the above notice has been mailed.[96]

Several states that allow for a court order exception for disclosure condition that order upon a specific requirement such as public safety. In Missouri, Nevada, and South Carolina a court order is allowed if "disclosure is necessary to protect the public safety or to prosecute a crime."[97] Ohio accomplishes a similar intention: "to law enforcement . . . investigating a matter involving public safety in exigent circumstances."[98] Montana requires the court to balance the need for release against general principles of privacy: "disclosure is necessary because the merits of public disclosure clearly exceed the demand for individual privacy."[99] In these states a challenge to the court order could be made claiming in specific terms that the impending disclosure order fails to meet the criteria set forth in the statute.

Library staff must be instructed as to the proper response or procedure that should be followed, since disclosure situations can rapidly become complicated. Legal counsel might be from two governmental authorities with overlapping jurisdictions, i.e., county district attorney (representing law enforcement) versus the city attorney's office or county corporation counsel (representing the library). It is suggested that the library director meet with the appropriate legal representative, most likely a city attorney or corporation counsel, to review the applicable statute (including its legislative history if available), current library policy if there is one, as well as applicable court or administrative rulings on the matter. Arriving at a consistent and coordinated plan of action with respect to the governing law or applicable library policy and then relaying that information to staff in the form of a formalized library procedure is also advisable for effective representation and enforcement. The library director, library staff, and legal representative must agree or have a similar understanding of the daily application of state law and implementation of library policy.

Applying Library Confidentiality Statutes in Practice

Patrick appears at the circulation desk with Josephine's library card claiming to be a family member. Does this entitle Patrick access to check out items on the hold shelf intended for Josephine? What if Patrick, a neighbor of Josephine, brings in a note signed by Josephine granting permission to Patrick to check on the status of an item on hold or check out an item? What if the library knows that Josephine is a family member of Patrick's and the family routinely dispatches one member every day to collect and bring home the hold items? Should the library accommodate the patron and allow family members to check out each other's reserve items?

Providing such access or circulating hold items to a person other than the patron (e.g., to a third party such as a family member or friend) without the informed consent of the patron violates the library privacy statutes in many states. Minnesota is the only state to allow for this situation: "to a family member or other person who resides with a library patron and who is picking up the material on behalf of the patron."[100] In contrast, Arkansas would seem to prohibit this even if family member Patrick brought in a signed note from Josephine, since the "the informed, written consent of the patron [must be] given at the time the disclosure is sought,"[101] i.e., the written consent must be made contemporaneous with the release.

It is entirely possible that giving a book on hold to a family member involves no disclosure of a patron's record. Yet the disclosure of information contained in Josephine's circulation record did occur. Even in those states that prohibit the release of any information contained in a registration or circulation record, does merely circulating a hold item to a third party violate the statute? In other words, is the circulation of a hold item construed as the release of information contained in a patron record? Arguably, it is a disclosure of circulation information or "hold-shelf" information, which may not be protected by a statute as a circulation record. It is not clear that what has been disclosed is a record, at least for those states that protect only the "record" from disclosure. It may depend on what a particular statute protects, the record itself, or the information contained in the record.

New York includes "title reserve requests" in its definition of library records.[102] In New York, the hold shelf information would be protected. Recall also that New York does not have a consent provision, so a note from Josephine would not help resolve the matter.

One way to meet patrons' needs to have others pick up their materials is to offer a "written" consent or permission form, whereby the patron indicates who may retrieve and check out hold items or pick up interlibrary loan materials. Much like a registration record at a video store that lets a customer indicate which family members may rent movies on his or her card, this consent can be incorporated into the library records. This of course is acceptable only in those states that allow for a consensual release. In those states that do not have a consent exception and protect any information in a record, is there no way to argue that the third party check-out of hold items is acceptable? Of course, one can imply consent where the statute is silent. Perhaps a library could decide to circulate hold items to a third party only if the third party specifically identified the hold item by title. The implication here is that Josephine shared the information with Patrick and that the library is revealing no information that third party Patrick (family, spouse, friend, neighbor, etc.) does not already possess. This again underscores the need to have front-line (including clerical) staff well trained so that patron privacy is not inadvertently compromised.[103]

Q20   What if faculty members would like others to pick up materials for them?

If faculty members (or others) desire this type of sharing, the library may record consent forms and comply with privacy concerns of the library or legislature as articulated in most statutes. This accommodation may depend on how strictly a statute should be read. For those states that list some exceptions, such as a court order, but do not include one for consent of the data subject,[104] a very strict reading may be that the legislature deliberately did not intend to include consent as an exception. However, others may find that consent is inherently implied: the information release has been delegated by the patron in question. The final step after adoption of a policy is the training of staff so that front-line employees are familiar with the policy and its application in the various scenarios discussed herein.

Library Administration

A second type of exception allows libraries to disclose patron information to library staff or others as needed, in what might be called an ordinary course of business exception. This might take the form of a general exception related to the daily operation of the library,[105] or it might relate to specific functions, such as interlibrary loan,[106] the collection of fines and overdue books,[107] or aggregate statistical reporting (but without personally identifiable information).[108] It could be argued that releasing fines (overdue or damaged books) information to parents is allowed. This would solve the dilemma of financial responsibility without access, but still permit routine monitoring by parents.

General exceptions for internal and external administration would allow the library to release patron information to third parties for internal business purposes, the billing of online database usage, for example. Release to third parties for the external provision of services such as interlibrary loan, where a patron's name and the item or items requested are released to another library, can also be included. In those states where a statute is silent on the matter, does that mean such releases are not allowed? It would seem logical to allow for such releases. However, deriving authorization for this form of release without specific enabling language in those states lacking such language would appear to obviate or make superfluous the purpose or existence of the same language in other states' statutes where it does in fact exist. It can be legally unsound to compare statutes from different states in terms of statutory construction (which is like comparing legal apples and oranges). Yet an overview of state statutes suggests that in cases where these sorts of administrative exceptions are not apparent, the best course of action is to include language on a library card application that allows the patron to consent by signature to these types of routine releases of patron information. It should be noted, however, that patrons may wish to consent to some information releases, and not to others. It is not a trivial problem to keep track of such preferences. In other words, do not read statutory silence on the matter of administrative-related releases as prohibiting such releases if not specifically allowed, but rather consider obtaining patron permission in writing before incorporating such releases into the ordinary course of business at the library. As a practical matter, this can be done at the time the patron registers for library privileges.

Criminal or Civil Legal Proceedings

The third major exception to the release of patron information is for matters related to a criminal investigation or other legal proceeding; this would include a warrant as part of a criminal investigation,[109] or record production via subpoena[110] or court order,[111] whether in a civil or criminal matter. A court order is some direction or command delivered by a court. A subpoena can be a writ (written court order) commanding a person to appear before a court subject to a penalty for noncompliance (contempt, for example). A warrant is a form of court order that authorizes someone to do something, such as directing a law enforcement officer to make an arrest, conduct a search, or perform a seizure (of certain library records). As a practical matter, staff need to be aware of what to do when a court order, subpoena, or warrant is served. This is the thorniest of the exceptions, and is discussed in more detail below.

Q21   What is a subpoena duces tecum?

A subpoena is a call to come before a court or other tribunal. A subpoena duces tecum (pronounced "sa-pee-na doo-sez tay-kem") is a subpoena ordering a witness to appear and to bring specified documents or records.[112] For example, a library director may be required to appear before the court and bring specified documents or records (such as the registration or circulation records of a particular patron).

Q22   My state requires a court order. Is that the same as a subpoena?

Some states require a court order, while others require either a subpoena or a court order. Although it will have a court caption and appear to be an official court document, *a subpoena is not a court order unless it is issued by the court.* A subpoena is often issued at the request of an attorney or a law enforcement officer, and may not have been reviewed by a judge. A subpoena generally does not require an immediate response, although it may require one within a few days.

Q23   Must any court order be complied with immediately?

Even the issue of compliance with a court order to release patron information may not be that apparent. Pennsylvania restricts the "court order [to those arising] in a criminal proceeding."[113] The South Carolina statute, on the other hand, clearly includes civil court orders within the reach of the court order: "judicial order . . . upon showing of good cause before the presiding Judge in a civil matter."[114] Likewise, Arkansas indicates that release may be made to a "law enforcement agency or civil court, pursuant to a search warrant."[115] Most states appear to allow the release of patron information pursuant to any "court order."[116] However, one New York state court has held that a discovery order in a civil proceeding is not sufficient to override the protection afforded by the library privacy statute, since the matter must involve an order in conjunction with a criminal case.[117] Moreover, the statute at issue in the New York case ("subpoena, court order or where otherwise required by statute")[118] failed to specify, as do most "court order" exception statutes, the type of court order, criminal or civil or either, to which the court exception applies. Yet the restriction to criminal matters only is what the New York court read into the "court order" exception. Armed with nonspecific language in a statute that fails to include civil orders, a library involved in a civil proceeding could attempt to convince the state court to adopt a similar interpretation of a similarly worded, nonspecific court order statute.

Q24   My state only requires "a lawfully issued subpoena." How do I know if it is "lawfully issued"?

There is no clear-cut answer to this, as it varies from state to state. Check with your attorney to make sure the subpoena complies with state law.

Q25   Is a search warrant a court order?

Yes. The court orders a search warrant. The execution of a search warrant can be abrupt, and effected by force or the threat of it. There generally is no legal mechanism to quash (cancel) the search warrant once the wheels are in motion.[119] Nevertheless, a library should try to get a short delay in order to have counsel present.

Q26   What should the library do if law enforcement (or someone else) comes into the library with a subpoena?

The library should inform the requester that it cannot comply without consulting an attorney.

Staff should know never to turn over any information to anyone without first referring the matter to appropriate supervisory personnel. Train "front-line" staff that although they may have to comply with a search warrant, signed by a judge, they must *always* refer a subpoena for library records to the library director, who acts as the official custodian of the records. This is essential, even if that staff member is "in charge" of a branch library, for example, and normally handles all other matters of crisis. Again, unlike a search warrant, a subpoena for records does not need immediate compliance.

In many cases, the library director should challenge the subpoena in court. This is true, even if the patron has allegedly committed a heinous crime, and the community (including the library director) wants to see the patron brought swiftly to justice.

Q27   How should the library challenge the subpoena in court?

The library's attorney should be familiar with the landmark subpoena case, *Branzburg* v. *Hayes,* in which the Supreme Court held that "grand juries must operate within the limits of the First Amendment as well as the Fifth."[120] Also critical is *United States* v. *R Enterprises,* in which the Court reaffirmed that "[g]rand juries are not licensed to engage in arbitrary fishing expeditions, nor may they select targets of investigation out of malice or an intent to harass."[121]

Supreme Court precedent offers support for a right to receive information and for a right to speak anonymously, from which the rights to read and to read anonymously are derived. The First Amendment "necessarily protects the right to receive" information. It protects the anonymity of the author, and the anonymity of members of organizations. Without the right to receive information, the right to express information can be an empty right.[122] After examining the state's confidentiality statute and the library's policy, the attorney may wish to show that patrons will be "chilled" in exercising their First Amendment rights if they believe their reading habits can be given out to law enforcement.[123] Affidavits from library personnel, library board trustees, and others can help here. Because there is a First Amendment interest, the government must show a compelling need for the information.

Some courts, applying *Branzburg*, are protective of the First Amendment in asking questions such as the following ones:[124]

(1) Is the information sought relevant to the investigation?
(2) Can the information be obtained by alternative means?
(3) Is there a compelling need for the information?

Other courts (a minority) ask whether there has been an abuse of a grand jury function, such as government harassment or bad faith.[125]

An important recent case on this issue is *Tattered Cover, Inc.* v. *City of Thornton*,[126] decided by the Supreme Court of Colorado in 2002. While it is not a library privacy case, it raises many of the same issues and concerns. Looking to its state constitution rather than the federal Constitution, the court held "that the Colorado Constitution requires that the innocent book seller be afforded a possibility for an adversarial hearing prior to execution of a search warrant seeking customer purchase records."[127] The suspect in question was suspected of engaging in the manufacture of controlled substances, since two books from the Tattered Cover stock list—*Advanced Techniques of Clandestine Psychedelic and Amphetamine Manufacture* and *The Construction and Operation of Clandestine Drug Laboratories*—were found on the premises, in addition to a mailing envelope from the Tattered Cover addressed to the suspect, who was the target of the warrant.

The court established a four-part test to determine the legality of the search warrant:

(1) Was there a legitimate and significant government interest in acquiring the information?
(2) Was there a strong nexis between the matter investigated and the material sought?
(3) Was the information available from other sources?
(4) Was the intrusion limited in scope so as to prevent exposure of other constitutionally protected matters?

The Colorado court concluded the four factors were not met, since the city "failed to demonstrate that its need for this evidence is sufficiently compelling to outweigh the harmful effects of the search warrant."[128] In its analysis the court recognized the value of anonymous speech and the right to read anonymously. It also observed the chilling effect such investigations foster and noted the lack of legal precedent in a case that involved the competing interests of free speech and the investigatory authority of law enforcement.

Q28   *What if the librarian wants to comply with the subpoena?*

Perhaps a librarian believes or has evidence that a library patron is involved in illegal activity, such as downloading child pornography. There may be situations in which a librarian believes that the public interest in disclosure outweighs the individual's interest in privacy. Law enforcement officials may be conducting legitimate investigations.

Yet, *even if the request seems legitimate,* librarians are generally well advised to ask their attorneys to quash the subpoena. The court will consider whether there is a particularized harm to First Amendment principles if the information is produced. The court will consider the following questions: Is the information relevant to the investigation? Can the information be obtained by alternative means? Is there a compelling need for the information?

A court may quash (terminate) the subpoena if it is unduly burdensome on First Amendment concerns. Alternatively, it may grant the subpoena, and the library would then be compelled to turn over the records. In either event, by challenging a subpoena, and waiting for a court order, the library is not at risk of violating the library privacy statute. Furthermore, its patrons are far less likely to feel their privacy is at risk than if the library readily turned over records on request.

Q29   *Can you give an example of a case where law enforcement successfully obtained library records?*

In *Brown* v. *Johnston,*[129] an agent of the Iowa Division of Criminal Investigation (DCI) was investigating a series of cattle mutilations. The DCI brought a subpoena duces tecum to the Des Moines Public Library, requesting library records containing the names of persons who had checked out any of sixteen titles dealing with witchcraft and related topics. The application for the subpoena did not show that the books were related to the investigation. The library and Steven Brown, a patron, sued, claiming that forced disclosure of the circulation records would chill library patrons' First Amendment rights to read and acquire information. However, the Iowa Supreme Court permitted the state to obtain the library circulation records. The court held that if a library patron's right to privacy existed, it was outweighed by the state's interest in a criminal investigation.[130] The decision of the *Brown* court has been strongly criticized by some commentators.[131]

Q30   *Can you give an example of a case where law enforcement was unsuccessful in obtaining library records?*

A police officer served a librarian with a subpoena in Decatur, Texas, in a child abandonment case. The subpoena directed the library to find the names of all patrons who had borrowed books on child bearing in the previous nine months. The library challenged the subpoena in court, and succeeded because the court found no compelling need or nexus.[132]

Q31   *My library belongs to a consortium, and I'm concerned that my patrons' records are out of my control. How can I ensure that each library in the consortium adheres to the same privacy guarantees that my library does?*

This is a tough issue. One should be aware that consortia need to adopt privacy policies just as do individual libraries.[133] Consortia that have all their members in the same legal jurisdiction need only wrestle with the privacy policies that their individual institutions use to supplement legislation. The American Library Association recommends a policy on the confidentiality of library records that all types of libraries and consortia can use as a start. It also has a recommended policy on the confidentiality of personally identifiable information about library users. At a minimum, there arises an ethical obligation to tell patrons who might otherwise be unaware of it that their records are shared, as needed, with consortia members.

Q32   *What does the American Library Association recommend when drafting a library confidentiality policy?*

The American Library Association has a wealth of information on its website, http://www.ala.org, that helps librarians draft policies, including the ALA's "Policy on Confidentiality of Library Records" at http://www.ala.org/alaorg/oif/policyconfidentiality.pdf.[134]

CONCLUSION

A variety of laws protect the privacy of library and archive patrons. The federal PATRIOT Act has made it easier for federal law enforcement to obtain court orders for a wide range of information, including library records. State laws protect library patron records, and a careful review of the governing state statute in conjunction with reviewing or implementing a library's privacy policy is recommended.

First, the library should be proactive. The director should meet with the library's legal counsel from time to time to discuss possible courses of action in various legal scenarios, not just privacy, but censorship, patron behavior problems, etc. In the matter of patron privacy, this helps to prepare the director as the responsible legal custodian of the record or information. During these meetings, it is advisable to review the statute, policy, and library codes of ethics under which a particular policy may operate. This provides the library with an opportunity to have its legal representative understand the context (professional culture) of concern in these matters. Relate this information to staff and indicate to them what your decided plan of action will be in these situations so everyone acts in a consistent matter. Often the public is unaware of the restrictions imposed by the applicable state statute or the library's privacy policy. This may lead to misunderstandings or discomfort among patrons, parents, etc. Having the staff prepared to answer and briefly explain the restrictions and options that may exist can diffuse a problem situation or serve as an educational opportunity for the library. At this time the staff may be able to offer the patrons several options, including the opportunity to sign a consent form that allows family members to pick up items on hold. Alternatively, a parent should not allow a child to have his or her own card if the parent is uncomfortable with a statute that also protects the privacy of minor children.

There is great variation among state library privacy statutes, and one statute does not fit all situations. Although a library cannot contradict a provision in a state statute (override a parental right of access explicitly granted in a statute, for example), it may be able to clarify what sorts of records and persons are protected and how the statute would operate in specific situations, indicating the conditions under which written consent will be accepted. A well-articulated policy can also provide staff with a valuable tool in protecting the privacy rights of patrons, as it assists in the staff's understanding of the potential nuances in application of a state statute. Depending on the wording of a particular applicable statute, the library may desire to protect other types of records under its own policy in addition to the types of records (circulation and registration records only, as opposed to any record containing patron information) protected by statute. In this way, a library policy may supplement the protection provided by a state library statute. Finally, libraries should disclose their privacy policies to their patrons. It is suggested that all policies be reviewed and authorized by the responsible legal representative and governing board or body of a library before implementation.

APPENDIX

State Library Confidentiality Statutes

State/Statute(s)	Protection	Significant Exceptions
Alabama Ala. Code §36-12-40 (2000); §41-8-10 (2000)	"registration and circulation records and information concerning the use of the . . . libraries of this state"	"any parent of a minor child shall have the right to inspect the registration and circulation records of any school or public library that pertains to his or her child"
Alaska Alaska Stat. §40.25.140 (2000)	"names, addresses, or other personal identifying information of people who have used materials made available to the public by a library"	"records of a public elementary or secondary school library identifying a minor child . . . to a parent or guardian of that child"; court order
Arizona Ariz. Rev. Stat. §41-1354 (2000)	"any record or other information which identifies a user of library services as requesting or obtaining specific materials or services or otherwise using the library"	court order; written consent; "necessary for the reasonable operation of the library"
Arkansas Ark. Code Ann. §§13-2-701–704 (1999)	"library records which contain the names or other personally identifying details regarding the patrons"	"informed, written consent"; "law enforcement agency or civil court, pursuant to a search warrant"

State/Statute(s)	Protection	Significant Exceptions
California Cal. Gov't Code §6267 (2000)	"all registration and circulation records" "'registration records' includes any information which a library requires a patron to provide in order to become eligible to borrow books and other material and the term 'circulation records' includes any information which identifies the patrons borrowing particular books and other material"	"authorized, in writing"; "order of the appropriate superior court"; "a person acting within the scope of his or her duties within the administration of the library"
Colorado Colo. Rev. Stat. §24-90-119 (2000)	"any record or other information which identifies a person as having requested or obtained specific materials or service or as otherwise having used the library"	"written consent"; "subpoena, upon court order"; "necessary for the reasonable operation of the library"
Connecticut Conn. Gen. Stat. §11-25 (1999)	"personally identifiable information contained in the circulation records of all public libraries"	none
Delaware Del. Code Ann. tit. 29, §10002(d)(12) (2000)	"any records of a public library which contain the identity of a user and the books, documents, films, recordings or other property of the library which a patron has used"	none listed, but part of open records laws, so general exceptions may apply
District of Columbia D.C. Code Ann. §37-106.2 (1999)	"circulation records . . . which can be used to identify a library patron who has requested, used, or borrowed identified library material . . . and the specific material that patron has requested, used, or borrowed"	written permission of the affected library patron; court order, but requires notice to the record sent to the record subject, but court may waive notice requirement pursuant to §37-106.2(b)(6)(A)–(C); "proper operation of the public library"

State/Statute(s)	Protection	Significant Exceptions
Florida Fla. Stat. Ann. §257.261 (1999)	"registration and circulation records"; "a person may not make known in any manner any information contained in such records"	"may only release confidential information relating to the parent or guardian of the person under 16"; "does not prohibit . . . disclosing information to municipal or county law enforcement officials, or to judicial officials, for the purpose of recovering overdue books, documents, films, or other items or materials . . . " similar release allowed for the "purpose of collecting fines or overdue books, documents . . ."
Georgia Ga. Code Ann. §24-9-46 (2000)	"circulation and similar records of a library which identify the user of library materials"	written consent; court order or subpoena; "to members of the library staff in the ordinary course of business"
Hawaii Haw. Rev. Stat. §92F-13 (2000)	no specific library provision, but government records law exempts "records which, if disclosed, would constitute a clearly unwarranted invasion of personal privacy"	no specific library provisions, but general exceptions may apply
Idaho Idaho Code §9-340E (2000)	"records of a library which, when examined alone, or when examined with other public records, would reveal the identity of the library patron checking out, requesting, or using an item"	none
Illinois 75 Ill. Comp. Stat. 70/1 (2001)	"registration and circulation records" registration: "any information a library requires a person to provide . . ." circulation: "all information identifying the individual borrowing particular books or materials"	court order; "reasonable statistical reports regarding library registration and book circulation . . . so that no individual is identified therein"

State/Statute(s)	Protection	Significant Exceptions
Indiana Ind. Code Ann. §5-14-3-4(b)(16) (2001)	"library or archival records which can be used to identify any library patron"	none listed, but part of open records law, so general exceptions may apply
Iowa Iowa Code §22.7(13) (1999)	"records of a library which, by themselves or when examined with other public records, would reveal the identity of the library patron checking out or requesting an item or information from the library"	none listed, but part of open records law, so general exceptions may apply
Kansas Kan. Stat. Ann. §45-221(23) (1999)	"library patron and circulation records which pertain to identifiable individuals"	none listed, but part of open records law, so general exceptions may apply
Kentucky 81 Op. Att'y Gen. Ky. 159 (1981)*	no statute, but attorney general opinion indicates that state privacy law would protect circulation and registration records	none indicated
Louisiana La. Rev. Stat. §44:13 (2000)	". . . indicating which of its documents or other materials regardless of format, have been loaned to or used by an identifiable individual or group of individuals"	"to a parent or custodian of a minor child seeking access to that child's records"; overdue and fines collection
Maine Me. Rev. Stat. Ann. tit. 27, §121 (1999)	"that contain information relating to the identity of a court order library patron relative to the patron's use of books or other materials at the library"	"express written permission";

State/Statute(s)	Protection	Significant Exceptions
Maryland Md. State Gov't Code Ann. §10-616 (1999); Md. Educ. Code Ann. §23-107 (1999)	"prohibit inspection, use, or disclosure of any circulation record or other item, collection, or grouping of information about an individual that"; "maintained by a library"; "contains an individual's name or the identifying number, symbol, or other identifying particular assigned to the individual," and "identifies the use a patron makes of that library's materials, services or facilities"	"circulation record of an individual only in connection with the library's ordinary business and only for the purpose for which the record was created"
Massachusetts Mass. Ann. Laws chap. 78, §7 (2000)	"records of a public library which reveal the identity and intellectual pursuits of a person using such library"	"inter-library cooperation and coordination"
Michigan Mich. Comp. Laws §397.601 et seq. (2001)**	"library record, which means a document, record, or other method of storing information retained by a library that contains information that personally identifies a library patron"	"written consent of the person liable for payment for or return of the materials identified in the library record"; court order, but requires notice be given to the library with a right "to be heard" and "be represented by counsel"
Minnesota Minn. Stat. §13.40 (1998)	"data that link a library patron's name with materials requested or borrowed or that link a patron's name with a specific subject about which the patron has requested information or materials"; "data in applications for borrower cards"	"to a family member or other person who resides with a library patron and who is picking up the material on behalf of the patron"; court order; "library purposes"
Mississippi Miss. Code Ann. §39-3-365 (2000)	"relating to the identity of a library user, relative to the user's use of books or other or other materials"	"express written consent"; court order

State/Statute(s)	Protection	Significant Exceptions
Missouri Mo. Rev. Stat. §§182.815–817 (1999)**	"any document, records, or other method of storing information retained, received or generated by a library that identifies a person or persons as having requested, used, or borrowed library material, and all other records identifying the names of library users"	"written request"; "order issued by a court . . . necessary to protect the public safety or to prosecute a crime";
Montana Mont. Code Ann. §22-1-1101 to -1103 (2001)	"document, record, or any other method of storing information retained, or received or generated by a library that identifies a person or person as having requested, used, or borrowed library material, or other records identifying the names or other personal identifiers of library users"	"written request"; "order issued by a court . . . necessary because the merits of public disclosure clearly exceed the demand for individual privacy"; "overdue or stolen materials or collect fines"
Nebraska Neb. Rev. Stat. §84-712.05(10) (2000)	"records or portions of records kept by a publicly funded library which, when examined with or without other records, reveal the identity of any library patron using the library's materials or services"	none listed, but part of open records law, so general exceptions may apply
Nevada Nev. Rev. Stat. Ann. §239.013 (2000)**	"any records of a public library or other which contain the identity of a user and the books, documents, films, recordings or other library property of the library which he used"	"order issued by a court upon a finding that the disclosure of such records is necessary to protect the public safety or to prosecute a crime"
New Hampshire N.H. Rev. Stat. Ann. §201-D:11 (2000)**	"library records which contain the names or other personal identifying information regarding the users of public or other than public libraries"	consent of the user; subpoena; court order; "necessary for the proper operation of such library"

State/Statute(s)	Protection	Significant Exceptions
New Jersey N.J. Stat. §18A:73-43.1 and .2 (2000)**	"document or record, how-ever maintained, the primary purpose of which is to provide for control of circulation or other public use of library material"; "which contain the names or other personally identifying details regarding the users"	subpoena issued by a court; court order; requested by user; "necessary for the proper operation of the library"
New Mexico N.M. Stat. Ann. §18-9-4 to -5 (2000)	"patron records shall not be disclosed or released"	"written consent"; court order; ("library shall have the right to be represented at any hearing on disclosure or release of its patron records") by school libraries to the "legal guardian of the patron records of unemancipated minors"
New York N.Y. C.P.L.R. §4509 (2000)	"records which contain names or other personally identifying details regarding the users of . . . including but not limited to records related to the circulation of library materials"	subpoena; court order; "to the extent necessary for the proper operation of such library"
North Carolina N.C. Gen. Stat. §125-18 and -19 (2000)**	"library record (document, record, or other method of storing information retained by a library) that identifies a person as having requested or obtained specific materials, information, or services or as otherwise having used the library"	"written consent of the user"; subpoena; court order; "or where otherwise required by law" "necessary for the reasonable operation of the library"; "nonidentifying material that may be retained for the purpose of studying or evaluating the circu-lation of library materials in general"
North Dakota N.D. Cent. Code §40-38-12 (2000)	"record maintained or received by a library receiving public	court order; subpoena

State/Statute(s)	Protection	Significant Exceptions
North Dakota (Cont'd)	funds, which provides a library patron's name or information sufficient to identify a patron together with the subject about which the patron requested information"	
Ohio Ohio Rev. Code Ann. 149.432 (2001)**	"record in any form . . . that contains any of the following types of information: . . . requires an individual to provide in order to be eligible to use . . . or borrow . . . identifies an individual as having requested or obtained specific materials or materials on a particular subject . . . provided by an individual to assist a library staff member to answer a specific question or provide information on a particular subject"	"library record information pertaining to a minor child is requested from a library by the minor child's parent, guardian, or custodian"; subpoena; search warrant; court order; "to law enforcement . . . investigating a matter involving public safety in exigent circumstances"
Oklahoma Okla. Stat. tit. 65, §1-105 (1999)	"having records indicating which of its documents or other materials, regardless of format, have been loaned to or used by an identifiable individual or group"	"persons authorized to inspect such records, in writing, by the individual or group"; by order of a court of law; "within the scope of their duties in the administration of the library" possible middle and elementary school exception
Oregon Or. Rev. Stat. §§192.501 and .502 (1999); 41 Op. Att'y Gen. Or. 435 (1981)	"records of a library, including circulation records, showing use of specific library material by a named person or consisting of the name of a library patron together with the address or telephone number, or both of the patron"	none listed, but part of open records law, so general exceptions may apply

State/Statute(s)	Protection	Significant Exceptions
Pennsylvania 24 Pa. Cons. Stat. §4428 (1999)	"records related to the circulation of library materials which contain the names or other personally identifying details regarding the users"	"court order in a criminal proceeding"
Rhode Island R.I. Gen. Laws §38-2-2(4)(u) (2000)	"library records which by themselves or when examined with other public records, would reveal the identity of the library user requesting, checking out, or using any library materials"	none listed, but part of open records law, so general exceptions may apply
South Carolina S.C. Code Ann. §60-4-10 (1999)	"records related to registration and circulation of library materials which contain names or other personally identifying details regarding the users . . . records which by themselves or when examined with other public records would reveal the identity of the library patron checking out or requesting an item from the library or using other library services"	"persons authorized by the library patron" "judicial order upon a finding that the disclosure of the records is necessary to protect public safety, to prosecute a crime, or upon showing of good cause before the presiding Judge in a civil matter" "scope of their duties in the administration of the library or library system"
South Dakota S.D. Codified Laws §14-2-51 (2001)	"all public library records containing personally identifiable information are confidential . . . any information contained in public library records may not be released"; "'personally identifiable' means any information a library maintains that would identify a patron"	"upon request of a parent of a child who is under eighteen years of age"; court order

State/Statute(s)	Protection	Significant Exceptions
Tennessee Tenn. Code Ann. §§10-8-101 and 102 (2000)**	"record means a document, record, or other method of storing information retained by a library that identifies a person as having requested or obtained specific information or materials from such library"	"written consent"; order of a court; "to seek reimbursement for or the return of lost, stolen, misplaced or otherwise overdue library materials"
Texas Att'y Gen. Texas, Open Rec. Dec. No. 100 (July 10, 1975)	no statute, but attorney general opinion indicates that state privacy laws would protect library circulation records	none indicated
Utah Utah Code Ann. §63-2-302 (2000)	"records of publicly funded libraries that when examined alone or with other records identify a person"	none listed, but part of open records laws, so general exceptions may apply
Vermont Vt. Stat. Ann. tit. 1, §317(c)(19) (2000)	"records relating to the identity of library patrons or the identity of library patrons in regards to the circulation of library materials"	none listed, but part of open records laws, so general exceptions may apply
Virginia Va. Code Ann. §2.1-342.01 (2000)	"library records which can be used to identify both (i) any library patron who has borrowed material from a library and (ii) the material such patron borrowed"	none listed, but part of open records laws, so general exceptions may apply
Washington Wash. Rev. Code Ann. §42.17.310- (1)(l) (1999)	"any library record, the primary purpose of which is to maintain control of library materials, or to gain access to information, which dis- closes or could disclose the identity of a library user"	none listed, but part of open records laws, so general exceptions may apply

State/Statute(s)	Protection	Significant Exceptions
West Virginia W. Va. Code Ann. §10-1-22 (2000)	"circulation and similar records . . . which identify the user of library materials"	"written consent of the user of the library materials or the user's parents or guardian if the user is a minor or ward"; court order; subpoena; "to members of the library staff in the ordinary course of business"
Wisconsin Wis. Stat. §43.30 (2000)	"records . . . indicating the identity of any individual who borrows or uses the library's documents or other materials, resources or services"	court order; "persons acting within the scope of their duties in the administration of the library"; "persons authorized by the individual"
Wyoming Wyo. Stat. §16-4-203(d)(ix)	"library circulation and registration records"	"as requested by a custodial parent or guardian to inspect the records of his minor child" "administration of the library"

* "We think that the individual's privacy rights as to what he borrows from a public library (books, motion picture film, periodicals and any other matter) is overwhelming. In fact we can see no public interest at all to put in the scales opposite the privacy rights of the individual. We would point out, however, that Kentucky has no privacy statute and that the exceptions to mandatory disclosure of public records are permissive and no law is violated if they are not observed by the custodian. In summary, it is our opinion that the custodian of the registration and circulation records of a public library is not required to make such records available for public inspection under the Open Records Law." 81 Op. Att'y Gen. Ky. 159 (1981).

** A statute may apply to libraries beyond merely "public" ones or those supplied with public monies or funds. *See* Mich. Stat. Ann. §15.1795(2)(h) (1999) ("or any private library open to the public"); Mo. Rev. Stat. §182.815 (1999) ("private library open to the public"); Nev. Rev. Stat. Ann. §239.013 (2000) ("public library or other library"); N.H. Rev. Stat. Ann. §201-D:11 (2000) ("regarding the users of public or other than public libraries"); N.J. Stat. Ann. §18A:73-43.1 (2000) ("whether public or private"); N.C. Gen. Stat. §125-18 (1999) ("or any private library open to the public"); H.R. 389, 1999 Leg. (Ohio 2000) ("open to the public"); Tenn. Code Ann. §10-8-101 (2000) ("any private library that is open to the public").

Notes

1. For a close look at digital monitoring in copyright management systems and its effect on the right to read anonymously, *see* Julie E. Cohen, *A Right to Read Anonymously: A Closer Look at "Copyright Management" in Cyberspace*, 28 CONNECTICUT LAW REVIEW 981 (SUMMER 1996).

2. See *Griswold v. Connecticut*, 381 U.S. 479 (1965).

3. U.S. CONST. amend. IV.

4. U.S. CONST. amend. IX.

5. U.S. CONST. amend. X. *See* Michael C. Dorf, *SUPREME COURT 4— CONGRESS 0: How the Court Has Rejected Congress's View of Civil Rights in Four Recent Cases*, FINDLAW'S LEGAL COMMENTARY, March 21, 2001, *at* http://writ.news.findlaw.com/dorf/20010321.html (visited Feb. 24, 2002).

6. Pub. L. No. 107-56, 115 Stat. 272 (2001).

7. 50 U.S.C. §§1801–1863.

8. Jennifer C. Evans, *Hijacking Civil Liberties: The USA PATRIOT Act of 2001*, 33 LOYOLA UNIVERSITY OF CHICAGO LAW JOURNAL 933, 972 (2002).

9. Section 215 of the PATRIOT Act deletes the current §§501–503 of 50 U.S.C. and replaces them with new §§501 and 502.

10. 50 U.S.C. §§501–502.

11. See ALA. CODE §36-12-40 and §41-8-10 (2000); ALASKA STAT. §40.25.140 (2000); ARIZ. REV. STAT. §41-1354 (2000); ARK. CODE ANN. §§13-2-701 to -704 (1999); CAL. GOV'T CODE §6267 (2000); COLO. REV. STAT. §24-90-119 (2000); CONN. GEN. STAT. §11-25 (1999); DEL. CODE ANN. tit. 29, §10002(d)(12) (2000); D.C. CODE ANN. §37-106.2 (1999); FLA. STAT. ANN. §257.261 (1999); GA. CODE ANN. §24-9-46 (2000); HAW. REV. STAT. §92F-13 (2000); IDAHO CODE §9-340E (2000); 75 ILL. COMP. STAT. 70/1 (1999); IND. CODE ANN. §5-14-3-4(b)(16) (2000); IOWA CODE §22.7(13) (1999); KAN. STAT. ANN. §45-221(23) (1999); LA. REV. STAT. §44:13 (2000); ME. REV. STAT. ANN. tit. 27, §121 (1999); MD. STATE GOV'T CODE ANN. §10-616 and §23-107 (1999); MASS. ANN. LAWS ch. 78, §7 (2000); MICH. COMP. LAWS §397.601 et seq. (2001); MINN. STAT. §13.40 (2000); MISS. CODE ANN. §39-3-365 (2000); MO. REV. STAT. §§182.815 to .817 (1999); MONT. CODE ANN. §§22-1-1101 to -1103 (2000); NEB. REV. STAT. §84-712.05(10) (2000); NEV. REV. STAT. ANN. §239.013 (2000); N.H. REV. STAT. ANN. §201-D:11 (2000); N.J. STAT. §§18A:73-43.1 AND .2 (2000); N.M. STAT. ANN. §§18-9-4 AND -5 (2000); N.Y. C.P.L.R. §4509 (2000); N.C. GEN. STAT. §§125-18 and -19 (1999); N.D. CENT. CODE §40-38-12 (2000); OHIO REV. CODE ANN. 149.432; OKLA. STAT. tit. 65, §1-105 (1999); OR. REV. STAT. §192.501 (1999); 24 PA. CONS. STAT. §4428 (1999); R.I. GEN. LAWS §38-2-2(4)(u) (2000); S.C. CODE ANN. §60-4-10 (1999); S.D. CODIFIED LAWS §14-2-51 (2000); TENN. CODE ANN. §§10-8-101 and -102 (2000); UTAH CODE ANN. §63-2-302 (2000); VT. STAT. ANN. tit. 1, §317(c)(19) (2000); VA. CODE ANN. §2.1-342.01(A)(10) (2000); WASH. REV. CODE ANN. §42.17.310(1)(l) (2000); W. VA. CODE ANN. §10-1-22 (2000); WIS. STAT. §43.30 (1999); WYO. STAT. §16-4-203(d)(ix) (2000).

12. 81 Op. Att'y Gen. Ky. 159 (1981); Att'y Gen. Texas, Open Rec. Dec. No. 100 (July 10, 1975).

13. See, e.g., DEL. CODE ANN. tit. 29, §10002(d)(12) (2000); IND. CODE ANN. §5-14-3-4 (b)(16) (2000); IOWA CODE §22.7(13) (1999).

14. First tier (Top 10): California, Connecticut, Florida, Hawaii, Illinois, Massachusetts, Minnesota, New York, Rhode Island, Wisconsin. Second tier (14 states): Alaska (close to the Top 10), Arizona, Colorado, Georgia, Maine, Maryland, Montana, Nevada, Ohio, Oklahoma, Oregon, Utah, Virginia, Washington. Third tier (5 states): Indiana, Michigan, New Jersey, New Mexico, Pennsylvania. Fourth tier (17 states, plus the District of Columbia): Alabama, Arkansas, Delaware, Iowa, Kansas, Kentucky, Louisiana, Mississippi, Nebraska, New Hampshire, North Carolina, North Dakota, South Dakota, Tennessee, Vermont, West Virginia, Wyoming. Not on the radar screen (4 states): Idaho, Missouri, South Carolina, Texas. *Compilation of State and Federal Privacy Laws,* PRIVACY LAW JOURNAL (1997, with 2000 supplement); findings summarized *at* http://www.townonline.com/specials/privacy/ under "Ranking of the States" (visited April 29, 2001).

15. The interplay of privacy and open records laws is surveyed and discussed in Shirley A. Wiegand, LIBRARY RECORDS: A RETENTION AND CONFIDENTIALITY GUIDE (1994).

16. *James M. Knight v. School Administrative Unit #16,* No. 00-E-307, Rockingham (S.S. Super. Ct. N.H.). See *Exeter Internet Ruling, Complete Ruling,* PORTSMOUTH HERALD, Jan. 8, 2001, *at* http://www.seacoastonline.com/news/1_8specialhtm (visited April 30, 2001); ESchool news staff and wire service reports, *Court: Schools Must Let Parents View Internet-Use Logs* (Nov. 20, 2000), *at* http://www.eschoolnews.org (visited April 30, 2001).

17. For example, see *In re Subpoena Duces Tecum to America Online, Inc.,* 52 Va. Cir. 26 (2000).

18. *See* Electronic Privacy Information Center (EPIC) Freedom of Information Request (Jan. 16, 2001), *at* http://www.epic.org/open_gov/dodfoian2h2.html (visited April 30, 2001).

19. *Quad/Graphics, Inc. v. Southern Adirondack Library System,* 664 N.Y.S.2d 225, 227 (1997).

20. N.Y. C.P.L.R. §4509.

21. *Quad/Graphics, Inc.,* 664 N.Y.S.2d at 227.

22. WIS. STAT. §43.30 (1999); compare MONT. CODE ANN. §22-1-1101 (2000) ("document, record, or any other method of storing information retained, or received or generated by a library that identifies a person or persons"); NEV. REV. STAT. ANN. §239.013 (2000) ("any records of a public library or other which contain the identity of a user").

23. See, e.g., ARIZ. REV. STAT. §41-1354 (2000) ("identifies a user"); COLO. REV. STAT. §24-90-119 (2000) ("identifies a person"); D.C. CODE ANN. §37-106.2 (1999) ("can be used to identify a library patron"); N.D. CENT. CODE §40-38-12 (2000) ("or information sufficient to identify a patron together with the subject about which"); S.D. CODIFIED LAWS §14-2-51 (2000) ("any information that would identify

a patron"); VT. STAT. ANN. tit. 1, §317(c)(19) (2000) ("records relating to the identity of library patrons"); W. VA. CODE §10-1-22 (2000) ("records . . . which could identify the user of library materials").

24. OR. REV. STAT. §192.502(22) (1999).

25. *See* 41 Op. Att'y Gen. Or. 435 (1981) (interpreting Or. Rev. Stat. §192.501 (1999).

26. See, e.g., ARIZ. REV. STAT. §41-1354 (2000) ("a library or library system supported by public monies"); CAL. GOV'T CODE §6267 (2000) ("any library which is in whole or in part supported by public funds"); COLO. REV. STAT. §24-90-119 (2000) ("publicly supported library or library system"); N.D. CENT. CODE §40-38-12 (2000) ("a library receiving public funds"); OKLA. STAT. tit. 65, §1-105 (1999) ("any library which is in whole or in part supported by public funds"); S.C. CODE ANN. §60-4-10 (1999) ("supported in whole or in part by public funds").

27. See, e.g., ALASKA STAT. §40.25.140 (2000) ("libraries operated by the state, a municipality, or a public school, including the University of Alaska"); 24 PENN. CONS. STAT. §4428 (1999) ("the State Library or any local library which is established or maintained under any law of the Commonwealth or the library of any university, college or educational institution chartered by the Commonwealth or the library of any public school or branch reading room, deposit station or agency operated in connection therewith").

28. 75 ILL. COMP. STAT. 70/1 (1999) ("any public library or library of an educational, historical or eleemosynary institution"); LA. REV. STAT. §44:13 (2000) ("in whole or in part supported by public funds, including the records of public, academic, school, and special libraries, and the State Library of Louisiana"); MONT. CODE ANN. §22-1-1102 (2000) ("a library that is established by the state, a county, city, town, school district, or a combination of those units of government, a college or university").

29. ARK. CODE ANN. §13-2-703(a) (1999).

30. OHIO REV. CODE ANN. 149.432.

31. MICH. COMP. LAWS §397.601 (2001) ("any private library open to the public"); MO. REV. STAT. §182.815 (1999) ("private library open to the public"); TENN. CODE ANN. §10-8-101 (2000) ("any private library that is open to the public").

32. N.C. GEN. STAT. §125-18 (1999). See also MO. REV. STAT. §182.815 (1999) ("private library open to the public").

33. N.H. REV. STAT. ANN. §201-D:11 (2000).

34. S.C. CODE ANN. §60-4-10 (1999) ("supported in whole or in part by public funds or expending public funds").

35. NEV. REV. STAT. ANN. §239.013 (2000).

36. N.J. STAT. §18A:73-43.1 (2000).

37. 75 ILL. COMP. STAT. 70/1 (1999).

38. S.C. CODE ANN. §60-4-10 (1999).

39. See, e.g., ARK. CODE ANN. §13-2-703 (1999); CAL. GOV'T CODE §6267 (2000); WIS. STAT. §43.30 (1999).

40. N.D. CENT. CODE §40-38-12 (2000).

41. WIS. STAT. §43.30 (1999).

42. *See* Robert J. Paul, *Access: Statutes Outline Requirements Regarding School Library Circulation Records*, EDUCATION FORWARD, August 1991, at 17 ("In a previous departmental legal opinion in 1984, DPI [Department of Public Instruction] counsel concluded as a threshold matter that this statute applied to school libraries because they are supported by public funds and there was no language suggesting exclusion of school libraries. . . In summary, §43.30, WIS. STAT., allows only library employees acting within the scope of their duties access to individual identifying library circulation records and general public school administrative personnel, teachers and others, may have access to non-individual identifying circulation information. Parents may not have access to the historic individual circulation records of their children."). *See also* Donald Lamb, *Library Circulation Records Must Protect Privacy of Borrowers*, CHANNEL DLS, October 1989, at 5 (making reference to an opinion issued by the Wisconsin attorney general's office) ("Only school library and public library administrators—not school or municipal administrators—and persons granted permission by the borrower or ordered by a court of law may inspect a public or school library's circulation records").

43. Family Educational Rights and Privacy Act (FERPA), 34 C.F.R. pt. 99 (as amended July 6, 2000). See also 20 U.S.C. §1232g (2001).

44. See, e.g., ALA. CODE §36-12-40 and §41-8-10 (2000); CAL. GOV'T CODE §6267 (2000); FLA. STAT. ANN. §257.261 (1999) 75 ILL. COMP. STAT. 70/1 (1999).

45. See, e.g., CONN. GEN. STAT. §11-25 (1999); D.C. CODE ANN. §37-106.2 (1999). See also KAN. STAT. ANN. §45-221(23) (1999) ("library patron and circulation records"); OR. REV. STAT. §§192.501 and .502 (1999) ("records of a library, including circulation records"); WYO. STAT. ANN. §16-4-203(d)(ix) (2000).

46. MD. STATE GOV'T CODE ANN. §23-107 (1999).

47. GA. CODE ANN. §24-9-46 (2000); W. VA. CODE §10-1-22 (2000).

48. 24 PA. CONS. STAT. §4428 (1999).

49. S.D. CODIFIED LAWS §14-2-51 (2000).

50. S.C. CODE ANN. §60-4-10 (1999).

51. ARK. CODE ANN. §13-2-703(A) (1999).

52. N.Y. C.P.L.R. §4509 (2000).

53. CAL. GOV'T CODE §6267 (2000). See also 75 ILL. COMP. STAT. 70/1 (1999) ("circulation records include all information identifying the individual borrowing particular books or materials").

54. FLA. STAT. ANN. §257.261 (1999).

55. "Borrow" is defined as "1. to receive with the implied or expressed intention of returning the same or an equivalent. 2. To appropriate for one's own use." WEBSTER'S SEVENTH NEW COLLEGIATE DICTIONARY 98 (1971).

56. MD. EDUC. CODE ANN. §23-107 (1999).

57. ALASKA STAT. §40.25.140 (2000).

58. S.D. CODIFIED LAWS §14-2-51 (2000).

59. MD. EDUC. CODE ANN. §23 -107 (1999).

60. LA. REV. STAT. §44:13 (2000).

61. OKLA. STAT. tit. 65, §1-105 (1999).

62. FLA. STAT. ANN. §257.261 ("known in any manner any information contained in such records," but then limits protection to "registration and circulation" records).

63. MINN. STAT. §143.40 (1998) ("the following data ["data that link a library patron's name with materials requested or borrowed or that link a patron's name with a specific subject about which the patron has requested information or materials"] maintained by a library are private data on individuals and may not be disclosed for other than library purposes").

64. ALASKA STAT. §40.25.140 (2000) ("the names, addresses, or other personal identifying information of people who have used materials made available to the public by a library shall be kept confidential").

65. COLO. REV. STAT. §24-90-119 (2000). See also, e.g., ARIZ. REV. STAT. §41-1354 (2000) ("record or other information which identifies a user"); COLO. REV. STAT. §24-90-119 (2000) (any record of other information which identifies a person"); DEL. CODE ANN. tit. 29, §10002(d)(12) (2000) ("any records of a public library which contain the identity of a user "); GA. CODE ANN. §24-9-46 (2000) (circulation and similar records which identify the user of library materials"); KAN. STAT. ANN. §45-221(23) (1999) ("library patron and circulation records which pertain to identifiable individuals").

66. COLO. REV. STAT. §24-90-119 (2000).

67. ARIZ. REV. STAT. §41-1354 (2000).

68. ARK. CODE ANN. §13-2-703(A).

69. ARIZ. REV. STAT. §41-1354 (2000) ("class 3 misdemeanor"); COLO. REV. STAT. §24-90-119 (2000) ("class 2 petty offense" and up to a $300 fine); FLA. STAT. ANN. §257.261 (1999) ("misdemeanor of the second degree").

70. Richard Winton, Books: *Others Turn to Bill Collectors and Threats of Public Humiliation, but City System Has Lagged Behind,* LOS ANGELES TIMES, July 30, 2000, at A1.

71. See, e.g., ARIZ. REV. STAT. §41-1354 (2000) ("written consent of the user"); ARK. CODE ANN. §13-2-704 (1999) ("with the informed, written consent of the patron given at the time the disclosure is sought"); CAL. GOV'T CODE §6267 (2000) ("by a person authorized, in writing, by the individual to whom the records pertain"); COLO. REV. STAT. §24-90-119 (2000) ("upon written consent of the user"); GA. CODE ANN. §24-9-46 (2000) ("upon written consent of the user"); MICH. COMP. LAWS §397.601 (2001) ("without the written consent of the person liable for payment for or return of the materials identified in that library record"); MISS. CODE ANN. §39-3-365 (2000) ("express written permission of the respective library user"); MO. REV. STAT. §182.817 ("written request of the person identified"); MONT. CODE ANN. §22-1-1103 ("written request of the person identified in that record, according to procedures and forms giving written consent as determined by the library"); N.M. STAT. ANN. §18-9-4 (2000) ("except upon written consent of the person identified in the record"); N.C. GEN. STAT. §125-19 (1999)

("upon written consent of the user"); OKLA. STAT. tit. 65, §1-105 (1999) ("persons authorized to inspect such records, in writing, by the individual or group"); TENN. CODE ANN. §§10-8-101 and -102 (2000) ("written consent"); W. VA. CODE § 10-1-22 (2000) ("upon written consent of the user of the library materials").

72. ME. REV. STAT. ANN. tit. 27, §121 (1999).

73. MISS. CODE ANN. §39-3-365 (2000).

74. MONT. CODE ANN. §22-1-1103 ("written request of the person identified in that record, according to procedures and forms giving written consent as determined by the library").

75. MICH. COMP. LAWS §397.601 (2001).

76. N.H. REV. STAT. ANN. §201-D:11 (2000) ("consent of the user"); N.J. STAT. §18A:73-43.2 (2000) ("requested by the user"); WIS. STAT. §43.30 (1999) ("to persons authorized by the individual").

77. College Center for Library Automation, *Maintaining LINCC Borrower Privacy* (prelim. ed. December 1993), citing FLA. STAT. ANN. §§257.261 and 228.093 (ca. 1993), *at* http://www.ccla.lib.fl.us/reports/borrower_privacy.pdf (visited April 30, 2001).

78. See, e.g., CONN. GEN. STAT. §11-25 (1999); IDAHO CODE §9-340E (2000).

79. See, e.g., DEL. CODE ANN. tit. 29, §10002(d)(12) (2000); IND. CODE ANN. §5-14-3-4(b)(16) (2000); IOWA CODE §22.7(13) (1999); KAN. STAT. ANN. §45-221(23) (1999); VT. STAT. ANN. tit. 1, §317(c)(19) (2000); VA. CODE ANN. §2.1-342.01 (A)(10) (2000); WASH. REV. CODE ANN. §42.17.310(1)(l) (2000); W. VA. CODE §10-1-22 (2000).

80. See, e.g., ALASKA STAT. §40.25.140 (2000) (exception for parental access); D.C. CODE ANN. §37-106.2 (1999) (exception for "proper operation of the public library"); 75 ILL. COMP. STAT. 70/1 (1999) (exception for court order and "reasonable statistical reports"); N.D. CENT. CODE §40-38-12 (2000) (court order or subpoena); MASS. ANN. LAWS chap. 78, §7 (2000) (exception for "purposes of interlibrary cooperation and coordination"); PA. CONS. STAT. §4428 (1999) (court order in a criminal proceeding).

81. See WIS. STAT. §19.32(1)(m) (1999) ("Person authorized by the individual [to inspect the record] means the parent, guardian as defined in . . . or legal custodian ").

82. See, e.g., ALA. CODE §§36-12-40 and 41-8-10 (2000); ALASKA STAT. §40.25.140 (2000); FLA. STAT. ANN. §257.261 (1999) (only applies to records of minors "under 16"); LA. REV. STAT. §44:13 (2000); N.M. STAT. ANN. §§18-9-4 and -5 (2000); OHIO REV. CODE ANN. 149.432; S.D. CODIFIED LAWS §14-2-51 (2000); W. VA. CODE §10-1-22 (2000); WYO. STAT. ANN. §16-4-203(d)(ix) (2000).

83. *Quad/Graphics, Inc. v. Southern Adirondack Library System,* 174 Misc. 2d 291, 294, 664 N.Y.S.2d 225, 228 (1997) ("Were this application to be granted, the door would be open to other similar requests made, for example, by a parent who wishes to learn what a child is reading or viewing on the Internet via WWW or by a spouse to learn what type of information his or her mate is reviewing at the public library").

84. MICH. COMP. LAWS §397.601 (2001).

85. Library of Michigan, *Trustee Corner: Library Privacy Act Issues* (Aug. 29, 1996), *at* http://www.libofmich.lib.mi.us/publications/trusteesept96.html (visited April 29, 2001).

86. MICH. COMP. LAWS §397.601 (2001).

87. Santa Clara County Library, California, *at* http://www-lib.co.santa-clara.ca.us/services/schedule.html#children (visited July 8, 2001).

88. MICH. COMP. LAWS §397.601 (2001).

89. MICH. STAT. ANN. §27A.2913 (2000). Wisconsin has a similar parental financial responsibility statute, but no additional library specific provision, See WIS. STAT. §895.035.

90. *See* Jeffrey L. Skaare, *The Development and Current Status of Parental Liability for the Torts of Minors,* 76 NORTH DAKOTA LAW REVIEW 89 (2000).

91. ALA. CODE §§36-12-40 and 41-8-10 (2000); S.D. CODIFIED LAWS §14-2-51 (2000).

92. See, e.g., ALASKA STAT. §40.25.140 (2000) (parent or guardian); FLA. STAT. ANN. §257.261 (1999) (only applies to records of minors "under 16"); LA. REV. STAT. §44:13 (2000) (parent or custodian); N.M. STAT. ANN. §§18-9-4 and -5 (2000) (legal guardian); OHIO REV. CODE ANN. 149.432 (parent, guardian or custodian); W. VA. CODE ANN. §10-1-22 (2000) (parent or guardian); WYO. STAT. ANN. §16-4-203(d)(ix) (2000) (custodial parent or guardian).

93. N.M. STAT. ANN. §18-9-4 (2000).

94. MICH. COMP. LAWS §397.601 (2001).

95. D.C. CODE ANN. §37-106.2(B)(4) (1999).

96. D.C. CODE ANN. §37-106.2(B)(5).

97. MO. REV. STAT. §§183.815 to .817 (1999); NEV. REV. STAT. ANN. §239.013 (2000); S.C. Code Ann. §60-4-10 (1999).

98. OHIO REV. CODE ANN. 149.432.

99. MONT. CODE ANN. §22-1-1101 (2000).

100. MINN. STAT. §13.40 (1998).

101. ARK. CODE ANN. §§13-2-704 (1999).

102. N.Y. C.P.L.R. §4509 (2000).

103. *See* Bruce S. Johnson, *"A More Cooperative Clerk": The Confidentiality of Library Records,* 81 LAW LIBRARY JOURNAL 769 (1989).

104. See, e.g., FLA. STAT. ANN. §257.261 (1999) (overdue materials, fines, and parental access if minor under age of sixteen, but no consent provision); 75 ILL. COMP. STAT. 70/1 (1999) (court order and reasonable statistical reports, but no consent provision); MASS. ANN. LAWS chap. 78, §7 (2000) (interlibrary cooperation and coordination, but no consent provision); N.Y. C.P.L.R. §4509 (2000) (proper operation of the library, subpoena, court order, or where otherwise required by statute, but no consent provision) (the absence of any other type of implied consent is also supported by judicial interpretation; see *Quad/Graphics, Inc. v. Southern Adirondack Library System,* 174 Misc. 2d 291, 294, 664 N.Y.S.2d 225, 228 (1997) ("Were this application to be granted, the door would be open to

other similar requests made, for example, by a parent who wishes to learn what a child is reading or viewing on the Internet via WWW or by a spouse to learn what type of information his or her mate is reviewing at the public library."); 24 PA. CONS. STAT. §4428 (1999) (court order in a criminal proceeding is the only exception listed).

105. See, e.g., ARIZ. REV. STAT. §41-1354 (2000) ("reasonable operation of the library"); CAL. GOV'T CODE §6267 (2000) ("person acting within the scope of his or her duties within the administration of the library"); COLO. REV. STAT. §24-90-119 (2000) ("when necessary for the reasonable operation of the library"); MD. EDUC. CODE ANN. §23-107 (1999) ("disclosure of the circulation record of an individual only in connection with the library's ordinary course of business and only for the purposes for which the record was created"); N.H. REV. STAT. ANN. §201-D:11 (2000) ("to the extent necessary for the proper operation of such libraries"); N.J. STAT. §18A:73-43.1 (2000) ("necessary for the proper operation of the library"); N.Y. C.P.L.R. §4509 (2000) ("to the extent necessary for the proper operation of such library"); N.C. GEN. STAT. §125-18 (1999) ("not include nonidentifying material that may be retained for the purpose of studying or evaluating the circulation of library materials in general"); OKLA. STAT. tit. 65, §1-105 (1999) ("persons acting within the scope of their duties in the administration of the library"); W. VA. CODE §10-1-22 (2000) ("member of the library staff in the ordinary course of business").

106. See, e.g., WIS. STAT. §43.30(2) (1999) ("may disclose an individual identity to another library for the purpose of borrowing materials").

107. See, e.g., FLA. STAT. ANN. §257.261 (1999) ("to any business for the purpose of collecting fines or overdue books, documents, films, or other items or materials"); MONT. CODE ANN. §22-1-1103(b)(3) (2000) ("to the extent necessary to return overdue or stolen materials or collect fines"); TENN. CODE ANN. §10-8-102(b)(3) (2000) ("when used to seek reimbursement for or the return of lost, stolen, misplaced or otherwise overdue library materials").

108. See, e.g., 75 ILL. COMP. STAT. 70/1 (1999) ("This section does not prevent a library from publishing or making available to the public reasonable statistical reports regarding library registration and book circulation where those reports are presented so that no individual is identified therein"); MONT. CODE ANN. §22-1-1103 (2000) ("A library is not prevented from publishing or making available to the public reasonable statistical reports regarding library registration and book circulation if those reports are presented so that no individual is identified therein"); N.C. GEN. STAT. §125-18 (1999) ("'Library record' does not include nonidentifying material that may be retained for the purpose of studying or evaluating the circulation of library materials in general").

109. See, e.g., ARK. CODE ANN. §§13-2-701 to -704 (1999); OHIO REV. CODE ANN. 149.432; W. VA. CODE §10-1-22 (2000).

110. See, e.g., COLO. REV. STAT. §24-90-119 (2000); GA. CODE ANN. §24-9-46 (2000); N.H. REV. STAT. ANN. §201-D:11 (2000); N.J. STAT. ANN. §18A:73-43.1 and .2 (2000); N.Y. C.P.L.R. §4509 (2000); N.C. GEN. STAT. §125-19 (1999); N.D.

CENT. CODE §40-38-12 (2000); OHIO REV. CODE ANN. 149.432; W. VA. CODE §10-1-22 (2000).

111. ALASKA STAT. §40.25.140 (2000); CAL. GOV'T CODE §6267 (2000); COLO. REV. STAT. §24-90-119 (2000); D.C. CODE ANN. §37-106.2 (1999); GA. CODE ANN. §24-9-46 (2000); ME. REV. STAT. ANN. tit. 27, §121 (1999); MICH. COMP. LAWS §397.601 et. seq. (2001); MISS. CODE ANN. §39-3-365 (2000); MO. REV. STAT. §§182.815 to .817 (1999); MONT. CODE ANN. §22-1-1101 (2000); NEV. REV. STAT. ANN. §239.013 (2000); N.H. REV. STAT. ANN. §201-D:11 (2000); N.J. STAT. §18A:73-43.1 and .2 (2000); N.M. STAT. ANN. §18-9-4 (2000); N.Y. C.P.L.R. §4509 (2000); N.C. GEN. STAT. §125-19 (1999); N.D. CENT. CODE §40-38-12 (2000); H.R. 389, 1999 Leg. (Ohio 2000); OKLA. STAT. tit. 65, §1-105 (1999); 24 PA. CONS. STAT. §4428 (1999) ("court order in a criminal proceeding"); S.C. CODE ANN. §60-4-10 (1999) ("judicial order . . . public safety, to prosecute a crime, or upon showing of good cause . . . in a civil matter"); S.D. CODIFIED LAWS §14-2-51 (2000); TENN. CODE ANN. §§10-8-101 and -102 (2000); W. VA. CODE §10-1-22 (2000); WIS. STAT. §43.30 (1999).

112. BLACK'S LAW DICTIONARY 1440 (7th ed. 1999).

113. 24 PA. CONS. STAT. §4428.

114. S.C. CODE ANN. §60-4-10 (1999).

115. ARK. CODE ANN. §§13-2-701 to -704 (1999).

116. See, e.g., ARIZ. REV. STAT. §41-1354; N.C. GEN. STAT. §125-19.

117. *Quad/Graphics, Inc. v. Southern Adirondack Library System,* 174 Misc. 2d 291, 294, 664 N.Y.S.2d 225 (1997).

118. N.Y. C.P.L.R. §4509 (2000).

119. H. Morley Swingle, *Criminal Investigative Subpoenas: How to Get Them, How to Fight Them,* 54 JOURNAL OF THE MISSOURI BAR 15 (January/February, 1998).

120. *Branzburg v. Hayes,* 408 U.S. 665 (1972).

121. *United States v. R Enterprises,* 498 U.S. 292 (1991).

122. The First Amendment "necessarily protects the right to receive" information, *Martin v. City of Struthers,* 318 U.S. 141, 143 (1943). It protects the anonymity of the author, *Talley v. California,* 362 U.S. 60 (1960); the anonymity of members of organizations, *Gibson v. Florida Legislative Investigation Committee,* 372 U.S. 539 (1963); *Bates v. City of Little Rock,* 361 U.S. 516 (1960); *NAACP v. Alabama,* 357 U.S. 449 (1958); the right to ask persons to join a labor organization without registering to do so, *Thomas v. Collins,* 323 U.S. 516 (1945); the right to dispense and to receive birth control information in private, *Griswold v. Connecticut,* 381 U.S. 479 (1965); the right to have controversial mail delivered without written request, *Lamont v. Postmaster General,* 381 U.S. 301 (1965); the right to go to a meeting without being questioned as to whether you attended or what you said, *DeGregory v. Attorney General of New Hampshire,* 383 U.S. 825 (1966); the right to give a lecture without being compelled to tell the government what you said, *Sweenzy v. New Hampshire,* 354 U.S. 234 (1957); and the right to view a pornographic film in the privacy of your own home without govern-

mental intrusion, *Stanley v. Georgia*, 394 U.S. 557 (1969). This summary of cases is taken from Hugh R. Jones, Staff Attorney, "Public Access to Library Patron Circulation and Fine Records," Memorandum addressed to The Honorable Bartholomew A. Kane (Oct. 23, 1990), *at* http://www.hsba.org/Hawaii/Admin/Info/90-30.htm (visited April 28, 2001). *See also* Julie E. Cohen, *A Right to Read Anonymously: A Closer Look at "Copyright Management" in Cyberspace,* 28 CONNECTICUT LAW REVIEW 981 (Summer 1996); and Tomas A. Lipinski, *To Speak or Not to Speak: Developing Legal Standards for Anonymous Speech on the Internet,* 5 INFORMING SCIENCE 95 (2002).

123. Theresa Chmara, "Unrestricted Access: Internet Privacy, Workplace Harassment and Professionalism," Memorandum for the Lawyers for Libraries Training Seminar (Chicago, Ill., Nov. 14, 1988).

124. See *In re Grand Jury Subpoena Duces Tecum,* 78 F.3d 1307 (8th Cir. 1996), *cert. denied,* 117 S. Ct. 432 (1996); In re Grand Jury Proceedings, 776 F.2d 1099 (2d Cir. 1985); *In re Grand Jury Subpoena,* 701 F.2d 115 (10th Cir. 1983); *Bursey v. United States,* 446 F.2d 1059 (9th Cir. 1972), *overruled in part on other grounds; In re Grand Jury Proceedings,* 863 F.2d 667 (9th Cir. 1988). These cases are given as examples in Chmara, "Unrestricted Access: Internet Privacy, Workplace Harassment and Professionalism."

125. *In re Grand Jury P87-3 Subpoena Duces Tecum,* 955 F.2d 229 (4th Cir. 1992). This case is given as an example in Chmara, "Unrestricted Access: Internet Privacy, Workplace Harassment and Professionalism."

126. *Tattered Cover, Inc. v. City of Thornton,* 44 P.3d 1044 (Colo. 2002).

127. *Tattered Cover, Inc.,* 44 P.3d at 1047.

128. *Tattered Cover, Inc.,* 44 P.3d at 1063.

129. *Brown v. Johnston,* 328 N.W.2d 510 (Iowa 1983).

130. *Brown,* 328 N.W.2d at 512–13.

131. *See* Comment, *Brown v. Johnston: The Unexamined Issue of Privacy in Public Library Circulation Records in Iowa,* 69 IOWA LAW REVIEW 535 (1983). A legal memo to the state librarian of Hawaii in 1990 stated: "The constitutional uncertainty that appears in the *Brown* decision is reflected in several opinions issued by the attorneys general of various states. The attorneys general of Nevada, Tennessee, and Texas have opined that the United States Constitution protects the confidentiality of library circulation records. See Op. Att'y Gen. Nev. 80-6 (1980); Op. Att'y Gen. Tenn. 87-04 (1987); Att'y Gen. Tex. Open Records Decision No. 100 (July 10, 1975). The attorneys general for two other states, Iowa and Mississippi, have taken the opposite view. See Op. Att'y Gen. Iowa No. 71-8-22 (1971); Op. Att'y Gen. Iowa No. 78-8-25 (1979); Op. Att'y Gen. Miss. (May 10, 1985)." Hugh R. Jones, Staff Attorney, "Public Access to Library Patron Circulation and Fine Records," Memorandum addressed to The Honorable Bartholomew A. Kane (Oct. 23, 1990), *at* http://www.hsba.org/Hawaii/Admin/Info/90-30.htm (visited April 28, 2001).

132. Theresa Chmara, *Privacy and Confidentiality Issues,* FREEDOM TO READ FOUNDA-TION NEWS 23, no. 2, at 6 (n.d.); Chmara, "Unrestricted Access: Internet Privacy, Workplace Harassment and Professionalism."

133. An excellent article on drafting general library policies applicable to privacy, con-troversial material, etc., is Claire Weber, *Designing, Drafting and Implementing New Policies,* in LIBRARIES, MUSEUMS AND ARCHIVES: LEGAL ISSUES AND CHAL-LENGES IN THE NEW INFORMATION ERA 303 (Tomas Lipinski ed., 2002).

134. American Library Association, *Policy on Confidentiality of Library Records, at* http://www.ala.org/alaorg/oif/policyconfidentiality.pdf (visited April 27, 2001).

6 MEETING ROOMS AND DISPLAYS
The Public Soapbox inside the Library

Q1 Are all library meeting rooms and display areas protected by the First Amendment?

Q2 Must all library meeting rooms and display areas in public institutions be open to all users?

Q3 If my meeting room or display area is open to the public, is it a "public forum"?

Categories of Public Forum

Traditional Public Forum: The Library's Sidewalks

Designated Public Forum: The Spaces Government Opens to Public Expression

Limited Public Forum: The Library and Its Public Meeting Rooms and Display Areas

Nonpublic Forum: The Library's Technical Services Areas and Offices

Q4 What speech is protected in the library meeting rooms and display areas that are considered "public forums"?

Speech Content Regulations

Case Study: Manhasset Public Library

Speech Regulations: Content-Neutral

Meeting Rooms: Special Considerations

Appendix

Cases

Further Resources

Notes

uthor's story: When I worked as a public librarian, booking meeting rooms and setting up displays, it never occurred to me that I was acting as a government agent, and that my bookings were subject to First Amendment review. I shudder to recall one Saturday when I got a flurry of phone calls from churches, vociferously complaining that the group Eckankar was planning to show a film in our community room that afternoon. If I didn't cancel it, I was told, there would be pickets and demonstrations.

I immediately checked into the situation. Yes, Eckankar had booked the room. The churches were not opposed to Eckankar's message—it teaches about the eternal soul and "soul travel." The churches were upset because they themselves had wanted to use the community room and had been turned away by our policy that said "no religious groups" could use the room. Eckankar, said the protesters, was a religious group, and we had let its followers in. What did I do? I talked to Eckankar, made a determination that, yes, indeed, it was a religious group. I felt fortunate that the group did not dispute that characterization. This meant that under our policy, they could not use the room. I told them that we would honor today's booking, but they would need to look elsewhere for future meetings. The protesters accepted my solution, and I felt I had solved a crisis.

I didn't realize how lucky I was that Eckankar's followers—and the churches, for that matter—did not file a lawsuit against us. Had they done so, they would have won, even though our policies were not unusual. I didn't know that I had been acting as an agent of the government and was a custodian of a "public forum," a soapbox where citizens have First Amendment rights of expression. I had no idea that my library's community room was such a sacred space, virtually guaranteed to all community members on an equal basis, regardless of the content of their meetings.

This chapter describes the legal context of public library spaces that have been opened up to public expression, such as community rooms, auditoriums, public-display walls, and exhibit cases. These public spaces, known in legal parlance as "public forums," trigger a "strict scrutiny" First Amendment analysis whenever content restrictions are placed on their use.

Q1   Are all library meeting rooms and display areas protected
by the First Amendment?

No. If your library is private, or part of a private institution, the First Amendment is not applicable, with few exceptions.[1] The First Amendment restricts *government* from abridging free speech. Private institutions are not constrained, even if their meeting rooms are open to the public.

Q2   Must all library meeting rooms and display areas in public institutions be open to all users?

No. First of all, each library can designate certain rooms or display areas to be off-limits to users. Not all government spaces are open to all—you needn't entertain all groups in your office space, technical services area, etc. However, once a library opens a room or display area for public use, it is considered a "designated public forum." Designated forums are treated as though they are "public forums" and the library may not control which messages are expressed there (unless the forum is also determined to be "limited").

Second, each library may restrict its resources to a "limited" purpose, such as serving a defined community. That is, a public or private academic college may limit its meeting rooms to its academic community. A school library may limit its space to the school community. A public library, open to the public, must welcome the public into its meeting rooms.

Q3   If my meeting room or display area is open to the public, is it a "public forum"?

Yes. According to court cases, public library meeting rooms are *designated public forums*.[2] That is, if a meeting room is open to the public for expressive activity, it may not be restricted on the basis of the content or viewpoint of a group's speech. To take one example of an impermissible content restriction: a library may not make a policy that expressly forbids groups that wish to discuss birth control while at the same time allowing the chess club to book the room. An impermissible viewpoint restriction example: a library may not allow a pro-choice group to use the room while denying access to a pro-life group.

The term "public forum" emerged in First Amendment jurisprudence in 1939, when the Supreme Court held that the government does not have absolute discretion to control speech in public places.[3]

Two recent court cases found public library meeting rooms to be a type of "public forum," and struck down rules that denied religious groups the use of the public space.[4]

CATEGORIES OF PUBLIC FORUM

Current public forum doctrine applies a three-tiered system: government property is either a "traditional public forum," a "designated public forum," or a "nonpublic forum."[5]

Traditional Public Forum: The Library's Sidewalks

The first category, "traditional public forums," are places traditionally used for purposes of assembly, communication, and public debate: parks, streets, and sidewalks.[6] Library meeting rooms and display areas do not fit into this category. However, some library sidewalks fit into this category, and library rules restricting leafleting or other speech in such areas should only be made after consultation with an attorney.

Designated Public Forum: The Spaces
Government Opens to Public Expression

The second category, the "designated public forum," is public property that the government has opened for use by the *public* as a place for expressive activity, such as a public auditorium.[7] This term is used differently by different courts; some library meeting rooms and display areas fit into this category, if the public is allowed to use the spaces. Library rooms and display areas that are used *only* by the library itself are not considered part of the public forum. For example, perhaps a book display case is only used by the library, or even by a library support group such as the Friends of the Library to house its book sale. An outside group would not have a right to put its displays in that area. Perhaps a meeting room is used only for staff meetings, but is available for Friends group meetings, or for a volunteer literacy program that the library participates in. The library may say that such spaces will only support library group activities. Other public groups may not use the facilities for their own expressive activities, and the space is not a designated public forum.

Limited Public Forum: The Library and
Its Public Meeting Rooms and Display Areas

The term "limited public forum" is not used in a consistent manner. Some courts discuss a limited public forum as though it is a nonpublic forum; others treat it more as a subcategory of the "designated public forum," subject to the full protections of the public forum, and limited only by purpose. The *Kreimer* case examined the mission of the public library, and discussed the difference between a library reading room and a street corner—the library was open for a "limited purpose," that of *reading* or *receiving information*. The reading room was not open for expressive activity, that is, making speeches in the reading room. The court said that the public library was a limited public forum, a type of designated public forum.[8] Even the library meeting rooms and display areas are open for limited expressive activity; for example, the display areas may be limited to printed materials.

What if the library policy goes one step further and says that the space may only be used for "educational purposes"? The *Mainstream Loudoun* court found that content-based restrictions in limited public forums are treated with the same strict scrutiny as traditional public forums.[9] Some commentators think there is legal justification in limiting a limited public forum by purpose; others do not.[10] One way to approach limited forums is to think of them on a sliding scale basis. In general, the more restrictive the criteria for admission and the more administrative control over access, the less likely a forum will be deemed public.[11] This is a very gray area, and any restrictions on the basis of purpose should be carefully reviewed by legal counsel.

One commentator sees limited public forums as places that by design are content-based—after-school use of classrooms by the public for educational purposes only—but without viewpoint neutrality imposed, i.e., God-centered parenting and "humanist"-centered parenting classes must both be allowed.[12]

Nonpublic Forum: The Library's Technical Services Areas and Offices

The third category is the "nonpublic forum." Library property such as technical service areas, staff offices, and the like are included here. Libraries may also have meeting rooms and display areas that fit into this category. For example, a library may have a room that is only used for library staff meetings, or a display that is only used to show library books. Library regulation of public speech in these areas must meet an extremely low legal hurdle, known as the "reasonable" test. That is, if a library can make any justification that isn't wholly arbitrary, it is likely to be upheld in any legal challenge.

*Q4   What speech is protected in the library meeting rooms and
display areas that are considered "public forums"?*

Almost all speech is protected by the First Amendment in these areas. This
includes controversial, religious, and political speech as well as most hate
speech. This means that once the library opens up its meeting rooms and
display areas to public use, it cannot then discriminate on the basis of
content, with rare exceptions.

SPEECH CONTENT REGULATIONS

When the government restricts speech in a public forum (including designated public forums and limited public forums) on the basis of content or
viewpoint, the courts generally apply a tough legal test to the restriction,
known as "strict scrutiny." When this standard is used, the courts usually
overturn the governmental speech restriction. As law professor Gerald
Gunther famously put it, strict scrutiny is "strict" in theory and often
"fatal" in fact.[13] In order to survive a case that is judged under the strict
scrutiny standard, the government (i.e., a library that restricts speech) must
show that there is a "compelling interest" and that the measure is narrowly
tailored to use the "least restrictive means" to meet that interest.[14]

*Q5   How should the library treat displays or meetings
that concern controversial issues?*

The heart of the First Amendment is the protection of controversial
speech. As librarians know from book selection, one person's vulgarity is
another person's lyric.[15] In 2001, for example, the mayor of Anchorage,
Alaska, ordered the removal of a gay-pride exhibit at the city's Loussac
Library. The American Civil Liberties Union filed suit, and a federal judge
ordered its reinstallation. The city agreed to revise its meeting room policy
and to pay $10,000 in legal fees to settle.[16]

*Q6   How should the library treat displays or meetings
that concern religious issues?*

There are court cases that deal precisely with this issue. In a recent
Wisconsin court case, a library patron wished to book the meeting room
for a presentation on creationism but was turned away. He sued and won;
the library had to allow him to use its meeting room.[17] The court found

significant the fact that the mission statement of the library indicated that it served a wide variety of community educational interests. This was reflected in its collection development policies and practices, and was found inconsistent with the library's unwillingness to extend the same attitude to the use of its meeting room, i.e., it had books on evolution as well as creationism in its collection. The decision provides an excellent case study of the legal scrutiny that a court might apply to library policies and practices. In a Fifth Circuit case in 1989, the Concerned Women for America (CWA) wished to use a library auditorium for a prayer chapter's meeting and to pray over abortion. The CWA won; the library had to allow the prayer chapter into its meeting room. As this book went to press, two women from Light Ministries filed a federal lawsuit against the city of Pensacola, Florida, for prohibiting the use of its meeting room for religious purposes.[18]

The U.S. Supreme Court recently held that religious speech in public school classrooms used after hours is viewpoint (not content) based. This means that even if a forum is determined to be a nonpublic forum, it *still* cannot limit religious speech.[19]

Q7   Isn't there a conflict between church and state?

No. You are referring to the Establishment Clause of the Constitution, which provides the legal basis for the separation of church and state. According to a federal court in Wisconsin, the Establishment Clause did not justify the library's ban on religious instruction. Because the library granted access to a wide variety of nonreligious private organizations, there was no "realistic danger that the community would think that the [library] was endorsing religion or any particular creed, and any benefit to religion or the Church would have been incidental."[20]

A federal appellate court in Mississippi also said that the Establishment Clause was not at issue. "In the absence of empirical evidence that religious groups will dominate the use of the library's auditorium, causing the advancement of religion to become the forum's 'primary effect,' an equal access policy will not offend the Establishment Clause."[21]

Q8   How should the library treat displays or meetings that concern political issues?

Political speech is at the core of the First Amendment. It is strongly protected by the Constitution. The case in Wisconsin was centered on religious speech, but in passing, the court discussed the library's restriction on "politically partisan" groups. It said that the "political partisan" exclusion was narrow, covering only a small subcategory of political speech, apparently covering only political party meetings. "Thus, the exclusion appears to leave untouched a substantial amount of political speech, including discussion of all manner of controversial subjects such as abortion, homosexuality, flag burning, school prayer and race relations, so long as the speech does not occur at a politically partisan meeting."[22]

It would not be surprising if a politically partisan group were to challenge a restrictive policy and win.

Q9   How should the library treat displays or meetings that use hate speech?

The term "hate speech" covers a range of speech—most of it protected by the First Amendment, but some that is not. *Black's Law Dictionary* defines "hate speech" as "speech that carries no meaning other than the expression of hatred for some group, such as a particular race, esp. in circumstances where the communication is likely to provoke violence."[23] Library policies should not treat hate speech any differently from other controversial speech.

Q10   Can you give an example of a library that allowed a hate speech group to use its facilities?

Yes. Matt Hale, leader of the World Church of the Creator, a racist organization, was allowed to use the meeting room of the Bloomington (Ill.) Public Library on October 28, 2000. The library's attorneys said that the library could not ban Hale from the meeting room. The library could limit a group's use of the meeting room to six times a year and no more than once a month. This would apply, however, to any group.[24]

Hale filed a federal lawsuit against the Schaumburg Township District Library on March 29, 2001, when it would not let him speak in its meeting room on the topic of "white pride." Reportedly, the library board cited its policy disallowing meetings that might disrupt library functions and presented a potential for violence. Hale charged that the board could not refuse the request because of potential actions by demonstrators. "It's the police's job and the library's job to make sure that I can give a speech without having altercations or disturbances," he said.[25] Five months after the library trustees canceled his meeting, the library and Hale came to an agreement that allowed Hale to hold a meeting on a Saturday evening after the library was closed. Director Mike Madden told *American*

Libraries that it became apparent that the presiding judge saw the over-riding issue as the First Amendment and not public safety. As this book went to press, Hale had recently spoken at libraries in Wallingford, Connecticut; York, Pennsylvania; and Yorktown, Virginia.[26]

Q11   May a library demand extra fees or deposits for security expenses if a speaker is expected to draw an angry crowd?

Probably not. The Supreme Court has ruled that a fee based on the anticipated crowd *response* necessarily involves the examination of the content of the speech, making it nearly impossible to enforce (i.e, the strict-scrutiny standard applies).[27]

Q12   I don't understand. Surely you don't mean that I must allow a group into the library that is threatening my patrons?

The First Amendment does not protect actual, specific "threats." A threat must be a "true threat" with a specific target, however. This must be distinguished from political hyperbole. Political hyperbole, even if "vituperative, abusive and inexact," is protected by the courts against a "background of a profound national commitment to the principle that debate on public issues should be uninhibited, robust, and wide-open, and that it may well include vehement, caustic, and sometimes unpleasantly sharp attacks on government and public officials."[28]

For example, if a library patron says all civil servants are scum, he is participating in robust debate. But if he says to a clerk, "I'm going to knock your head off, you government scum," these are likely to be "fighting words."

Q13   So the library does not have to put up with "fighting words"?

That's right. According to the Supreme Court, "fighting words" are epithets reasonably expected to provoke a violent reaction if addressed toward an "ordinary citizen." The Supreme Court held that "such utterances are no essential part of any exposition of ideas, and are of such slight social value as a step to truth that any benefit that may be derived from them is clearly outweighed by the social interest in order and morality."[29]

Q14   What if the group is inciting a riot?

The key question here is whether the group's program is merely one of teaching abstract doctrines, or is it actual incitement? The first is protected by the First Amendment, even if it includes the advocacy of force against another group, for example, like that of the Nazis marching in Skokie, Illinois. The line is drawn, however, "where such advocacy is directed to inciting or producing *imminent lawless action* and is likely to incite or produce such action."[30] This is incitement, and can be illegal. Much as you might find it abhorrent, offensive leaflets in your giveaway racks do not incite imminent lawless action. In the community room, with live speakers, the possibility of incitement is increased. If, for example, a white-power group is using your community room and says, "Nonwhite children shouldn't be mixing with white children," that is protected free speech. If the speaker said, "Let's go into the children's room and round up all the nonwhites," that would be incitement.

Q15   *How should the library treat displays or meetings
        that concern sexual issues?*

Most speech that concerns sexual issues is protected by the First Amendment and should be permitted by the library. Three narrow categories of sexual speech, however, are not protected, and federal and state laws may outlaw it: child pornography, obscenity, and "harmful to minors" material. These categories are much more narrowly defined by law than the general public conception of "pornography," a term which defies legal definition; members of the public may use the term to describe anything from the latest XXX-rated website to the current *Sports Illustrated* swimsuit edition.

CASE STUDY

MANHASSET PUBLIC LIBRARY

A "no nudes" policy at a public library was challenged by an artist who had been invited to exhibit in the library, and then asked to remove her work when it was discovered that three paintings included "semi-nude females." The library lost the case in court. In an unpublished opinion, a federal district court awarded the artist an undisclosed sum and a guarantee that she would be allowed to display her work in the library. The court prohibited the removal of paintings of "semi-nude females" from the community room of a public library.[31]

Q16 Are there any situations in which the library can stop a
program or a display if it is really, really upsetting to patrons
and staff?

Yes, but this is generally not enough of a reason. To restrict speech, a
library must show that (1) *it has a compelling state interest,* and (2) *the*
speech restrictions are narrowly drawn to achieve that end.[32] This standard is extraordinarily difficult to reach, and libraries should amass a
great amount of evidence to support both of these factors before pursuing
a content-based speech restriction. A meeting with an attorney is definitely
advised before a library takes such an action.

Speech Regulations: Content-Neutral

Q17 Our policy limits the amount of time for which a group can
reserve the meeting room or display space. Is that okay?

The library may include reasonable "time, place, and manner" restrictions
on the use of its meeting rooms and display areas. Such regulations must
be content-neutral, both in the written policy and as it is applied. For
example, the library may state that "No group may reserve the room more
than one time per week." A content-neutral regulation will be upheld if "it
furthers an important or substantial governmental interest; if the governmental interest is unrelated to the suppression of free expression; and if
the incidental restriction on alleged First Amendment freedoms is no
greater than is essential to the furtherance of that interest."[33]

The library should be prepared to show that it applied the policy uniformly, without singling out groups it liked or disliked. Even content-
neutral time, place, and manner restrictions can be applied in such a
manner as to stifle free expression. Adequate standards must be set to
avoid a standardless discretion by the library staff.[34]

Meeting Rooms: Special Considerations

Q18 I see a big difference between hate speech spewed forth
live in a meeting room and hate speech quietly sitting
on a giveaway rack. Does the law?

It does to a certain extent. Only live speakers, not quiet print, can "incite
imminent lawless action." That is why virtually all books containing hate
speech that the library might buy are protected. The recent *Hit Man* case is

an exception, but it is so narrow that it's mentioned here only because it was a high-profile case. In that case, the book was used as a manual to kill three people. Its publisher, Paladin Press, stipulated that its book was marketed to potential hired killers, and was enjoined by the court from distributing further copies.[35]

Q19   What if the meeting gets out of hand—too loud or worse?

This is a good opportunity to enforce content-neutral meeting room regulations, such as caps on noise levels. The regulations must be enforced evenly, to all groups, abiding by the same criteria. A summer reading celebration with music would need to meet the same noise restrictions as a meeting with an angry crowd.

Although restrictions based on expected audience reactions are content-based, restrictions based on the group's *own* past behavior can be constructed as content-neutral. For example, a rule that an applicant may not use a room if it has damaged library property and not paid for it in the past is based on verifiable behavior, not speech content. The Supreme Court recently examined content-neutral rules enforced by the Chicago Park District, and allowed the government a wide berth in enforcing such rules.[36]

APPENDIX

Cases

2000

WISCONSIN. FEDERAL DISTRICT COURT DECISION:

RESTRICTED-ACCESS LIBRARY POLICY STRUCK DOWN.
Pfeifer v. City of West Allis, 91 F. Supp. 2d 1253 (E.D. Wis. 2000).
Decision: April 10, 2000.

A federal court ruled that the West Allis (Wis.) Public Library violated a man's First Amendment rights when it refused him permission to use the library's Constitution Room for a presentation about creationism. The library policy excluded the following uses of the room:

1. Meetings that are politically partisan. 2. Religious services or instructions. 3. Commercial sales or presentations promoting specific companies or products. 4. Regular meetings of clubs, groups or organizations etc.—not to include educational or cultural activities open to the general public that are sponsored by the clubs, groups, organizations, etc.[37]

The court found the library's meeting room to be a designated public forum, subject to the same standards as a traditional public forum. "Concern by forum administrators about potentially controversial applicants is surely understandable, but it should not be an incentive to restrict communicative activity." *Pfeifer*, 91 F. Supp. 2d at 1267.

1999

FLORIDA. SETTLEMENT AGREEMENT:

RESTRICTED-ACCESS LIBRARY POLICY CHANGED.
Settlement Agreement: October 6, 1999.

The Tampa-Hillsborough County (Fla.) Public Library System settled a lawsuit filed October 3 by Concerned Women for America (CWA). The CWA wanted to use a library meeting room to discuss and pray about abortion. The library's policy prohibited religious, partisan political, for-profit, and discriminatory groups from using library meeting rooms. Under the settlement, the library agreed to allow religious groups to use the library, but kept the ban on partisan political, for-profit, and discriminatory groups.[38]

1989

MISSISSIPPI. FEDERAL FIFTH CIRCUIT DECISION:

RESTRICTED-ACCESS LIBRARY POLICY STRUCK DOWN.
Concerned Women for America v. *Lafayette County*, 883 F.2d 32; 1898 U.S. App. LEXIS 13864 (5th Cir. 1989). Decision: September 14, 1989.

A federal appellate court struck down the Lafayette County (Miss.), Oxford, Library's policy that did not allow the Concerned Women for America (CWA) Prayer Chapter the use of the library auditorium. The library policy, which required groups to get permission from the head librarian, was found unconstitutional:

The Auditorium of the Oxford branch of the First Regional Library is open for use of groups or organizations of a civic, cultural or educational character, but not for social gatherings, entertaining, dramatic productions, money-raising, or commercial purposes. It is also not available for meetings for social, political, partisan or religious purposes, or when in the judgment of the Director or Branch Librarian any disorder is likely to occur. *Concerned Women for America,* 883 F.2d at 33; 1898 U.S. App. LEXIS 13864.

The court found that by allowing diverse groups to use its auditorium, there was a substantial likelihood that the library had created a public forum. *Concerned Women for America,* 883 F.2d at 34; 1898 U.S. App. LEXIS 13864.

The Establishment Clause was not implicated, in the absence of evidence that religious groups would dominate the use of the library's auditorium, causing the advancement of religion to become the forum's "primary effect." *Concerned Women for America,* 883 F.2d at 35; 1898 U.S. App. LEXIS 13864 (5th Cir., Sept. 14, 1989), citing *Widmar* v. *Vincent,* 454 U.S. 263, 275, 102 S. Ct. 269, 277, 70 L. Ed. 2d 440 (1981).

Further Resources

American Library Association, *Meeting Rooms: An Interpretation of the LIBRARY BILL OF RIGHTS, available at* http://www.ala.org/alaorg/oif/meet_rms.html.

American Library Association, *Exhibit Spaces and Bulletin Boards: An Interpretation of the LIBRARY BILL OF RIGHTS, available at* http://www. ala.org/alaorg/oif/exh_spac.html.

Notes

1. It is generally accurate to say that the First Amendment does not apply to private libraries. In California, however, the state Education Code applies the First Amendment to private secondary and post-secondary educational institutions. It provides that "School districts operating one or more high schools and private secondary schools shall not make or enforce any rule subjecting any high school pupil to disciplinary sanctions solely on the basis of conduct that is speech or other communication that, when engaged in outside of the campus, is protected from governmental restriction by the First Amendment to the United States Constitution or Section 2 of Article 1 of the California Constitution." CAL. EDUC. CODE §48950(a) (2001). Student Robert J. Corry sued Stanford University based on a Stanford Speech Code that prohibited "discriminatory intimidation by threats of violence and also includes personal vilification of students on the basis of their sex, race,

color, handicap, religion, sexual orientation, or national and ethnic origin." *Corry v. Stanford University,* No. 740309 (Super. Ct., Cal., Santa Clara County, Feb. 27, 1995) (order granting preliminary injunction), *available at* http://lawschool.stanford. edu/library/special/corrym.shtml. Also, a private library or its parent institution may have adopted First Amendment principles in its policies.

2. *Kreimer v. Bureau of Police for the Town of Morristown,* 958 F.2d 1242 (3d Cir. 1992); *Concerned Women for America v. Lafayette County,* 883 F.2d 32 (5th Cir. 1989); *Pfeifer v. City of West Allis,* 91 F. Supp. 2d 1253 (E.D. Wis. 2000); *Mainstream Loudoun v. Loudoun County Library,* 2 F. Supp. 2d 783 (E.D. Va. 1998).

3. See *Hague v. Committee for Indus. Org.,* 307 U.S. 496, 516 (1939) (reversing police officer's refusal to issue permit to lease banquet halls to an organization with suspected communist associations).

4. *Pfeifer,* 91 F. Supp. 2d at 1253; *Concerned Women for America,* 883 F.2d at 32.

5. *Perry Education Ass'n v. Perry Local Educators' Assn.,* 460 U.S. 37 (1983).

6. *Perry Education Ass'n,* 460 U.S. at 45 (calls streets and parks "quintessential." "At one end of the spectrum are streets and parks which 'have immemorially been held in trust for the use of the public and, time out of mind, have been used for purposes of assembly, communicating thoughts between citizens, and discussing public questions.' *Hague,* 307 U.S. at 515").

7. *Perry Education Ass'n,* 460 U.S. at 45.

8. See *American Library Association v. United States,* 201 F. Supp. 2d 401 (E.D. Pa. 2002), equating designated public forums with limited public forums when analyzing Internet access in a public library; see *Kreimer v. Morristown,* 958 F.2d 1242, 1259 (3d Cir. 1992), for a discussion of a library as a limited public forum, a type of designated public forum.

9. *Mainstream Loudoun v. Loudoun County Library,* 2 F. Supp. 2d 552, 561 (E.D. Va. 1998).

10. *See* Theodore George, Legal Update, *Censoring Internet Access at Public Libraries: First Amendment Restrictions,* 5 BOSTON UNIVERSITY JOURNAL OF SCIENCE & TECHNOLOGY LAW 11 (1999) (libraries as limited public forums are subject to strict scrutiny when making content-based restrictions). For the opposing view, *see* Mark S. Nadel, *The First Amendment's Limitations on the Use of Internet Filtering in Public and School Libraries: What Content Can Librarians Exclude?,* 78 TEXAS LAW REVIEW 1117 (2000) (argues that even if libraries are classified as limited public forums, they make content-based decisions in book purchasing); and Brent L. VanNorman, Comment and Note, *The Library Internet Filter: On the Computer or on the Child?,* 11 REGENT UNIVERSITY LAW REVIEW 425 (1998/1999) (argues that libraries are nonpublic forums).

11. *Hopper v. Pasco,* 241 F.3d 1067 (9th Cir. 2000).

12. Matthew D. McGill, *Unleashing the Limited Public Forum: A Modest Revision to a Dysfunctional Doctrine,* 53 STANFORD LAW REVIEW 929 (2000) ("'limited public forum' will refer to a forum that the government has opened for particular subjects or speakers," at 935). *See* decisions of *Lamb's Chapel v. Center Moriches Union Free School District,* 508 U.S. 384 (1993); and *Rosenberger v. Rector and Visitors*

of University of Virginia, 515 U.S. 819 (1995);   and discussion of those cases in McGill, *Unleashing,* 943–945.

13. Gerald Gunther, Foreword, *In Search of Evolving Doctrine on a Changing Court: A Model for a Newer Equal Protection,* 86 HARVARD LAW REVIEW 1, 8 (1972). It should be noted that this standard might be changing. See, e.g., *Adarand Constructors, Inc. v. Pena,* 515 U.S. 200, 201(1995) ("Finally, we wish to dispel the notion that strict scrutiny is 'strict in theory, but fatal in fact'").

14. *Sable Communications of Cal., Inc. v. FCC,* 492 U.S. 115, 126 (1989). See also *American Library Association v. United States,* 201 F. Supp. 2d 401, 410 (E.D. Pa. 2002).

15. See *Cohen v. California,* 403 U.S. 15 (1971) ("one man's vulgarity is another's lyric").

16. *Anchorage Exhibits Policy Stalled,* News Briefs for January 7, 2002, AMERICAN LIBRARIES, *at* http://www.ala.org/alonline/news/2002/020107.html (visited Feb. 27, 2002); *New Anchorage Library Policy to Allow Outside Exhibits,* News Briefs for August 6, 2001, AMERICAN LIBRARIES, *at* http://www.ala.org/alonline/news/2001/010806.html (visited Feb. 27, 2002); *Anchorage Lawsuit Settled, but Exhibits Are in Limbo,* News Briefs for July 23, 2001, AMERICAN LIBRARIES, *at* http://www.ala.org/alonline/news/2001/010723.html (visited Feb. 27, 2002).

17. *Pfeifer v. City of West Allis,* 91 F. Supp. 2d 1253 (E.D. Wis. 2000).

18. *Two Women File Suit Challenging Library Policy after Being Told They Could Not Use a Library Community Room to Discuss Women's Issues from a Religious Viewpoint,* Liberty Counsel Press Release (April 9, 2001), *at* http://www.lc.org/pressrelease/religion-in-public-places/nr040901.htm (visited June 30, 2001). See also *Good News Club v. Milford Central School,* No. 99-2036, U.S. (June 11, 2001) (public middle school's exclusion of Christian organization from meeting in its building after school violated the First Amendment). For an updated listing of litigated and nonlitigated cases concerning the use of library (and other public) meeting rooms for religious purposes, *see* Liberty Counsel's website *at* http://www.lc.org/caseupdate/caseindex.htm (visited Feb. 27, 2002).

19. *Good News Club v. Milford Cent. Sch.,* 533 U.S. 98 (2001).

20. *Pfeifer,* 91 F. Supp. 2d at 1266, citing *Lamb's Chapel v. Center Moriches Union Free School District,* 508 U.S. 384, 385 (1993).

21. *Concerned Women for America v. Lafayette County,* 883 F.2d 32, 35 (5th Cir. 1989), citing *Widmar v. Vincent,* 454 U.S. 263, 275, (1981).

22. *Pfeifer,* 91 F. Supp. 2d at 1263.

23. BLACK'S LAW DICTIONARY 1407–1408 (7th ed. 1999).

24. *Library Can Limit Supremacist but Not Bar Him,* News Briefs for November 20, 2000, AMERICAN LIBRARIES, *at* http://www.ala.org/alonline/news/2000/001120.html (visited Dec. 20, 2000); Steve Arney, *Library Advised Not to Block Hale,* PANTA-GRAPH (Bloomington, Ill., Nov. 15, 2000).

25. *White Supremacist Sues Library after Speech Cancelled,* News Briefs for April 2, 2001, AMERICAN LIBRARIES, *at* http://www.ala.org/alonline/news/2001/010402.html#matthale (visited June 30, 2001).

26. *Supremacist Draws Angry Crowd in Connecticut,* News Briefs for March 19, 2001, AMERICAN LIBRARIES, *at* http://www.ala.org/alonline/news/2001/010319.html (visited July 14, 2002); *White-Rights Speech in Pennsylvania Library Triggers Violence; 25 Arrested,* News Briefs for January 21, 2002, AMERICAN LIBRARIES, *at* http://www.ala.org/alaonline/news/2002/020121.html (visited July 14, 2002); *Police Ensure Peaceful Supremacist Meeting in Virginia,* News Briefs for May 13, 2002, AMERICAN LIBRARIES, *at* http://www.ala.org/alonline/news/2002/020513. html (visited July 14, 2002).

27. *Forsyth County v. Nationalist Movement,* 505 U.S. 123 (1992).

28. *Watts v. United States,* 394 U.S. 705 (1969), citing *New York Times Co. v. Sullivan,* 376 U.S. 254, 270 (1964).

29. *Chaplinsky v. New Hampshire,* 315 U.S. 568, 572 (1942).

30. *Brandenburg v. Ohio,* 395 U.S. 444, 446 (1969) (per curiam) (Ohio statute restricting speech was unconstitutional because it did not distinguish between persons calling for the immediate use of violence and those teaching an abstract doctrine about the use of force, at issue when a film showed a speech by a Ku Klux Klan chapter, asserting that revenge might be taken against the U.S. government if it "continues to suppress the white . . . race").

31. *Bellospirito v. Manhasset Public Library,* No. 93-CV-4484, at 13–14 (E.D.N.Y. July 31, 1994), unpublished opinion (finding the library community room to be a "public forum that has been opened to the general public for at least certain categories of speech" and therefore subject to the "same standards as apply in a traditional public forum." Cited in Daniel Mach, Note, *The Bold and the Beautiful: Art, Public Spaces, and the First Amendment,* 72 NEW YORK UNIVERSITY LAW REVIEW 383 (May 1997). *See also* Marilyn C. Mazur, *Sex and Censorship: Dangers to Minors and Others? A Background Paper* (March 1999), *at* http://www.ncac. org/issues/sex_censorship.html (visited Feb. 28, 2002); and Charles P. Wiggins, *Censorship and Visual Images: Issues with Examples from Public Libraries,* LIS 615, Instructor: Beatrice Kovacs (Sept. 4, 1999), *at* http://home.att.net/~cpwiggins/librarianship/portfolio/censor_vis.html (visited Feb. 28, 2002). This student paper cites various sources from the professional library literature about the case.

32. *Perry Education Ass'n v. Perry Local Educators' Assn.,* 460 U.S. 37, 45 (1983).

33. *Turner Broadcasting System, Inc. v. FCC,* 512 U.S. 622, 662 (1994) (quoting *United States v. O'Brien,* 391 U.S. 367, 377 (1968)).

34. See *Thomas v. Chicago Park Dist.,* 534 U.S. 316 (2002) (No. 00-1249).

35. *Rice v. Paladin Enterprises,* 128 F.3d 233 (4th Cir. 1997), *cert. denied* 523 U.S. 1074 (1998).

36. *Thomas v. Chicago Park District,* 534 U.S. 316 (2002).

37. *Pfeifer v. City of West Allis,* 91 F. Supp. 2d 1253, 1256 (E.D. Wis. 2000).

38. Three days after the lawsuit was filed, the two sides reached a settlement agreement, supervised by U.S. District Judge William J. Castagna. *See* Bruce Vielmetti, *Religious Groups Gain Use of Library,* ST. PETERSBURG TIMES, Oct. 6, 1989. The library's current policy can be found *at* http://www.thpl.org/thpl/webmaster/ forms/mtgrm_policy.html (visited June 30, 2001).

7

PROFESSIONAL LIABILITY
Reference, Collection, Book Reviews, Latchkey Children

Q1   Can a librarian ever be held legally responsible for giving inaccurate information to a patron?

Q2   What might a patron claim, in filing a lawsuit against a librarian for poor reference or research service?

Q3   How do I know if poor reference service could be a "tort" in my jurisdiction?

Q4   What kind of poor reference service can lead to harm?

Resource Errors

Service Errors

Q5   Should a librarian remove a book if it has erroneous information?

Q6   We don't charge for reference service or write contracts for service. Does this protect us if we give incorrect information?

Gratuitous Nature of Information Services Provided at the Library

Gratuitous Services Shield the Librarian from Claims of "Economic Harm"

Gratuitous Services Do Not Shield the Librarian from Claims of "Personal Harm"

240

Understanding Negligence Concepts

Q7   Does a librarian have a legal duty of care to provide accurate information?

Q8   If the librarian has such a duty, what constitutes failure to meet that duty?

Q9   Must the patron show a direct connection between the librarian's failure to provide accurate information and the harm suffered by the patron?

Q10   What harm must a patron show?

Q11   Since there aren't any legal cases on libraries and information liability, what cases in related areas might provide guidance?

Understanding Malpractice Concepts

Q12   Does a professional librarian have a greater obligation to provide accurate information than a nonprofessional does?

Q13   Is a librarian legally considered to be a professional?

Q14   What would be needed to establish privity between a librarian and a patron?

Liability for Defamatory, Harmful, or Dangerous Information in the Library Collection

Q15   Are libraries responsible for libel if they unknowingly make a book available to the public that is defamatory?

Q16   Are libraries under any obligation to investigate the contents of their collections for libel?

Q17   Are libraries responsible for libel if they do know that an author or publisher is known to publish defamatory information?

Q18   Are libraries responsible for libel if they do know that a particular item on their shelves is defamatory?

Q19   Is a library liable for "dangerous" items in its collection?

Q20   Does a library have an obligation to discover whether any of its items has "dangerous" information?

Q21   Should a library put warning labels on "dangerous" or inaccurate books?

Q22   Are there laws designed to protect librarians from information liability?

Q23   Can you summarize librarian liability for giving out inaccurate information?

Q24   What if the library edits or alters the information that contains errors—has doing this now somehow made it the library's own?

Legal Information and Liability for the Unauthorized Practice of Law

Q25   When answering questions related to the law, at what point should a librarian worry that he or she is engaging in the unauthorized practice of law?

Q26   Should the library give disclaimers to patrons when helping them with medical or legal information?

Book Reviews

Q27   Can a librarian be liable for writing a bad book review?

Q28   Can a librarian freely express an opinion when writing a book review, no matter how scathing?

Latchkey Children

Q29   My library constantly has children left after closing. If they are left alone in the parking lot after hours and we do nothing, are we responsible? What if we have a policy to wait with the child until a ride comes or else call the police?

Q30   Could it be considered "premises liability" if something happens to a child left after hours in a library parking lot?

Q31   Does the "no duty" rule apply to me as a public employee?

Q32   Do libraries generally have a duty to aid someone after hours?

Q33   Have there been any court cases on latchkey children left at libraries?

Q34   What happened to the crossing guard?

Q35   You mean he was not liable, even though he knew that children often arrived early and could be in danger?

Q36   What do you mean by "special relationship"?

Q37   Does that mean that librarians have no duty to make sure that children are safely picked up after closing?

Q38   What if the child is very young, like three or four years old?

Q39   If the librarian could be liable for leaving a child in a darkened library parking lot after closing, could she go to jail?

Q40   So are you suggesting that a parent could be sent to jail for leaving a child alone at the library after closing?

Q41   What if I feel a moral duty to wait with the child, or my library has a policy to wait with the child until a ride comes?

Q42   You mean I have greater liability when I wait with a child?

Q43   Am I *personally* liable?

Notes

᠅᠅᠅

Other chapters have discussed whether a librarian and a library might be liable for violating copyright, state privacy law, etc. This chapter examines the interesting question of whether a librarian might be professionally liable for giving inaccurate information to a patron, for keeping inaccurate information on library shelves, or for writing scathing book reviews. And although librarians are generally not responsible for children left at their libraries after hours, a discussion of latchkey children is included.

Q1   *Can a librarian ever be held legally responsible for giving inaccurate information to a patron?*

This question has never been tried in court. This chapter will offer a framework for analysis that a court might use in deciding whether the librarian could be legally responsible for giving bad, incomplete, or inaccurate information to a patron. Of course, a librarian's poor performance might lead to some sort of negative action by the library—a cut in pay, transfer to a less desirable position, or even loss of employment altogether. But what about lawsuits from a patron? For example, could a lack of thoroughness in the reference or research process ever rise to a level such that a lawsuit could be brought against the librarian or the library?

Q2   *What might a patron claim, in filing a lawsuit against a librarian for poor reference or research service?*

A patron might claim that he or she suffered some form of *personal harm* (physical or mental) or *economic loss,* or both, as a result of receiving the incorrect information. In law these harms are known as "torts." In some circumstances, such as an information brokerage service within the library, a patron may have a contract with the library, and can then claim breach of contract. The language of the contract becomes crucial in such cases, and the legal analysis, including remedy, would be conducted under contract principles as opposed to tort law.[1] This chapter focuses on non-profit library settings that typically do not write contracts when providing service.

Q3   How do I know if poor reference service could be a "tort" in my jurisdiction?

Tort law, the law of personal injury, generally is state law and varies from state to state. To date, there have not been any reported legal cases on this topic, and librarians who are concerned about this topic will need to look to their state laws and court cases to find similar cases that might apply. A good place to get an overview of tort law for all the states is the second edition of the *Restatement of Torts*.[2] Restatements are compiled on various subjects in an attempt to summarize an area of law across the country. A formal group of scholars, known as the American Law Institute, began compiling and updating the restatements in the 1920s.[3] The books' topics include contracts, property, agency, conflict of laws, etc. The *Restatement of Torts* summarizes tort law across the United States, but reliance should not be made on this source alone without first consulting the local law in your specific state jurisdiction.

Q4   What kind of poor reference service can lead to harm?

Harm could arise under two general fact patterns, "resource errors" (inaccurate information on the shelf) and "service errors" (neglecting to consult the correct source).

Resource Errors

The first type of harm could arise because the librarian had referred the patron to information that is inaccurate. For example, a patron requesting information on state capitals is correctly pointed to a book on United States geography. Unfortunately, the book mistakenly identifies the capital of Wisconsin as Milwaukee and not the correct city of Madison. Or a librarian responds to a travel question by referring to a travel book on Hawaii that fails to mention the dangerous conditions such as submerged rocks and reefs or an undertow at a particular beach.[4] Perhaps a cookbook fails to indicate proper preparation and cooking techniques for exotic foods.[5] This is a resource error or fault.

Service Errors

A second type of harm might be due to the failure to properly perform the reference or research task. The correct information indeed exists, but the librarian fails to locate it. This is a service error or fault. Pritchard and Quigley[6] further break this "service" error into two subcategories: parameter errors and omission errors. A "parameter" service error is when the librarian "neglected to consult the correct source." An "omission" service error occurs when the librarian "consulted the correct source, but failed to locate the correct answer(s)."

Q5   Should a librarian remove a book if it has erroneous information?

Some libraries are filled with books that are out-of-date. Some libraries have "historical collections" that serve as a repository of knowledge. Is there a legal duty to remove ("weed") out-of-date material from the active collection, or at least alert patrons if a particular item is outdated, when there is no knowledge of a specific error but the material is otherwise suspect (out-of-date, disreputable publisher, etc.)?

   A reasonable librarian would assume that a geography book on Africa published before the political upheavals of the 1970s and 1980s is likely to have outdated information. A library book on treating AIDS published in 1985 would similarly have outdated information. Is there a *duty* to weed it from the collection? To leave it in the collection might be a hybrid fault, combining both a resource error with a service error. Since liability would ultimately rest on the lack of affirmative acts to remove the erroneous information, an "omission" of sorts in the failure to remove the book occurs (a "resource error," but only if the librarian continued to refer patrons to it as a contemporary source of material) and might also be labeled a "parameter error" (failed to consult the correct source, i.e., an up-to-date source) under Pritchard and Quigley's dual taxonomy.

Q6   We don't charge for reference service or write contracts for service. Does this protect us if we give incorrect information?

It helps quite a bit, if the harm claimed is merely economic. Most public, nonprofit, and academic libraries do not charge fees for reference service, but provide the service "gratuitously."

Gratuitous Nature of Information Services
Provided at the Library

The information provided in public and other nonprofit libraries is "gratuitous" in the sense that a person does not pay for the information product or service. This is in contrast with for-profit information contracting or brokering settings, where the collection and dissemination of information to the patron or customer are paid for either in particular or as part of the overall service interaction.

The *Restatement of Torts* recognizes a lower standard of care for gratuitous transfers.[7] However, if the information is given freely as an enticement to enter into a commercial exchange, then it may not be considered "gratuitous." For example, free legal or medical advice given with the purpose of securing later clients may not be truly "gratuitous."[8]

In any case, the *Restatement* raises the standard when one is a public servant under a duty to supply information: "The liability of one who is under a public duty to give the information extends to loss suffered by any of the class of persons for whose benefit the duty is created, in any of the transactions in which it is intended to protect them."[9]

However, the illustrations and the harms described in the *Restatement*—a notary public who makes an incorrect signature acknowledgment, the designated county clerk who provides incorrect tax arrears information, a U.S. government food inspector who incorrectly grades or marks a food product—appear quite different from the "public duty" a librarian might be said to perform.[10] The notary public, the tax clerk, and the food inspector all make some legal or official certification upon which others may be bound to rely. This is quite different than dispensing information on a variety of subjects at the reference desk.

The usual case in which the exception arises is that of a public officer who, by his acceptance of his office, has undertaken a duty to the public to furnish information of a particular kind. Typical is the case of a recording clerk, whose duty it is to furnish certified copies of the records under his control. The rule stated is not, however, limited to public officers, and it may apply to private individuals or corporations who are required by law to file information for the benefit of the public.[11]

The information liability expert Raymond Nimmer wrote: "The fact that an information service operates without commercial interest in the transaction affects the level of care that might be reasonable under the circumstances even under general negligence standards. Clearly such situations do not create an environment in which ordinary expectations are that free information maintains high levels of quality and integrity."[12] Free information services promote a public policy "in favor of the availability and circulation of information in our society."[13] This policy extends beyond mere traditional sources of information. "The theory of limited or no duty for general distribution [of] information applies equally well where the distribution involves electronic databases or news services. The principle involved invokes the general public policy of fostering broad distribution of information."[14] Thus a strong public policy argument can be made against holding librarians in a public setting accountable for the information harms that result.

Gratuitous Services Shield the Librarian from Claims of "Economic Harm"

A patron conceivably might claim "personal harm" to his or her own self or property, or a patron might claim "economic harm" to his or her business, for example. A higher legal standard is generally imposed before one can make a claim for economic harm only.

The *Restatement of Torts* recognizes this distinction: gratuitously provided information that results in economic loss alone cannot form the basis of a lawsuit. Again note that it is no longer considered "gratuitous" if the librarian or information broker gives out information without charge in the hope of establishing a later fee-for-service arrangement.[15]

Gratuitous Services Do Not Shield the Librarian from Claims of "Personal Harm"

However, where bodily injury results from gratuitously supplied information, then the law does recognize the potential for liability.[16] "The rationale is that personal safety is more important than property."[17] Before understanding the nuances of this distinction and the circumstances under which each concept might apply at the library reference desk, a basic concept of negligence must be understood.

The *Restatement of Torts* says:

> Where, as under the rule stated in this Section, the harm which results is bodily harm to the person, or physical harm to the property of the one affected, there may be liability for the negligence even though the information is given gratuitously and the actor derives no benefit from giving it.[18]

UNDERSTANDING NEGLIGENCE CONCEPTS

To analyze whether a court might ever hold a librarian liable for resource errors (library resources are inaccurate) or service errors (librarian missed important information in the resource), a look at the meaning of the term "negligence" in tort law is in order. "[N]egligence is conduct which falls below the standard established by law for the protection of others against unreasonable risk of harm. It does not include conduct recklessly disregardful of an interest of others."[19] While much of tort law is state law and thus varies from state to state, several basic statements can be made regarding the elements of a claim for negligence. Stated in its simplest form, there must be (1) a duty, (2) a breach of that duty which involves a failure to exercise reasonable care in the execution of that duty, (3) some sort of measurable harm, and (4) a legal relationship (called "proximate cause") between the breach and the harm.

In a lawsuit against a librarian for information liability, a patron must show (1) the librarian had a legal duty of care, (2) the librarian failed to meet that duty, (3) there was a legal nexus between the violation of the duty and the resulting harm (known in law as "proximate cause"), and (4) the patron suffered actual (i.e., measurable) loss or harm.[20]

Even if librarians are under a legal duty to provide absolutely error-free information, the question still would be one of reasonableness in the reliance on information given for free at the public library. The fact that the information is gratuitous may, however, affect the reasonableness of the patron's reliance upon it in taking action. There may be no reasonable justification for taking the word of a casual bystander, who has no special information or interest in the matter, as to the safety of a bridge or a scaffold. Yet a plaintiff would be fully justified in accepting the statement of one who purports to have special knowledge of the matter, or special reliability, even though the plaintiff knows that he is receiving gratuitous advice.[21] It could be argued that a librarian answering questions at a reference desk meets this reasonableness of reliance standard. The lack of reasonableness of a patron's reliance on the information impacts the proximate-cause assessment. Is it reasonable for a patron to rely on the information? Patrons might of course desire to hold the librarian responsible, which is indicative of a general trend in society and the popular press to hold someone else accountable for the harms that befall one, but this is not the same as establishing legal responsibility or proximate cause. Commentators such as Gray and Healey both believe it is not.[22]

Q7   Does a librarian have a legal duty of care to provide accurate information?

Do librarians have a legal duty to supply accurate information? The legal duty would be a recognized obligation to conform to a particular standard of conduct. No court has addressed this issue, or defined a librarian's legal duty. Within the occupation of librarianship, a reasonable person would expect librarians to provide the most accurate information possible. But is attempting to provide the most accurate information possible the same as a guarantee that all information provided is in fact correct and subject to reasonable reliance, a guarantee upon which we'd like others to legally rely?

Courts have addressed a publisher's legal duty of care. In *Gale* v. *Value Line, Inc.*,[23] for example, a federal district court refused to find a publisher responsible for errors in a report that ranked convertible securities. It wrote: "Furthermore, the imposition of a duty that required absolute and completely correct information as to every detail, including the requirement that nothing be left out would establish an intolerable and probably unachievable standard of conduct." Extrapolating from this reasoning, it seems unlikely that a court would apply an absolute standard and therefore conclude that a librarian had no duty to supply information that is 100-percent accurate. However, this issue has not yet been litigated, and each library may present a unique set of circumstances. For example, an affluent medical library used by members of the public may present a stronger case for a duty to have accurate information than a public library faced with the same medical reference question.

In the law library arena, one commentator wrote:

> Even as a publisher, the Library [the Law Library of Congress] may not be liable for negligence. Although it may have a duty to provide accurate information, where omissions or mistakes are not obvious on their face and the burden of discovering them would be unreasonable under a "risk utility balancing test," at least one court would not find liability, especially if a danger existed that the Library would not act at all rather than risk untoward liability.[24]

Furthermore, even if errors do exist in materials, it is unlikely that librarians would be required to label such items as "in error" or "out of date." In one case, involving a publisher of mislabeled entries in a mushroom field guide, the Ninth Circuit rejected placing a burden on the publisher to investigate for errors or even to place a disclaimer on the book stating that it might contain erroneous information. If publishers do not have such a duty, then librarians who might have such information on their shelves would not be held to such a duty either.[25] Therefore, it seems unlikely that a court would conclude, as a matter of law, that such a duty exists.

Q8   *If the librarian has such a duty, what constitutes failure to meet that duty?*

In legal reasoning, it is customary to continue the analysis, even if one concludes early that there is no duty. This is because a different court may find differently, particularly since each situation presents a unique set of facts and circumstances. Thus, if a court were to find such a duty to provide accurate information did exist, the next question in the inquiry is whether or not a librarian fails to meet the duty (of providing correct information) by presenting a patron with information that has errors. Whatever is reasonable, a failure to perform or meet the standards of the duty would meet the second element of a negligence claim.

Q9   *Must the patron show a direct connection between the librarian's failure to provide accurate information and the harm suffered by the patron?*

The third element, "proximate cause," means that the reliance the patron places upon the information, correct or otherwise, is reasonable and foreseeable. Even if a patron is able to demonstrate the first two elements of his or her claim of negligence, a court might still conclude that there is no "proximate cause" or close connection between the incorrect information supplied by a librarian and the harm suffered by the patron.

The question is whether it is reasonable for patrons to rely on information received from the public library. "By making a claim against a librarian, the plaintiff is not just saying that the information was somehow inadequate, but also that the librarian knew or should have known this was the case and supplied it anyway, and further that it was reasonable to rely on the librarian without any further analysis or judgment on the patron's part."[26] This would appear to be the main barrier to the success of claims against public librarians. Again, a court might conclude as a matter of law that no such reliance is reasonable.

Q10   *What harm must a patron show?*

Regarding the fourth element, there must be actual harm, not merely potential harm. Being led to believe that Milwaukee is the capital of Wisconsin may not mean much in the scheme of things—unless one used a lifeline on the television game show *Who Wants to Be a Millionaire* and called the local library and received the incorrect answer, but this would still raise a question of reasonableness, i.e., is it reasonable to rely on the answer from a public librarian when a million dollars is at stake? It might also depend on whether the librarian consulted what one would expect to be a reputable source, i.e., there was no indication that the book would contain errors, so it was reasonable for the librarian to rely on the information. In this case the librarian would have performed his or her duty, checked appropriate sources, and passed the information along to the patron. If a patron booked a nonrefundable airline flight to Milwaukee for a conference that he or she was informed was going to be held at the state capital, then there might be some measurable harm, i.e., the price of the lost ticket. The crux of the negligence issue would still be whether it was reasonable for the patron to rely on only one source of information before booking his or her ticket, and not, for example, consult with the airline first or simply look at another map. Several commentators, such as Gray[27] and Healey,[28] would answer in the negative, i.e., such reliance is not reasonable.

Q11   Since there aren't any legal cases on libraries and information liability, what cases in related areas might provide guidance?

It might be helpful, as Healey does, to look at a field related to libraries, public education, to see if actions against teachers for not teaching students properly have had any success in the courts. Courts have been resounding in their rejection of suits against educators for failing to properly educate students.[29] Logic would suggest that if courts are not receptive to suits against licensed teachers, whose relationship with students is much closer than that of a librarian and patron, then it would be logical to conclude that librarians owe no such duty either to the general public.[30] Moreover, public education is more or less compulsory; it could be argued that there is a legal duty on the part of the state to offer schooling to children without cost. On the other hand, the claim in these cases is not that teachers taught the wrong information, i.e., that the capital of Wisconsin was Milwaukee in a geography class or that an incorrect method of long division was demonstrated, but rather that the student failed to learn from the teacher's presentation of proper information. The scenario at issue in the educational malfeasance cases is therefore somewhat different from the resource or service error of the reference librarian.

The idea forwarded by the courts in defense of teachers and the educational system is that it is the student who must learn and carry the ultimate responsibility for learning or not learning; the teacher is merely the facilitator in the process. However, it is not clear in those cases whether the claim included assertions that the teacher relayed incorrect information. It might also suggest that the proper response to poor teaching, like poor reference service, should be some negative action by the teacher's (or librarian's) employer based on the low level of performance, rather than on encouraging students or patrons to seek direct legal remedy from the court system. Likewise, with librarians a court might conclude that it is against public policy to hold public librarians accountable for the information, however flawed, they dispense, because the negative impact on the willingness of librarians to provide similar services in the future would be compromised to the point that librarians would be reluctant to even provide an answer for fear of being sued.

UNDERSTANDING MALPRACTICE CONCEPTS

The use of professional licensing raises another issue. In law, a slightly higher standard of care is required of individuals who act in their professional capacity to render a service. Tort cases arising under a breach of this higher standard of practice or duty of care are known as "malpractice" cases. The *Restatement of Torts* expresses the principle as follows: "Unless he represents that he has greater or less skill or knowledge, one who undertakes to render services in the practice of a profession or trade is required to exercise the skill and knowledge normally possessed by members of that profession or trade in good standing in similar communities."[31] However, "[m]alpractice liability is not usually imposed when professionals fail to achieve certain results, but rather when they fail to exercise due diligence and reasonable care in their practices."[32] In other words, a malpractice standard changes the "reasonableness" of whether third parties (such as a library patron) may rely on what the actor says or does, the product or service he or she supplies or renders, from one of ordinary care (negligence) to one of professional care (malpractice).

*Q12   Does a professional librarian have a greater obligation
to provide accurate information than a nonprofessional
does?*

If librarians are legally considered to be *professionals,* then a lawsuit may
be evaluated by a standard that takes into account the librarian's training
and certification. Theoretically, since the librarian is a professional, it is
more reasonable for the patron to rely on the information or service provided by the librarian. The lesser negligence standard only requires that
there be some duty of general care (which a court might not identify),
coupled with the unresolved issue of whether patron reliance on the information provided is reasonable. *Malpractice,* on the other hand, requires
that the librarian comport with professional standards of care, and it is
therefore reasonable for others to rely on his or her professional product
or service.

One commentator, William Nasri, defines "professional liability/mal-
practice" as "any professional misconduct or unreasonable lack of skill in
the performance of professional duties through intentional carelessness or
simple ignorance."[33]

Q13   Is a librarian legally considered to be a professional?

Again, this has not been tested in the courts, and commentators can not
agree. Healey does not believe a court would conclude a librarian is a professional and apply malpractice standards.[34] Nasri concludes in the affirmative based upon the following characteristics common to professions:
"unique, definite and recognized social service," "intellectual techniques"
for performing the social service, specific training, "autonomy balanced
by personal responsibility . . . and acts performed within the scope of this
autonomy," service orientation, and professional organizations and codes
of conduct.[35] But a court may be less likely to do so. What other factors
might a court consider? While librarians may want to view themselves as
professionals as preferred within our own literature, a court using a different set of factors, as described above, may reach a different result.
"There must be more to becoming subject to malpractice than the mere
incantation of an ancient rule."[36]

Commentator Donald R. Ballman lists a number of factors that make
one a professional:

(1) Control (patrons relinquish control for decision-making and the
professional retains control over the work)

(2) Reliance (client relies on representations and expertise of the professional)
(3) Standards (identifiable professional standards)
(4) Privity (some sense of a fiduciary relationship with the customer, one based on trust)
(5) Impact (a direct effect of product or service on patron)
(6) Public policy (societal interest in deterring negligent acts, potential for harm is great)
(7) Service orientation of the profession (output or work products are intangible)[37]

Applying this to librarians, most would not be a "professional" in Ballman's taxonomy:

Library patrons do not typically relinquish control for decision-making, such as the purchase of the plane ticket to Milwaukee in the previous scenario. The reliance issue is dependent on the facts of the situation; the greater the disclaimers that a library presents regarding its materials and services, the lesser the risk of liability. Libraries are especially likely to issue verbal or written disclaimers when it comes to responding to inquiries on topics such as medicine and law or even ready reference or phone reference in public settings. It would appear that for many librarians, especially those in public institutions other than schools, licensing does not exist, although many places require a master's degree accredited by the American Library Association. Within the library profession, no clear standards of conduct exist. Furthermore, no clear punitive recourse for failing to comport to standards, such as taking away a license, has ever been articulated by professional organizations such as the ALA. "Professional standards are more easily discernible when a profession is licensed, or when lawsuits have provided a body of case law that defines professional duty of care. Because librarianship is not licensed and has no case law, there are no formal standards of this type."[38] Privity in the typical public library scenario does not appear to exist. Again, the potential impact upon a library patron's life quality or the potential for harm do not appear to tilt the weight of public policy factors in favor of professional status. However, the intangible nature of library service would suggest the existence of a profession. Yet plaintiffs in the closely analogous field of computer science and computing have had difficulty in establishing the professional status of programmers, computer consultants, etc., in so-called computer malpractice cases.[39]

*Q14   What would be needed to establish privity between
a librarian and a patron?*

"Privity" means a legally recognized mutual interest or a joint knowledge of something private or secret.[40] In this case, the question is whether the mutual interest in serving and being served could constitute privity. Yet the patron-librarian relationship does not seem to rise to a level contemplated by other professions such as medicine, law, or accounting, where in some sense there is privity due to the sensitive nature of the information revealed during the course of the relationship.[41] The privity analysis shifts, however, if the transaction is part of a business, like that of an information broker, where it is more possible that a court could conclude that privity exists. "[I]f the defendant is in the business of providing information and there is privity between a particular information provider and a recipient of such information, courts are likely to recognize a duty of care owing from the former to the latter."[42]

At least one court has suggested a lack of equal privity between a doctor and a medical librarian when compared to a duty owed a patient:

> This court is particularly suspicious here of the reliability of any opinions based on Dr. Kavalier's literature review, because the court found it troubling that Dr. Kavalier based his belief that certain articles on gender identity disorder were reliable on a medical librarian's statement that articles on Medline were generally reliable. Thus, the factual basis, data, principles, methods, and their application upon which Dr. Kavalier relied are sufficiently called into question that they cannot form a reliable basis in the knowledge and experience of the relevant discipline.[43]

In fact, the court noted that a mere literature review, often the task assigned to a medical librarian, is an insufficient basis or methodology on which to render a reliable expert opinion.[44]

A similar quandary is presented in libraries that, in an effort to eliminate misunderstanding, post notices or otherwise make patrons aware that the information provided is for "educational or personal use only" and should not be relied upon. It may help insulate the library, but does little in terms of building confidence in the "professional" stature of the librarian or the importance of the library to the wider community.

Of course, the entire issue of liability under negligence and malpractice standards is a bit of a double-edged sword. Librarians may be subject to a lesser legal standard, which is good from a liability perspective, but it means that librarians are not considered professionals in the eyes of the law. Moreover, if the lesser standard applies, liability is also unlikely, since patron reliance (proximate cause) upon the information received from the librarian is not reasonable. This is akin to saying courts should never hold librarians responsible, since no patron should ever rely on or pay any attention to what the librarian says or give any credence to the sources referred by the librarian in the first place—again, not much of a reflection on the quality of or regard for the profession of librarianship, but perhaps a blessing in disguise.

LIABILITY FOR DEFAMATORY, HARMFUL, OR DANGEROUS INFORMATION IN THE LIBRARY COLLECTION

In addition to inaccurate information, the question as to whether libraries are responsible for defamatory or even *dangerous* content can arise. Libraries may have books promoting the use of guns, cigar smoking, consuming alcoholic beverages, or even on bomb making. Again the question is one of reasonableness. In a more general sense, is the library or librarian responsible for the content of the material in the collection?

Q15   Are libraries responsible for libel if they unknowingly make a book available to the public that is defamatory?

The general rule is that distributors such as libraries, bookstores, and news vendors are not responsible for the errors in content they disseminate.[45] The vendor or lender is not liable if there are no facts or circumstances known to him that would suggest to him, as a reasonable person, that a particular book contains matter that upon inspection, he would recognize as defamatory.[46] "This distributor liability is rarely invoked because a plaintiff cannot often prove that a distributor had the knowledge required to impose fault."[47] Numerous courts have found publishers or other information media providers not responsible for the erroneous information in their publications, programs, etc., even when that error caused serious injury.[48] "With very few exceptions, a pattern of nonliability pervades case law dealing with publishers of general dissemination products."[49]

Q16   Are libraries under any obligation to investigate the contents of their collections for libel?

No. The *Restatement of Torts* explains that "[s]o far as the cases thus far decided indicate, the duty arises only when the defendant knows that the defamatory matter is being exhibited on his land or chattels, and he is under no duty to police them or to make inquiry as to whether such a use is being made. He is required only to exercise reasonable care to abate the defamation, and he need not take steps that are unreasonable if the burden of the measures outweighs the harm to the plaintiff."[50] This might mean that a plaintiff might have to contact each library that has the book in its collection and request that the defamatory book be removed. The impracticability of this suggests the unlikelihood of a library ever being in the position of having to remove a book that is defamatory. Furthermore, abatement might entail the insertion of a retraction notice or label, similar to a publisher's more typical "error" or "omission" addendum, into the defamatory item in the collection. However, either scenario, removal or notice, may raise serious ethical issues for libraries as well.

At least one court has concluded that "actual knowledge or facts giving rise to a duty to investigate"[51] would have to be alleged in order for a case based on distributor liability to go forward. "If a distributor can ever bear the burden of liability for libel, such detailed allegations must be required in order to insure the unrestricted distribution of newspapers and magazines which is at the heart of the First Amendment."[52]

Q17   Are libraries responsible for libel if they do know that an author or publisher is known to publish defamatory information?

They can be. First, if an author or publisher is known to publish defamatory literature, the library has a higher burden of responsibility than usual. The *Restatement of Torts* offers this instruction: "Thus, when the books of a reputable author or the publications of a reputable publishing house are offered for sale, rent or free circulation, [a library] is not required to examine them to discover whether they contain anything of a defamatory character. If, however, a particular author or a particular publisher has frequently published notoriously sensational or scandalous books, a shop or library that offers to the public such literature may take the risk of becoming liable to any one who may be defamed by them."[53] Again, a court might be tempted as a matter of law to hold that for public policy reasons or in light of overriding First Amendment concerns, the library would not be liable.[54] Second, would a tell-all author like Kitty Kelley or a scandal sheet like *The Star* or the *National Enquirer* be sufficient to trigger liability, or is a pattern of repeated and pervasive defamatory publishing required before a red-flag duty is created?

Q18   Are libraries responsible for libel if they do know that a particular item on their shelves is defamatory?

They can be. Although an individual's accusation that a book is defamatory is not proof that the book is actually defamatory, once presented with concrete evidence (court order or judgment), the library must either remove, redact, retract, or otherwise abate the defamatory portion or face potential liability as a republisher. The *Restatement of Torts* indicates that liability for defamation extends to one who fails to remove defamatory material: "One who intentionally and unreasonably fails to remove defamatory matter that he knows to be exhibited on land or chattels in his possession or under his control is subject to liability for its continued publication."[55]

Again, no court case has addressed this matter in a library setting. Overriding public policy arguments may persuade a court to hold that a library, unlike other distributors, would not be liable, even after an item in its collection has been found to be defamatory. The court's jurisdiction is also a factor. For example, a California appellate court that finds a book is defamatory does not necessarily mean the book is defamatory (against a library acting as a distributor with knowledge or as a "republisher" by keeping it on its shelf through "continued publication") in Wisconsin, since Wisconsin's law on defamation may vary from that of California. It would suggest rather that a library in California could, under a strict reading of the *Restatement,* be open to liability for defamation due to the continued access to material determined to be defamatory by a California court applying California law. The impracticality of multiple litigation in every jurisdiction where the defamed desires to prevent publication or more accurately republication (continued publication) might account for the dearth of case law on the matter.

Q19   Is a library liable for "dangerous" items in its collection?

Generally, no. It is exceptionally rare for even a publisher, much less a distributor, to be found negligent for the publication of dangerous items. Lawsuits based on perceived dangerous or harmful material have not met with success, such as those against various rock or rap groups, whose music plaintiffs claim has incited violent behavior, crimes, suicide attempts, etc.[56] A thorough discussion of these cases is beyond the scope of this book, but these lawsuits are generally unsuccessful.[57] The one instance in which a publisher was held liable was the *Hit Man* case, in which the publisher *stipulated* that its how-to-do-it manual on murder for hire was written and marketed to "would-be criminals."[58] Such a stipulation precluded more benign explanations such as offering information to detectives who pursue assassins or to crime novelists. Far more often, courts note that the broader First Amendment concerns (the "chilling effect" that such suits would have on the free flow of information) override any personal claims of harm.[59] Often courts imply that the economic cost of investigating every publication for potential error would be just too great.[60]

Q20   Does a library have an obligation to discover whether any of its items has "dangerous" information?

No. Libraries, like bookstores, are considered "distributors," and the courts do not expect them to be aware of the contents of all their items. Such an expectation would severely limit the information made available to the public. In *Smith* v. *California,* a case involving the sale of obscene material, the U.S. Supreme Court struck down an ordinance that imposed a criminal liability on booksellers for possessing and offering the material for sale.[61] The Court observed the danger of holding distributors strictly liable for the contents of their collections:

> By dispensing with any requirement of knowledge of the contents of the book on the part of the seller, the ordinance tends to impose a severe limitation on the public's access to constitutionally protected matter. For if the bookseller is criminally liable without knowledge of the contents, and the ordinance fulfills its purpose, he will tend to restrict the books he sells to those he has inspected; and thus the State will have imposed a restriction upon the distribution of constitutionally protected as well as obscene literature.[62]

The inability of plaintiffs to be successful in these cases rests as much on public policy as on legal principles: the negative effect that holding the intermediary publisher, bookstore, or library liable for erroneous information would have on future dissemination and the free flow of information.[63] If a bookstore would have no criminal liability for the content of material on its shelves, this logic might also apply to civil liability as well as the criminal obscenity at issue in *Smith.*

One can of course argue that this policy argument should not extend to the library and librarian once they know of the errors or are aware of the harm that reliance on the erroneous item might cause. Regardless of the reasonableness of this assessment, "[i]n most jurisdictions, courts hold that publishers or distributors of third-party content owe no duty of care . . . to their public readership."[64] This public policy perspective can work to protect librarians from liability. There would certainly be a disastrous effect on the availability of information services if librarians were suddenly to be held accountable for the accuracy of material or for all negative effects of the services they render.

Q21   Should a library put warning labels on "dangerous" or inaccurate books?

No. Courts have rejected labeling as a remedy for publishers, and it would seem likely that if a publisher does not need to place a warning notice on dangerous books, a library should not be required to do so either.[65]

The Ninth Circuit has declined to make publishers responsible for checking or verifying the information content of books, or even to place warning notices on books:

> Finally, plaintiffs ask us to find that a publisher should be required to give a warning (1) that the information in the book is not complete and that the consumer may not fully rely on it or (2) that this publisher has not investigated the text and cannot guarantee its accuracy. With respect to the first, a publisher would not know what warnings, if any, were required without engaging in a detailed analysis of the factual contents of the book. This would force the publisher to do exactly what we have said he has no duty to do—that is, independently investigate the accuracy of the text. We will not introduce a duty we have just rejected by renaming it a "mere" warning label. With respect to the second, such a warning is unnecessary given that no publisher has a duty as a guarantor.[66]

Other commentators, however, have suggested that imposing this burden is proper.[67]

If the case law supported this result (the placement of warning labels), librarians would face another problem. Labeling a book as dangerous would contradict the *Library Bill of Rights* as interpreted by the Intellectual Freedom Committee of the American Library Association and as adopted by the ALA Council.[68]

However repugnant to concepts of library ethics a warning notice or disclaimer might be, it can mitigate liability for harm that might arise from the information. For example, in *Herceg* v. *Hustler Magazine, Inc.,* the Fifth Circuit concluded that the First Amendment protected *Hustler* magazine from an article it ran on autoerotic asphyxia that was alleged to have "incited" a teenager to attempt the procedure that resulted in his death.[69] The *Hustler* article contained numerous and explicit warnings as to the dangerous nature of the information contained in the article.

Q22   Are there laws designed to protect librarians from information liability?

Neither case law, the *Restatement,* nor commentators' opinions suggest that immunity from liability exists at present, but standards of duty may evolve in time to hold librarians accountable. The most likely scenario requiring duty would be cases in which the error, omission, or harmful or dangerous information is identified, notice exists, and a duty to do something about it, such as no longer referring patrons to it or placing a warning notice upon it, might be required in the future.

However, at least one state, Illinois, has contemplated this unfortunate potential and has protected librarians under a "misrepresentation or false information" law:

> A public employee acting in the scope of his employment is not liable for an injury caused by his negligent misrepresentation or the provision of information either orally, in writing, by computer or any other electronic transmission, or in a book or other form of library material.[70]

This statute would protect the librarian from failing to remove out-of-date material as well as more straightforward service errors, i.e., failing to locate or provide the correct information.

Q23   Can you summarize librarian liability for giving out inaccurate information?

Under existing law, a library would not be liable for errors contained in its collections, i.e., a resource error. The public policy implications of legal rules establishing such liability would be too disastrous for the free flow of information. It is also unlikely that a court would find that librarians have a legal duty to give out accurate information. Further, it is unlikely that a court would find that librarians are like doctors or lawyers and have a higher level of care to the patrons, creating a risk of malpractice.

Finally, overriding First Amendment concerns might preclude courts from ever holding libraries responsible for information that is erroneous (a book on handgun cleaning omits the important safety step of clearing the chamber), misused, or taken out of context (a book on handguns is used to modify a pistol which is then used in a shooting).

Q24   *What if the library edits or alters the information that*
         contains errors—has doing this now somehow made it
         the library's own?

This question was asked by the law librarian of Congress, Kathleen Price, about errors in a legal database the library was considering making available on the World Wide Web.

> Conversely, if the Library and its partners exercise content control over the information available over the Internet they may be held liable for the transmission of inaccurate or harmful material. Under Perritt's analysis,[71] the decision to exercise control may well bring with it tort liability. If the Library exercises content control it has reason to know of inaccuracies in, or harmful content of, the information it makes available over the Internet. This knowledge can establish the scienter [i.e., sufficient knowledge or awareness to establish liability] necessary to support a tort claim against the Library. In short, the Library becomes a "publisher." Publishers enjoy editorial control and First Amendment protection, but do not have tort immunity.[72]

Assuming that a proper legal nexus between the reliance on the information and the harm can be established, then the question may still be whether the librarian exercised care in getting the information for the patron and whether the librarian knew or should have known the patron would rely on it. It's logical to assume that a patron would rely on the information, since he or she asked for it in the first place. The reasonableness of the reliance is still at issue. Suppose a patron wants to know whether she should have a medical procedure performed, or whether it's safe to mix two powerful medications. The patron wants accurate information, to be sure, but is it reasonable for the patron to make a possibly life-threatening decision based only upon information obtained from the local public library, as opposed to contacting a physician or pharmacist? If the patron does rely on that information, the responsibility would still not rest with the library, as the foregoing discussion has demonstrated.

Legal Information and Liability
for the Unauthorized Practice of Law

Q25   *When answering questions related to the law, at what*
         point should a librarian worry that he or she is engaging
         in the unauthorized practice of law?

This is not usually a concern for librarians, because in general, one of the defining characteristics of an "unauthorized practice of law" scenario is that the person holds himself or herself out as a lawyer or as having a specialized knowledge of law.

Commentators take differing views on the subject, however. Some say that when one considers providing reference information regarding legal or medical topics, the potential for liability is increased.[73] Other commentators suggest that this concern is overstated.[74] Helping patrons with legal information raises two liability issues: the first is the (unlikely) possibility that the librarian may be accused of practicing law without a license, and the second is the possibility that the topic raises the standard of care with which a librarian must act (also unlikely). While the same concepts could be applied to medical information (unauthorized practice of medicine and importance of medical information to patrons), this discussion only relates to legal information. Moreover, the increased concern may in part be a reaction to patron perception, i.e., a legal question is more important (and probably more complex and confusing, thus requiring more assistance) to the patron, therefore the librarian had better get it right. However, the obvious unreasonableness of this perception seems to underscore the lack of reasonable reliance the patron should legally place upon it.

First, the typical reference librarian in a public library does not hold himself or herself out as a lawyer or as having a specialized knowledge of law. Second, given the discussion regarding the reasonableness of any negligence claim against a librarian for faulty information or service, those legal standards would be even less applicable in a case of legal information dispensed at a public library's reference desk. If it is not reasonable for patrons to rely on information received from their local public library on topics of general concern, it would seem to be an even further stretch of the law and of common sense to accept a claim that it is reasonable to rely on highly specialized or important (in terms of the patrons' well-being) legal or medical information, similarly dispensed at the general library reference desk.

However, this may oversimplify the matter. A number of related professions or occupations have been the subject of litigation and commentary for the unauthorized practice of law, such as accountants,[75] social workers,[76] and real estate agents.[77] Furthermore, as noted earlier, several commentators discuss the heightened potential for liability in medical and legal reference.[78]

One concern is whether one engages in the unauthorized practice of medicine or law by dispensing medical or legal reference service.[79] Another reason for the heightened potential for liability in the medical and legal area is that cases do exist in which both doctors and lawyers have been found legally responsible for failing to use adequate up-to-date technology or research methods.[80] Commentator Paul Healey writes:

> Confusion and fear arise when questions asked by pro se users in their pursuit of legal information require answers that constitute, in whole or in part, a legal opinion by the reference librarian. The law regulating the unauthorized practice of law is exceedingly vague, and theoretically the rendering of any legal opinion or judgment could be considered as engaging in the practice of law. Because answering a reference question could result in giving a legal opinion, and because the rendering of a legal opinion can be seen as practicing law, law librarians fear that assisting pro se users could result in being accused of engaging in unauthorized practice of law.[81]

This possibility, coupled with the medical or law librarian's role in the medical and legal research process, cause some commentators to hypothesize that liability for librarian negligence is only a matter of time. Complicating this potential is the fact that in a number of medical and law libraries, the librarians may have some level of medical expertise in nursing, medical technology, or some other health science field, or may have some legal training such as a law degree, paralegal certificate, or attorney's license.

The benchmark of unauthorized practice for a licensed profession is usually based in part upon the presentation of oneself as a doctor, lawyer, etc. Other elements in the unauthorized practice of law include activities that fall into one of three categories:

(1) Representing another in a legal or administrative proceeding
(2) Preparing legal documents
(3) Providing legal advice regarding another's rights and responsibilities[82]

Q26   Should the library give disclaimers to patrons when helping them with medical or legal information?

This is a good idea. Libraries and librarians that make clear (through notices and the use of signed waivers) that no medical or legal advice will be given and patrons are to rely on the reference information that is given at their own risk will reduce the possibility of claims on these grounds. Furthermore, libraries may institute a policy of providing service only instead of information or answers. This moves the library away from an appearance of engaging in elements of medical or legal practice. A patron is instructed on how and where to locate information but is not provided an answer to a medical or legal question. Another common practice of many libraries is to only "read" and never interpret from a legal source, and not to perform any research for the patron. However, a patron who already has the legal citation may be provided with the location or even a copy of the material that is sought.

BOOK REVIEWS

A number of librarians write book reviews for professional journals and popular media. Is there any potential liability associated with this practice, if someone were to compose a negative review and it could be proved that the negative review somehow resulted in a loss of sales for the book? For some reviewers this may not be a problem, since some review sources only publish positive reviews.[83]

Q27   Can a librarian be liable for writing a bad book review?
When a librarian serves as an author, he or she must be careful not to copy someone else's work (copyright violation), or defame another person. A court case centering on alleged defamation in a book review was heard by a federal appeals court in *Moldea* v. *New York Times Co.*[84] It is a significant case not only because of its subject matter but also because of the somewhat unique procedural aspects of the case.

In 1989 the *New York Times* published a scathing review of *Interference: How Organized Crime Influences Professional Football,* by Dan E. Moldea. Reviewer Gerald Eskanazi claimed the book was the result of "too much sloppy journalism to trust the bulk of this book's 512 pages—including its whopping 64 pages of footnotes." Moldea sued the *New York Times* for defamation and lost.[85] An initial appellate decision was rendered in favor of Moldea, holding that some of the reviewer's characterizations went beyond opinion and could in fact be proved or disproved. If the facts proved to be unsupportable, there could be a finding of defamation.[86] Both the publishing and reviewing community were aghast at the impact of the opinion: write too nasty a review (of a book, movie, restaurant, etc.) and you might get sued, successfully![87] In a rare move, the federal appellate court withdrew the opinion and issued a substitute opinion complete with an introductory mea culpa—an uncommon, almost rare sequence of events in court jurisprudence.

In the end, the Court of Appeals for the District of Columbia concluded that as long as the opinion of the review is confined to the book, and is not an attack on the author, one person's opinion is as good as another. An opinion (a review) cannot rise to the level of false statement required for defamation unless the opinion implies a demonstrably false fact or relies upon statements that are provable as false. In making this assessment, the appellate court focused upon the book review's context, observing that "a book review, in which the allegedly libelous statements were made were evaluations quintessentially of a type readers expect to find in that genre."[88] In an extended commentary, the court explained what is and what is not acceptable: "We believe that the Times has suggested the appropriate standard for evaluating critical reviews: 'The proper analysis would make commentary actionable only when the interpretations are unsupportable by reference to the written work.'"[89]

Q28   Can a librarian freely express an opinion when writing
a book review, no matter how scathing?

Yes. But the reviewer should understand the distinction between mere opinion, which is legally protected, and assertion of unsupportable facts, which is not. In a seminal defamation case, *Gertz* v. *Robert Welch, Inc.,*[90] the Supreme Court appeared to give broad constitutional protection to statements of opinion. According to the Court, "Under the First Amendment there is no such thing as a false idea. However pernicious an opinion may seem, we depend for its correction not on the conscience of judges and juries but on the competition of other ideas. But there is no constitutional value in false statements of fact."[91]

Later, in *Milkovich* v. *Lorain Journal Co.,*[92] the Supreme Court reiterated that there is no blanket immunity for "opinions." The court described a "supportable interpretation" standard which says that a reviewer's interpretation must be rationally supportable by reference to the actual text he or she is evaluating. This standard also establishes boundaries even for textual interpretation. A reviewer's statement must be a rational assessment or account of something the reviewer can point to in the text, or omitted from the text, being critiqued:

> For instance, if the *Times* review stated that *Interference* was a terrible book because it asserted that African-Americans make poor football coaches, that reading would be "unsupportable by reference to the written work," because nothing in Moldea's book even hints at this notion. In such a case, the usual inquiries as to libel would apply: a jury could determine that the review falsely characterized *Interference,* thereby libeling its author by portraying him as a racist (assuming the other elements of the case could be proved).[93]

The legal standard in a review is therefore whether the "interpretation" of the reviewer is in any way "supportable" by reference to the actual item reviewed. Keeping within these boundaries should minimize, if not eliminate, the liability for librarians who choose to engage in service to the profession by writing reviews and who should at some point write a negative one.

LATCHKEY CHILDREN

*Q29   My library constantly has children left after closing.
If they are left alone in the parking lot after hours and
we do nothing, are we responsible? What if we have
a policy to wait with the child until a ride comes or
else call the police?*

It depends. Legally, these are two very different questions, both of which are explored below. The general legal principle to guide us here is that under the common law, there is a principle that a person has *no duty to come to the aid of others.* However, under the "Good Samaritan" rule, a person *could be liable* if she comes to another's aid, and *doesn't exercise due care in administering the aid.* One can be liable by failing to exercise due care and increasing the risk of harm, or by causing another to rely on aid and thereby suffer harm.

*Q30   Could it be considered "premises liability" if something
happens to a child left after hours in a library parking lot?*

The majority of cases concerning public entity liability hold that third party conduct, by itself, unrelated to the condition of the property, does not constitute a "dangerous condition." These cases rely on the definition of "dangerous condition" as a "condition of property."[94]

Q31   Does the "no duty" rule apply to me as a public employee?

Yes. As a general rule, public employees, like ordinary persons, have no duty to come to the aid of others. A person who has not created a peril is not liable for failure to take affirmative action to assist or protect another unless there is some relationship between them, which gives rise to a duty to act.[95]

Q32   Do libraries generally have a duty to aid someone after hours?

No. But again note: If a librarian begins to aid a child, she has essentially undertaken that duty and must see it through.

Q33   Have there been any court cases on latchkey children left at libraries?

No, none that are reported. A relevant case, however, concerned the legal responsibility of a crossing guard who saw a girl, who appeared to be nine or ten years old, attempt to cross a street, but did not help her because he had not yet begun duty. She was struck by a car and injured.

Q34   What happened to the crossing guard?

He won his case. The court found the crossing guard had no special relationship with the girl, and his "[mere] failure to take affirmative action to assist or protect another, no matter how great the danger in which the other is placed, or how easily he could be rescued," did not make him liable.[96]

Q35   You mean he was not liable, even though he knew that children often arrived early and could be in danger?

Yes. The court said that no special relationship existed that would impose a duty on the crossing guard to help the girl. His knowledge that the children would arrive early was immaterial.

Q36   What do you mean by "special relationship"?

The evidence that he was not authorized to work before 7:30 A.M. was sufficient to establish that he had no special relationship earlier than that time.[97]

*Q37   Does that mean that librarians have no duty to make
sure that children are safely picked up after closing?*

Unfortunately, the common law is decided on a case-by-case basis, and the
only way to know for sure is to have a case brought to court. However, the
similarity between the crossing guard case and a librarian is persuasive.

Q38   What if the child is very young, like three or four years old?

The courts sometimes do find exceptions to this principle of "no duty"
when the child is particularly young or vulnerable. A court could conceivably find a special relationship, i.e., that a librarian has assumed supervisory care over a very young child during the open hours. It's possible a
court would find that a duty extended after closing if a librarian knowingly left the child alone in the dark.

In the abstract, a librarian's knowledge that the child is alone and in
danger should not impose liability. But sometimes courts extend the law
to mitigate harsh results, and it is possible, despite this principle of law,
that a court could find the librarian had a duty of care. There is no clear
legal authority until a case comes to trial.

*Q39   If the librarian could be liable for leaving a child in a dark-
ened library parking lot after closing, could she go to jail?*

Extremely unlikely. "Criminal endangerment laws" are aimed at parents,
legal guardians, or others specifically entrusted with caring for the child's
well-being. There are criminal penalties for parents who desert a child in
any place with the intent to abandon it.[98]

*Q40   So are you suggesting that a parent could be sent to jail
for leaving a child alone at the library after closing?*

Only in the unlikely event that the parent intended to abandon the child.

*Q41   What if I feel a moral duty to wait with the child, or my
library has a policy to wait with the child until a ride comes?*

If you help the child, you assume a duty of due care and trigger a liability
analysis for breach of duty. This brings us back to the first question; *once
a librarian assumes the duty to aid another, she must exercise due care.*

> One who, having no initial duty to do so, undertakes to come to the aid
> of another is under a duty to exercise due care in performance of that

duty and is liable if (a) his failure to exercise such care increases the risk of harm or (b) the harm is suffered because of the other's reliance upon the undertaking.[99]

Q42   You mean I have greater liability when I wait with a child?

Yes. By taking on the responsibility of waiting with unattended children, the library has assumed a duty of due care. Examples of breaching "due care" might include waiting with the child for awhile and then leaving her alone, or taking the child into your car and then driving recklessly.[100]

Q43   Am I personally liable?

The short answer is, it depends. If your library has a policy that its employees should wait with the child, your actions are likely to be within the scope of your employment and are legally considered an "exercise of discretion." Each state has some protection for state and government employees, shielding them from personal liability even if they make poor decisions.[101]

Contrast this with the librarian whose library has no policy, or who otherwise voluntarily assumes the duty on her own time. She is less likely to be shielded by public employee protections, such as governmental defenses or insurance. Her liability is more likely to be that of a private person—as if she found a child in a park and offered to help.[102]

Notes

1. John A. Gray, *Personal Malpractice Liability of Reference Librarians and Information Brokers,* 9 JOURNAL OF LIBRARY ADMINISTRATION 71, 74–76 (1988).
2. RESTATEMENT (SECOND) OF TORTS (1999).
3. *See* J. Myron Jacobstein, LEGAL RESEARCH ILLUSTRATED 391–396 (7th ed. 1998), discussing the restatements.
4. *Birmingham v. Fodor's Travel Publications, Inc.,* 833 P.2d 70 (Haw. 1992) (book: FODOR'S HAWAII).
5. *Cardozo v. True,* 342 So. 2d 1053 (Ga. 1981) (book: TRADE WINDS COOKERY).
6. Teresa Pritchard and Michelle Quigley, *The Information Specialist: A Malpractice Risk Analysis,* ONLINE, May 1989, at 57, 60.
7. RESTATEMENT (SECOND) OF TORTS §552(1) (1999) (Information Negligently Supplied for the Guidance of Others).
8. Raymond T. Nimmer, INFORMATION LAW ¶10.14[4], at 10-59 (2001).
9. RESTATEMENT (SECOND) OF TORTS §552(3).
10. RESTATEMENT (SECOND) OF TORTS §552 illus. 16, 17, and 18.
11. RESTATEMENT (SECOND) OF TORTS §552 cmt. k.

12. Nimmer, INFORMATION LAW ¶10.14[4], at 10-58.

13. John A. Gray, *Personal Malpractice Liability of Reference Librarians and Information Brokers,* 9 JOURNAL OF LIBRARY ADMINISTRATION 71, 77 (1988). See also RESTATEMENT (SECOND) OF TORTS §552(1) cmt. a ("By limiting the liability for negligence of a supplier of information to be used in commercial transactions to cases in which he manifests an intent to supply the information for the sort of use in which the plaintiff's loss occurs, the law promotes the important social policy of encouraging the flow of commercial information upon which the operation of the economy rests. The limitation applies, however, only in the case of information supplied in good faith, for no interest of society is served by promoting the flow of information not genuinely believed by its maker to be true").

14. Nimmer, INFORMATION LAW ¶10.14[2][b], at 10-53.

15. RESTATEMENT (SECOND) OF TORTS §552.

16. RESTATEMENT (SECOND) OF TORTS §311 (Negligent Misrepresentation Involving the Risk of Physical Harm) (Restatement §311 states: "(1) One who negligently gives false information to another is subject to liability for physical harm caused by action taken by the other in reasonable reliance upon such information, where such harm results (a) to the other, or (b) to such third persons as the actor should expect to be put in peril by the action taken. (2) Such negligence may consist of failure to exercise reasonable care (a) in ascertaining the accuracy of the information, or (b) in the manner in which it is communicated").

17. Gray, *Personal Malpractice Liability,* 77.

18. RESTATEMENT (SECOND) OF TORTS §311 cmt. c.

19. RESTATEMENT (SECOND) OF TORTS §282 (1999) (Negligence Defined).

20. Adapted from Page Keeton et al., PROSSER AND KEETON ON THE LAW OF TORTS §30, at 164–65 (5th ed. 1984).

21. RESTATEMENT (SECOND) OF TORTS §311 cmt. c.

22. Gray, *Personal Malpractice Liability;* Paul D. Healey, *Chicken Little at the Reference Desk: The Myth of Librarian Liability,* 87 LAW LIBRARY JOURNAL 515, 524 (1995).

23. *Gale v. Value Line, Inc.,* 640 F. Supp. 967, 971 (D.R.I. 1986).

24. Kathleen Price, *The International Legal Information Network (ILIN)—A Practical Application of Perritt's "Tort Liability, the First Amendment, and Equal Access" to Electronic Networks,* 38 VILLANOVA LAW REVIEW 555, 570 n.17 (1993) (citing and referring to *Braun v. Soldier of Fortune Magazine, Inc.,* 968 F.2d 1110 (11th Cir. 1992) (applying risk-utility analysis to issue of negligent publishing). *See also* Brian Cullen, Note, *Putting a "Chill' on Contract Murder: Braun v. Soldier of Fortune and Tort Liability for Negligent Publishing,* 38 VILLANOVA LAW REVIEW 625 (1993).

25. *Winter v. G. P. Putnam's Sons,* 938 F.2d 1033 (9th Cir. 1991).

26. Healey, *Chicken Little at the Reference Desk,* 524.

27. Gray, *Personal Malpractice Liability,* 77 ("It is my 'educated guess' that common law courts will hold that reference librarians do not have a duty of care when acting as information intermediaries on behalf of their patrons").

28. Healey, *Chicken Little at the Reference Desk,* 524.
29. Julie O'Hara, *The Fate of Educational Malpractice,* 14 EDUCATION LAW REPORTER 887 (1986); Laurie S. Jamison, *Educational Malpractice: A Lesson in Professional Accountability,* 32 BOSTON COLLEGE LAW REVIEW 899 (1991); John G. Culhane, *Reinvigorating Educational Malpractice Claims: A Representational Focus,* 67 WASHINGTON LAW REVIEW 349; Ryland F. Mahathey, Note, *Tort Law: Can an Educator Be Liable for a Student's Failure? The Tort of Educational Malpractice,* 34 WASHBURN LAW JOURNAL 147 (1994).
30. Healey, *Chicken Little at the Reference Desk,* 529.
31. RESTATEMENT (SECOND) OF TORTS §299A (1999) (Undertaking in Profession or Trade).
32. Marianne Puckett and James Pat Craig, *Information Malpractice,* in 52 ENCYCLOPEDIA OF LIBRARY AND INFORMATION SCIENCE 141, 146 (1993).
33. William Z. Nasri, *Professional Liability,* in LEGAL ISSUES FOR LIBRARY AND INFORMATION MANAGERS 141, 141 (William Z. Nasri ed., 1987).
34. Healey, *Chicken Little at the Reference Desk,* 521–522, 525–526.
35. Nasri, *Professional Liability,* 142.
36. Donald R. Ballman, *Software Tort: Evaluating Software Harm by Duty of Function and Form,* 3 CONNECTICUT INSURANCE LAW JOURNAL 417, 456 (1996/ 1997).
37. Ballman, *Software Tort,* 456.
38. Paul D. Healey, *Chicken Little at the Reference Desk: The Myth of Librarian Liability,* 87 LAW LIBRARY JOURNAL 515, 526 (1995).
39. Kevin S. McKinnon, *Computer Malpractice: Are Computer Manufacturers, Service Bureaus, and Programmers Really the Professionals They Claim to Be?,* 23 SANTA CLARA LAW REVIEW 1065 (1983); William D. Horgan, Comment, *The Y2K Problem: A Proposed Statute to Guide Triers of Fact in Determinations of Negligence,* 6 RICHMOND JOURNAL OF LAW & TECHNOLOGY 15 (Winter 1999), *available at* http://www.richmond.edu/jolt/v6i3i/note3.html; Ballman, *Software Tort,* 426; Andrew S. Crouch, *When the Millennium Bug Bites: Business Liability in the Wake of the Y2K Problem,* 22 HAMLINE LAW REVIEW 797, 812 (1999).
40. BLACK'S LAW DICTIONARY 1217–1218 (7th ed. 1999).
41. Joel Rothstein Wolfson, *Electronic Mass Information Providers and Section 552 of the "Restatement (Second) of Torts": The First Amendment Casts a Long Shadow,* 29 RUTGERS LAW JOURNAL 67, 73–82 (1997).
42. Kent D. Stuckey, INTERNET AND ONLINE LAW §3.01[1][b][i], at 3-4 to 3-5 (2000).
43. *Smith v. Rasmussen,* 57 F. Supp. 2d 736, 767 (N.D. Iowa 1999).
44. *Smith,* 57 F. Supp. 2d at 767.
45. John N. Talbot, NEW MEDIA: INTELLECTUAL PROPERTY, ENTERTAINMENT AND TECHNOLOGY LAW §10.5, at 10-4 (1999); Raymond T. Nimmer, INFORMATION LAW ¶10.05[2][b][ii] (2001).
46. RESTATEMENT (SECOND) OF TORTS §581 cmt. e (1999) (Transmission of Defamation Published by Third Parties).
47. Michelle J. Kane, Business Law: Electronic Commerce: Internet Service Provider Liability: *Blumenthal v. Drudge,* 14 BERKELEY TECHNOLOGY LAW JOURNAL 483, 487 (1999) (footnote omitted).

48. See, e.g., *Winter v. G. P. Putnam's Sons*, 938 F.2d 1033 (9th Cir. 1991) (book: ENCYCLOPEDIA OF MUSHROOMS); *Mark v. Zulli*, No. CV 075386 (Cal. Super. Ct. Oct. 7, 1994); and *David v. Jackson*, No. 540624 (Cal. Super. Ct. Sept. 8, 1994) (unpublished opinions discussed in News Notes, 22 MEDIA LAW REPORTER no. 42 (Nov. 1, 1994); *Barden v. HarperCollins Publishers, Inc.*, 863 F. Supp. 41 (D. Mass. 1994) (book: THE COURAGE TO HEAL and THE COURAGE TO HEAL WORK-BOOK); *Gutter v. Dow Jones, Inc.*, 490 N.E.2d 898 (Ohio 1992) (WALL STREET JOURNAL); *First Equity Corp. v. Standard & Poor's Corp.*, 869 F.2d 175 (2d Cir. 1989) (Corporation Records); *Gale v. Value Line, Inc.*, 640 F. Supp. 967 (D.R.I. 1986) (Value Line convertibles); *Birmingham v. Fodor's Travel Publications, Inc.*, 833 P.2d 70 (Haw. 1992) (book: FODOR'S HAWAII); *Alm v. Nostrand Reinhold Co.*, 134 Ill. App. 716, 480 N.E.2d 1263 (1985) (THE MAKING OF TOOLS); *Lewin v. McCreight*, 655 F. Supp. 282 (E.D. Mich. 1987) (THE COMPLETE METALSMITH); *Jones v. J. B. Lippincott Co.*, 694 F. Supp. 1216 (D. Md. 1988) (HANDBOOK OF NURSING); *Libertelli v. Hoffman-LaRoche*, 7 MEDIA LAW REPORTER 1734 (S.D.N.Y. 1981) (PHYSICIAN'S DESK REFERENCE); *Cardozo v. True*, 342 So. 2d 1053 (Ga. 1981) (TRADE WINDS COOKERY); *Smith v. Linn*, 386, Pa. Super. Ct. 392, 563 A.2d 123 (1989) (LAST CHANCE DIET); *Roman v. New York*, 110 Misc. 2d 799, 442 N.Y.S.2d 944 (Super. Ct. 1981) (Planned Parenthood pamphlet); *Demuth Development Corp. v. Merkt Co.*, 432 F. Supp. 990 (E.D.N.Y. 1977) (ENCYCLOPEDIA OF CHEMICALS AND DRUGS); *Walter v. Buer*, 439 N.Y.S.2d 821 (Sup. Ct. 1981) (*Discovering Science* television program).

49. Nimmer, INFORMATION LAW ¶10.14[2][a], at 10-52. See also Joel Rothstein Wolfson, *Electronic Mass Information Providers and Section 552 of the "Restatement (Second) of Torts": The First Amendment Casts a Long Shadow*, 29 RUTGERS LAW JOURNAL 67, 81–103 (1997).

50. RESTATEMENT (SECOND) OF TORTS §577 cmt. p (1999) (What Constitutes Publication).

51. *Lewis v. Time, Inc.*, 83 F.R.D. 455, 465 (E.D. Cal. 1979).

52. *Lewis*, 83 F.R.D. at 465.

53. RESTATEMENT (SECOND) OF TORTS §581 cmt. e (Transmission of Defamation Published by Third Parties).

54. Wolfson, *Electronic Mass Information Providers*, 81–103.

55. RESTATEMENT (SECOND) OF TORTS §577(2).

56. *McCollum v. Columbia Broadcasting System*, 249 Cal. Rptr. 187 (Cal. Ct. App. 1988) (court rejected negligence claim based on harmful nature of Ozzy Osbourne music (*Blizzard of Oz, Diary of a Madman,* and *Speak of the Devil*): the works were protected by the First Amendment, "Osbourne's music was not directed and intended toward the goal of bringing about the imminent suicide of listeners and . . . it was not likely to produce such a result"); *Davison v. Time Warner*, 1997 U.S. Dist. LEXIS 21559, 1997 WL 405907 (S.D. Tex. 1997); *Vance v. Judas Priest*, 1990 WL 130920 (D.C. Nev. 1990); *Waller v. Osbourne*, 763 F. Supp. 1144 (M.D. Ga. 1991), *aff'd without opinion* 958 F.2d 1084 (11th Cir. 1992), *cert. denied* 508 U.S. 916 (1992).

57. *See* Patricia R. Stembridge, *Adjusting Absolutism: First Amendment Protection for the Fringe*, 80 BOSTON UNIVERSITY LAW REVIEW 907 (2000); Robert Firester and

Kendall T. Jones, *Catchin' the Heat of the Beat: First Amendment Analysis of Music Claimed to Incite Violent Behavior*, 20 LOYOLA OF LOS ANGELES ENTERTAIN-MENT LAW REVIEW 1 (2000); Gregory Akselrud, *Hit Man: The Fourth Circuit's Mistake in* Rice v. Paladin Enterprises, Inc., 19 LOYOLA OF LOS ANGELES ENTERTAINMENT LAW REVIEW 375 (1999); David Crump, *Camouflaged Incitement: Freedom of Speech, Communicative Torts, and the Borderland of the Brandenburg Test*, 29 GEORGIA LAW REVIEW 1 (1994). *See also* Robert N. Houser, *Allegedly Inciteful Rock Lyrics—A Look at Legal Censorship and Inapplicability of First Amendment Standards*, 17 OHIO NORTHERN UNIVERSITY LAW REVIEW 323 (1990); Peter Alan Block, *Modern-Day Sirens: Rock Lyrics and the First Amendment*, 63 SOUTHERN CALIFORNIA LAW REVIEW 777 (1990); John W. Holt, *Protecting America's Youth: Can Rock Music Lyrics Be Constitutionally Regulated?*, 16 JOURNAL OF CONTEMPORARY LAW 53 (1990); John A. Gray, *Strict Liability for the Dissemination of Dangerous Material*, 82 LAW LIBRARY JOURNAL 497 (1990).

58. *Rice v. Paladin Enterprises, Inc.*, 128 F.3d 233, 241 (4th Cir. 1997). *See also* Akselrud, *Hit Man*, 375.

59. Wolfson, *Electronic Mass Information Providers*, 73–82 (discussing the overriding First Amendment concern that permeates court analysis in many of these cases).

60. *Birmingham v. Fodor's Travel Publications, Inc.*, 833 P.2d 70, 75 (Haw. 1992).

61. *Smith v. California*, 361 U.S. 147 (1959).

62. *Smith*, 361 U.S. at 153.

63. See, e.g., Jennifer L. Phillip, *Information Liability: The Possible Chilling Effect of Tort Claims against Producers of Geographic Information Systems Data*, 26 FLORIDA STATE UNIVERSITY LAW REVIEW 743 (1999).

64. Raymond T. Nimmer, INFORMATION LAW ¶10.14[2][a], at 10-51 to -52 (2000).

65. *Winter v. G. P. Putnam, Sons*, 938 F.2d 1033, 1037–1038 (9th Cir. 1991).

66. *Winter*, 938 F. 2d at 1037–1038.

67. *But see* Lars Noah, *Authors, Publishers, and Products Liability: Remedies for Defective Information in Books*, 77 OREGON LAW REVIEW 1195 (1998).

68. See 2.16, *Statement on Labeling: An Interpretation of the Library Bill of Rights*, reprinted in American Library Association, Office for Intellectual Freedom, INTEL-LECTUAL FREEDOM MANUAL (6th ed. 2002).

69. *Herceg v. Hustler Magazine, Inc.*, 814 F.2d, 1017, 1204 (5th Cir. 1987).

70. 745 ILL. COMP. STAT. §10/2-210 (2000) ("Misrepresentation or False Information").

71. Referring to Henry J. Perritt Jr., *Tort Liability, the First Amendment, and Equal Access*, 5 HARVARD JOURNAL OF LAW & TECHNOLOGY 65 (1992).

72. Kathleen Price, *The International Legal Information Network (ILIN)—A Practical Application of Perritt's "Tort Liability, the First Amendment, and Equal Access" to Electronic Networks*, 38 VILLANOVA LAW REVIEW 555, 559–560 (1993).

73. Allan Angoff, *Library Malpractice Suit: Could It Happen to You?*, 7 AMERICAN LIBRARIES 489 (1976); Martha J. Dragich, *Information Malpractice: Some Thoughts on the Potential Liability of Information Professionals*, 8 INFORMATION TECHNOLOGY & LIBRARIES 265 (1989); Susan Dunn, *Society, Information Needs, Library Services and Liability*, 26 IOWA LIBRARY QUARTERLY 18 (1989); John A.

Gray, *Personal Malpractice Liability of Reference Librarians and Information Brokers,* 9 JOURNAL OF LIBRARY ADMINISTRATION 74 (1988); Gerome Leone, *Malpractice Liability of a Law Librarian?,* 73 LAW LIBRARY JOURNAL 45 (1980); Robin K. Mills, *Reference Service vs. Legal Advice: Is It Possible to Draw the Line?,* 72 LAW LIBRARY JOURNAL 188 (1979); Anne P. Mintz, *Information Practice and Malpractice: Do We Need Malpractice Insurance?,* 9 ONLINE 20 (1984); William Z. Nasri, *Malpractice Liability: Myth or Reality?,* 1 JOURNAL OF LIBRARY ADMINISTRATION 4 (1980); Thomas Steele, *Liability of Librarians for Negligence,* 26 PUBLIC LIBRARIES 8 (1987).

74. Gray, *Personal Malpractice Liability,* 71.

75. Elijah D. Farrell, *Accounting Firms and the Unauthorized Practice of Law: Who Is the Bar Really Trying to Protect?,* 33 INDIANA LAW REVIEW 599 (2000).

76. Anthony Bertelli, *Should Social Workers Engage in the Unauthorized Practice of Law?,* 8 BOSTON UNIVERSITY PUBLIC INTEREST LAW JOURNAL 15 (1998).

77. Shane L. Goudey, *Too Many Hands in the Cookie Jar: The Unauthorized Practice of Law by Real Estate Brokers,* 75 OREGON LAW REVIEW 889 (1996).

78. Marianne Puckett and James Pat Craig, *Information Malpractice,* in 52 ENCYCLOPEDIA OF LIBRARY AND INFORMATION SCIENCE 141, 152–161 (1993); Mark Mackler and Michael Saint-Onge, *The Sky May Yet Fall on Firm Librarians: A Reply to "Chicken Little at the Reference Desk,"* 88 LAW LIBRARY JOURNAL 456 (1996); Paul D. Healey, *Chicken Little at the Reference Desk: The Myth of Librarian Liability,* 87 LAW LIBRARY JOURNAL 515, 527–529 (1995).

79. Wayne Moore, *Are Organizations That Provide Free Legal Services Engaged in the Unauthorized Practice of Law?,* 67 FORDHAM LAW REVIEW 2397 (1999); William H. Brown, *Legal and the Unauthorized Practice of Law: Protection or Protectionism,* 36 CALIFORNIA WESTERN SCHOOL OF LAW 157 (1999).

80. *Helling v. Carey,* 519 P.2d 981 (Wash. 1974) (failure to use technology in administering glaucoma test); *Smith v. Lewis,* 530 P.2d 589 (Cal. 1975) (failure to use computerized technology in researching a legal question); *Harbeson v. Parke Davis,* 746 F.2d 517 (9th Cir. 1984) (failure to use computer technology in researching a medical issue).

81. Paul D. Healey, *In Search of the Delicate Balance: Legal and Ethical Questions in Assisting the Pro Se Patron,* 90 LAW LIBRARY JOURNAL 129, 129–130 (1998).

82. Derel A. Denckla, *Nonlawyers and the Unauthorized Practice of Law: An Overview of the Legal and Ethical Parameters,* 67 FORDHAM LAW REVIEW 2581, 2588 (1999).

83. *See* G. Edward Evans, DEVELOPING LIBRARIES AND INFORMATION CENTER COLLECTIONS 111–115 (2000).

84. *Moldea v. New York Times Co.,* 22 F.3d 310 (D.C. Cir. 1994).

85. *Moldea v. New York Times Co.,* 793 F. Supp. 335 (D.D.C. 1992).

86. *Moldea v. New York Times Co.,* 15 F.3d 137 (D.C. Cir. 1994).

87. Martin Garbus, *My Mother, Book Reviews, and the First Amendment,* LEGAL TIMES, March 14, 1994, at 19; Martin Garbus, *My Mother, Book Reviews, and the First Amendment,* PUBLISHERS WEEKLY, April 25, 1994, at 28.

88. *Moldea,* 22 F.3d at 315.

89. *Moldea,* 22 F.3d at 315, quoting Petition for Rehearing at 8.

90. *Gertz v. Robert Welch, Inc.,* 418 U.S. 323 (1974).

91. *Gertz,* 418 U.S. at 339–340.

92. *Milkovich v. Lorain Journal Co.,* 497 U.S. 1 (1990).

93. *Moldea,* 22 F.3d at 315.

94. See, e.g., *Peterson v. San Francisco Community College District,* 36 Cal. 3d 799, 811 (1984).

95. *Westbrooks v. State of California,* 173 Cal. App. 3d 1203, 1208 (1985), citing *Williams v. State of California,* 34 Cal. 3d 18, 23 (1983); RESTATEMENT (SECOND) OF TORTS §314 (1999).

96. *Scott v. Farar,* 139 Cal. App. 3d 462, 466 (1985), citing *Davidson v. City of Westminster,* 32 Cal. 3d 197 (1982). There are also a number of cases that show public schools have no duty to supervise students on their way to and from school. For example, see *Gilbert v. Sacramento Unified School District,* 65 Cal. Rptr. 913, 916 (Ct. App. 1968) (no liability was imposed on school personnel when a child was injured; "an indispensable condition of liability for negligence is that a duty of care be owed to the person injured").

97. *Scott,* 139 Cal. App. 3d at 466–467.

98. See, e.g., CAL. PENAL CODE §271 and §273(b) (2000) ("Every parent or any child under the age of 14 years, and every person to whom any such child has been confided for nurture, or education, who deserts such child in any place whatever with intent to abandon it, is punishable by imprisonment in the state prison or in the county jail not exceeding one year or by fine not exceeding one thousand dollars ($1,000) or both").

99. *Westbrooks,* 173 Cal. App. 3d at 1208, citing *Williams v. State of California,* 34 Cal. 3d 18 (1983).

100. By analogy, see *Gonzales v. City of San Diego,* 130 Cal. App. 3d 882 (1982). In *Gonzales,* the court held that by voluntarily providing lifeguard services on a public beach, the city assumed a duty of care and then breached its duty after failing to warn swimmers about dangerous riptide conditions.

101. See, e.g., CAL. GOV'T CODE §820.2 (2000) ("Except as otherwise provided by statute, a public employee is not liable for an injury resulting from his act or omission where the act or omission was the result of the exercise of the discretion vested in him, whether or not such discretion be abused").

102. See, e.g., CAL. GOV'T CODE §820.2 (2000) ("Except as otherwise provided by statute (including Section 820.2), a public employee is liable for injury caused by his act or omission to the same extent as a private person").

8 ISSUES IN LIBRARY EMPLOYMENT

Employment Reference Inquiries and Requests

Q1   What are the major pitfalls that library employers should be aware of when it comes to giving letters of reference?

Q2   It sounds like the library is damned if it gives good references and damned if it gives bad ones. What should it do?

Defamation

Tortious Interference with a Prospective Contractual Relationship

Fair Employment Laws

Negligent Referrals

Q3   Is there any immunity for employers who give out negative references that they believe are truthful?

Q4   What are the major pitfalls that library employers should be aware of when it comes to asking for references when they are hiring new employees?

Q5   How far does the library need to go when investigating a potential new employee?

Office Romance: Employee Fraternization Rules

Q6   What are the legal ramifications of employees who are involved in romantic relationships with each other?

No Policy Scenario

Policy in Place

Q7   Can a library policy ban office romances?

Q8   In setting office romance policies, does it matter whether the library is in the public or the private sector?

Q9   What if the library employee is an "at will" worker?

Q10   Can libraries make policies that say spouses can't work together?

Q11   Can libraries prohibit employees' romantic behavior in their free time?

Q12   What should a library do if it wants to have an anti-fraternization policy, especially to shield itself from sexual harassment claims?

Q13   What elements should be in a "love contract"?

Q14   How can an employer enforce a non-fraternization policy?

Employees and Free Speech

Public Sector v. Private Sector

Parameters of First Amendment Protections
for Public Employee Speech

Q15   What is "protected speech"?

Q16   How does a court determine if the employee's speech is a "substantial or motivating factor" behind the adverse employment action?

Q17   How can the employer prove it would have made the same decision even if the employee had not engaged in the protected conduct?

Q18   How do courts balance an employee's rights to speech on matters of public concern and the employer's need for a nondisruptive workplace?

Case Study: Library Technical Services Supervisor
May Make Complaints about Library Safety

Political Speech

Q19   What political speech rights do public library employees have?

Political Campaigns

Q20   Can library staff that work for the government participate in political campaigns?

Q21   May library staff run for public office?

Q22   May staff put political campaign literature on their desk in the office if they do not actively circulate it?

Q23   Can an employee use a union leave of absence for partisan political activity?

Q24   Could library staff go to jail for violating laws that restrict public employees' political activities?

Legislation and Ballot Measures

Q25   May a library employee take a position on a ballot measure?

Q26   Can library staff inform patrons regarding pending library budget cuts or urge patrons to contact their local officials to support library funding initiatives?

Q27   What is the difference between "providing information" and "advocacy"?

Q28   May library staff generally discuss politics with the public?

Q29   How does a library employee know precisely what restrictions are in place?

Q30   If the library worker is a *contractor,* rather than an *employee,* does this affect his or her rights?

Discrimination in the Workplace

Free Speech and Harassment

Q31   Is there a conflict between free speech and laws against harassment?

Q32   What do the federal and state laws prohibiting "harassment speech" restrict?

Q33   How would a library employee show sexual harassment?

Q34   How is a "hostile work environment" defined?

Q35   What is the employer's responsibility when faced with a "hostile environment" claim?

Q36   Here's the million dollar question. Is it possible for *library patrons* to cause a "hostile environment" for staff by viewing pornographic images on library computers?

Q37   How would a court analyze the hostile environment claim when pornography is on library computers, according to the First Amendment?

Case Study: Loudoun County Public Library

> The Policy on Internet Sexual Harassment
>
> Policy Was Not a Time, Place, and Manner Restriction
>
> Policy Failed Strict Scrutiny Test
>
> Policy Not Narrowly Tailored to Achieve Its Goal

Case Study: Minneapolis Public Library

Q38   What are examples of other types of employment discrimination suits?

Case Study: Library Technician Sues High School for Discrimination under the ADA, ADEA, Civil Rights Act, and the Maine Human Rights Act

> Facts and Claims of the Case: Library Technician Files for Discrimination
>
> (1) Americans with Disabilities Act (ADA)
>   Shoulder Tendonitis
>   Obesity as Perceived Disability
> (2) Age Discrimination in Employment Act of 1967 (ADEA)
> (3) 42 U.S.C. §1981 and §1981a
> (4) Maine Human Rights Act (MHRA)

Q39   What should an employer do when an employee expresses religious convictions in the workplace and others feel harassed by that expression?

Case Study: Evangelical Christian Factory Employee's Dismissal Upheld

Notes

This chapter discusses a variety of legal issues related to employee management. It addresses several trends and recent developments in employment law, as well as situations unique to libraries. It is not meant as a comprehensive treatment of fair employment law.

EMPLOYMENT REFERENCE INQUIRIES AND REQUESTS

Q1   What are the major pitfalls that library employers
should be aware of when it comes to giving letters
of reference?

From time to time, library managers may be asked to provide letters of reference or act as a reference for departing employees. As an employer, the library will also want references regarding potential future employees. In the past, this process may have been somewhat routine—an employee asked a manager to serve as a reference, and the manager did so.

Today, however, a prudent manager should tread carefully before agreeing to serve as a reference and when making the actual reference or recommendation. Employees and former employees are increasingly suing employers for providing negative references.[1]

Employers also face liability from the subsequent employer if they fail to provide accurate information or omit crucial information about a former employee that led another employer to hire an individual in error.[2]

Q2   It sounds like the library is damned if it gives good
references and damned if it gives bad ones. What
should it do?

This is true. By disclosing negative information, employers potentially expose themselves to claims of defamation[3] or tortious interference with a prospective contractual relationship.[4] By intentionally failing to include negative information, employers face possible negligent referral or misrepresentation claims.[5]

Truth, good faith, and non-retaliatory motives, however, should see the library through this catch-22.

Defamation

Truth is always a defense against a claim of defamation.[6] Employers should be careful to tell the entire truth, not hide behind it, as a half-truth is as bad as a lie.[7] Opinion[8] and consent[9] are also defenses to a charge of defamation. If information provided in a reference is mere opinion or fact and the employee has consented to the release of the information, the employer providing the referral or reference will have complete insulation from a later claim of defamation.[10]

Tortious Interference with a Prospective Contractual Relationship

Good faith is key to the library here. A claim of tortious interference requires malice or some evidence of ill intent. Tortious interference with prospective advantage is "an intentional, damaging, intrusion on another's potential business relationship, such as the opportunity of obtaining customers or employment."[11]

Fair Employment Laws

Depending on the surrounding circumstances, providing a substantiated negative reference can open the employer to other liability as well. For example, if the employee has made claims under Title VII of the Civil Rights Act of 1964—i.e., that the employer discriminated against the employee on the basis of race, religion, gender, or any of the other protected categories—a post-employment negative reference may be viewed as an impermissible retaliation. The Supreme Court has recently found that an employer could be liable under the federal fair employment laws if the employer provided the negative information (even if it was truthful) as a retaliation for the employee filing a discrimination claim.[12] This suggests that in those limited instances where the library is involved in employment discrimination, it should restrict any reference to name and dates of employment only, in order to avoid any chance of liability under federal discrimination law.

Negligent Referrals

Employers that give negative references that are truthful will generally be free of liability. Yet many employers may still be intimidated by the possibility of litigation or other trouble from the former employee, or by the legal expense and time it might require even to prepare a motion to dismiss the lawsuit. As a result, employers may give a neutral or positive referral where one is not warranted.[13] Employers may err on the side of caution by *not revealing,* for example, the dangerous propensity of a former employee and providing a neutral or even a positive recommendation. In these circumstances, liability may arise under a concept known as "negligent referral."

Consider the following cases. In *Randi* v. *Muroc Joint Unified School District*,[14] several letters of recommendation were written on behalf of a former employee. The letters described the employee in very positive terms and recommended him without reservation for a vice-principal position at another school. In truth, the man had been forced to resign due to complaints filed by several female students who claimed that he had acted inappropriately toward them. The man later molested a female student while in his new position. The California Supreme Court ruled that coupled with the unsupportable recommendations given, this amounted to an affirmative misrepresentation. The court stressed that liability will apply only where there is a substantial, foreseeable risk of physical harm to the prospective employer or to third parties, such as future coworkers or patrons.

Nondisclosure of pertinent facts may also give rise to liability on the part of a less than forthright former employer.[15] In *Jerner* v. *Allstate Insurance Company*,[16] the employer had a policy of not giving recommendations. The employer indicated in writing, however, that the employee was released due to corporate restructuring. In reality, the employee was let go because he brought a gun to work. After he was fired from his next employer, Fireman's Fund Insurance Company, the employee returned to work and shot and killed several coworkers. Cases like *Jerner* v. *Allstate Insurance Company* demonstrate that "employers who think they are playing it safe by handing out good references to bad employees may later be held liable for misrepresentations or omissions."[17]

Consider providing additional information beyond dates of employment only on condition of a signed release of liability from the prospective employer against any claims of negligent referral. This avoids the invariably problematic "don't ask-don't tell" scenario and provides the referring employer with the necessary basis upon which to make an informed decision as to whether the information, if omitted, would pose a substantial risk of foreseeable harm to third parties. Any time the former employee would expose an "at risk" population to harm (safety-sensitive positions and care or custody situations), the former employer should be forthcoming with relevant information. The work experience of the employee can form the basis of this determination.

Q3   *Is there any immunity for employers who give out negative references that they believe are truthful?*

Yes. This is known as a "qualified privilege." This privilege dates back to the common law, and is now part of state statutes throughout the country. It gives an employer civil immunity against defamation claims that may occur when the employer makes defamatory statements about a departing employee or former employee.

Under qualified privilege protection, employers may convey statements to the departing employee or former employee and to the employee's coworkers through an exit interview or in a staff meeting with other employees discussing the circumstances of their coworker's recent departure. An employer may also share a writing regarding a former employee, such as a performance evaluation, with a prospective employer of the employee. The statutory qualified privilege gives employers a defense against defamation claims brought by disgruntled employees or former employees. This is to encourage employers to communicate employment information to prospective employers.[18] Most of these statutes require some sort of good faith on the part of the employer; thus the qualified privilege is countered by a showing that the employer abused the privilege.

Q4   *What are the major pitfalls that library employers should be aware of when it comes to asking for references when they are hiring new employees?*

Employers have been sued for "negligent hiring" when the employer failed to make reasonable inquiry into the information provided by a potential employee, proceeded to make the hire, and the employee later committed some harm to fellow employees or to third parties.[19]

When libraries are in the position of hiring, they have a duty to make a reasonable inquiry into the background of prospective employees. Failure to do so may result in a claim of negligent hiring. As in all theories of liability based on negligence, the employer is under a duty of reasonable care when hiring individuals "who, because of the employment, may pose a threat of injury to members of the public."[20] For example, an employer of an apartment manager failed to make any inquiry into the employee's background other than performing a credit check and having him complete a standard application form. The manager had a record of burglary and later committed several offenses against fellow apartment residents.[21] In a similar case, an employment agency failed to investigate the background surrounding the sexual assault history of an employee. The agency relied on the explanation given by the employee, who claimed innocence when in fact he was convicted of raping a military coworker.[22]

Q5   How far does the library need to go when investigating
a potential new employee?

The key here is reasonableness: the scope of the employer's duty to investigate a prospective employee is "directly related to the severity of risk third parties are subjected to by an incompetent employee."[23] Employment situations with at-risk populations or where the employee exercises some sort of custody or care would qualify. While a position at the adult reference desk at a public library would not qualify, one in the children's services area or as a media specialist in a K–12 setting would arguably meet this standard.

This area is based in state law, so a check of your state's case law should be made, since the cases discussed in this section are only representative of the developing law, and may not be the controlling law in your jurisdiction. The *Randi* and *Jerner* cases received national attention, at least in the employment community, and many state legislatures responded. As a result, many states have passed laws that hold employers harmless for liability arising from an employment reference.[24] A so-called errors and omissions clause (i.e., in negligent referral cases) in such statutes makes the immunity generally conditional on the reference being truthful and made in good faith. In other words, the employer must not distort in any way the work record of the employee, or leave out information that if omitted would pose a substantial risk of foreseeable harm to third parties. For example, failing to reveal to a prospective employer that a children's librarian was let go because of questionable behavior toward grade school-age patrons, which was supported by several written complaints from parents, may give rise to a claim of intentional (fraudulent) or negligent misrepresentation.[25] Some of the statutes also protect the subsequent employer from a mistake in hiring (i.e., the negligent hiring cases). However, this reliance must still be reasonable under the circumstances.

In summary, it is recommended that libraries consider or adopt the following policies and procedures:

Consider limiting references to verification information only: name, dates, position title and job description, pay range if public employee.

Provide references, but only with the signed consent of the employee and a release from liability from the soliciting future employer.

If you decide to provide a reference, you cannot be selective in what you say. The reference must be truthful, containing both the bad and the good; it must not contain errors or omit any significant facts, in light of the "errors and omissions" rule and the concept of a substantial risk of foreseeable harm.

Be especially careful when potentially involved with at-risk employment settings, safety-sensitive ones, or caregiver or custodial situations.

OFFICE ROMANCE: EMPLOYEE FRATERNIZATION RULES

Office romance is an issue of growing importance as Americans spend more and more time at work. Studies indicate that a third of all romantic relationships begin at work.[26] One study shows as many as 80 percent of employees have been involved at one time or another in a romantic relationship at work.[27]

Q6   What are the legal ramifications of employees who are involved in romantic relationships with each other?

The goal of this section is to alert readers to the potential legal issues raised by office romances. Should a policy be in place regulating this type of conduct? If so, what should its parameters be? What happens if the romance is ignored?

No Policy Scenario

Consider the following scenario in a setting without any such policy. Two employees begin dating and fall hopelessly in love. They spend months together outside of work. The first issue is whether their romance interferes with their work. If this is not a concern, there may be no other problem. However, if one of the employees is a supervisor, then sexual harassment can become a serious issue. This can arise in several ways.

First, fellow employees may sense that the paramour is given favorable treatment by the supervisor because of the romantic affinity. While this may not be harassment, it tends to have a negative impact on employee morale and gives a poor impression of the organizational climate, i.e., that one can "sleep one's way to the top" or to at least favorable treatment. "An isolated instance of favoritism to a 'paramour' (or spouse, or a friend) may be unfair, but it does not discriminate against women or men in violation of Title VII, since both are disadvantaged for reason other than their genders."[28] If the conduct is widespread, however, it may rise to the level of a "hostile work environment."[29]

Second, if the relationship ends, one partner may attempt to restore the relationship, thus giving rise to a claim of harassment (hostile work environment) for the subsequent repeated and unwanted contact.

Finally, the jilted partner may claim that the relationship was not consensual after all, and raise a quid pro quo claim of harassment, especially if the relationship was a supervisory one.

Another concern, though rare, is the prevention of workplace violence by the jilted partner. If the employer knew of the romance and knew when it ended (through a disclosure policy), then the employer might have been able to take steps to diffuse the negative relational and emotional fallout and prevent a tragedy.[30]

Policy in Place

The prudent approach is to operate with a policy in place. "The best approach to drafting an office romance policy requires striking an appropriate balance between the employees' rights to privacy and employer noninterference in their personal off-duty behavior and the employers' legitimate interests in preventing sexual harassment, avoiding or minimizing litigation and liability, and promoting a positive and conflict-free work environment with high morale and maximum productivity."[31] Most experts believe that a policy is prudent for the purpose of preventing sexual harassment or addressing favoritism and morale issues when the relationship involves a supervisor-subordinate situation.[32]

There are two main options one can use to augment an organization's sexual harassment policy. First, a policy could ban all employee romances. There are legal problems with this approach which are discussed below. Second, the policy could allow such romances, but when the parties are at different levels within the organization, the romance may continue, but only on the parties' agreement to certain conditions. In the latter case, the conditions are sensitive to employee privacy and other rights, while protecting the organization from liability should the relationship sour. This approach often includes disclosure and accommodation, and is favored by commentators.[33] "Rather than broad prohibition of workplace relationship, the proscription of relationships between supervisors and subordinates or between employees in the same department often makes the most sense."[34] A less restrictive approach is to prohibit differential romances only among those in direct supervisor-subordinate relationships. A more restrictive approach would be to prohibit romances between all employees who work in the same unit or department, whether supervisory or not.[35]

Q7   Can a library policy ban office romances?

Aside from the fact that absolute enforcement is nearly impossible, there are a variety of legal problems with banning employee romance, particularly in public employee settings. A variety of constitutional rights may protect librarians who work in a public setting such as a public, school, or court library. In addition, some states protect the relationships or "recreational" activities of public employees outside of work.

There is little case law in the area, and none with a library setting. In one public sector case, a police officer was dismissed for living with a married woman. He won his suit, making a right to privacy claim.[36] However, in a similar case, the Fifth Circuit said that while public employees have a right to privacy, it is not an unqualified right. The court focused on the "rational connection" between the prohibitions on cohabitation among officers of different ranks and the "exigencies" of department discipline in its duty to protect the public at large.[37]

Q8   In setting office romance policies, does it matter whether the library is in the public or the private sector?

In the public sector, be aware that the library is a government agency. As a government agency, the library must not violate an employee's due process, that is, a fair and consistent application of any rules and a hearing and right to be heard. Dating rules are tough to enforce consistently, due to the fact that some romances are more secretive than others.

Private sector employees may also raise a variety of legal claims against office romance rules. Although a well-drafted private employer's no-fraternization policy is generally upheld, managers need to be aware of the potential for liability nonetheless. Legal claims may rest upon a legal theory known as "intentional infliction of emotional distress."

Intentional infliction of emotional distress requires that the library intentionally or recklessly cause another person "severe emotional distress through [its] extreme or outrageous acts."[38] Proving the elements of intentional infliction of emotional distress (e.g., that the harm was intentional) is difficult, but where the employer's conduct is "extreme and outrageous" or is "beyond all possible bounds of decency," courts have been receptive to such claims.[39] However, some jurisdictions also require that some physical manifestation of the emotional harm must also be present, increasing the difficulty of such suits.

The Fifth Circuit approved an employer's anti-dating rule, and upheld its dismissal of employees for violating it. The court found that the rule was not "outrageous," "atrocious," or "utterly intolerable."[40]

Q9   What if the library employee is an "at will" worker?

When the employment is "at will" (even in the public sector, library director positions may be "at will"), a claim can be made that there is a wrongful discharge. This is a difficult case to make. "Employment at will" means that employees work at the whim of the employer, absent a formal contract. Most courts have allowed wrongful discharge lawsuits, however, if the act is based upon a violation of public policy or of an implied covenant of good faith and fair dealing.

Q10   Can libraries make policies that say spouses can't work together?

It depends. Many states have statutes that may prohibit discrimination based upon "marital status."[41] A minority of states take a narrow view— they make sure that employers do not discriminate solely on the basis of a person's *marital status*.[42] That is, a library in one of these states merely needs to make sure its hiring policy does not discriminate against an employee because he or she is single, divorced, separated, or married.

An emerging majority of states take a broad view of what "marital status" discrimination means.[43] These states not only ensure that employers do not discriminate based on whether someone is single, divorced, etc., but also prohibit employers from making policies that say the employer cannot hire an employee's spouse. Courts in these states reason that because the employer would not have problems hiring both spouses if they were not married to each other, their status as husband and wife (marital status) causes them to be discriminated against, violating this statute. The term "marital status" is subject to two interpretations: the status of being married or not, and the status of being married to a particular person, i.e., another employee. Some of these state laws have business necessity exemptions, allowing reasonable regulations for the purpose of safety or security.[44]

*Q11   Can libraries prohibit employees' romantic behavior
in their free time?*

Some states have laws that stop employers from interfering with employees' "recreational activities." However, these statutes may contain an exception for activities that are detrimental to the company or that impact an employee's job performance unfavorably. Is dating after hours protected in these states? It's difficult to assess this. New York, for example, has a law that prohibits discharge on the basis of "legal recreational activities outside work hours, off of the employer's premises and without use of the employer's equipment or other property." [45] It does allow, however, discharge for recreational activity that is detrimental to the company or that impacts an employee's job performance. New York courts interpreting this statute have come to opposite conclusions concerning dating. At least one court says dating is protected,[46] and another says it is not.[47]

*Q12   What should a library do if it wants to have an anti-
fraternization policy, especially to shield itself from
sexual harassment claims?*

Legal as well as practical problems abound when an employer attempts to regulate office romances. It is difficult to turn the tide of human nature. If it would seem odd for an employer to ban the development of friendships among coworkers, then based on the social nature of the human being, the same must be said for the amorous tendencies of coworkers. The practical and legal issues here are related. Employers may be aware of some romances and not others. Even with awareness, it's problematic at best to define the prohibited contact. Is it dating? Cohabitating? Inconsistent enforcement can further undermine the point of the policy. Regardless, some employers are moving toward the encouragement of self-reporting and the use of consensual relationship agreements known as "kiss and tell" or "love contracts."[48] There can be advantages to these agreements, especially when coupled with reasonable additional measures, such as a no direct supervisor-employee romancing rule, or an option of transfer to another department so the supervisor is no longer supervising his or her paramour.[49]

This minimizes the potential for legal retribution from a sexual harassment suit once the romance sours, since the consent is clearly stated. For the record, soured affairs constitute a minuscule share of sexual harassment charges actually brought. According to the Equal Employment Opportunity Commission, only 5 percent of the sexual harassment charges it investigates are due to a failed affair between a boss and subordinate.[50]

The "love contract" will require the parties to notify the employer when the romance has ended. This helps the employer to heighten its awareness of potential sexual harassment claims at the most sensitive time. From a practical perspective, it can also maintain employee morale. The employer is not seen as "the heavy," but the employer's emphasis on maintaining productivity (through the option of transfer, for example) retains some sense of managerial integrity.

Q13   What elements should be in a "love contract"?

If the library or its governing entity considers adopting and enforcing a "love contract," the following elements should be considered for inclusion in a contract which both parties sign:

(1) Expression of the voluntary nature of the relationship
(2) A non-retaliation clause in case the relationship should end
(3) The organization's sexual harassment policy
(4) The voluntary nature of entering into this agreement
(5) Opportunity to consult with legal counsel before signing
(6) Revocation procedures
(7) Indication that the superior will never have decision-making authority of any kind over the subordinate paramour
(8) Agreement by both parties to refrain from engaging in any "romantic" conduct in the workplace or when acting in a professional capacity, such as at a conference or presentation
(9) Waiver of all rights to claim sexual harassment up to the signing of the agreement
(10) An agreement to submit all disputes that arise out of the relationship to binding arbitration[51]

Q14   How can an employer enforce a non-fraternization policy?

The key to enforcing such a policy is threefold. First, a policy should respect employees' privacy rights but accomplish the organizational goals of efficiency and effectiveness. Second, the policy should clearly state what is prohibited, what is allowed and under what conditions, and if disclosure is required, what options employees have, such as transfer. The rationale for all these should be stated. Third, library management must be prepared to apply the policy in a consistent manner.[52]

EMPLOYEES AND FREE SPEECH

This section applies primarily to public employees—library staff employed by federal, state, and local government libraries. When noted, employees at private institutions are included. It considers speech issues ranging from staff complaints to political speech rights to the complicated conflict between employees' rights of free speech and the right to be free from workplace harassment.

Public Sector v. Private Sector

Work in the public sector differs markedly from work in the private sector. On the one hand, public employees are subject to legislative restraints regarding their political activities. On the other hand, federal and state constitutional guarantees of freedom of speech and freedom of association *limit* the restrictions that public employers can place on their employees. In other words, library staff in the public sector enjoy greater safeguards concerning their rights to speak than their colleagues in the private sector. Nevertheless, the law surrounding a public employee's First Amendment free speech rights is complicated and unpredictable. The key inquiry is whether the library employee's speech is characterized as a matter of "public concern," and if so, the employee's rights are balanced against the employer's interests, with varying results.

Library employees in private settings may be regulated by their institutions' policies, including "gag orders" and the like, without recourse to the First Amendment in the U.S. Constitution. This is because the First Amendment limits *government* restrictions on speech.

Parameters of First Amendment Protections for Public Employee Speech

Restrictions on library employee speech may be made at the federal, state, local, and departmental levels. At each of these levels, speech restrictions will be judged by the courts on the basis of whether or not the restrictions encompass speech on matters of "public concern." Public employee speech that is not a matter of "public concern" is generally not protected by the First Amendment, perhaps harking back to an aphorism in 1892 penned by Justice Oliver Wendell Holmes, then on the Massachusetts Supreme Court: "[The policeman] may have a constitutional right to talk politics, but he has no constitutional right to be a policeman."[53] This is called the "doctrine of privilege," i.e., that government employment is a privilege and not a right; therefore the government can impose whatever conditions, including "unconstitutional" conditions, it wants on its employment.

Today, however, the courts have found a significant degree of protection for public employee speech, at least so far as the speech touches on matters of "public concern." The landmark Supreme Court case on this issue, *Pickering* v. *Board of Education,* strongly endorsed the value of free speech for a teacher who was fired for writing a letter to a newspaper critical of the local school board. The letter was found to be of "public concern," i.e., important to public discourse at large. The court found this speech to be under the umbrella of the First Amendment, and thus the letter could not be the basis for discharge—unless it was found to cause a substantial interference with the ability of the teacher to continue to do his job.[54] Later cases refined the "public concern" doctrine, and today the inquiry that courts undertake look like this:

(1) Was the speech protected?[55]
(2) Was the protected speech a "substantial or motivating factor" behind the adverse employment action?[56]
(3) If the employee can establish the first two elements, can the employer prove that it would have made the same decision to terminate even if the employee had not engaged in the protected conduct?[57]

In addition, the courts will apply a balancing test that sometimes allows employers to restrict speech *even on matters of public concern,* if it might disrupt the workplace.

Q15   What is "protected speech"?

In the employment context, "protected speech" must meet a legal standard that shows the speech is a matter of "public concern." It is crucial to understand this: if the employee's speech does not qualify as "protected speech," he or she can be discharged *even if the decision is unfair*. The government employer is given a wide berth when it comes to managing its offices.

To be considered a matter of "public concern," a library employee's speech must relate to a matter of "political, social, or other concern to the community."[58] The court considers "the content, form and context of a given statement, as revealed by the whole record."[59] This can be a difficult hurdle for a library employee to overcome, since not every conversation made within the public employment context rises to this level of public concern. "To presume that all matters which transpire within a government office are of public concern would mean that virtually every remark . . . would plant the seed of a constitutional case."[60]

Speech that rises to the legal standard of "public concern" often involves the reporting of corruption or wrongdoing to higher authorities.[61] Comments made in a personal conversation may be "too remote from the political rally, the press conference, the demonstration, the theater, or other familiar emporia of the marketplace of ideas" to activate the guarantees of the First Amendment.[62] The audience for the speech is also an important factor. An audience of a few, "rather than the press," weighs against a claim of protected speech.[63]

Q16 *How does a court determine if the employee's speech is a "substantial or motivating factor" behind the adverse employment action?*

This is a factual determination. A library employee's mere claim that he or she said something and was subsequently demoted or terminated fails to satisfy the requirement of a well-pleaded complaint, since the burden of proof requires specific evidence.[64]

**Three-Part Inquiry to Determine
If a Public Employee Has the Right
to Free Speech in the Workplace**

(1) Is the speech protected?

(2) Was the protected speech a "substantial or motivating factor" behind the adverse employment action?

(3) Once the employee has established the first two elements, can the employer prove that it would have made the same decision to terminate even if the employee had not engaged in the protected conduct?

Q17   How can the employer prove it would have made the same decision even if the employee had not engaged in the protected conduct?

This is also a factual determination. The employer must now rebut. The employer's records showing the employee's work performance are critical. The employer must demonstrate that the decision would have been made in any event. Documentation of work performance, discipline records, etc., are used.

Q18   How do courts balance an employee's rights to speech on matters of public concern and the employer's need for a nondisruptive workplace?

Courts balance the employee "as a citizen, in commenting upon matters of public concern and the interest of the State, as an employer, in promoting the efficiency of the public services it performs through its employees."[65] This requires "particularized balancing on the unique facts presented in each case."[66] Employers' interests may include efficiency, ensuring loyalty, and fostering positive morale in the workplace.[67] In applying the balancing test from *Pickering,* the following questions are asked:

(1) Whether the speech at issue impairs discipline by superiors or harmony among coworkers

(2) Whether the speech has a detrimental impact on close working relationships for which personal loyalty and confidence are necessary

(3) Whether the speech impedes performance of the speaker's duties,

(4) Whether the speech interferes with the regular operation of the public employee's enterprise[68]

Furthermore, it has been held that an employer need not establish that the employee's speech actually disrupts the workplace. The Supreme Court has given substantial weight to government employers' "*reasonable predictions of disruption,* even when the speech involved is on a matter of public concern, and even though when the government is acting as sovereign our review of legislative predictions of harm is considerably less deferential" (emphasis added).[69]

——————————— CASE STUDY ———————————

LIBRARY TECHNICAL SERVICES SUPERVISOR MAY MAKE COMPLAINTS ABOUT LIBRARY SAFETY

Donna Kennedy, the automation coordinator and technical services supervisor of the Tangipahoa Parish Library in Amite, Louisiana, was fired after complaining about safety concerns. The U.S. Fifth Circuit Court of Appeals upheld her right to sue the director and trustees for violating her First Amendment rights.

Kennedy was demoted and then fired after she wrote a letter to the board asking for improved library security. A patron with a criminal record and a history of mental illness had entered the Independence Branch library and raped an employee. The man severely beat the employee about her head, fracturing several bones in her face.

Kennedy became extremely concerned and wrote a letter urging that the library keep at least two library employees in the branch at all times when the library was open to the public. She sent the letter to the library board and the library branch managers. She also gave a copy to the victim. On October 23, 1997, Kennedy spoke about the security issue at a library board meeting, and was demoted by the library director that afternoon.

Kennedy's comments to the library board, as reported in the court decision citing the local newspaper, were: "I appreciate the fact that Buddy [Ridgel] brought this up. We're all wondering what's going to be happening. It's good to let the employees and the public know that you're talking about this and doing something about it."[70] The library director's letter to Kennedy said, "It has become apparent that you have assumed far too much authority for your position as Automation Coordinator and Technical Supervisor. Your assigned role does not include discussing opening and closing of branches, nor does include [sic] discussing with other employees what I, as the appointed Director, do correctly or, in you [sic] opinion, incorrectly . . ."[71]

The federal appellate court sided with Kennedy, noting that "Kennedy spoke on a matter of public concern" and that her demotion raised First Amendment concerns.[72]

Political Speech

A review of state laws by Rafael Gely and Timothy D. Chandler shows that thirty-five states have some form of explicit restriction on state employees' participation in politics.[73] Of the thirty-five states, four are more restrictive than the federal Hatch Act (see below): Louisiana, New Mexico, Ohio, and West Virginia. These states limit the ability of public employees to take an active part in political campaigning. Louisiana and Ohio broadly prohibit covered employees from taking part in the management of the affairs of a political party or any political campaign. New Mexico and West Virginia, on the other hand, have adopted a somewhat less restrictive approach by allowing political participation in general, but prohibiting covered employees from becoming members or officers of political parties.

Thirty-one states have statutes that are less restrictive than the Hatch Act. Of these, fourteen states prohibit using an employee's official authority to interfere with or affect political processes or outcomes. Twenty-three states prohibit public employees from providing or soliciting financial or worker contributions to any political organization or candidate. In addition, thirteen states prohibit public employees from holding elected offices, and twenty-two states specifically prohibit them from engaging in political activities while on duty, in uniform, or on state property.[74]

Q19   What political speech rights do public library employees have?

Political speech, by definition, is likely to touch on matters of public concern. Nevertheless, some political speech, particularly partisan campaign activity, can interfere with the smooth administration of public employment. The courts are all over the map on political speech by public employees.[75] It can make a big difference whether the political speech at issue is running for office, supporting political candidates or legislative measures, or merely expressing political opinions.

Generally, courts have upheld public employee speech restrictions when they are seen to serve legitimate local or state interests in maintaining discipline and providing for the effectiveness of employees. An overriding concern of the courts is whether the government can show that *legitimate government interests are at stake* in restricting the speech. Evidence of the government's actual reasons for imposing restrictions is not required.

On the one hand, restrictions on high-level participation in partisan politics, such as running for office or using one's public position to influence campaigns, are more likely to be upheld as "reasonable restrictions."

On the other hand, restrictions that forbid mere discussion of politics are less likely to be upheld.[76]

Political Campaigns

The government has taken two approaches to regulate the political involvement of public employees. One approach has been to enact laws restricting the ability of public employees to engage in various political activities, such as campaigning, soliciting contributions, or running for political office. The political activity of public employees is regulated by the federal Hatch Act[77] and by state "Little Hatch Acts." When challenged by employees as violative of free speech, courts often uphold the regulation of public employees' political activities. Courts justify these restrictions based upon the need for an efficient workplace.[78] The second approach is political patronage—hiring and firing based on an employee's political affiliations. Libraries should not use the political patronage system any more, particularly since a series of Supreme Court rulings in the 1980s and 1990s struck down such systems, leaving only narrow exceptions.[79]

Q20   Can library staff that work for the government participate in political campaigns?

It depends. The Hatch Act restricts the political activity of executive-branch employees of the federal government, the District of Columbia (D.C.) government, and certain state and local agencies. In 1993 Congress passed legislation that substantially amended the Hatch Act, allowing most federal and D.C. employees to engage in many types of political activity, including active participation in political campaigns. However, some federal agencies and categories of employees continue to be prohibited from engaging in partisan political activity.[80]

Although it is a federal act, the Hatch Act covers certain state and local agencies that have programs financed in whole or in part by federal loans or grants. Such state and local employees may not use their official authority or influence to affect an election, contribute anything of value to a political organization, or run for elective office.[81] The 1993 amendments that allow federal employees greater leeway did not affect the provisions restricting state and local employees.

Q21   May library staff run for public office?

It depends on the jurisdiction.[82] Courts have held it is within the legislative discretion to restrict political campaigning as a measure to bring about an efficient civil service system, relieved of political pressure. Such provisions are common at the state, local, and even departmental levels and have the purpose of promoting efficiency and integrity in the discharge of official duties.[83]

In some cases, courts have said that while it is permissible to forbid a local employee from running for a local elective office, it is impermissible to restrict employees from running for state or national offices, stating that there is no compelling need to restrict on such a sweeping scale. One court held that a city home-rule charter prohibiting a city employee's candidacy for any public office was unconstitutionally broad, since a national campaign did not use the contacts and information provided by his or her job.[84]

*Q22   May staff put political campaign literature on their desk in
        the office if they do not actively circulate it?*

That may vary by the circumstance and how the state or local law is written. In Illinois, for example, a case held that the state prohibition on the "distribution of campaign literature" meant more than mere acquiescence in the placement of literature in the office.[85]

*Q23   Can an employee use a union leave of absence for partisan
        political activity?*

Probably. In one case, a state prohibited union leaves of absence for partisan political activity. The court found this prohibition violated both the state's Political Freedom Act and the First Amendment.[86]

*Q24   Could library staff go to jail for violating laws that restrict
        public employees' political activities?*

Not likely. In one case, the state of Florida had a statute that made it a misdemeanor for public employees to willfully circulate petitions, work at the polls, or distribute badges, colors, or indicators favoring or opposing a candidate. The court held that imposing a criminal penalty went beyond what was necessary to insure the public interest and infringed on the individual's rights.[87]

Legislation and Ballot Measures

Sometimes localities issue restrictions on political activity by public employees regarding local measures, but do not restrict it on state or federal issues.

Q25   May a library employee take a position on a ballot measure?

While library employees may take positions on their own time, it is common to find a restriction on the use of public resources for such purposes. For example, a Nebraska Accountability and Disclosure Commission opinion stated:

> A public official or public employee may express his or her position with regard to a ballot question and may even urge voters to vote for or against the ballot question, provided that government personnel, resources, property or funds under that official's care and control are not used for that purpose, and provided further in the case of a public employee that he or she does not engage in such political activity during office hours or when otherwise engaged in the performance of his or her official duties.[88]

Q 26   Can library staff inform patrons regarding pending library budget cuts or urge patrons to contact their local officials to support library funding initiatives?

This kind of activity involves public resources in the form of paid time. Libraries are in the business of providing information, however, and many libraries put together fact sheets that show budget-cut impacts or potential funding initiative impacts. Library staffs are usually advised to refrain from actual advocacy while using public resources. "Advocacy" may be defined as taking a particular position. Friends of the Library or other support groups, however, may distribute literature that takes a position, so long as all other positions are given the same distribution opportunities.

Q27   What is the difference between "providing information" and "advocacy"?

This is certainly a gray area, but some useful guidance may be found in a document issued by the secretary of state of Oregon explaining the state statute that restricts public employees' political activities. In summary, it identifies the factors necessary to determine if a document is advocacy or merely informational:

Timing—is the material only published at election time?

Balance—are both negative and positive facts mentioned?

Overall impression—is the reader informed or persuaded?

Tone of the publication—is it dispassionate or enthusiastic?

Use of the word "will"—in describing the passage of a measure, the word "would" is a better alternative since it suggests that voters have a choice.

Use of the word "need"—in describing the purpose of a measure, the word "need" is often emotionally charged.

Headings' or lead lines' "tone"—should not favor or oppose a measure.

Quotes about the measure—should not be included.

Graphics, checkmarks, and photographs—photos can be emotional; checkmarks often indicate what someone should do.

Use of phrases similar to campaign slogans—should not be used.

Contact information for political committees—should not be used.

Information about voter turnout requirements—may be used if neutrally stated, e.g., don't use a phrase like "double majority."

Finally, the document must not explicitly urge a yes or no vote. It should not have phrases such as "Why I should vote for Measure 99."[89]

Q28 May library staff generally discuss politics with the public?

There may be a fine line between using public resources for political purposes and general political discussions. Nevertheless, an Illinois court held that a police captain who had discussed politics, specifically the upcoming mayoral election, with an elderly woman while he was on duty could not be dismissed, even though he violated an internal police regulation which prohibited him from discussing politics. The court said that the free discussion of governmental affairs included discussions of candidates, structures and forms of government, and all matters relating to political processes. The court added that policemen, like teachers and lawyers, were not relegated to a watered-down version of constitutional rights.[90]

Q29 How does a library employee know precisely what restrictions are in place?

This is an important question. Although an employee is presumed to know the laws and policies that guide him or her in the workplace, if a law or policy doesn't clearly enunciate what is forbidden, it might be challenged as "void for vagueness." When a restriction is so vague that the employee does not know exactly what conduct is restricted, it becomes impossible to comply with the restriction. On the other hand, if adequate warning is given of what activities are proscribed, along with explicit standards, restrictions may be upheld.

Q30   If the library worker is a contractor, *rather than an* employee, *does this affect his or her rights?*

It can. The *contractor's* First Amendment rights are actually *stronger* than those of a regular employee. The Supreme Court recently held that the First Amendment protects public contractors who speak out on a matter of public concern. The government may not stop a contract in retaliation for doing so. The government's interest in running an efficient workplace is not as strong with contractors as it is with its own employees.[91]

DISCRIMINATION IN THE WORKPLACE

Free Speech and Harassment

Q31   Is there a conflict between free speech and laws against harassment?

Yes. State and federal anti-harassment laws seek to ensure that employees enjoy a "hostile-free" workplace. In both the public and private sectors, employers may restrict employees from speaking on certain subjects by such means as rules against racial slurs in employee workrooms, hanging up posters of scantily clad women, etc. In setting rules that involve expression, the employer must balance workplace efficiency and employee morale.

Q32   What do the federal and state laws prohibiting "harassment speech" restrict?

Under both federal and state law, severe on-the-job harassment is not limited to physical conduct such as unwanted touching. Verbal statements may be considered a form of discrimination, such as harassing statements based on race, color, religion, sex, national origin, age, or disability.[92]

Q33   How would a library employee show sexual harassment?

The employee has two ways to show harassment. The first, known as "quid pro quo," applies when a "tangible adverse employment action" is taken against an employee, such as firing, demoting, transferring, or refusing to promote—because of a refusal to submit to the supervisor's sexual demands.[93] The second is when the plaintiff is subjected to a "hostile and abusive work environment," i.e., one in which an employee is subjected to severe or pervasive verbal or physical behavior.

The Supreme Court recently blurred the distinction between the two theories. It said the only real difference between the two is that there is an "explicit" alteration in employment conditions in quid pro quo cases, whereas there are "constructive" alterations in hostile environment cases due to threats, even if unfulfilled.[94] The requirements to show a "hostile work environment," however, are more difficult than those to show a "quid pro quo."

Q34   How is a "hostile work environment" defined?

This requires a showing of "severe or pervasive conduct."[95] The factors for this determination are set forth in *Harris* v. *Forklift Systems, Inc:*

- The frequency of the conduct
- Its severity
- Whether it is physically threatening or humiliating or a mere offensive utterance
- Whether it unreasonably interferes with an employee's work performance[96]

The Supreme Court wrote: "This standard, which we reaffirm today, takes a middle path between making actionable any conduct that is merely offensive and requiring the conduct to cause a tangible psychological injury."[97]

Q35   What is the employer's responsibility when faced with a "hostile environment" claim?

The employer is responsible for taking immediate corrective action if it knew or should have known about the behavior. The employer will not be liable if it "exercised reasonable care to prevent and correct promptly any . . . harassing behavior" and the "employee unreasonably failed to take advantage of any preventive or corrective opportunities."[98]

Q36   Here's the million dollar question. Is it possible for library patrons *to cause a "hostile environment" for staff by viewing pornographic images on library computers?*

This is a cutting-edge question. Traditionally, sexual harassment claims were based on a supervisor's behavior. This has been extended to coworkers' behavior, and now the question arises whether *the public's behavior* can give rise to a hostile environment. This is further complicated in a library setting, since libraries are obliged to honor the free speech of library patrons, as defined by the First Amendment. That is, although a public employer has considerable latitude in restricting its own employees' speech to avoid harassment, *the restriction of the public's speech* triggers a fuller First Amendment analysis.

Q37 *How would a court analyze the hostile environment claim when pornography is on library computers, according to the First Amendment?*

Any given situation may be judged differently, depending on its facts. A court will look at the library's policy and how it's enforced. On one end of the spectrum, *behavior* regulations (e.g., no lewd behavior such as masturbation in the library) are not *speech,* and libraries may enforce reasonable patron conduct policies without running into the First Amendment. On the other end, a policy prohibiting a patron from quietly observing adult sites at a library computer equipped with a privacy screen, with automated time-out software that refreshes the screen (placing the library's home page on it, for example), has little chance of successfully meeting strict-scrutiny First Amendment tests. In the middle are patron-librarian interactions ranging from a single request for assistance in reaching an adult website to repeated requests for a librarian to look at a screen, asking the librarian which sites she enjoyed the most. A recent district court CIPA decision resolved the conflict between sexual harassment and free speech clearly in favor of speech. It focused on *behavior,* and said that the proper method for a library to deter unlawful or inappropriate patron conduct, such as harassment, is to impose sanctions on such conduct, either by removing the patron from the library, revoking the patron's library privileges, or, in the appropriate case, calling the police.

If a library policy merely places time, place, and manner restrictions on Internet use, such as "one hour per day" or "identification required," these restrictions are considered "content-neutral" and will usually be upheld.

On the other hand, if the library's policy restricts on the basis of the *content* of the Internet viewing, a court will generally hold the policy to the highest legal hurdles, known as "strict scrutiny," which is exceptionally difficult to pass. In a nutshell, to pass strict scrutiny, the policy must address a *compelling interest,* be *necessary to further those interests,* and use *the least restrictive means.*

---------------------------- CASE STUDY ----------------------------

LOUDOUN COUNTY PUBLIC LIBRARY

In *Mainstream Loudoun* v. *Loudoun County Public Library* (1998), a federal court struck down a Virginia library's policy of installing filtering software on all of its public Internet computers as a violation of First Amendment rights on free speech. The library had based its policy on concerns that pornography viewed over the Internet by patrons could create a "hostile environment" for other patrons and staff.

The Policy on Internet
Sexual Harassment

The board of the Loudoun County Public Library had adopted a "Policy on Internet Sexual Harassment":

> Library pornography can create a sexually hostile environment for patrons or staff. Pornographic Internet displays may intimidate patrons or staff . . . Such displays would transform the library environment . . . to one which invited unwelcome sexual advances and sexual harassment. . .[99]

The library installed blocking software, X-Stop, to prevent access to such sites. Although the software was designed to block sites containing child pornography, obscenity, and materials harmful to minors, it also blocked many innocuous sites, such as "Let's Have an Affair Catering," the *San Francisco Chronicle,* and Kentucky tax forms.

Policy Was Not a Time, Place,
and Manner Restriction

The court analyzed the library board's argument that the restrictions on Internet access were merely time, place, and manner restrictions. The library board pointed to a line of Supreme Court cases that had upheld zoning ordinances restricting adult movie theaters to certain locations, on the theory that the purpose was to control "secondary effects" such as crime, and *not* because of the content of the movies. The *Loudoun* court found that the purpose of avoiding a "hostile environment" was *not* a secondary effect, but focused on the very speech itself.

Policy Failed Strict Scrutiny Test

Hostile environment was a compelling interest. The court recognized that the avoidance of a "sexually hostile environment" was a "compelling interest," as determined by other courts in other contexts.[100]

The policy was not necessary to further the compelling interest. The court wrote that the library did not show evidence that the policy was necessary to further the interest of avoiding a "sexually hostile environment." The library had on record a single complaint that a patron had observed a boy viewing what she believed were pornographic pictures on the Internet. The incident was the only one the defendant discovered within Virginia and had not occurred at the Loudoun County Library. David Burt, a filter advocate, served as an expert witness and pointed to only three libraries that had experienced similar problems.

Policy Not Narrowly Tailored to Achieve Its Goal

The court said that *even if* the library board could show the policy *was* necessary to further the interest of a nonhostile environment, it would still need to show that the policy was narrowly tailored, using *the least restrictive means available*. The X-Stop filtering software was found not to be the least restrictive alternative. Although the court did not evaluate the constitutional strength of the following, it did mention a variety of less restrictive alternatives: privacy screens, casual staff monitoring, adopting a policy that threatens loss of library privileges or prosecution for accessing illegal sites, and limiting filters to only those terminals used by minors.

——————————————— CASE STUDY ———————————————

MINNEAPOLIS PUBLIC LIBRARY

The Equal Employment Opportunity Commission (EEOC) issued a preliminary ruling or "determination" for a complaint filed by library staff (known as "the Minneapolis 12") that the Minneapolis Public Library had created a hostile environment. The librarians claimed they were subjected to "repeated exposure to sexually explicit materials and sexual activity." The images were printed on library Internet printers by members of the public and left for staff to pick up. Furthermore, the complaint alleged that "It is not uncommon for obscene and vulgar language to be directed at us if we attempt to enforce the time limit. In addition, the ready availability of such materials at the library has been accompanied by a sexual activity [*sic*] at the library including masturbation."[101] Critics say the EEOC went beyond its bounds and was in direct conflict with the patrons' rights to view even "inappropriate" (though not legally obscene) material under the First Amendment.[102] As this book went to press, the U.S. Department of Justice conducted interviews with the employees to determine whether it would represent the EEOC on the employees' behalf. The plaintiffs' attorney said that if the Department of Justice declined, the plaintiffs would file suit on their own behalf.

———

*Q38   What are examples of other types of employment
       discrimination suits?*

Sexual harassment, racial harassment, age, disability, and other types of discrimination are complicated, fact-based cases, and it is always difficult to predict the outcomes. Moreover, a lawsuit will frequently pose multiple claims, such as age, sex, and disability discrimination, all in one suit. This is an area that employment attorneys are well versed in, and the library setting does not pose particularly unique circumstances. Nevertheless, it may be helpful to examine in depth an illustrative case brought by a library employee. The case is of special interest because one of the claims involved a repetitive stress injury,[103] an increasing affliction among library workers.

It is crucial to note that one may not draw specific conclusions out of any discrimination case, since these cases are heavily fact-dependent. Instead, look at the modes of analysis used by the court.

—————————————— CASE STUDY ——————————————

LIBRARY TECHNICIAN SUES HIGH SCHOOL FOR DISCRIMINATION UNDER THE ADA, ADEA, CIVIL RIGHTS ACT, AND THE MAINE HUMAN RIGHTS ACT

Facts and Claims of the Case: Library Technician Files for Discrimination

A high school library technician who was terminated filed suit in federal court for discrimination (*Ridge* v. *Cape Elizabeth School Dept.*). The technician, Ridge, suffered shoulder tendonitis related to the repetitive motions of continually remagnetizing "truckloads of books." As is often the case with discrimination lawsuits, the plaintiff filed multiple claims under (1) the Americans with Disabilities Act, (2) the Age Discrimination in Employment Act of 1967, (3) the Civil Rights Act of 1991, and (4) a state claim under the Maine Human Rights Act.[104]

(1) Americans with Disabilities Act (ADA)

The court wrote that the library technician would have to prove that (1) she was disabled within the meaning of the ADA; (2) she was nevertheless able to perform the meaningful functions of her job, either with or without reasonable accommodation; and (3) her employer terminated her in whole or in part because of her disability.

If unable to prove her case directly, the technician could do so indirectly by using prima facie burden-shifting methods. That is, she could move the case forward if she could show, by a preponderance of the evidence, that she: (1) had a disability within the meaning of the act; (2) was nevertheless qualified to perform the essential functions of her job, with or without reasonable accommodations; (3) was subject to an adverse employment action by a company subject to the act; (4) was replaced by a nondisabled person or was treated less favorably than nondisabled employees; and (5) suffered damages as a result.[105]

At that point, the school would need to offer a legitimate nondiscriminatory reason for the termination. Finally, the technician would have the opportunity and the burden of proving that the school library's "proffered reason is merely a pretext for disability discrimination." Ridge claimed discrimination on the basis of two physical syndromes: (1) shoulder tendonitis, an actual disability, and (2) obesity, a perceived disability.

SHOULDER TENDONITIS

The Americans with Disabilities Act defines a "disability" as:

(A) a physical or mental impairment that substantially limits one or more of the major life activities of such individual;

(B) having a record of such an impairment; or

(C) being regarded as having such an impairment.[106]

The court examined the medical records, and found that in Ridge's case, the "major life activities" limited by her tendonitis included lifting. She was thus able to make out a *"prima facie* case of discrimination,"* and it was then up to the employer to show a legitimate, non-discriminatory reason for her termination. The school successfully offered evidence that Ridge was terminated because she was unable to accept constructive criticism and work productively with her supervisor. At that point, Ridge needed to prove that the real reason for her termination was her physical disability, but failed. In fact, the court found no evidence to indicate that the head librarian was even aware that the repetitive motion of remagnetizing books bothered the plaintiff's arms.

OBESITY AS PERCEIVED DISABILITY

Ridge's case continued, since she claimed discrimination due to a perception of her obesity as a disability, and the ADA considers it discrimination if an employer "regards" one as having an impairment. The court determines:

(1) the nature and severity of the impairment;

(2) the duration or expected duration of the impairment; and

(3) the permanent or long-term impact or the expected permanent or long-term impact of or resulting from the impairment.[107]

Ridge stated that the head librarian posted an article in the library on drawing illustrations for a "librarianism" magazine that stated

> all publications today want to avoid sexism, racism, and ageism in illustrations as well as in text . . . . Most librarians are modern-looking, modern-thinking, service oriented professionals who

strongly favor equal opportunities for all. These guidelines should help you prepare illustrations that will edify and delight our readers: . . . 3. Librarians should never be depicted as spinsters or "little old ladies." Male librarians do not ordinarily wear bow ties. Exaggerated breasts and buttocks, shushing fingers, and SILENCE signs are unacceptable in *American Libraries*.[108]

Ridge also said the librarian discussed breast reduction surgery with her, asked if she could fit under a table to unplug a computer, asked if she could handle all the walking required in the expanded library, and made numerous comments about the weight of teachers and students. The court found the only relevant inquiry was whether the plaintiff could handle all the walking required in the expanded library. The court noted that Ridge was terminated well over one year from the time the librarian made her isolated inquiry into her walking ability.

It is exceptionally difficult to make a successful claim as to the major life activity of "working." An impairment does not substantially limit the ability to work unless it significantly restricts an employee's ability to perform either a class of jobs or a broad range of jobs in various classes, as compared with the average person having comparable training, skills, and abilities. The inability to perform a single, particular job does not constitute a substantial limitation in the major life activity of working.[109] The court found that Ridge did not produce evidence that the school regarded her as being incapable of working generally in a broad range of jobs because of her obesity. As such, Ridge failed to meet her burden of proof with respect to the ADA.

(2) Age Discrimination in Employment Act of 1967 (ADEA)

In Ridge's discrimination complaint on the basis of her age, the court noted that she bore the ultimate burden of proving that, but for her age, she would not have been fired.[110] Where direct evidence of discrimination is lacking, a burden-shifting framework similar to the ADA scenario governs a plaintiff's ADEA claim. Ridge had to show (1) she was a member of a protected age group, i.e., at least forty years old; (2) she was meeting legitimate job expectations; (3) she was fired; and (4) the employer had a continuing need for the same services, which subsequently were performed by an individual with the same or similar qualifications. To be successful, the employer had to provide a legitimate, nondiscriminatory reason for firing Ridge. If it did, then the employee had to show by a preponderance of the evidence that the stated reason was merely a pretext.[111]

The only dispute here was on the second factor, that of meeting legitimate job expectations. The school argued that Ridge was unable to work cooperatively with her supervisor. Ridge offered evidence that she performed the technical, everyday functions of her position in a competent manner. Her performance review showed that she was "clearly academically qualified to do her job," and that she "accurately completes most tasks required of her." The court decided that Ridge established her case well enough to require that the employer show a legitimate, non-discriminatory reason for the plaintiff's dismissal. Ridge then had to prove that the employer's reasons were mere pretext. Ridge's evidence included:

(1) She had been asked if she could handle all the walking in the library.

(2) The head librarian indicated that she was going to "trade" Ridge in for "two twenty-fivers."

(3) The head librarian made repeated comments about the age of faculty, and their unwillingness to keep up.

(4) Ridge found an advertisement for another school system in her mailbox.

(5) The head librarian made comments about a teacher who had retired, and the teacher was close in age to the plaintiff.

The court found these were stray comments and insufficient evidence to show pretext.[112]

(3) 42 U.S.C. §1981 and §1981a

These civil rights statutes, which form part of the Civil Rights Act of 1991, forbid racial discrimination in the making and enforcement of private contracts. Here, Ridge made no allegation she was discriminated against on the basis of her race. Consequently, the plaintiff's claim under 42 U.S.C. §1981 in Count 3 of the Amended Complaint was meritless. Furthermore, 42 U.S.C. §1981a is wholly dependent on other substantive Acts, such as the ADA and the ADEA.[113] Section 1981a merely expands on the remedies available under these other substantive acts. Because Ridge's ADA and ADEA claims failed, 42 U.S.C. §1981a also failed.

(4) Maine Human Rights Act (MHRA)

The MHRA is the state of Maine's analog to the Americans with Disabilities Act, and prohibits "discrimination in employment, housing or access to public accommodations on account of race, color, sex, physical or mental handicap."[114] Here the court found it did not need to continuously distinguish between the two statutes as to their scope and general intent because Maine courts consistently look to federal law in interpreting state anti-discrimination statutes.

Q39   *What should an employer do when an employee expresses religious convictions in the workplace and others feel harassed by that expression?*

The law offers no clear resolution to this conflict. Such cases show a chronic tension between competing interests—the rights of employees to express their religious beliefs and yet be free from discrimination in the workplace. Two recent commentators note that the courts have largely ignored the "uniquely significant tension in religious harassment, treating all types of harassment identically."[115] Recent Supreme Court decisions expanding employer liability for sexual harassment may, therefore, have significant implications for cases of religious harassment. What if a library employee is telling coworkers that they are doing immoral things and need God's forgiveness? Under current workplace speech doctrines, a library employer that restricts this type of speech is likely to be on solid ground.

——————————— CASE STUDY ———————————

EVANGELICAL CHRISTIAN FACTORY EMPLOYEE'S DISMISSAL UPHELD

The federal appellate court in the Fourth Circuit recently upheld the dismissal of Charita Chalmers, an evangelical Christian factory employee, who wrote personal letters to coworkers, asserting that they had done immoral things and needed to ask God for forgiveness. Chalmers was fired, and sued for discrimination on the basis of religious activity under 701(j) of Title VII of the Civil

Rights Act of 1964, claiming that the company failed to "reasonably accommodate" her religion. The court said no accommodation was required because she had not informed the company of the need for an accommodation.

Notes

1. *See* John Bruce Lewis et al., *Defamation and the Workplace: A Survey of the Law and Proposals for Reform,* 54 MISSOURI LAW REVIEW 797 (1989); Ramona L. Paetzold and Steven L. Willborn, *Employer (Ir)rationality and the Demise of Employment References,* 30 AMERICAN BUSINESS LAW JOURNAL 123 (1992); O. Lee Reed and Jan W. Henkel, *Facilitating the Flow of Truthful Personnel Information: Some Needed Change in the Standard Required to Overcome the Qualified Privilege to Defame,* 26 AMERICAN BUSINESS LAW JOURNAL 305 (1988); Ann M. Barry, Comment, *Defamation in the Workplace: The Impact of Increasing Employer Liability,* 72 MARQUETTE LAW REVIEW 264 (1989); Deborah Daniloff, Note, *Employer Defamation: Reasons and Remedies for Declining References and Chilled Communications in the Workplace,* 40 HASTINGS LAW JOURNAL 687 (1989).

2. *See* Valerie L. Acoff, *References Available upon Request . . . Not!—Employers Are Being Sued for Providing Employee Job References,* AMERICAN JOURNAL OF TRIAL ADVOCACY 755 (Spring 1994).

3. See, e.g., *Linafelt v. Bev, Inc.,* 662 So. 2d 986 (Fla. 1st Dist. Ct. App. 1995). *See also* Daniloff, *Employer Defamation,* 687; Edward R. Horkan, *Contracting around the Law of Defamation and Employment References,* 79 VIRGINIA LAW REVIEW 517 (1993).

4. See, e.g., *Eastus v. Blue Bell Creameries L.P.,* 97 F.3d 100 (5th Cir. 1996); *Brainerd v. Governors of the University of Alberta,* 873 F.2d 1257 (9th Cir. 1989).

5. Alex B. Long, *Addressing the Cloud over Employee References: A Survey of Recently Enacted State Legislation,* 39 WILLIAM AND MARY LAW REVIEW 177, 188 (1997).

6. RESTATEMENT (SECOND) OF TORTS §581(A) (1997) ("One who publishes a defamatory statement of fact is not subject to liability for defamation if the statement is true"). See also RESTATEMENT (SECOND) OF TORTS §581(A) cmt. d (1997) ("Truth of a defamatory statement of fact is a complete bar to recovery for an action for harm caused to another's reputation"). *See also* chapter 2, "Designing the Library Web Page," for more on defamation.

7. *O'Brien v. Papa Gino's America, Inc.,* 780 F.2d 1067 (1st Cir. 1986). An employee was discharged for drug abuse. The "truth" defense was unavailable to the employer, however, because facts revealed that the discharge was also in retaliation for the employee's failing to promote the owner's relative when ordered to do so.

The court concluded that the incomplete explanation of the circumstances surrounding the discharge was equivalent to a falsity.

8. RESTATEMENT (SECOND) OF TORTS §566 (1977) ("A defamatory communication may consist of a statement in the form of an opinion, but a statement of this nature is actionable only if it implies the allegation of undisclosed facts as the basis for the opinion").

9. RESTATEMENT (SECOND) OF TORTS §583 (1977). Few cases exist applying the consent defense to defamation in employment settings. *See* Ramona L. Paetzold and Steven L. Willborn, *Employer (Ir)rationality and the Demise of Employment References,* 30 AMERICAN BUSINESS LAW JOURNAL 123, 132 (1992).

10. Roger B. Jacobs and Cora S. Koch, LEGAL COMPLIANCE GUIDE TO PERSONNEL MANAGEMENT 272–273 (1993).

11. BLACK'S LAW DICTIONARY 1148 (7th ed. 1999).

12. *Robinson v. Shell Oil Co.,* 519 U.S. 337 (1997).

13. Andrew W. Martin Jr., *Legal Malpractice: Negligent Referral as a Cause of Action,* 29 CUMBERLAND LAW REVIEW 679 (1998/1999); Janet Swerdlow, *Negligent Referral: A Potential Theory for Employer Liability,* 64 SOUTHERN CALIFORNIA LAW REVIEW 1645 (1991).

14. *Randi W. v. Muroc Joint Unified School District,* 929 P.2d 582, 60 Cal. Rptr. 2d 263 (1997); *contra Cohen v. Wales,* 133 A.D.2d 94, 95 (N.Y. App. Div. 1987) (no duty owed by former employer to a third party victim; former employer failed to disclose that the employee-teacher had been charged with sexual misconduct); *Moore v. St. Joseph Nursing Home, Inc.,* 459 N.W.2d 100 (Mich. Ct. App. 1990) (no duty of a former employer to disclose information in a favorable reference to a prospective employer regarding a former employee's dangerous and violent propensities).

15. Anthony J. Sperber, *When Nondisclosure Becomes Misrepresentation: Shaping Employer Liability for Incomplete Job References,* 32 UNIVERSITY OF SAN FRANCISCO LAW REVIEW 405 (1998).

16. See, e.g., *Jerner v. Allstate Insurance Company,* No. 93-09472 (Fla. Cir. Ct. filed Dec. 7, 1993), *cert. denied,* 650 So. 2d 997 (Fla. 1995), *settled,* Fla. Cir. Ct. Order (August 10, 1995) (referral failed to reveal that employee had been fired for bringing a gun to work; employee later shot and killed several employees of subsequent employer) (discussed in Allan H. Weitzman and Kathleen M. McKenna, *Employees' References May Spawn Litigation,* NATIONAL LAW JOURNAL, May 19, 1997, at B4.

17. David E. Rovella, *Laws May Ease the Risky Business of Job References,* NATIONAL LAW JOURNAL, Oct. 23, 1995.

18. Susan Oliver, *Opening the Channels of Communication among Employers: Can Employers Discard Their "No Comment" and Neutral Job Reference Policies?,* 33 VALPARAISO UNIVERSITY LAW REVIEW 687, 715 (1999).

19. *See* Ronald M. Green and Richard J. Reibstein, EMPLOYER'S GUIDE TO WORKPLACE TORTS: NEGLIGENT HIRING, FRAUD, DEFAMATION, AND OTHER EMERGING AREAS OF EMPLOYER LIABILITY 5 (1992).

20. *Ponticas v. K.M.S. Invs.*, 331 N.W.2d 907, 911 (Minn. 1983).

21. *Ponticas*, 331 N.W.2d at 911.

22. *Gutzan v. Altair Airlines, Inc.*, 766 F.2d 135 (3d Cir. 1985).

23. *Ponticas*, 331 N.W.2d at 913.

24. A number of states have employment reference statutes that provide varying levels of immunity to employers: ALASKA STAT. §09.65.160 (Michie 1996); ARIZ. REV. STAT. ANN. §23-1361 (West Supp. 1996); CAL. CIV. CODE §47(c) (West Supp. 1997); COLO. REV. STAT. §8-2-114 (Supp. 1996); DEL. CODE ANN. tit. 19, §708 (Supp. 1996); FLA. STAT. ANN. §768.095 (West. Supp. 1997); GA. CODE ANN. §34-1-4 (Supp. 1996); IDAHO CODE §44-201 (Michie 1996); 745 ILL. COMP. STAT. ANN. 46.10 (West Supp. 1997); IND. CODE ANN. §22-5-3-1 (West Supp. 1997); KAN. STAT. ANN. §44-199a (West Supp. 1997); LA. REV. STAT. ANN. §23:291 (West Supp. 1997); ME. REV. STAT. ANN. tit. 26, §598 (West Supp. 1996); MD. CODE ANN. §5-423 (Michie 1997); MICH. COMP. LAWS §423.452 (West Supp. 1997); NEB. REV. STAT. §48-2304 (1998); N.M. STAT. ANN. §50-12-1 (Michie Supp. 1996); N.C. GEN. STAT. §1-539.12 (1997); N.D. CENT. CODE §34-02-18 (Supp. 1997); OHIO REV. CODE ANN. §4113.71 (Banks-Baldwin Supp. 1998); OKLA. STAT. ANN. tit. 40, §61 (West Supp. 1997); OR. REV. STAT. §30.178 (Supp. 1996); R.I. GEN. LAWS §28-6.4-1 (Supp. 1996); S.C. CODE ANN. §41-1-65 (Law, Co-op., Supp. 1996); S.D. CODIFIED LAWS §60-4-12 (Michie 1998); TENN. CODE ANN. §50-1-105 (Supp. 1998); UTAH CODE ANN. §34-42-1 (Supp. 1996); WIS. STAT. ANN. §895.487 (West 1997); WYO. STAT. ANN. §27-1-113 (Michie Supp. 1996). *See also* Alex B. Long, *Addressing the Cloud over Employee References: A Survey of Recently Enacted State Legislation,* 39 WILLIAM AND MARY LAW REVIEW 177 (1997); Julie Forster, *Twenty-Five States Adopt "Good Faith" Job Reference Laws to Shield Businesses from Liability,* WEST'S LEGAL NEWS, July 2, 1996, *available at* 1996 WL 3633240; Markita D. Cooper, *Beyond Name, Rank, and Serial Number: "No Comment" Job Reference Policies, Violent Employees and the Need for Disclosure-Shield Legislation,* 5 VIRGINIA JOURNAL OF SOCIAL POLICY AND THE LAW 287 (1998).

25. See, e.g., *Randi W. v. Muroc Joint Unified School District,* 929 P.2d 582, 60 Cal. Rptr. 2d 263 (1997) (officials from three different schools failed to disclose that the employee in question had been the subject of several parental complaints and student accusations of sexual harassment, improper touching, and sexual remarks to female students; employee later assaulted a student of subsequent employer).

26. Sheldon N. Sandler, *Discouraging Sexual Harassment and Favoritism in the Workplace,* DELAWARE EMPLOYMENT LETTER, NOVEMBER 1998.

27. Mary Loftus, *Frisky Business,* PSYCHOLOGY TODAY, March-April 1995, at 34.

28. Equal Employment Opportunity Commission, *Policy Guidance on Employer Liability under Title VII for Sexual Favoritism,* reprinted in DAILY LABOR REPORTER (BNA) No. 32, Feb. 15, 1990, at D1.

29. Marc L. Silverman et al., *Employers as Cupid's Squad: Navigating the Office Romance Minefield,* NEW YORK LAW JOURNAL, Feb. 14, 2000, at S1.

30. Jennifer L. Dean, *Employer Regulation of Employee Personal Relationships,* 76 BOSTON UNIVERSITY LAW REVIEW 1051, 1056 (1996).

31. Gary M. Kramer, *Limited License to Fish Off the Company Pier: Toward Express Employer Policies on Supervisor-Subordinate Fraternization*, 22 WESTERN NEW ENGLAND LAW REVIEW 77, 78 (2000).

32. Randi Wolkenbreit, *In Order to Form a More Perfect Union: Applying No-Spouse Rules to Employees Who Meet at Work*, 31 COLUMBIA JOURNAL OF LAW AND SOCIAL PROBLEMS 119 (1997).

33. Dean, *Employer Regulation*, 1051.

34. Melinda Socol Herbst, *Employers May Police Some Workplace Romances*, NATIONAL LAW JOURNAL, Feb. 26, 1996, at C19.

35. Perkins Coie, *Handling Romance in the Workplace*, OREGON EMPLOYMENT LAW LETTER, January 2000.

36. *Briggs v. North Muskegan Police Department*, 563 F. Supp. 585 (W.D. Mich. 1983), *aff'd* 746 F.2d 1475 (6th Cir. 1984).

37. *Shawgo v. Spradin*, 701 F.2d 470 (5th Cir. 1983). A similar result occurred when plaintiffs argued unsuccessfully that the constitutionally protected right to marry prevented the enforcement of police department regulations that prevented employees from cohabiting in *Kukla v. Village of Antioch*, 647 F. Supp. 799 (N.D. Ill. 1986).

38. BLACK'S LAW DICTIONARY 814 (7th ed. 1999).

39. *Rulon-Miller v. International Business Machines Corp.*, 208 Cal. Rptr. 524 (Cal. Ct. App. 1984); *Watkins v. United Parcel Service, Inc.*, 797 F. Supp. 1349 (S.D. Miss.), *aff'd* 979 F.2d 1535 (5th Cir. 1992).

40. *Watkins*, 797 F. Supp. at 1361, *aff'd* 979 F.2d 1535.

41. ALASKA STAT. §18.80.220 (1991); CAL. GOV'T CODE §12940 (1992); CONN. GEN. STAT. §46A-60 (1992); DEL. CODE ANN. tit. 19, §711 (1985); D.C. CODE ANN. §1-2512 (1987); FLA. STAT. ANN. §760.10 (1986); HAW. REV. STAT. §378-2 (1991); ILL. COMP. STAT. 5/1-102 (1989); MD. ANN. CODE art. 49B, §16 (1991); MICH. COMP. LAWS ANN. §37.2202 (1992); MINN. STAT. ANN. §363.03 (1991); MONT. CODE ANN. §49-2-303 (1991); NEB. REV. STAT. §48-1104 (1988); N.H. REV. STAT. ANN. §354-A:8 (1991); N.J. REV. STAT. §10.5-12 (1992); N.Y. EXEC. LAW §296 (1982); N.D. CENT. CODE §§14-02 and -03 (1991); OR. REV. STAT. §659.030 (1991); VA. CODE ANN. §2.1-716 (1992); WASH. REV. CODE §49.60.180 (1990); WIS. STAT. §111.311 (1988). See also ME. REV. STAT. ANN. tit. 5, §7051(2) (1989) (prohibiting marital status discrimination for all civil service positions); IDAHO CODE §33-4407 (1992) (prohibiting marital status discrimination by educational institutions); IND. CODE ANN. §20-6.1 TO 6-11 (1992); IOWA CODE ANN. §601A.9 (1988).

42. *Miller v. C.A. Muer Corp.*, 362 N.W.2d 650 (Mich. 1985); *Thomson v. Sandborn's Motor Express*, 382 A.2d 52 (N.J. 1977); *Manhattan Pizza Hut, Inc. v. New York State Human Rights Appeal Board*, 415 N.E.2d 950 (N.Y. 1980); *Townsend v. Board of Education of County of Grant*, 396 S.E.2d 185 (W. Va. 1990).

43. *Thompson v. Board of Trustees*, 627 P.2d 1229, 1231 (Mont. 1981); *Kraft, Inc. v. State*, 284 N.W.2d 386 (Minn. 1979) (no bona fide occupational qualification demonstrated); *Washington Power Co. v. Washington State Human Rights Com-*

mission, 586 P.2d 1149 (Wash. 1978) (insufficient evidence of business necessity); *Ross v. Stouffer Hotel Co.*, 879 P.2d 1037 (Haw. 1994) (lack of business justification for rule).

44. See, e.g., Cal. Gov't Code §12940(a)(3) (2000).

45. See N.Y. Lab. Law §201-d (McKinney 2000); N.D. Cent. Code §14-02.4-08 (Michie 2000); Colo. Rev. Stat. §24-34-402.5 (2000).

46. *Carey v. de Souza*, 678 N.Y.S.2d 264 (N.Y. App. Div. 1998).

47. *State v. Wal-Mart Stores, Inc.*, 621 N.Y.S.2d 158 (N.Y. App. Div. 1995) (dating is not protected as an employee recreational activity in N.Y. Lab. Law §201-d).

48. Marc L. Silverman et al., *Employers as Cupid's Squad: Navigating the Office Romance Minefield*, New York Law Journal, Feb. 14, 2000, at S1.

49. Lisa I. Fried, *Office Romance: Employers Fear Liaisons Lead to Harassment Suits*, New York Law Journal, Jan. 28, 1999, at 5.

50. Dennis M. Powers, *The Office Romance: What's a Business to Do?*, at http://careers. altavista.com/emp/articles/romance.html (visited May 13, 2001).

51. Gary M. Kramer, *Limited License to Fish Off the Company Pier: Toward Express Employer Policies on Supervisor-Subordinate Fraternization*, 22 Western New England Law Review 77, 140–143 (2000) (including discussion of sample language and additional points to include).

52. Melinda Socol Herbst, *Employers May Police Some Workplace Romances*, National Law Journal, Feb. 26, 1996, at C19.

53. *McAuliffe v. Mayor of City of New Bedford*, 29 N.E. 517, 517–518 (1892).

54. *Pickering v. Board of Education*, 391 U.S. 563 (1968).

55. *Pickering*, 391 U.S. at 568; *Connick v. Myers*, 461 U.S. 138, 145–146 (1983).

56. *Board of County Commissioners v. Umbehr*, 518 U.S. 668 (1996).

57. *Mt. Healthy City School District Board of Education v. Doyle*, 429 U.S. 274 (1977).

58. *Connick v. Myers*, 461 U.S. 138, 146 (1983).

59. *Connick*, 461 U.S. at 147–148.

60. *Connick*, 461 U.S. at 149.

61. *Wallace v. Texas Tech University*, 80 F.3d 1042, 1051 (5th Cir. 1996).

62. *Swank v. Smart*, 898 F.2d 1247, 1251 (7th Cir. 1990).

63. *Johnson v. Multnomah County*, 48 F.3d 420, 425 (9th Cir. 1995).

64. *Board of County Commissioners v. Umbehr*, 518 U.S. 668 (1996).

65. *Pickering v. Board of Education*, 391 U.S. 563, 568 (1968).

66. *Voigt v. Savell*, 70 F.3d 1552, 1560–1561 (9th Cir. 1995).

67. *Kaluczky v. White Plains*, 57 F.3d 202, 210 (2d Cir. 1996).

68. *Rankin v. McPherson*, 483 U.S. 378, 388 (1987).

69. *Waters v. Churchill*, 511 U.S. 661, 663 (1994).

70. Sylvia Schon, *Libraries Take Safety Measures*, Daily Star, Oct. 24, 1997, at 1, cited in *Kennedy v. Tangipahoa Parish Library Board of Control*, 224 F.3d 359 (5th Cir. 2000).

71. *Kennedy,* 224 F.3d 359.

72. *Kennedy,* 224 F.3d 359.

73. Rafael Gely and Timothy D. Chandler, *Public Employees' Political Activities: Good Government or Partisan Politics?,* 37 HOUSTON LAW REVIEW 775, 791 (2000).

74. *See also* charts on Little Hatch Act restrictions, state by state: Public Service Research Foundation, *Charts on Little Hatch Acts, at* http://www.psrf.org/hatch.html (visited July 5, 2001).

75. Keith G. Munro, *Constitutional Protection: Freedom of Speech and Public Employees,* 8 NEVADA LAWYER 10 (January 2000). Note: Many of the cases that follow were taken from Munro's article.

76. See *De Stefano v. Wilson,* 96 N.J. Super. 592 (1967) (a state statute forbidding political activity by public employees, and a police department regulation forbidding police officers from discussing politics have been held to violate the First Amendment).

77. 5 U.S.C. §§1501 *et seq.;* the major portions of the amended act are 5 U.S.C. §§7323 and 7324.

78. See, e.g., *United States Civil Service Commission v. National Association of Letter Carriers,* 413 U.S. 548, 556 (1973) (holding that restricting the political activities of public employees is constitutionally permitted if it is justified by the need to provide efficient government); *United Public Workers of America v. Mitchell,* 330 U.S. 75, 99 (1947) (holding that Congress can constitutionally restrict active partisan political activity of federal employees), cited in Gely and Chandler, *Public Employees' Political Activities,* 775.

79. See *O'Hare Truck Service v. City of Northlake,* 518 U.S. 712, 720–721 (1996) (holding that decisions prohibiting patronage discharges extend to prohibit the discharge of independent contractors); *Rutan v. Republican Party,* 497 U.S. 62, 79 (1990) (pointing out that the prohibition against discharge based on patronage also extends to promotion, transfer, recall, and hiring decisions); *Branti v. Finkel,* 445 U.S. 507, 518 (1980) (noting that patronage may be exercised only if party affiliation is required for the effective performance of the office involved); *Elrod v. Burns,* 427 U.S. 347, 367 (1976) (holding that employees may be discharged under patronage practices only if the employees held policy-making positions). All these cases are cited in Gely and Chandler, *Public Employees' Political Activities,* 775.

80. U.S. Office of Special Counsel, *Federal Hatch Act, at* http://www.osc.gov/hatch_a.htm (visited July 5, 2001). This site lists the agencies that are still prohibited from partisan activity, and a clearly written list of "Hatch Act Do's and Don'ts." See 5 U.S.C.§§1501 *et seq.;* the major portions of the amended act are 5 U.S.C. §§7323 and 7324.

81. 5 U.S.C. §1502 (2000).

82. The Public Service Research Foundation has tracked states' rules on civil service employees running for office and has found that the following states place no restrictions on it (other than using no state resources, including state time): Alabama, California, Colorado, Delaware, Hawaii, Iowa, Kansas, Massachusetts, Montana, Nevada, New Jersey, New York, North Carolina, North Dakota,

Oregon, Rhode Island, South Carolina, Tennessee, Utah, Vermont, Virginia, Washington, Wyoming. For specific restrictions placed on civil service employees by other states, *see* Public Service Research Foundation, *States' Rules on Civil Service Employees Running for Office, at* http://www.psrf.org/chart1.html (visited July 6, 2001). Local restrictions may apply.

83. *Ricks v. Department of State Civil Service,* 8 So. 2d 49 (La. 1942). State or local statutes that require public employees to resign upon filing for public office have been upheld as serving the public interest. See *Johnson v. State Civil Service Dept.,* 157 N.W.2d 747 (Minn. 1968).

84. Cases in which courts have struck down restrictions on local employees' running for state and national office include *Mancuso v. Taft,* 476 F.2d 197 (R.I. 1973) (construing Rhode Island law), which held that a city home-rule charter prohibiting city employees' candidacy to any public office was unconstitutionally broad, since running for U.S. Congress did not pose the same threat as running for local office, where the contacts and information provided by the employee's job related directly to the position he was seeking.

85. *Gibbs v. Orlandi,* 189 N.E.2d 233 (Ill. 1963), held that a state civil service employee had not violated the Illinois Political Activity Act by distributing campaign literature on behalf of a candidate when he merely permitted political literature to remain on his desk, stating that "distributing" political literature would commonly mean more than mere acquiescence in the placement of literature in the office.

86. MICH. COMP. LAWS ANN. §15.401 *et seq.; Michigan State AFL-CIO v. Michigan Civil Service Commission,* 566 N.W.2d 258 (Mich. 1997).

87. *Swinney v. Untreiner,* 272 So. 2d 805 (Fla. 1973).

88. Nebraska Accountability and Disclosure Commission, *Conflict of Interests; A Public Official Taking a Position in Opposition to a Ballot Question, Op. 068* (July 20, 1984), *at* http://nadc.nol.org (visited June 26, 2001).

89. Bill Bradbury, Secretary of State, Oregon, *Restrictions on Political Campaigning by Public Employees,* ORS 260-432, *at* http://www.sos.state.or.us/elections/Publications/respubemp.html (visited July 7, 2001).

90. *Rogenski v. Board of Fire & Police Commissioners,* 285 N.E.2d 230 (Ill. 1972).

91. *Board of County Commissioners v. Umbehr,* 518 U.S. 668 (1996). *See also* Hansen Clarke, *Contract Law II: The First Amendment Rights of Government Contractors,* 76 MICHIGAN BAR JOURNAL 1205 (November 1997).

92. 42 U.S.C. §2000e-2(a)(1) (2001); 42 U.S.C. §12101 *et seq.;* 42 U.S.C. §1981.

93. *Burlington Industries v. Ellerth,* 524 U.S. 742 (1998).

94. *Burlington Industries,* 524 U.S. 742.

95. *Harris v. Forklift Systems,* 510 U.S. 17, 21 (1993).

96. *Harris,* 510 U.S. at 23.

97. *Harris,* 510 U.S. at 19.

98. *Burlington Industries,* 524 U.S. 742.

99. Loudoun County Public Library Internet Use Policy (n.d.), quoted in Kim Hough-
ton, *Internet Pornography in the Library: Can the Public Library Employer Be
Liable for Third-Party Sexual Harassment When a Client Displays Internet
Pornography to Staff?*, 65 BROOKLYN LAW REVIEW 827, 855–856 (1999).

100. *Johnson v. Los Angeles Fire Dept.*, 865 F. Supp. 1430, 1439 (C.D. Cal. 1994)
("There is no doubt that the prevention of sexual harassment is a compelling gov-
ernment interest"), cited in *Mainstream Loudoun v. Loudoun County Library*, 2
F. Supp. 2d 783 (E.D. Va. 1998).

101. Complaint filed with the Equal Employment Opportunity Commission against
the Minneapolis Public Library (May 2, 2000), from fax from the Halagan Law
Firm, *at* http://www.techlawjournal.com/internet/20010523com.asp (visited July 2,
2001).

102. See, e.g., Eugene Volokh, *Squeamish Librarians*, REASON ONLINE (June 4, 2001),
at http://www.reason.com/hod/ev 060401.html (visited July 2, 2001).

103. A related case is now before the Supreme Court, *Toyota Motor Manufacturing,
Kentucky, Inc. v. Ella Williams*, 2000 Fed. App. 0287A (6th Cir.), *cert. granted*
(U.S. Jan. 5, 2001) (No. 00-1089).

104. *Ridge v. Cape Elizabeth School Department*, 77 F. Supp. 2d 149 (D. Me. 1999);
claims filed were 42 U.S.C. §12101 *et seq.*; 42 U.S.C. §§1981 and 1981a; ME.
REV. STAT. ANN. tit. 5, §4551 *et seq.*

105. *McDonnell Douglas Corp. v. Green*, 411 U.S. 792 (1973), cited in *Ridge*, 77 F.
Supp. 2d 149.

106. 42 U.S.C. §12102(2), cited in *Ridge*, 77 F. Supp. 2d 149.

107. 29 C.F.R. §1630.2(j)(2), cited in *Ridge*, 77 F. Supp. 2d 149.

108. *Ridge*, 77 F. Supp. 2d at 163.

109. 29 C.F.R. §1630.2(j)(3)(i), cited in *Ridge*, 77 F. Supp. 2d at 164.

110. *Jimenez v. Bancomercio de Puerto Rico*, 174 F.3d 36, 40 (1st Cir. 1999), cited in
Ridge, 77 F. Supp. 2d at 164.

111. *Jimenez*, 174 F.3d at 41, cited *in Ridge*, 77 F. Supp. 2d at 164.

112. *Thomas v. Sears, Roebuck & Co.*, 144 F.3d 31, 34 (1st Cir. 1998); *Ayala-Gerena
v. Bristol Myers-Squibb Co.*, 95 F.3d 86, 96 (1st Cir. 1996), cited in *Ridge*, 77 F.
Supp. 2d 149.

113. See *Presutti v. Felton Brush, Inc.*, 927 F. Supp. 545, 550 (D.N.H. 1995), cited in
Ridge, 77 F. Supp. 2d 149.

114. ME. REV. STAT. ANN. tit. 5, §4552, cited in *Ridge*, 77 F. Supp. 2d 149.

115. Kimball E. Gilmer and Jeffrey M. Anderson, *Zero Tolerance for God? Religious
Expression in the Workplace After Ellerth and Faragher*, 42 HOWARD LAW
JOURNAL 327, 328 (Winter 1999).

9 FRIENDS, THE INTERNET, AND LOBBYING

Q1   Can Friends of the Library, foundations, and other library support groups lobby by using the Internet?

Q2   Why does the government give tax breaks to 501(c)(3) organizations?

Q3   How do I know if my group is a 501(c)(3) organization?

Q4   What are the requirements to become a 501(c)(3) organization?

Q5   Do Friends and foundations automatically qualify for 501(c)(3) status if they are organized for charitable purposes?

Q6   Can the library itself qualify as a 501(c)(3) organization?

Q7   What types of organizations may become 501(c)(3)s?

Q8   What types of restrictions are imposed on library support groups that are organized as 501(c)(3)s?

Q9   Do nonprofit organizations have the same free speech rights as anyone else, guaranteed by the First Amendment?

Q10   How is it that labor unions, civic leagues, and chambers of commerce freely engage in lobbying for legislation?

Q11   What is a 501(c)(4) organization?

Q12   Can a Friends or foundation group organized as a 501(c)(3) ever contribute to or work in a candidate's political campaign?

Q13   Does this mean a Friends or foundation group that qualifies as a 501(c)(3) organization can do no lobbying?

"Substantial Part" Test

"Expenditure" Test

Q14   What is the distinction between direct and grassroots lobbying?

Q15   Under the expenditure method, must I calculate how much we spend on direct vs. grassroots lobbying?

Types of Lobbying Expenditures

Q16   How do the "substantial part" and the "expenditure" tests apply to lobbying on the Internet?

Q17   How is the IRS expected to measure Internet use for lobbying by tax-exempt organizations in the future?

Q18   Do Friends and foundations usually choose the "substantial part" test or the "expenditure" measure?

Q19   What are the penalties for lobbying activities that go beyond the substantial part test?

Q20   Are the penalties the same for those that use the expenditure test?

Lobbying Amounts

Q21   How does the IRS regulate lobbying activities on the Web?

Q22   Would the development, maintenance, and use of websites be considered lobbying expenditures?

Q23   Is there any guidance from past technologies that indicate how the IRS might treat Internet use for lobbying?

Q24   What if our posting is merely information, and doesn't urge anyone to take a particular position?

Q25   Does the IRS restrict mass media communications?

Q26   Are all 501(c)(3) organizations treated alike in terms of restrictions?

Q27   What are private foundations?

Q28   Does the IRS treat private foundations differently from other charities?

Q29   Should we determine if our library foundation is considered a "private foundation"?

Q30   Do we have to register as lobbyists?

Notes

his book concludes with a brief discussion of an emerging issue for
library supporters concerning the legal limits on lobbying by nonprofit
organizations such as Friends of the Library, foundations, library associations, and others. A fundamental change is occurring in the way nonprofit
organizations engage in grassroots activism, driven by the growth of the
Internet. The law governing these activities has been slow in expanding to
encompass these new techniques for advocacy. At present, library-support
nonprofit organizations that are eligible and wish to enjoy tax-exempt
status may choose between two sets of rules set forth by the Internal
Revenue Service under its regulations for exempt organizations authorized
by 26 U.S.C. §501(c)(3). The organizations described in §501(c)(3) are
commonly referred to under the general heading of "charitable organizations," although other some other organizations are eligible as well.[1]

One rule the organization may choose is that no "substantial part" of
its activities can consist of lobbying. Alternatively, the organization can
choose to use an "expenditure test" using a sliding scale. Small charitable
organizations that are certified as 501(c)(3)s may spend up to 20 percent
of their expenditures on lobbying activities. With volunteers and inexpensive technology at the helm, this amount can allow an organization to
have a far greater impact on lobbying than ever before.

*Q1   Can Friends of the Library, foundations, and other library
support groups lobby by using the Internet?*

In essence, when a library support group qualifies and chooses to attain
tax-exempt status as a 501(c)(3) charitable organization, it sacrifices a
great deal of its freedom to lobby.We begin our analysis with an explanation of the tax code. After a series of questions and answers that build a
foundation for the tax code's restrictions on lobbying by charitable organizations (and it is not a total ban), we will explore its application to
Friends' and others' activities in cyberspace.

There is one surprising conclusion: the IRS regulations state that "no
substantial part of the organization's activities may be attempts to influence legislation."[2] Yet an organization may opt for an alternative "expenditure" measure. If properly filed, small charitable organizations may then
devote up to 20 percent of their expenditures to lobbying activities, a
remarkable amount in this era of inexpensive websites and listservs.

*Q2   Why does the government give tax breaks to 501(c)(3)
organizations?*

The tax breaks are awarded on the basis that the organization confers a public benefit—a benefit which society or a community may not itself provide. In other words, those organizations which relieve the government of obligations it would otherwise bear itself should not be taxed.[3]

Q3 How do I know if my group is a 501(c)(3) organization?

The treasurer of the group has this information. The group is a 501(c)(3) if it applied to the Internal Revenue Service and received approval of tax-exempt status from the IRS. The designation "501(c)(3)" refers to the section of the Internal Revenue Code of 1986 that exempts qualifying organizations from having to pay federal income tax. The most advantageous benefit, however, is that donors may deduct contributions made to the organization from their income, estate, and gift taxes.[4]

The IRS offers detailed instructions on how to achieve 501(c)(3) status in its Publication 557, *Tax Exempt Status for Your Organization*.[5]

Q4 What are the requirements to become a 501(c)(3) organization?

There are four basic requirements for any such organization:

(1) It must be organized exclusively for charitable, religious, educational, scientific, or literary purposes. The statement of this purpose may be "as broad as, or more specific than, the purposes stated in section 501(c)(3)."[6]

(2) It must meet organizational and operational tests.

A. The *organizational test* requires the use of several key provisions in its articles of incorporation. First, the organization may not "engage, otherwise than as an insubstantial part of its activities, in activities which in themselves are not in furtherance of one or more exempt purpose."[7] Second, the articles of incorporation must mandate that the organizational documents dedicate corporate assets to an exempt purpose.[8]

B. The *operational test* states than an organization will be regarded as "operated exclusively" for an exempt purpose if it engages only in activities primarily intended to accomplish the purpose specified in section 501(c)(3).[9]

(3) It must ensure that its net income is not used to make payments,

other than reasonable compensation for goods and services, to private shareholders or individuals.[10]

(4) No substantial part of the organization's activities may be attempts to influence legislation or participate in political campaigns.[11] Alternatively, an organization may elect to apply an expenditure test.

> **Requirements of a 501(c)(3) Organization**
>
> - It must show charitable purpose (or equivalent).
> - It must meet organizational and operational tests.
> - It may not make payments to private individuals beyond reasonable costs for goods or services.
> - It must follow IRS restrictions on lobbying.

Q5 Do Friends and foundations automatically qualify for 501(c)(3) status if they are organized for charitable purposes?

No. These organizations must apply in writing, using the appropriate forms, directly to the Internal Revenue Service. The IRS's Publication 557, *Tax Exempt Status for Your Organization,* provides specific information on the application process, filing requirements and disclosures, and descriptions of qualifying organizations.[12]

Q6 Can the library itself qualify as a 501(c)(3) organization?

If it is a unit of local government, it is already exempt from federal income tax under section 170 of the Internal Revenue Code.[13] Under certain conditions, however, an instrumentality of government may qualify as a 501(c)(3) if it is organized as a separate entity and does not enjoy governmental powers. The question comes down to whether the library is a unit of local government, an integral part of that unit, or an instrumentality of local government.[14]

Q7 What types of organizations may become 501(c)(3)s?

Essentially, charitable organizations may become 501(c)(3)s. The 501(c)(3) text states:

> Corporations, and any community chest, fund, or foundation, organized and operated exclusively for religious, charitable, scientific, testing for public safety, literary, or educational purposes, or to foster national or international amateur sports competition (but only if no part of its activities involve the provision of athletic facilities or equipment), or for the

prevention of cruelty to children or animals, no part of the net earnings of which inures to the benefit of any private shareholder or individual, no substantial part of the activities of which is carrying on propaganda, or otherwise attempting, to influence legislation (except as otherwise provided in subsection (h)), and which does not participate in, or intervene in (including the publishing or distributing of statements), any political campaign on behalf of (or in opposition to) any candidate for public office.[15]

Q8   What types of restrictions are imposed on library support groups that are organized as 501(c)(3)s?

The IRS limits "attempts to influence legislation," including contacting or urging the public to contact members of a legislative body for the purpose of proposing, supporting, or opposing legislation. "Legislation" includes federal, state, and local government actions, as well as public action involving initiatives, constitutional amendments, city charter amendments, and the like.

The IRS defines "attempts to influence legislation" as any attempt to influence any legislation through an effort to affect the opinions of the general public or any segment thereof (grassroots lobbying), and any attempt to influence any legislation through communication with any member or employee of a legislative body or with any government official or employee who may participate in the formulation of legislation (direct lobbying).

Notably, the following activities are *not* restricted:

Making available the results of nonpartisan analysis, study, or research examining and discussing broad social, economic, and similar problems

Providing technical advice or assistance (where the advice would otherwise constitute the influencing of legislation) to a governmental body or to a committee or other subdivision thereof in response to a written request by that body or subdivision

Appearing before, or communicating with, any legislative body about a possible decision of that body that might affect the existence of the organization, its powers and duties, its tax-exempt status, or the deduction of contributions to the organization

Communicating with a government official or employee, other than:

A communication with a member or employee of a legislative body (when the communication would otherwise constitute the influencing of legislation), or

A communication with the principal purpose of influencing legislation

Communications between an organization and its bona fide members about legislation or proposed legislation of direct interest to the organization and the members, unless these communications directly encourage the members to attempt to influence legislation or directly encourage the members to urge nonmembers to attempt to influence legislation[16]

Q9   *Do nonprofit charitable organizations have the same free speech rights as anyone else, guaranteed by the First Amendment?*

They do if they choose not to file for tax-exempt status. But if they do, the federal government may limit their lobbying activities. The U.S. Supreme Court has twice upheld the Treasury Department's regulations on lobbying, despite challenges under the First Amendment.[17]

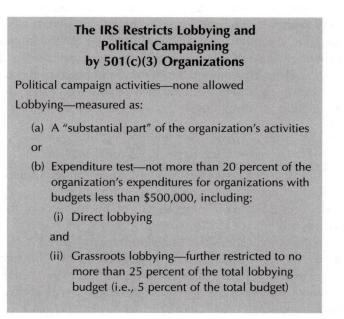

**The IRS Restricts Lobbying and
Political Campaigning
by 501(c)(3) Organizations**

Political campaign activities—none allowed

Lobbying—measured as:

(a) A "substantial part" of the organization's activities

or

(b) Expenditure test—not more than 20 percent of the organization's expenditures for organizations with budgets less than $500,000, including:

 (i) Direct lobbying

and

(ii) Grassroots lobbying—further restricted to no more than 25 percent of the total lobbying budget (i.e., 5 percent of the total budget)

*Q10   How is it that labor unions, civic leagues, and chambers
of commerce freely engage in lobbying for legislation?*

The Internal Revenue Code assigns such organizations 501(c)(4) status, which allows a nonprofit organization that doesn't fit the 501(c)(3) requirements to be tax-exempt and lobby for legislation that affects the organization's ability to accomplish its exempt purpose.[18]

Q11   What is a 501(c)(4) organization?

The 501(c)(4) designation is for nonprofit civic organizations and local associations of employees (unions). They are allowed greater latitude in political activities than are 501(c)(3)s. Their direct tax liabilities are virtually the same as those for 501(c)(3)s, but the crucial difference is that only 501(c)(3)s can receive donations (either material or monetary) and provide the donor with a tax-deductible receipt for their tax records. Many groups set up both a 501(c)(3) and a 501(c)(4) in order to take advantage of the benefits of each type of designation.[19]

*Q12   Can a Friends or foundation group organized as a
501(c)(3) ever contribute to or work in a candidate's
political campaign?*

No. *Any* participation or intervention in a candidate's campaign for political office will disqualify the organization for 501(c)(3) status. Such participation includes the publishing or distribution of statements on behalf of or in opposition to a candidate. Certain voter education activities may be conducted in a nonpartisan manner, but if the organization is unsure of whether the activity is acceptable, the IRS recommends that the group request a letter ruling from the IRS.

*Q13   Does this mean a Friends or foundation group that qualifies
as a 501(c)(3) organization can do no lobbying?*

Not at all. Charitable organizations may not engage in any political campaign activities, but may engage in a limited amount of activities attempting to influence legislation.[20] The organization has a choice to make, one that is especially important if it intends to use the Internet for lobbying purposes. The default choice is the "substantial part" test. Of potentially greater use to volunteer organizations that wish to use the Internet to lobby is the "expenditure test." In order to choose the expenditure test, an organization must file Form 5768,[21] with a postmark within the first tax year to which it applies.

"Substantial Part" Test

If an organization does not file for the "expenditure" method, the IRS will look to make sure "no substantial part of [the organization's] activities [constitutes] carrying on propaganda, or otherwise attempting to influence legislation."[22] The IRS looks at the totality of the circumstances, not just financial indicators.[23]

The term "substantial part" has never been explicitly defined by the IRS or in the code.[24] Courts have found the test difficult to apply, and use a balancing test. The U.S. Court of Claims wrote in 1974:

> The political efforts of an organization must be balanced in the context of the objectives and circumstances of the organization to determine whether a substantial part of its activities is to influence, or is an attempt to influence, legislation. A percentage test to determine whether the activities are substantial is not appropriate. Such a test obscures the complexity of balancing the organization's activities in relation to its objectives and circumstances in the context of the totality of the organization.[25]

The balancing test takes into consideration all the activities of the organization and examines its attempts to influence legislation in light of several factors, including the percentage of the organization's budget (or employee time) spent on lobbying; the continuous or intermittent nature of the organization's legislative involvement; the nature of the organization and its aims; and, realistically, the controversial nature of the organization's position and its visibility.[26]

The ambiguity of this provision led Congress to provide an alternative for organizations that desire clearer guidelines, and devised the "expenditure" test.

"Expenditure" Test

The second method is the "expenditure" method, provided for in section 501(h) of the code. A formula is calculated on a percentage of expenditures that may be spent on lobbying activities.[27] The sole inquiry is into expenditure amounts. Organizations with annual expenditures under $500,000 can devote up to 20 percent of their exempt-purpose expenditures to lobbying. The IRS looks at two categories to determine the calculation, direct and grassroots lobbying.

Q14   What is the distinction between direct and grassroots lobbying?

Direct lobbying is a direct attempt to influence legislation by communicating directly with the legislative body. It also includes expenditures for referendums and other ballot measures.

Grassroots lobbying is an attempt to affect the opinions of an organization's members or of the general public, with the intent of urging them to influence legislation. For example, if a Friends organization communicates with its members on legislation of direct interest to the Friends group, this is not lobbying, but if it urges its members to contact a legislative body, that is considered grassroots lobbying.

Q15   *Under the expenditure method, must I calculate how much we spend on direct vs. grassroots lobbying?*

Yes. The total of all direct and grassroots expenditures must not exceed 20 percent of all expenditures of the group's operating budget. From that base point, the organization determines for a given tax year the total amount it can spend on all lobbying activities, known as its "lobbying nontaxable amount."

Types of Lobbying Expenditures

Lobbying expenditures. This is the umbrella category that includes any expenditures made, direct or grassroots, for the purpose of attempting to influence legislation.

Direct expenditures. Direct lobbying is as it sounds—it is directed to anyone who has the authority to formulate or enact legislation.[28] It refers to communications that address specific legislation (either by name or general idea) and reflect a view on that legislation.[29]

Grassroots expenditures. Grassroots lobbying is an attempt to influence legislation by trying to affect the opinions of the general public or any segment thereof. It refers to communications that discuss specific legislation or encourage recipients to take action, such as contacting their elected representatives.[30] The restriction on *grassroots* lobbying expenditures is especially strict: no more than one-quarter of the total lobbying expenditures may be used for grassroots lobbying. That is, the "grassroots nontaxable amount" cannot exceed 25 percent of the *lobbying* nontaxable amount (or 5 percent of the total budget).

Q16   *How do the "substantial part" and the "expenditure" tests apply to lobbying on the Internet?*

This is a cutting-edge question, and one that is not yet determined. The costs are generally minimal for an organization to post information on the Internet, creating a real disparity in how the activity would be treated under the two tests. Commentator Pamela O'Kane Foster poses this hypothetical:

> Suppose an organization with an annual budget of $100,000 posts a statement regarding pending legislation on the Web, urging readers to call their representatives to vote a particular way. Suppose the cost of this posting is $1,000, including staff time to type it into a readable format and to submit it to the organization's Internet provider. Suppose further that the Web site on which this call to action is posted is visited by thousands of people, and the response in the legislators' offices is significant. Phone calls, letters, and e-mails come in regularly, asking legislators to vote as suggested in the posting. Under the expenditure test, the amount spent is only five percent of the annual allowable expenditures for an organization with a budget that size. Even considering this to be grass-roots lobbying, as it would be, the expenditures are well under the threshold, representing only twenty percent of the allowable grassroots expenditure. [Note that grassroots expenditures in this case could reach as high as $5,000.] There would not seem to be any problem, and the IRS would not question the expenditures.
>
> The substantial part test, however, paints a different picture. Under this test, the IRS looks at the other activities of the organization and could conceivably consider the impact of the lobbying. Although the organization might not lose its exemption for this one instance, it could be at risk. Under the expenditure test, on the other hand, the organization could engage in five times this amount and still remain safely within allowable limits.[31]

Q17   *How is the IRS expected to measure Internet use for lobbying by tax-exempt organizations in the future?*

As this book went to press, the IRS was examining the application of the Internal Revenue Code to the use of the Internet by tax-exempt organizations, not only for lobbying, but also for charitable solicitation, advertising, and other business activities. The questions posed by the IRS for public comment should be an indication of its future regulations. The questions (paraphrased here) include: (1) What facts are important in determining whether information on a website about candidates constitutes intervention in a political campaign? (2) Is a hyperlink on a website to an organization that engages in political campaigns prohibited? What facts are relevant in determining whether the link constitutes a political campaign intervention? (3) For charitable organizations that have not made the election under 501(h), what facts are relevant in determining whether lobbying and communications on the Internet are a substantial part of the organization's activities? Should the location of the communication or the number of hits be relevant? What facts are relevant in determining whether a listserv is a grassroots communication?[32]

Q18   *Do Friends and foundations usually choose the "substantial part" test or the "expenditure" measure?*

While that figure has not been calculated, as of 1995, only about one percent of all eligible charities elected the expenditure test, mainly because it is seen as too new and too rigid.[33] Many organizations say they feel it would be a disadvantage to lose the chance to argue that their level of lobbying activity is insubstantial, or else they fear an increased risk of audit under the expenditure test. Also, the "substantial part" test is the default option.

Q19   *What are the penalties for lobbying activities that go beyond the substantial part test?*

The penalty for lobbying activities deemed substantial is the loss of tax exemption. The punishment is absolute and can be imposed after only one year of substantial lobbying expenditures.[34]

Q20   *Are the penalties the same for those that use the expenditure test?*

No. Under the expenditure test, there is an intermediate level of penalty— an excise tax of 25 percent of the excess lobbying expenditures. If a Friends group elects the expenditures test, it will keep its tax-exempt status unless it normally makes lobbying expenditures that are more than 150 percent of the lobbying nontaxable amount for the organization for each tax year. Similarly, it will keep its status unless it normally makes grassroots expenditures greater than 150 percent of the grassroots nontaxable amount for the organization for each tax year. Only when the lobbying expenditures exceed these limits for four consecutive years, will the organization lose its tax exemption.[35]

Lobbying Amounts

The lobbying amount for any organization is measured on a sliding scale:

(1) 20 percent of the exempt-purpose expenditures if the exempt-purpose expenditures are not over $500,000

(2) $100,000 plus 15 percent of the excess of the exempt-purpose expenditures over $500,000 if the exempt-purpose expenditures are over $500,000 but not over $1,000,000

(3) $175,000 plus 10 percent of the excess of the exempt-purpose expenditures over $1,000,000 if the exempt-purpose expenditures are over $1,000,000 but not over $1,500,000, or

(4) $225,000 plus 5 percent of the excess of the exempt-purpose expenditures over $1,5000,000 if the exempt-purpose expenditures are over $1,500,000

In no event is spending on lobbying to exceed $1,000,000.

Under these rules, for example, a group with a budget of $25,000 could spend 20 percent of it for lobbying, of which 25 percent (i.e., 5 percent of the total budget) could be used for grassroots lobbying.

Q21 How does the IRS regulate lobbying activities on the Web?

It is difficult for the IRS to regulate lobbying activities on the Web using either test. Remember that the level of expenditure is still a significant part of the substantial part test. The IRS reporting requirements center on Form 990, the tax-exempt organization's annual tax-return form. This form does not show whether or not activities are charitable.

O'Kane Foster notes that Congress's use of the IRS to monitor tax-exempt organizations is an ill-chosen decision, since the IRS is not equipped to monitor anything from a vantage point other than an expenditure-based one.[36]

Q22 Would the development, maintenance, and use of websites be considered lobbying expenditures?

Under the current tests, it would seem the development of websites could not be considered a lobbying expenditure, *unless the stated purpose is to engage in grassroots lobbying.*[37] As long as the predominant use of the site is not lobbying, the maintenance of the site would not be considered exclusively a lobbying expenditure.

Specifically, under the 501(h) expenditure test, the code provides for the allocation of expenditures that are for multiple purposes under the three types of expenditures—non-lobbying, direct lobbying, and grass-roots lobbying. Allocable expenses generally include the salaries of employees who spend some of their time on lobbying activities, overhead costs, and costs of newsletters.[38]

Q23 Is there any guidance from past technologies that indicate how the IRS might treat Internet use for lobbying?

O'Kane Foster suggests the analogy of telephone costs. The installation of a phone system and the maintenance of that system (including repairs, general phone company charges, and the like) would not be thought of as lobbying expenditures.[39] But if an organization uses its telephones for little else besides calling members of the public and urging them to contact their representatives, then the phone costs would likely be considered lobbying expenditures.[40]

Q24 What if our posting is merely information, and doesn't urge anyone to take a particular position?

Merely posting information on the Web should not change the character of information that is not considered lobbying in the first place.

Q25 Does the IRS restrict mass media communications?

Yes. Any paid advertisement appearing in the "mass media" is presumed to be a "grassroots lobbying communication" if it appears within two weeks before a vote by a legislative body on a highly publicized piece of legislation, reflects a view on that legislation, and encourages the public to communicate with legislators.[41] Note that this refers to *paid advertisements*.

Q26 Are all 501(c)(3) organizations treated alike in terms of restrictions?

No. 501(c)(3) organizations are divided into public charities and private foundations. Only public charities can have contributions deductible under the tax code.[42]

Q27 What are private foundations?

A private foundation is a nongovernmental, nonprofit organization with funds (usually from a single source, such as an individual, family, or corporation) and program managed by its own trustees or directors. Private foundations are charitable organizations formed to distribute funds to further their own goals. They are established to maintain or aid social, educational, religious, or other charitable activities serving the public welfare, primarily through the making of grants.[43] The congressional presumption is that any 501(c)(3) is a private foundation, with the exception of organizations which have broad public support or actively function in a supporting relationship to such an organization. In order to overcome the private foundation presumption, the organization must show it meets the description of broad public support.

Q28   Does the IRS treat private foundations differently from other charities?

Yes. Private foundations are even more restricted. In response to a perceived threat of undue influence by wealthy contributors to private foundations, Congress enacted further restrictions on them.[44] Foundations are prohibited from providing *any* funding at all for lobbying activities. They must also distribute a percentage of their assets each year.[45] Note that using the word "Foundation" in an organization's name has little bearing on whether or not the IRS will treat the organization as a private foundation.

The Internal Revenue Code imposes two levels of excise taxes on a foundation—and on its managers who knowingly authorize a restricted expenditure for any lobbying activities engaged in by either the foundation or its grant recipients, whether or not it is necessary for the organization's exempt purpose. There are three very narrow exceptions to this:

(1) Providing "technical advice or assistance . . . in response to a written request by [a governmental] body"
(2) Lobbying about a possible legislative decision that "might affect the existence of the private foundation, its powers and duties, its tax-exempt status, or the deduction of contributions to such foundation" (commonly called the "self-defense" exception)
(3) "Nonpartisan analysis, study, or research"[46]

Q29   Should we determine if our library foundation is considered a "private foundation"?

It is important that you determine if your organization is a private foundation. Most organizations exempt from income tax (as organizations described in section 501(c)(3)) are presumed to be private foundations unless they notify the Internal Revenue Service within a specified period of time that they are not. This notice requirement applies to most section 501(c)(3) organizations regardless of when they were formed.[47]

Q30 Do we have to register as lobbyists?

This is unlikely. Look to state lobbying laws to answer that. In New York, for example, a lobbyist is defined as a person or organization employed or designated by another who attempts to influence pending legislation and who expends or receives more than $2,000 in a calendar year for that purpose. If a library pays a volunteer's expenses to a library legislative day, it may be time to look at your state law to see if registration with the state as a lobbyist is necessary.[48]

Notes

1. Treas. Reg. §1.501(c)(3)-1 (2001) includes organizations organized and operated for religious, charitable, scientific, testing for public safety, literary, or educational purposes, or for the prevention of cruelty to children or animals.
2. Treas. Reg. §1.501(c)(3)-1(b)(3) (2000).
3. *Regan v. Taxation with Representation of Washington,* 461 U.S. 540, 550 (1983).
4. I.R.C. §501(a) (2000).
5. For a detailed explanation of the process, *see* Internal Revenue Service, Publication 557, TAX EXEMPT STATUS FOR YOUR ORGANIZATION (rev. 1999), Cat. No. 46573C, *available at* http://www.irs.gov/pub/irs-pdf/p557.pdf (visited July 13, 2002).
6. Treas. Reg. §1.501(c)(3)-1(b)(1)(ii).
7. Treas. Reg §1.501(c)(3)-1(b)(1)(i).
8. Treas. Reg. §1.501(c)(3)-1(b)(4).
9. Treas. Reg. §1.501(c)(3)-1(c).
10. *Gemological Institute of America, Inc.,* 17 T.C. 1604 (1952), *aff'd per curiam,* 212 F.2d 205 (2d Cir. 1956), cited in Melissa Waller Baldwin, Comment, *Section 501(C)(3) and Lobbying: The Case for the Local Organization,* 23 OHIO NORTHERN UNIVERSITY LAW REVIEW 203, 208 n.37 (1996).
11. Treas. Reg. §1.501(c)(3)-1(b)(3).
12. Internal Revenue Service, Publication 557, TAX EXEMPT STATUS FOR YOUR ORGANIZATION (rev. 1999), Cat. No. 46573C, *available at* http://www.irs.ustreas.gov/prod/forms_pubs/pubs/p557toc.htm (visited June 27, 2001).
13. I.R.C. §170.
14. Ellen Richardson, *Comments on 501(c)(3) Status, Access (Library of Michigan)* (November-December 1997), *at* http://www.libofmich.lib.mi.us/publications/accessnov97.html#trustee (visited June 28, 2001).
15. I.R.C. §501(c)(3).

16. Internal Revenue Service, Publication 557, TAX EXEMPT STATUS FOR YOUR ORGANIZATION, *at* http://www.irs.gov/pub/irs-pdf/p557.pdf (visited July 13, 2002).

17. *Cammarano v. United States,* 358 U.S. 498 (1959); and *Regan v. Taxation with Representation of Washington,* 461 U.S. 540 (1983).

18. I.R.C. §501(c)(4) (2000).

19. 26 U.S.C. §501(c)(4) (2001). For specific eligibility, application information, and lobbying restrictions, *see* Internal Revenue Service, *Social Welfare Organizations, at* http://www.irs.ustreas.gov/bus_info/eo/soc-welf.html (visited July 7, 2001).

20. For a detailed explanation, *see* Judith Kindell and John Francis Reilly, *Lobbying Issues, at* \http://www.irs.gov/pub/irs-tege/topic-p.pdf (visited July 13, 2002).

21. Internal Revenue Service, Form 5768, *Election/Revocation of Election by an Eligible Section 501(c)(3) Organization to Make Expenditures to Influence Legislation, available at* http://www.irs.gov/pub/irs-pdf/f5768.pdf (visited July 13, 2002).

22. I.R.C. §501(c)(3).

23. *See* Lobbying by Charities; Lobbying by Private Foundations, 53 Fed. Reg. 51826, 51827 (1988) (codified at 26 C.F.R. pts. 1, 53, 56) ("In contrast to the substantial part test . . . the expenditure test imposes no limit on lobbying activities that do not require expenditures, such as certain unreimbursed lobbying activities conducted by bona fide volunteers").

24. Pamela O'Kane Foster, Note, *Lobbying on the Internet and the Internal Revenue Code's Regulation of Charitable Organizations,* 43 NEW YORK LAW SCHOOL LAW REVIEW 567, 595 (1999).

25. *Haswell v. United States,* 500 F.2d 1133, 1142 (Ct. Cl. 1974), *cert. denied,* 419 U.S. 1107 (1975), cited in O'Kane Foster, Note, *Lobbying on the Internet,* 595.

26. James J. Fishman and Stephen Schwarz, NONPROFIT ORGANIZATIONS: CASES AND MATERIALS 504 (1995), cited in O'Kane Foster, Note, *Lobbying on the Internet,* 595.

27. I.R.C. §501(h) (2000).

28. I.R.C. §4911(d)(1)(B) (2000).

29. 26 C.F.R. §56.4911-2 (1990).

30. 26 C.F.R. §51.836 (1990).

31. O'Kane Foster, Note, *Lobbying on the Internet,* 595.

32. *Request for Comments regarding Need for Guidance Clarifying Application of the Internal Revenue Code to Use of the Internet by Exempt Organizations,* Announcement 2000-84 (due Feb. 13, 2001), INTERNAL REVENUE BULLETIN (Oct. 16, 2000), *at* http://www.irs.gov/pub/irs-irbs/irb00-42.pdf (visited July 2, 2002).

33. "Some charities prefer the vagueness of the general rules to the specificity and record-keeping requirements of the 501(h) election. . . . In fact, it has been reported that fewer than 4,000 of approximately 380,000 eligible 501(c)(3) organizations have made the expenditure test election." James J. Fishman and Stephen Schwarz, NONPROFIT ORGANIZATIONS: CASES AND MATERIALS 532 (1995), cited in O'Kane Foster, Note, *Lobbying on the Internet,* 595.

34. I.R.C. §501(h) (2000).
35. I.R.C. §501(h).
36. O'Kane Foster, Note, *Lobbying on the Internet,* 595.
37. I.R.C. §4911(c)(3) (2000).
38. *See* Treas. Reg. §56.4911-3(a)(3) (1986), cited in O'Kane Foster, Note, *Lobbying on the Internet,* 595.
39. I.R.C. §501(h).
40. O'Kane Foster, Note, *Lobbying on the Internet,* 595.
41. See 26 C.F.R. §56.4911-6 (2001) ("Records of Lobbying and Grass Roots Expenditures").
42. I.R.C. §170 (2000).
43. *Glossary, The Foundation Center's User-Friendly Guide, Internet Edition, at* http://fdncenter.org/onlib/ufg/ufg gloss.html (visited Feb. 22, 2000), cited in O'Kane Foster, Note, *Lobbying on the Internet,* 595.
44. O'Kane Foster, Note, *Lobbying on the Internet,* 595, citing a discussion of congressional fears of and "assaults" on large private foundations in Waldemar A. Nielsen, The Big Foundations 7–17 (1972).
45. I.R.C. §509, 4940–4946 (2000).
46. I.R.C. §4945(e) (2000).
47. Internal Revenue Service, Publication 557, Tax Exempt Status for Your Organization (rev. 1999), Cat. No. 46573C, *available at* http://www.irs.gov/pub/irs-pdf/p557.pdf (visited July 13, 2002).
48. Rebekkah Smith, *New York State's Local Lobbying Law and Public Library Trustees, at* http://www.nysalb.org/news0104/smith.htm (visited May 19, 2001).

~ Index

References to notes are indicated by "n" after the page number, e.g., 7 n14. Endnotes are found at the end of each chapter.

MARY MINOW is a consultant with LibraryLaw.com. She has worked as an attorney, as a public library branch manager, and as an online database consultant. She has taught as an adjunct professor of library law at San Jose State University's School of Library and Information Science. In addition, she has served as a library commissioner for the Cupertino (Calif.) Public Library, and is currently the president of the California Association of Library Trustees and Commissioners.

Minow received an A.M.L.S. from the University of Michigan, Ann Arbor, and a J.D. from Stanford University.

TOMAS A. LIPINSKI is an assistant professor and co-director of the Center for Information Policy Research at the University of Wisconsin–Milwaukee's School of Information Studies. He researches, teaches, publishes, and speaks widely on issues relating to information and Internet law and policy, especially copyright in schools, libraries, and other information settings. He holds a law degree from Marquette University, a master of laws degree from the John Marshall Law School, and a doctorate in library and information science from the University of Illinois at Urbana-Champaign. In the summer he is a visiting professor at the School of Information Technology and at the School of Mercantile Law, University of Pretoria, Pretoria, South Africa.